MONEY AND FINANCE IN THE INDIAN ECONOMY

This volume analyses the diverse and often unexpected financial developments during the two decades of the post-reforms period. It provides an overview of the challenges faced by monetary and fiscal authorities in relation to fiscal imbalances, monetary-cum-exchange rate policies, and management of cross-border capital flows in the liberalized regime.

The essays identify inter-sectoral linkages in terms of a coherent macro-theoretic framework relevant for the Indian economy. They examine diverse issues such as the transition from credit rationing to demand constraint in the loan market; fiscal problems with reference to the rising revenue and fiscal deficits; external sector developments and their links with other sectors; and the contribution of the banking sector in economic growth and containment of financial volatility

Mihir Rakshit is Director, Monetary Research Policy, ICRA Limited. In a teaching career spanning several decades, he has held appointments at Indian Statistical Institute, Kolkata, Presidency College, Kolkata, Delhi School of Economics, and Erasmus University, Rotterdam, the Netherlands.

To
Susmita and Shardul

Money and Finance in the Indian Economy

Selected Papers

Volume II

Mihir Rakshit

OXFORD
UNIVERSITY PRESS

OXFORD
UNIVERSITY PRESS

YMCA Library Building, Jai Singh Road, New Delhi 110 001

Oxford University Press is a department of the University of Oxford. It furthers the University's objective of excellence in research, scholarship, and education by publishing worldwide in

Oxford New York

Auckland Cape Town Dar es Salaam Hong Kong Karachi Kuala Lumpur Madrid Melbourne Mexico City Nairobi New Delhi Shanghai Taipei Toronto

With offices in

Argentina Austria Brazil Chile Czech Republic France Greece Guatemala Hungary Italy Japan Poland Portugal Singapore South Korea Switzerland Thailand Turkey Ukraine Vietnam

Published in India
by Oxford University Press, New Delhi

First published 2009
Oxford India Paperbacks 2011

ISBN-13: 0-19-807010-1
ISBN-10: 978-0-19-807010-8

Typeset in Aldine401 BT 10.5/13
By Excellent Laser Typesetters, Pitampura, Delhi 110 034
Printed in India at Rakmo Press, New Delhi 110 020
Published by Oxford University Press
YMCA Library Building, Jai Singh Road, New Delhi 110 001

Contents

List of Tables, Figures, and Box vi
Acknowledgments vii
List of Abbreviations ix

1. Introduction 1
2. Money and Public Finance under Structural Adjustment 9
3. Restoring Fiscal Balance through Legislative Fiat 35
4. Some Public Economics of Food Subsidy and Buffer Stock Operations 61
5. Perspectives on Correcting Fiscal Imbalances in the Indian Economy 96
6. Some Analytics and Empirics of Fiscal Restructuring in India 142
7. External Capital Flows and Foreign Exchange Reserves 167
8. Using Forex Reserves for Infrastructural Investment 207
9. On Liberalizing Foreign Institutional Investments 242
10. Banking under the Emerging Economic Environment 262

Author Index 285
Subject Index 286

Tables, Figures, and Box

Tables

2.1	Key Macroeconomic Indicators, 1990–4	10
2.2	Variation in Money and some of its Components	12
2.3	Interest Rates, 1992–4	13
4.1	Effects of Exports, Open Market Sales (OMS), and Increase in BPL Quotas	78
5.1	Fiscal Profile of the Indian Economy	97
5.2	Indicators of Fiscal Sustainability—1999–2000	117
5.3	Macroeconomic Indicators of India—1990–1 to 1999–2000	122
5.4	Fiscal Restructuring Programme	135
7.1	A Profile of India's External Sector, 1990–2003	170
7.2	Some Indicators of Balance-of-Payments Viability	175
7.3	A Macroeconomic Profile of India	177
7.4	Monetary Developments	194
9.1	Some Macroeconomic (including External Sector) Indicators	247
10.1	Financial Profile of Banks in India	273

Figures

7.1	Some External Sector Indicators	172
7.2	Time Profile of some Macroeconomic Indicators	178

Box

7.1	Foreign Capital and Economic Development	179

Acknowledgements

Except for Chapters 1 and 8, all other essays in this book were published in *Economic and Political Weekly* and *Money & Finance*. I am grateful to these publications for permission to include the essays in the present volume.

It was at the instance of the late Amaresh Bagchi that I started writing on the Indian economic problems from the early 1980s. During all these years I gained immensely from our discussions on the emerging issues of the Indian economy and his candid comments on my papers. Amareshda also suggested bringing out some of my essays in collected volumes, but unfortunately missed their publication by a few months.

At various stages of my research over the last three decades I also have had the benefit of extremely fruitful interaction with the late Dipak Banerjee, Mrinal Datta-Chaudhuri, Amitava Bose, Basudev Biswas, Dipankar Dasgupta, Sumon Bhaumik, Suchismita Bose, Dipankor Coondoo, Pradip Maiti, Ro Naastepad, Susmita Rakshit, Soumyen Sikdar, and Servaas Storm. Particularly important in clarifying my thoughts on developing country macroeconomics in general and the Indian economy in particular was the intensive exchange of views I had with members of the fortnightly meetings at Presidency College, Calcutta, during the 1980s and of the Monthly Economics Workshop at ICRA, Calcutta. I am indebted for very helpful responses to the participants of the seminars I gave at Indian Statistical Institute, Calcutta and Delhi; Delhi School of Economics; Jawaharlal Nehru University, New Delhi; Centre for Development Studies, Trivandrum; Jadavpur University, Calcutta; Erasmus University, Rotterdam; and Cornell University, Itacha.

My work was greatly facilitated by the highly congenial environment at ICRA's Monetary Research Unit. Anup Kumar Bhandari, Sudipta Jha, and Sakuntala Sarkar spared no effort in helping me prepare numerous drafts of the essays and responding to the publisher's queries. The editorial staff of the Oxford University Press did a tremendous job of making my task hassle-free in the process of publication of this book and its companion volume.

The heaviest burden of the present venture was borne by members of my family who had to put up with my near-total inattention to their needs. My only plea is that they made the sacrifice cheerfully, and knew how I also sorely missed their company.

Abbreviations

AD	aggregate demand
ADB	Asian Development Bank
ADR	American Depositary Receipt
AIFI	all-India financial institution
APL	above poverty line
AS	aggregate supply
ATM	automated teller machine
BCBS	Basel Committee on Banking Supervision
BPL	below poverty line
BSE	Bombay Stock Exchange
CAD	current account balance
CAG	Comptroller and Auditor General of India
CRAR	capital to risk-adjusted assets ratio
CRR	cash reserve ratio
CR	credit rationing
DC	demand constraint
DFI	Development Financial Institution
DTL	demand and time liabilities
EFC	Eleventh Finance Commission
EG	Expert Group
EME	emerging market economy
FCI	Food Corporation of India
FDI	foreign direct investment
FFP	food-for-work programme
FG	fiscal gap
FII	Foreign Institutional Investment
FPI	foreign portfolio investment
FRBMA	Fiscal Responsibility and Budget Management Act
FRBMB	Fiscal Responsibility and Budget Management Bill

FRS	fiscal restructuring programme
GDP	gross domestic product
GDR	global depositary receipt
GFCE	government final consumption expenditure
GOI	Government of India
GNP	gross national product
HRD	human resource development
ICOR	incremental capital–output ratio
IDB	India Development Bond
IFL	Incremental Financial Liability
IMF	International Monetary Fund
KYC	know your client
LIC	Life Insurance Corporation
MODVAT	modified value-added tax
MSB	market stabilization bond
MSP	minimum support price
MSS	Market Stabilization Scheme
NAIRU	non-accelerating inflation rate of unemployment
NCAER	National Council for Applied Economic Research
NIRR	non-interest revenue–GDP ratio
NNML	net non-monetary liability
NNP	net national product
NPA	non-performing asset
NRI	non-resident Indian
NSC	National Savings Certificate
OMS	open-market sale
PCS	Planning Commission Scheme
PDS	public distribution system
PL	Public Liability
PN	participatory note
PPF	Public Provident Fund
PSB	public sector bank
PSE	public sector enterprise
PSU	Public Sector Undertaking
R&D	research and development
RBI	Reserve Bank of India
REER	real effective exchange rate
SAP	Structural Adjustment Programme
SEBI	Securities and Exchange Board of India
SHG	self-help group
SLR	statutory liquidity ratio

SPV	special purpose vehicle
STC	State Trading Corporation
TFC	Twelfth Finance Commission
TPDS	Targeted Public Distribution System
USD	United States dollar
UTI	Unit Trust of India
VAT	value-added tax
WPI	wholesale price index

1

Introduction

Everything should be made as simple as possible, but not simpler.

Einstein

The post-reforms period has witnessed rapid liberalization of the domestic money and capital markets; their growing integration with the global financial system; and the increasing importance of financial factors in driving the behaviour of the macroeconomy. Under the fast-changing market conditions both at home and abroad, monetary and fiscal authorities have been facing problems that are often qualitatively different from those encountered during the Plan period.[1] The most important of these problems relate to correction of fiscal imbalances; monetary-cum-exchange rate policies under the liberalized regime; and management of cross-border capital flows. These and similar issues constitute the theme of the essays included in the present volume.

For an in-depth appreciation of the various facets of developments in the spheres of money, banking, budgetary operation, and management of foreign exchange reserves, it is necessary to have in view inter-relations among all the major sectors of the economy, that is, a full-fledged macro model relevant for the Indian economy during the reference period. Such a theoretical framework was set forth in Chapter 2 of this book's companion volume *Macroeconomics of Post-reform India* and a perusal of this chapter is recommended for the more fastidious reader. However, the arguments and analysis in each of the subsequent chapters are self-contained, though the explanation of the underlying macroeconomic links is often terse and the theoretical reasoning necessarily selective, related as it is to the specific issue(s) at hand. Anyway, since practically all the essays in the volume were written in response to some intriguing developments or on-going

[1] From the Second to the Seventh Five-Year Plan (1955–90), to be more specific.

debate, and intended for non-specialists, readers with a nodding acquaintance with macroeconomics should have little trouble in following the basic argument and the chain of economic reasoning. The motivation of these essays and their sequencing in the rest of the volume are as follows.

A most remarkable development on the financial front almost on the heels of initiation of economic reforms was the transition, from a prolonged period of credit rationing,[2] to a situation of demand constraint in the loan market. Chapter 2 examines this phenomenon in the context of the structural adjustment policies pursued since 1991 and developments in other sectors of the economy, for example, poor growth in agriculture and industry; slowdown in fixed capital formation; inflow of foreign funds; and a booming stock market. A scrutiny of the financial and real sector behaviour of the economy during the reference period suggests that measures such as simplification of the tax system, removal or relaxation of bureaucratic control, and making PSUs subject to market discipline were necessary and long overdue; but at the same time quite a few of the policies, especially those related to the duty structure and differential degrees of protection, were half-baked and caused significant inefficiency and distortion in the pattern of production, investment, and imports. The most serious deficiency of the policy package arose from the lack of a coherent approach towards development of a fiscal, financial, and regulatory regime conducive to agricultural growth; rapid removal of infrastructural bottlenecks and promotion of economic activities consistent with the country's resource endowment and dynamic comparative advantage. It was the *ad hoc* nature of the measures sans such an approach that lay at the root of excess liquidity and stock market boom with sagging fixed capital formation; sharp decline in production of capital goods and consumer non-durables along with a rapid rise in output of consumer durables; and large inflow of foreign funds for purposes of retiring domestic debt and building up foreign exchange reserves even while domestic industries were saddled with excess capacity.

The next four chapters (3–6), written between 2000 and 2005, are on fiscal problems with special reference to the rising revenue and fiscal deficits, universally viewed as the Achilles heel of the Indian macroeconomy. Chapter 3 discusses some fundamental issues including normative ones relating to debt financing while reviewing the fiscal correction programme set forth in the Fiscal Responsibility and Budget Management Bill (FRBMB) 2000. The next three chapters are diagnostic as well as prescriptive. They examine the nature of the country's prolonged fiscal malady since the mid-1990s; evaluate the official measures for strengthening the fisc; and suggest

[2] From the early 1970s.

where deemed necessary alternative policy packages in the context of the major constraints operating in the Indian economy. Chapter 4 deals with a relatively narrow but important area of the Indian public finance, viz., fiscal implications of and policy issues related to food subsidy and stock-piling of foodgrains by Food Corporation of India (FCI). In contrast, Chapters 5 and 6 discuss practically all macroeconomic aspects of budgetary measures in the context of the fiscal restructuring schemes laid down by the Eleventh and the Twelfth Finance Commission (EFC and TFC).

The FRBMB was placed before the Parliament in 2000[3] in order to force the government to tackle the problem of burgeoning fiscal deficit, debt–gross domestic product (GDP) ratio, and interest payments. While laying down the course of fiscal correction, the background paper to the bill also raises some fundamental issues in respect of implications of debt financing for inter-generational equity apart from those of budgetary viability and growth. Chapter 3 provides a critique of the conceptual issues raised in the paper and examines how the provisions under FRBMB are likely to contribute towards the basic objectives of inter-generational equity, macro-stabilization, and growth. The bill, it is observed, breaks new ground in trying to promote transparency in framing budgetary measures and requiring the government to spell out their underlying assumptions and economic rationale. However, lack of conceptual clarity and weak analytical foundations seem to have made the core provisions of the bill inappropriate in the Indian context, especially from the viewpoint of the three aforementioned objectives.

An instructive example of how lack of an adequate appreciation of macroeconomic linkages can seriously distort policy initiatives is provided by the measures adopted in 2001 and 2002 for curbing the mounting food subsidy bill. In the late 1990s and the opening years of the new millennium, the fiscal stress arising from the huge accumulation of FCI's excess stock of foodgrains became a major policy concern and the government was busy devising the best way, from the viewpoint of promotion of fiscal health as well as primary economic goals, of bringing down the stock to its preferred level. However, as demonstrated in Chapter 4, the government policy of disposing of the excess stock partly through an increase in the ration quotas for below poverty line (BPL) families and largely through heavily subsidized export of foodgrains was far from optimal, based as it was on an overly partial view of the problem, without any consideration of the state of the macroeconomy and interdependence between the food and other markets.

[3] Based on *Report of the Committee on Fiscal Responsibility Legislation* (GOI, 2000). The bill was passed in 2003 with some modifications and these are discussed in Chapter 6 while examining the fiscal restructuring programme suggested by the Twelfth Finance Commission (2004).

Taking into account the prevalence of excess capacity and huge unemployment on the one hand and large shortfall of infrastructural facilities along with extremely poor indices for education and health on the other, the chapter suggests that FCI's excess food stocks (instead of being a problem) present a golden opportunity for correcting some of the government's past policy errors by stepping up social sector and infrastructural investments. On the basis of a macro-theoretic framework considered appropriate for the Indian economy at that juncture (2001), it is shown how the suggested policy package, apart from furthering the basic objectives, would also contribute substantially towards budgetary viability.

The last two chapters on budgetary issues (Chapters 5 and 6) analyse the sources of fiscal imbalance of the Indian economy and examine in the light of this analysis the efficacy of the fiscal restructuring schemes suggested by EFC (2000) and TFC (2004). The basic problem with both the schemes, it is found, arises from misdiagnoses of the fiscal ills, and more fundamentally, from the absence of an analytical framework for:

(a) identifying the major factors affecting the short- and the medium-run behaviour of the economy;
(b) estimating on the basis of (a) the effects of *primary* instruments[4] of budgetary policy on macro variables including the fiscal deficit and all that; and hence
(c) working out a package of primary policy instruments (and the associated ratios of debt and deficits) along with their phasing that are not only feasible and consistent, but also the most efficacious under the constraints facing the economy.

While there is little macroeconomic exercise behind EFC's fiscal adjustment programme, TFC does try to formulate its 'fiscal reform strategy (centring) on growth' and a framework relating growth, debt dynamics, and fiscal restructuring. However, apart from the fact that in the absence of the primitive chain of relations governing growth, interest rates, and primary deficits, TFC's analysis of debt dynamics degenerates into a tautology devoid of any explanatory or operational significance, there are other fundamental flaws in the TFC framework that seriously erode the efficacy of its programme of fiscal correction.

The analysis in the two chapters suggests that the economy's budgetary imbalances are attributable not so much to the overall fiscal deficit, but more to the composition of government expenditure and modes of its

[4] For example, tax rates and *nominal* expenditures over which the government has some *direct* control.

financing. Indeed, the nature of fiscal adjustment attempted during the 1990s seems to have played a significant role in creating difficulties on both the macroeconomic and budgetary front. The macroeconomic problems have been manifested in the decline and stagnation of aggregate capital accumulation and saving, low agricultural growth along with sharp fluctuations in foodgrains output and inflation, and deceleration of industrial growth. These problems are due in large part to the abdication of anti-cyclical fiscal responsibility, and more generally, to the counter-productive budgetary stance reflected in a cut-back in public investment, inadequate expenditure on education and health, a fall in the tax–GDP ratio, and reliance on high-cost borrowing instruments.

In the context of the aforementioned omissions and commissions, Chapters 5 and 6 chalk out fiscal correction measures that differ significantly from those of EFC and TFC in respect of both the instruments and their phasing. The thrust of the alternative approach is on specifying the primary instruments and dovetailing demand management measures in a developmental programme, taking into account the yawning gap as of now between the social and private returns on infrastructural and social sector investments and the short- and long-term costs of financing government expenditure through taxes, borrowing, and seignorage. The phasing of macro indicators under the suggested programme is characterized by a significant step up in public infrastructural and social sector investment along with greater reliance on borrowing and seignorage in the earlier phases and a gradual decline (as a ratio of full employment GDP) in such investments and modes of financing as the economy matures. On growth-theoretic considerations such a programme, it is shown, is not only feasible but also in consonance with inter-temporal optimality conditions.

As already noted, side by side with the worsening fiscal situation, the period since the mid-1990s has witnessed large capital inflows and burgeoning foreign exchanger reserves. Chapters 7, 8, and 9 are devoted to an examination of these external sector developments and their inter-relationship with other sectors of the macroeconomy. Chapter 7 provides a broader perspective, analyses the economic consequences of large capital inflows and reserves accretion, and discusses policy options in the context of the slowdown in growth, a significant output gap, and low absorption of foreign capital in the Indian economy. In particular, the chapter focuses on (a) the high cost of accumulation of excess reserves and (b) the deleterious impact of capital inflow in the presence of demand deficiency even when foreign funds are interest-free and used for investment (rather than reserves build-up). Reliance on foreign capital for supplementing domestic saving makes sense only when there is full employment of resources and at the margin the expected return on domestic capital accumulation exceeds the cost of servicing external liability including the risk associated therewith. The policy imperatives of this reasoning are fairly straightforward in the Indian context. In the absence of an economy-wide, well-functioning credit delivery system, the Reserve Bank's role in eliminating the output gap along with productive absorption of capital inflows and excess reserves can at best be supportive. The main initiative for this purpose has to be fiscal and take the form of building up infrastructural and other facilities that would provide a boost to private investment, both domestic and foreign. At the same time regulation of capital inflows, especially of the non-FDI variety, has to form an integral part of macro management for promotion of growth with balance-of-payments viability. It is these two policy issues that are discussed in some detail in Chapters 8 and 9.

The point of departure of Chapter 8 is the Planning Commission Scheme (PCS) mooted in 2004 for utilizing US dollar (USD) 10 billion worth of forex reserves over the next two years for purposes of infrastructural investment.[5] The scheme drew flak from practically the entire community of Indian economists as also from some in the IMF on the ground that it would (a) raise the inflationary potential; (b) enlarge fiscal deficit leading to crowding out of private investment and an increase in the burden of public debt; and (c) erode the balance-of-payments viability. However, none of the critics' concerns, the chapter demonstrates, stands up to a close scrutiny on the basis of the prevailing macrolinkages of the Indian economy. Even so, the chapter suggests some major modifications in PCS in the context of a near 15 per cent output gap and the extent of infrastructural deficiency bedevilling the economy. First, in the presence of an output gap, for stepping up public investment it is necessary neither to raise net imports (through depletion of reserves) nor to borrow from the public: net RBI credit to government in support of such expenditure will—apart from closing the output gap, promoting growth, and strengthening government finances—also help in management of capital inflows. Again, even when the output gap has been eliminated, a much bolder programme than what has been mooted by the Planning Commission is necessary; instead of being a bane, the capital inflows would then enable the economy to short-circuit the developmental process without putting pressure on the balance of payments.

While there can be no denying the positive role of capital inflows under a well-designed macroeconomic policy framework, it is also important to

[5] After much dithering the scheme was finally accepted by the Ministry of Finance in 2007. In the context of the quantum jump in forex reserves in the meantime, the analysis in the chapter has acquired greater significance as of now.

recognize that the various categories of these flows differ widely in respect of their volatility, transparency (cleanliness) as also their effects on real and financial sectors in general and balance-of-payments vulnerability in particular. It is on the basis of these considerations that Chapter 9 advocates strict control and regulation of foreign institutional investments. Curiously enough, the Ministry of Finance has for long been so besotted with FIIs that it constituted [first a Committee (2004) and then] an Expert Group (2005) with the express purpose of 'Encouraging FII Flows' albeit with measures for checking capital market vulnerability. The chapter examines the report of the Expert Group (EG) and unsurprisingly (given the terms of reference) finds it wanting in several important respects. In consonance with the ministry's wishes, EG proposes several measures of further liberalization of FIIs including participatory notes (PNs)—by far the most important, shady, and volatile form of FII—reposing a touching trust in the ability of the market regulator [Securities and Exchange Board of India (SEBI)] to contain the capital market vulnerability that might result therefrom. The basic deficiency of the report lies in its partial analysis (and that too of a highly unsatisfactory nature), sans any consideration of (a) the macroeconomic effects of FIIs or the monetary/fiscal problems they tend to engender; (b) the economy's investment needs (or absorptive capacity) in relation to its saving potential; and (c) the prospective supply and relative merits of different categories of capital inflows—factors which govern the optimal scale of FIIs. No wonder, the report ends up making suggestions without bothering to check their economic rationale or take cognizance of the fact that both theoretical arguments and empirical evidence militate against the proposals.[6]

The final chapter of the volume (Chapter 10) revisits some of the major issues related to banking and finance raised in Chapter 2, written (in 1994) shortly after the initiation of the financial sector liberalization programme. In the context of developments over the period 1994–2005, the chapter provides an appraisal of the sector's major attainments as also the serious shortcomings, many of which were evident as early as 1994. While some of

[6] Postscript: As might be expected, EG's recommendations were accepted with alacrity and the Indian capital market was flooded with FIIs of which nearly 80 per cent were PNs. It was only when these huge flows continued creating stock market bubble and large volatility, the Reserve Bank was being put under great stress in managing the exchange rate and money supply, and the rising fiscal burden due to the unrelenting increase in market stabilization bonds (MSBs) showed no sign of abatement, was there an end to the ministry's long-lasting affair with PNs. In October 2007 SEBI put a check on further FII inflows by way of PNs and required the existing ones to be phased out over the next eighteen months.

the shortcomings, it is noted, are structural or policy related, there have also been avoidable lapses in the organization and operation of the banks themselves. In light of this discussion, the chapter suggests measures that would enable the banking sector to effectively contribute towards economic growth and containment of financial volatility under the rapidly changing domestic and international economic environment.

The foregoing overview suggests how diverse and often unexpected the financial and other macro developments were during the first fifteen years of the post-reforms period. Indeed, it is such developments that pose ever changing challenges to economists and policymakers alike, and make the study and analysis of macroeconomic issues so fascinating. As the Indian economy matures and becomes more closely integrated with the rest of the world, the nature of the problems and challenges encountered would no doubt change in the future. However, a fruitful analysis of these problems would still require identification of intersectoral linkages in terms of a coherent macro-theoretic framework relevant for the economy under investigation—something the essays in the rest of the volume attempt.

2

Money and Public Finance under Structural Adjustment*

We must beware of Sirens' song and give their flowery meadow a wide berth. I alone, Circe suggested, might listen to their voices; but you must bind me hard and fast, so that I cannot stir from the spot where you will stand me, by the step of the mast, with the rope's ends lashed round the mast itself. And if I beg you to release me, you must tighten and add to my bonds.

Odyssey, Book XII.

I propose to phase out the government's access to ad hoc Treasury Bills over a period of three years. In 1994–95 the net issue of ad hoc Treasury Bills should not exceed Rs 9,000 crore for more that 10 continuous working days at any time during the year. If this happens the Reserve Bank will automatically sell Treasury Bills in the market to reduce the level of ad hoc Treasury Bills.

Budget Speech, Finance Minister,
Government of India, February 28, 1994.

State of the Macroeconomy: Some Puzzling Features

Since the initiation of the Structural Adjustment Programme (SAP) in July 1991, especially during 1993–4, the Indian economy has displayed a number of interesting features which have important implications for fiscal and monetary policies. First, for the first time since 1969, there appears to have occurred a switch from a regime of credit rationing to a situation of demand constraint in the loan market. Second, the excess liquidity in the system has failed to stimulate production and does not seem to have had a significant impact on the prices either (Table 2.1). Third, the increase in commercial

* Reprinted from *Economic and Political Weekly*, Vol. XXIX, Nos 16 and 17, April 16–23, 1994.

TABLE 2.1
Key Macroeconomic Indicators, 1990–4

	1990–1	1991–2	1992–3	1993–4
Variations in				
GDP	4.9	1.1	4	3.8
Agricultural production	3	–1.9	3.9	–0.9
Foodgrains production	3.2	–4.5	6.9	–0.5
Industrial production	8.3	0	1.8	1.6 (Apr–Jan)
Consumer price index	13.6	13.9	6.1	8.6 (Apr–Jan)
Wholesale price index (point-to-point)	12.1	13.6	7	7.6 (Apr–Jan)
Money suppy (M_3)	15.1	19.4	14.1 (Apr–Jan)	14.1
Gross domestic capital formation	11.2	–15.8	16.7	
Public	6.1	–7.1	26.4	
Private	17.3	–18.4	15.1	
Gross fixed capital formation	8.8	–4.1	1.7	
Public	6.5	0.2	–4.8	
Private	10.5	–7.1	6.7	
Ratios to GDP of				
Fiscal deficit	8.4	5.9	5.2	7.3
Revenue deficit	3.5	2.6	2.4	4.3
Monetized deficit	2.8	0.9	0.8	1
Current account balance	–3.3	–0.9	–2.1	–0.5
Gross dometic saving	24	23.1	22.3	
Public	1	1.7	2.1	
Private	23	21.4	20.2	
Gross domestic investment	27.4	24.2	24.5	
Public	10.5	10	10.3	
Private	16.2	14	14.6	

Sources: Government of India (1994), Reserve Bank of India (1993).

bank credit to the government has been far in excess of the requirement under the statutory liquidity ratio (SLR) (Table 2.2). Fourth, the fiscal deficit, after registering a decline in the first two years of SAP, has shot up to 7.3 per cent of GDP this year. Indeed, if one does not use the trick of (a) clubbing revenue receipts with some capital receipts such as recoveries of loans and sale proceeds of shares in public sector undertakings and (b) excluding market borrowing by public enterprises in the absence of loans routed through the treasury (Rakshit, 1991), the fiscal deficit will be close to 9 per cent of the GDP. However, contrary to the conventional wisdom this rise in fiscal deficit has been accompanied by a significant decline in the current account deficit, from 2.1 per cent to 0.5 per cent of GDP between 1992–3 and 1993–4 (Table 2.1). Fifth, the gross domestic saving ratio declined from 24 per cent to 22.3 per cent during 1990–3. The decline in private saving was steeper—from 23 per cent to 20.2 per cent—and occurred in the face of substantial tax concessions, especially in respect of income and other direct taxes (Table 2.1). Finally, production in the capital goods sector has fallen by 8.8 per cent during 1993–4 even though banks were flush with funds. The corporate sector raised Rs 29,000 crore from the primary market during 1993 (against Rs 16,600 crore in 1992); and there was a substantial inflow of foreign funds by way of euro-issues by Indian companies and foreign direct and institutional investment. What is no less important, despite the favourable turn of events on the trade front and the jump in foreign exchange reserves from $2.24 billion on April 1, 1992 to $13 billion by the third week of February 1994, the flow of foreign direct investment has been quite modest and the credit rating of India remains as low as it was in 1991.

An examination of the factors behind these developments appears necessary for an assessment of the policy package proposed by the Ministry of Finance. The importance of such an examination assumes urgency in view of the fact that the *Economic Survey 1993–4* and the Budget papers for 1994–5 display inadequate appreciation of the macroeconomic mechanism giving rise to the paradoxes noted above. In order to identify the economic forces behind the emerging scenario, we take the developments in the financial sector as our point of departure, mainly because the primary concern of the government remains reduction of fiscal and monetized deficits and the finance minister has proposed automatic sale of Treasury Bills by the Reserve Bank of India when its net credit to the government crosses a pre-specified limit. The second section summarizes the behaviour of money and credit during 1993–4 and draws attention to some serious inadequacies in the official explanation of major financial developments. The third section attempts a resolution of the paradoxes taking into account the interaction between the financial and real sectors. In terms of the analytical framework used in this context, the fourth section provides a critique of the budgetary proposals for 1994–5 and suggests some policy alternatives. The final section summarizes the main results.

Excess Liquidity and Its Manifestations

The most striking development in the financial sector during 1993–4 was the emergence of substantial excess supply. While it is not easy to provide a quantitative estimate of the extent of excess supply in the loan market, the symptoms of demand constraint faced by banks and other financial intermediaries are clearly revealed in the following developments.

During April–January 1993–4, the growth of reserve money, currency with the public, and money supply (M_3) were 20.4, 16.1, and 14.1 per cent, respectively (Table 2.2). Thus, the fairly steep fall in the (incremental) money multiplier occurred not only in the face of a cut in cash reserve ratio (CRR) on the net total demand and time liabilities (DTL) and of the removal of the 10 per cent incremental CRR imposed earlier, but also when the growth rate of currency with the public lagged far behind that of reserve money. Under the standard analysis these factors should have raised significantly the value of the incremental money multiplier. Indeed, deposits with scheduled commercial banks increased by only 13.8 per cent against a more than 25 per cent rise in their holding of reserve money. Rough and ready calculations on the basis of the prevailing base and incremental CRRs suggest that in the absence of any demand constraint in the loan market, the additional amount of bank deposits and credit (in all forms) during the first ten months of 1993–4 would have been larger by more than Rs 15,000 crore.[1]

Second, excess supply in the loan market has also been manifested in the remarkable change in the portfolio of scheduled commercial banks. During April–January 1993–4, non-food advances—constituting the most profitable asset of banks—rose by only 4.2 per cent while 'investments' recorded a growth of 18.8 per cent (Table 2.2). Priority sector advances in fact declined by Rs 210 crore, while investment in government securities jumped by Rs 18,796 crore against an increase of Rs 8,764 crore in the corresponding period in 1992–3 (*Economic Survey 1993–4*, p. 38). The interesting thing

TABLE 2.2
Variation in Money and some of its Components

(Per cent)

	1991–1	1992–3	1992–3 March 20 to January 8	1993–4 March 19 to January 7
Money supply (M_3)	19.4	14.1	12.4	14.1
Currency with the public	15.2	12.4	8.2	16.1
Commercial bank deposits	19.8	16.4	14	13.8
Advances	8	21	16.7	6.6
Non-food advances	8.2	20.1	16.3	4.2
Investments	20.2	17.1	12	18.8
Reserve money	12.4	11.5	14.6	20.4 (Jan 14)
Net RBI credit to centre	6.7	2.3	9.7	10.8

Source: Government of India (1994).

[1] Ignoring the cash drain from the banking system that would have occurred with the concomitant rise in the level of economic activity.

to note in this connection is that under SAP, reductions in SLR and CRR are deemed essential for diverting bank credit away from the government to finance productive investment in the private sector. However, while the incremental SLR has been reduced to 25 per cent, the rise in the ratio of investment in government securities to additional bank deposits during 1993–4 has been more than 50 per cent.

Third, symptoms of excess liquidity are also in evidence outside the banking sector. Large companies have repaid a substantial part of their debt in advance of the maturity date and/or invested their funds in units of the Unit Trust of India (UTI). UTI is having trouble with finding suitable outlets for its funds, has been forced to buy Commercial Papers, and refused to accede to the request of companies for premature retirement of non-marketable debentures acquired through special placement.

Finally, excess liquidity has caused a decline in the interest rates, but the decline is not enough to eliminate excess supply in the loan market. Of the three interest rates figuring in Table 2.3, only the call money rate may be regarded as market clearing and the fall in this rate is also the steepest. However, the significance of this interest rate in effecting the flow of funds from savers to the ultimate users of credit is severely limited. Of crucial importance in this regard are the institutional lending rate and the (minimum) interest on bank loans both of which are administered. The administered rates have, to be sure, responded to market forces, but the response has been sluggish and far from perfect (Table 2.3).

TABLE 2.3
Interest Rates, 1992–4

	Institutional Lending Rate	Call Money Rate	Banks' Minimum Lending Rate
Dec–1992	17.5	10.5	18
Dec–1993	15.5	5.5	15
Mar–1994	14.5	2	14

Source: Government of India (1993, 1994).

Official Misperceptions of Financial Developments

Before explaining the features noted above and seeking to relate them to factors operating in the real part of the economy, it is useful to clear the deck by dispelling some serious flaws in the official perception of current financial developments. The explanation of the Ministry of Finance of the slow growth of commercial bank credit, especially non-food advances, runs partly in terms of adherence to 'prudential norms' by banks in advancing loans, but mainly in terms of the rise in the yield on government securities and the zero risk weight assigned to them under the new norm (*Economic Survey 1993–4*, pp 38–9). The rise in fiscal deficit has in fact been identified as the villain of the piece: 'An important underlying reason for the limited increase in credit to the non-food commercial sector is the large borrowing requirement (fiscal deficit) of the government. A high fiscal deficit has led to high interest rates on bank advances to commercial sector, which has made some investments unviable, and also pushed the private sector looking for other sources of finance. Containment of fiscal deficit is, therefore, an important policy tool for freeing bank resources for injection into agriculture, industry and commerce' (*Economic Survey 1993–4*, p. 39).

Note first that during the period under consideration the return on government securities was around 11.5 per cent against the then prevailing minimum lending rate of 15 per cent on bank advances. Be that as it may, the official explanation would have made sense only if banks were fully loaned up or not burdened with excess reserves. We have drawn attention to the low growth of deposit in relation to accumulation of reserve money by the banks, even though the base CRR was reduced and the requirement relating to incremental CRR withdrawn. We have also provided a rough and ready estimate of the potential excess supply of bank credit. Indeed, excess reserves have induced banks to buy Commercial Papers at an yield of 11.5 per cent in violation of the tacit agreement that the yield should be 12.5 per cent. The point to note here is that even at the minimum lending rate there was not enough demand for loans by creditworthy borrowers to absorb the potential supply of bank advances. Under these circumstances, the increased investment in government securities by banks was not at the expense of bank advances to the commercial sector. A reduction in fiscal deficit would have raised excess reserves in the banking system without any enhanced deployment of bank resources to industry, agriculture, and commerce.

The most curious aspect of the explanation offered by the Ministry of Finance is its eloquent silence on the link between depressed conditions in industry and agriculture on the one hand and poor growth in bank advances on the other. Indeed, the phenomenon of the change in the relative importance of 'investments' in gilt-edged securities and advances in the portfolio of commercial banks during depressions has also been observed in countries such as the United States (Bernanke, 1983). The basic flaw in the finance ministry's view arises from not taking account of the fundamental difference in the economic mechanism under a regime of credit rationing and in a situation where the demand constraint is binding in the loan market. An implication of the official reading of the situation is that here the causation has run from low bank advances to stagnation of industrial and agricultural output, rather than the other way round. An instructive illustration of the preconceived theories distorting the view of the observer.

Towards a Resolution of Some Macroeconomic Paradoxes

Given the fairly widespread misconceptions regarding the links between budgetary operations and the behaviour of the financial and real sectors, we propose to summarize first the major elements of the theoretical framework that appears relevant for explaining some of the puzzling developments of the Indian economy during 1993–4. For simplifying the exposition we focus initially on the demand and supply sides of the credit market and suggest how the factors operating on the two sides are related with the rest of the economy.[2]

Demand and Supply Constrained Regimes in the Financial Market

When interest rates are administered (as most of them are in India) or slow to adjust, the loan market is characterized by a regime of credit rationing (CR) or of demand constraint (DC).[3] The importance of distinguishing between CR and DC arises from the fact that the behaviour of the economy and the effects of fiscal and monetary policies differ widely under the two regimes.

Whether the loan market will be characterized by CR or DC depends on the constellation of major economic forces operating in the credit as also the commodity market. Consider first the behaviour of the credit market. On the supply side it is useful to distinguish between two categories of loans, viz., bank and non-bank loans, and the latter may further be sub-divided into (a) direct loans from savers to investors and (b) loans routed through non-bank financial institutions. At given interest rates and no demand constraint, the maximum potential supply of bank credit, *a la* the textbook money multiplier analysis, is determined by the supply of reserve money, the CRR, and the demand for currency by the public. The potential supply of non-bank credit depends on the other hand upon the menu of financial assets available outside the banking sector, the structure of interest rates and the preference of the public between bank deposits and other forms of financial assets. An increase in reserve money, a scaling down of the CRR,

[2] For a more detailed exposition see Rakshit (1986a, 1994).

[3] Even when the central bank does not fix the structure of interest rates, strong oligopolistic elements in banking and finance tend to make the lending as also deposit rates fairly sticky. Neither does perfect competition by itself ensure market clearing interest rates since asymmetric information gives rise to the problems of adverse selections and moral hazard (Stiglitz and Weiss, 1981).

or a decline in the cash drain from the banking system augments the supply not only of bank but also of non-bank credit. Development of the capital market, financial innovation, introduction of new instruments of credit outside the banking sector, and an increase in yields on non-bank financial assets (supplied by the government, the corporate sector or non-bank financial institutions) relatively to interest rates on bank deposits—all tend to raise the relative importance of non-bank to bank credit. But this, contrary to the apprehension voiced by many a banker, does not entail disintermediation or a decline in the volume of bank deposits and credit (Rakshit 1986a, 1994).

The major users of credit are the government, producers, and investors. While the borrowing needs of the government may, as a first approximation, be regarded as a policy variable, the rest of the demand for credit is primarily for financing working capital and investment in fixed capital. Capital accumulation has not only a direct impact on the demand side of the credit market, but growth in investment also raises indirectly the demand for production loans with the operation of the investment multiplier in real or nominal terms.

Given the structure of interest rates and the financial network in the system, the loan market will be characterized by CR or DC according as the aggregate demand for credit exceeds or falls short of the total supply of bank and non-bank credit.[4] Under credit rationing some of the production and investment plans remain unfulfilled. The result is a supply side or a demand side failure in the commodity market depending upon whether it is the producers or the investors who are quantity constrained in the loan market (Blinder, 1987; Rakshit, 1986). When the economy is characterized by credit rationing, government borrowing through SLR has a one-to-one crowding-out effect, but the government expenditure through monetized deficit will have a (financial) crowding-in effect through the operation of the credit multiplier within and outside the banking system. When fiscal deficit is financed through the introduction of high-yield assets such as National Savings Certificates (NSCs) or funds are routed to borrowers (public or private) through establishment of mutual funds or other financial innovations, the supply of non-bank credit rises without any decrease in bank deposits and credit. Again, an across-the-board change in the borrowing rates of banks and financial institutions has little impact on the system; but an increase in interest rate on bank deposits relatively to that on other financial

[4] There could no doubt be excess demand in some sub-markets together with excess supply in others. Such coexistence does not invalidate the results relating to the overall working of the system.

assets reduces non-bank credit with no significant change in the supply of bank loans.

Radically different are the effects of fiscal deficits and monetary policies when the loan market is demand constrained. Under such a regime it is the aggregate demand for loan and its distribution that determine the levels of bank and non-bank credits. Additional holding of government securities by banks then does not have a crowding-out effect. The value of both the money multiplier and the credit multiplier (the incremental ratio of total credit to reserve money) assumes the value of unity.[5] When the government or private borrowers raise funds from non-bank sources, there occurs a corresponding decrease in money and bank credit.

Evidence and Theory

In terms of the framework outlined above, it is not difficult to resolve some of the puzzles listed in the first and second sections and to identify the sources of the fallacy in official reasoning. In the list of factors held responsible by the Ministry of Finance for slow growth of bank advances during 1993–4 (*Economic Survey 1993–4*, pp. 38–9), some operate under CR and others under DC; but the two sets of factors cannot operate simultaneously.[6] Hence our dismissal of fiscal deficit, of 'provisioning and capital adequacy norms' set for bank loans[7] and of the reduction in the gap between the banks' minimum lending rate and the yield on government securities, as explanatory factors when the loan market is characterized by demand constraint.

To appreciate the behaviour of the system consider first the supply side factors operating in the financial market. Between March 31, 1993 and January 7, 1994 the potential supply of bank credit increased substantially because of (a) the rise in reserve money by 16.9 per cent (the rise was 20.4 per cent during March 19–January 14); (b) a lower growth rate of currency with the public (viz., 16.1 per cent) *vis-à-vis* that of reserve money; and (c) a cut in CRR from 15 per cent to 14 per cent along with removal of the 10 per cent incremental CRR imposed earlier. The net RBI credit to the government increased by Rs 8,686 crore compared with Rs 7,491 crore during the corresponding period in the previous year. Of the Rs 18,731 crore change

[5] Ignoring the feedback from the commodity market associated with the use of credit.

[6] Or rather, cannot be used for explaining the overall behaviour of the financial market.

[7] Note that DC implies inadequate demand for loan by creditworthy borrowers. Apart from the fact that the imposition of norms can explain at best sectional but not overall demand constraint, there can be little doubt regarding the decline in the demand for loans in real terms by creditworthy borrowers. Be that as it may, a boost in profitability in agriculture and industry would turn a considerable section of borrowers currently shunned by banks eminently creditworthy.

in reserve money, net foreign exchange assets of the RBI (excluding revaluation of gold) accounted for Rs 11,270 crore against (-) Rs 3,261 crore in March 31–January 8, 1992–3 (*Economic Survey 1993–4*, p. 37). If we ignore the feedback from the commodity market through the incremental cash drain from banks, the *ex ante* variation in money supply (M_3) or total credit from the banking system (including the RBI) was about Rs 65,000 crore while the *ex post* variation amounted only to Rs 51,279 crore.

Given the structure of the capital market and the returns on financial assets other than bank deposits, an increase in M_3 is associated with a more or less proportional rise in non-bank credit as well. But the capital market itself has been undergoing rapid changes over the last few years. Some of the factors—for example, growth of the equity cult, introduction of convertible debentures, new schemes for attracting funds initiated by the government, operation of UTI, LIC, and other financial intermediaries, and setting up of mutual funds and finance companies—have been in operation since the mid-1980s and were instrumental in raising the value of the credit multiplier and in offsetting, to some extent, the crowding-out effect of growing fiscal deficit under a regime of credit rationing prevailing until fairly recently (Rakshit, 1994). Of special significance for the current scenario are the following developments during 1992–4:

(a) Repeal of Capital Issues (Control) Act, 1947 and removal of control over price and premium of shares.
(b) Permission to Indian companies to tap the international capital market through euro–equity shares.
(c) Extension of facilities to non-resident Indians (NRIs) and overseas corporate bodies for subscribing to shares and debentures of Indian companies.
(d) The permission to Foreign Institutional Investors (FIIs) to invest in the Indian capital market on registration with the Securities and Exchange Board of India (SEBI).
(e) Setting up of private mutual funds and finance companies.

These factors have produced a significant structural shift in the capital market. Given favourable conditions the potential supply of funds from non-bank sources can now increase enormously in relation to M_3. During 1993–4, the favourable circumstances consisted of: (a) a stock market boom leading to a sharp rise in the average price-earning ratio of the shares; (b) recession in major industrialized countries;[8] and (c) higher interest rates in India compared with those prevailing in the international financial markets.

[8] That made India an attractive destination of FIIs.

The conjunction of these events with the revised rules for the capital market under SAP has led to a substantial rise in the supply of funds from the primary market and in the inflow of foreign capital, mainly through euro-issues and foreign institutional investments. During April–December 1993 the corporate sector is reported to have raised Rs 21,600 crore from the primary market compared with Rs 16,500 crore during the calendar year 1992. Add to that the issue of Commercial Papers by companies and enhanced access of importers to suppliers' credit due to recession in advanced countries, and it is not difficult to explain the jump in the availability of funds outside the banking system.

So far as the demand side of the loan market is concerned, the major increase has come from the government sector. Fiscal deficit rose from Rs 40,173 crore in 1992–3 to Rs 58,511 crore in 1993–4 (*Budget at a Glance*, 1994–5, p. 1). Even allowing for the supply side effect of monetized deficit (via money and credit multipliers), budgetary operations seem on the whole to have had a larger impact on the demand than on the supply side of the credit market. The demand has also been boosted by the increase in the public food procurement credit to the tune of Rs 4,336 crore during March 19–January 7, 1993–4 (against Rs 824 crore during the corresponding period in 1992–3). The explanation of excess supply in the credit market thus lies primarily in an inadequate increase in demand from the commercial sector which in its turn may be traced to (a) stagnation in the agricultural and industrial output and (b) slow growth in investment, especially in gross fixed capital formation. Since an increase in the availability of credit has generally a favourable impact on production and investment, it is necessary to take into account the interdependence between the credit and the commodity markets. This we propose to do in the course of the resolution of puzzles noted in earlier sections.

Excess Liquidity, Composition of Bank Assets, and Money Supply

The simplest puzzle to resolve in terms of the framework presented above is the change in the composition of bank assets, making inoperative the reduction in SLR. With inadequate demand for loans from the commercial sector, it is only natural for banks to lap up government securities in order to reduce their excess reserves, even though the return on these securities is less than the minimum interest rates on bank advances. Again, while stagnation of agricultural and industrial production has had an adverse effect on aggregate demand for credit, the effect has been much more pronounced on the demand for bank advances. The major part of bank loan is used for financing working capital and the variation in this source of demand depends primarily on the growth of agriculture and industry, and not so much of services (where production loan per unit of output tends to be lower than that in the commodity producing sectors). However, the variation in non-food advances (in nominal terms) during 1993–4 was only 4.2 per cent while the inflation rate was about 9 per cent. The implication is that bank advances were not enough to sustain the production level reached in 1992–3. The explanation lies partly in the reduction in the use of fertilizer, but mostly in the switch from bank to non-bank sources of funds. Under conditions of excess supply in the loan market such a switch reduces the *ex post* supply of money as also the ratio of advances to 'investment' in the portfolio of banks. The phenomena of the fall in the incremental money multiplier and the change in the composition of bank assets are thus related both to the aggregate excess supply situation in the credit market and the substitution of bank loans by funds from other sources.

There appears in fact to have occurred a shift in the demand for credit by the commercial sector away not only from banks but also from the all-India financial institutions (AIFIs). Disbursements by AIFIs during April–December 1993 was only Rs 14,755 crore against Rs 15,393 crore during April–December 1992 (*Economic Survey 1993–4*, p 47). This works out to a more than 10 per cent decline in real terms and is due partly to inadequate demand for long-term investment. However, the corporate sector, as noted earlier, has at the same time mobilized substantial funds through capital issues in the domestic and international markets, and through issue of Commercial Papers.[9] Thus, for AIFIs and banks, the overall problem of demand constraint has been compounded by the shift to alternative sources of finance. In fact, the corporate sector has used some of the funds mobilized to repay (and often prepay) debts contracted earlier. The amount of repayment during 1993–4 is expected to be Rs 10,000 crore which, if realized, is estimated to reduce the interest cost of the corporate sector by Rs 1,500 crore per annum and would add consequently to the woes of financial institutions (*The Economic Times*, January 28).

The most important reason for the shift away from institutional credit lies in the sharp change in the relative cost of finance from different sources. Interest rates on domestic loans in the wake of financial liberalization under SAP were between 20 per cent and 22 per cent, while some forex loans carried interest rates in the range of 24 to 28 per cent. The jump in domestic rates was due to the unfreezing of maximum lending rates in a situation of credit rationing, and the interest on forex loans largely reflects the high risk premium under the serious balance-of-payments problem plaguing the

[9] Most of which have found their way in 'investments' on the asset side of the balance sheet of financial institutions including banks. However, the amount raised through Commercial Papers is fairly modest.

economy in 1991–2. By 1993–4 the situation in both the domestic and the international capital market changed dramatically. The domestic money market displayed symptoms of excess supply; recessionary conditions drove down interest rates in developed countries; and there was a considerable improvement in the external balance of India. However, the adjustment in institutional interest rates, which are administered, was extremely sluggish. By December 1993 the institutional lending rates and the minimum interest on bank loans[10] were brought down by only one to two percentage points, to 15.5 per cent and 15 per cent, respectively (Table 2.3). By contrast, there was a steep fall in the cost of raising funds from other sources. The yield on Commercial Papers was 11.5 per cent, and would have been much lower had financial institutions not indulged in oligopsonistic practices. Interest rates on suppliers' credit to importers hovered between 2 per cent and 3 per cent. Net earnings of companies as a ratio of the price of their shares came down to less than 4 per cent.[11] The interest rate on euro-convertibles was as low as 3.5 per cent. No wonder, it paid the importers and the corporate sector to opt for these cheaper sources of finance at the expense of loans from banks and AIFIs and to prepay debts contracted in the earlier period.

Excess Liquidity and Stagnation: Causal Links

The coexistence of excess liquidity and stagnation in agriculture and industry would appear odd to anybody steeped in mainstream macroeconomics: a sharp rise in reserve money and the *(ex ante)* supply of credit outside the banking system should normally generate an expansionary effect on production and investment, at least in the short run. Part of the explanation of the puzzle lies in the fact that in mainstream models, Keynesian or monetarist, all interest rates are assumed to be market clearing. However, in India interest rates charged by financial institutions (including banks), which still constitute by far the most important suppliers of credit, are administered and have been characterized by extremely slow and modest adjustment in the face of excess supply in the loan market.[12] While the existence of sticky interest rates throws some light on the connection between the money and the commodity markets in the Indian economy, a satisfactory resolution of the paradox requires us to distinguish between factors operating in industry and agriculture.

[10] In a situation of demand constraint it is the minimum interest rate that matters.

[11] The ratio was lower in the heydays of the stock market scam.

[12] To see the significance of administered interest rates in this context, note that an increase in the supply of reserve money or non-bank credit will have no impact on aggregate borrowing for production and investment when all interest rates are fixed and the credit market is demand constrained.

In explaining agricultural stagnation it appears appropriate to focus on the supply rather than the demand side factors.[13] We have already taken note of the decline in the cost of raising funds from non-institutional sources. But these sources could be tapped only by large producers in the organized sector, while the vast majority of farmers have still to rely on banks and monopolistic money-lenders in the rural areas. Adherence to the newly formulated prudential norms for banks might thus have been responsible for the denial of production loans to a section of the farming community and hence for the adverse supply side effect on agriculture (Blinder, 1987; Rakshit, 1986). The 0.7 per cent (nominal) growth in bank credit to agriculture during April–August 1993 (*Economic Survey 1993–4*, p. 39) lends some support to the hypothesis of sectoral (or sectional) credit rationing[14] operating in agriculture. The problem was aggravated by the steep rise in the prices of phosphatic and potassic fertilizers following their decontrol. While this rise in prices reduces the profit-maximizing quantity of fertilizer consumption (with no shortage of funds), the decline will be larger for producers facing the credit constraint.

The main source of agricultural stagnation seems, however, to lie elsewhere. In fact, stagnation in agriculture has set in since the late 1980s and continued in the 1990s in spite of a long spell of favourable weather conditions. The period 1990–4 was characterized by above average monsoon in all the years, but agricultural growth averaged only 1.1 per cent per annum against a more than 2 per cent increase in population. The reason lies in a decline in the agricultural investment, especially since the late 1980s (Rakshit, 1994). Gross investment in agriculture in real terms was Rs 4,636 crore in 1980–1, but came down to Rs 4,580 crore by 1991–2 (*Economic Survey 1993–4*, p. 124). Thus, while variations in monsoon, availability of credit, or relative prices of outputs and inputs can account for some changes in agricultural production around the trend in 'capacity output', over the last half a decade the growth in capacity itself has been extremely sluggish due to the declining trend in the investment–output ratio in agriculture.

So far as the industrial sector is concerned, excess capacity appears widespread; there is no shortage of production loan; nor are producers quantity constrained in respect of raw materials and components imported from abroad. For explaining the poor growth rate in industries we have thus to look for factors operating on the demand side. The improvement in trade balance during 1993–4 could conceivably have produced an expansionary

[13] The demand side factors are relevant more in explaining the composition of agricultural output than its total.

[14] As distinct from overall credit rationing.

effect. But the largest increase (amounting to 38 per cent during April–September 1993–4) occurred in the export of agricultural goods, the production of which is basically supply determined. It is also worth noting that out of the Rs 1,245 crore increase in exports of manufactured goods in April–September 1993–4, gems and jewellery[15] accounted for more than 40 per cent. Anyway, the rise in export demand was too small to have any perceptible impact on the domestic industrial sector. The largest boost to demand has been provided by the government. Between 1992–3 and 1993–4 the central government expenditure[16] in real terms increased by about 7 per cent. No less important was the cut in tax rates and the steep fall in government revenue both in absolute terms and as a ratio of GDP.

The expansionary forces unleashed by budgetary operations were not, however, strong enough to counter the recessionary tendencies in the system. Reduction in direct taxes, cuts in duties on items of luxury consumption both directly and indirectly (through reduction in tariffs on their raw materials and components), large transfers[17] by way of interest payments and subsidies, and the stock market boom, all have tended to benefit the middle- and upper-income groups, but not other sections of the community. The fall in agricultural production had, in fact, a negative effect on the demand for inputs and outputs supplied by the industrial sector. While the production of sugar is expected to go down by 5 per cent in 1993–4,[18] the fertilizer output recorded a decline of 10.6 per cent in April–December 1993–4. That the latter was due to the demand rather than the supply side factors is attested by the fact that even under the liberalized regime, fertilizer imports fell by 36.9 per cent during April–September 1993–4 (*Economic Survey 1993–4*, pp. 85, 105). Stockpiling by the Food Corporation of India (FCI) at enhanced procurement prices and the rise in the quantity and prices of agricultural goods sold abroad seem to have benefited the rural rich. At the same time, people in lower income groups must have been hit hard by the steep rise in issue prices of foodgrains and substantial addition to their stock by FCI.[19] These factors together with the boost to upper class demand

[15] Whose contribution to domestic value added is a small fraction of their exports.

[16] The whole of this does not constitute expenditure on final goods.

[17] Strictly speaking, the increase in emoluments of government servants should also be treated as transfers rather than public consumption, since they hardly raise the quality or quantity of public service.

[18] During April–October 1993–4 the decline in sugar production was more than 5.5 per cent.

[19] Since a larger stockholding leads to higher prices in the open market. Note also that the increase in food subsidy was largely due to higher interest and other costs of maintaining large stocks, and hence did not benefit lower income groups, at least in the short run.

provided by the budgetary policies and the stock market boom[20] go a long way in explaining the change in the production of industrial consumer goods. During April–January 1993–4 the growth of consumer durables was 14.3 per cent[21] while production of all consumer goods rose by only 1.4 per cent. There was in fact a negative growth (of -1.6 per cent) in the production of consumer non–durables.

The steepest fall (of -8.8 per cent) in output occurred in capital goods industries and may be attributed (proximately) to (a) low investment, especially in fixed capital and (b) diversion of demand from domestic to foreign sources of supply. During April–January 1993–4, the gross fixed capital formation in real terms is reported to have grown by only 1.75 per cent. The growth in investment in machinery and equipment seems, in fact, to have been negative. The demand constraint faced by the producers of these goods was made more severe by the then prevailing structure of taxes and policies relating to capital goods imports. The customs duties on capital goods and the project imports were much lower than those on raw materials and components required for their production. There were no countervailing duties to neutralize the excise and sales taxes imposed on domestic capital goods.[22] Finally, imports of second-hand machines and availability of suppliers' credit to importers at very low rates of interest have caused further diversion of demand away from the domestic capital goods sector.

Low Capital Accumulation, Excess Supply of Funds, and Stock Market Boom

The industrial recession is no doubt due partly to substitution of foreign capital goods for domestic capital goods; but much more important has been the stagnation of aggregate investment demand itself. This, in the context of the surfeit of finance at the disposal of the corporate sector and the prolonged increase in share prices, constitutes perhaps the greatest puzzle of the Indian economy in recent years.

We have already drawn attention to the fact that while banks and AIFIs are flush with funds, the corporate sector has raised substantial amount of capital from the primary market, both domestic and foreign. Part of this fund has been used for retiring old debts carrying high rates of interest. This

[20] Through the Pigou effect, with share prices rising at a faster rate than the consumer price index.

[21] Note that under the prevailing Exim policy there is no leakage by way of imports in respect of consumption goods (except through imports of their raw materials and components).

[22] As we will see, some of the anomalies are sought to be corrected in the Union Budget for 1994–5.

of course is an eminently sensible step from the viewpoint of individual enterprises. Also, it does not have any adverse macroeconomic consequence when the substitution is between domestic debts. But companies have also used funds raised through euro issues to pay off their domestic debt or to reduce their borrowing from banks and AIFIs. This, it may be noted, is an instance of the individual interest running contrary to the interest of the economy as a whole. To see why, note that given the demand constraint operating in the domestic money market, such substitution does not involve any increase in capital accumulation or future growth in GDP. There is only a redistribution of the operating surplus from domestic lenders to producers and foreign creditors. Though companies earn more profits, there is a decline in the gross national product and the country is burdened with the problem of servicing foreign debt.

What is puzzling is not so much the liquidation of costly debts with cheaper funds irrespective of their sources, but rather stagnation in investment notwithstanding the steep fall in the cost of finance. The phenomenon underlines bleak expectations of investors relating to prospective yields and seems to confirm the old adage used in the context of asymmetrical effects of monetary policies during depressions and booms: although a horse can always be prevented from drinking, it is not possible to force it to drink.

If investors indeed take a dim view of future prospects, how are we to account for the stock market boom? The answer to the question can at best be tentative and may perhaps be sought along Keynesian lines. Decisions regarding fixed capital formation are based on considerations of long-term fundamentals, and such investment, being lumpy and irreversible, attracts high risk premium. For 'investment' in the share market, on the other hand, what matters is expectations regarding the short-run movement of prices.

The bullish sentiment in the stock market may thus be traced to the following set of factors. First, reductions in corporate income and capital gains taxes, and exclusion of shares from taxable wealth of individuals, have raised the attractiveness of shares, especially of profit-making companies. Second, after the abolition of control over the price and premium of new capital issues, many companies have raised the ratio of dividend to profits in order to reduce the cost of raising funds from the primary market.[23] Third, liberalization and decontrol of (product) prices have raised earnings of relatively efficient companies, though others have suffered in the process. The market sentiment has been guided, as is often the case, more by the record of star performers than by the overall profitability of the corporate

[23] Most empirical studies suggest that an increase in dividends at the expense of retained profits tends to raise prices of shares.

sector. The bullish sentiment generated by the performance of the select group of companies has given a thrust to the share prices of other companies as well. Fourth, the market has come to expect more and more concessions from the government in view of its avowed policy of reducing over time all direct taxes to levels prevailing in advanced countries.[24] Fifth, easy availability of funds, especially against shares, has helped bullish operations in no small measure. Finally, the phenomenon of rising share prices, unsupported by long-run expectations of producers, seems to owe much of its origin to herd behaviour and to the benchmark of market expectations set by the dizzy height share prices reached during the scam days.

Investment and Public Policy

The perceptive reader must have realized that the factors listed above would hardly weigh much with hard-headed businessmen taking decisions on investment in fixed capital. They would no doubt be all praise for the finance minister for the bonanza by way of cuts in taxes on profits and capital gains. But what matters for investment is not simply the increase in net profit on current operations, but the expected (a) demand in relation to existing capacity and (b) the availability and/or prices of inputs used in the process of production. An analysis along these lines may provide some clue to the puzzle of low investment in the Indian economy.

Note first that to the extent expectations are influenced by current happenings, the endemic and substantial excess capacity, whatever be its source, cannot but have a depressive effect on the investment climate. The irony of the situation is that it is the slowdown in public investment and government policies relating to capital goods imports that have resulted in the sharp fall in capacity utilization of units producing capital goods and most of these units belong to the public sector.[25] Under the programme for reform undertaken by the government, it will not make sense to the management of these enterprises to go in for any project for expansion of capacity.

Second, government fiscal and other policies have no doubt given a thrust to the production of consumer durables. However, apart from the fact that the weight of these goods is relatively low in industrial output, their imports are still on the banned list. With the threat of demolition of the protective barrier looming large, it is idle to expect large-scale investment in these industries.

[24] This is partly borne out by the decline in share prices when the Union Budget for 1994–5 fell short of expectations.

[25] We have elaborated elsewhere on the macroeconomic implications of such policies on fiscal deficit and public sector saving (Rakshit, 1986a, 1991).

Third, an important development in this context is stagnation of agricultural output consequent upon the decline in investment in agriculture. The basic reason here, as widely suggested, is twofold: cut-back in government investment in irrigation and related areas; and presence of strong complementarity between public and private investment in agriculture. In a country like India viability of balance-of-payments, price stability, and prospects of industrial expansion depend crucially on the growth of agricultural output (Rakshit, 1991, 1994). The implication is that when investment decisions are based on the knowledge of relevant macroeconomic linkages, *a la* Lucas et al., bleak expectations concerning agricultural growth cannot but act as a deterrent to capital formation in industries.

Fourth, attention has repeatedly been drawn to the danger of serious infrastructural bottlenecks in the medium and the long run due to inadequate investment in power, transport, and communication. The gap created by the decline in public investment in these fields has, contrary to expectations of the government, not been filled by private investment. The reasons are not far to seek. Given the large size and indivisibility of infrastructural projects, private investors will consider them worthwhile only if they expect a substantial increase in the future demand for these services. But expectations in this regard are unlikely to be buoyant in view of stagnation of industrial investment which in its turn is due in part to uncertainty relating to the future availability of infrastructural services. Such coordination failures cannot be corrected through reliance on the free play of market forces.

Finally, long-run investment is influenced considerably by producers' perception of both the ability and the commitment of the government to promote growth and full capacity utilization. While the government's commitment to reform and liberalization appears undoubted, its pronouncements relating to its priorities and policies for tackling recession and promoting growth are unlikely to inspire much confidence in the medium- and long-run prospects of development of the economy. It is thus not too difficult to explain why foreign direct investment has so far been so modest and credit rating of India remains low in spite of an improvement in trade balance and substantial inflow of foreign funds into the stock market.

Union Budget 1994–5: Short-Term Responses and Long-Term Perspective

In analysing the budgetary proposals for 1994–5, it is useful to relate them to two basic questions. First, what are the policy responses of the government in tackling the problems of low capacity utilization, slow growth, and unabated inflation? Second, how far does the budget reflect a well thought-out programme of development of the economy and alleviation of poverty?

While the implicit analytical framework behind government policies remains basically the same as that under the IMF-proposed SAP, during 1993–4 there were, to the horror of the establishment, quite a few violations in the canons concerning fiscal deficit, monetized deficit, and food and fertilizer subsidy. Some of these violations, it is claimed, were part of a programme of macroeconomic stabilization in the context of the substantial slack prevailing in the economy. Let us see how far the budgetary measures for 1994–5 are addressed towards the solution of short-term macroeconomic problems and how or if these measures are dovetailed in the overall policy for long-term development of the economy.

Macroeconomic Stabilization

If the government indeed raised the fiscal and monetized deficits in 1993–4 to counter the recessionary tendencies in the system, the budget for 1994–5 shows a reversal of the policy in this regard. The absolute levels of fiscal and monetized deficits in 1994–5 are slated to go down by 8.5 per cent and 50 per cent, respectively, from their corresponding amounts in 1993–4 (revised estimates). This turnaround in policy, in the face of persistence of slack in the economy, is perhaps due to the fact that these measures were found ineffective (or even counterproductive) in tackling recession during 1993–4! The more charitable interpretation is that the net effect of the budgetary measures taken together is considered expansionary in spite of the significant cut-back in fiscal and monetized deficits. Let us consider the major provisions in the budget that can have important effects on the short-run macroeconomic behaviour of the system.

The direct impact of the budget in stimulating aggregate demand will be negative on two counts. First, while the total government expenditure in nominal terms is to increase by 5 per cent, the increase in revenue receipts is expected to be 13 per cent. With a 9 per cent inflation rate, this implies in real terms a decline in the government expenditure by 4 per cent against a 4 per cent rise in revenue collections. Again, while the estimated increase in the government expenditure is Rs 7,827 crore, the increase in interest payments by Rs 8,500 crore tilts the balance in favour of transfer payments against the government demand for final goods and services. Thus, given the size of the central government budget in relation to GDP,[26] there will be a sizeable contractionary impact, if the government can attain its expenditure and revenue targets.[27]

[26] The Central Government expenditure as a ratio of GDP is more than 20 per cent.

[27] The two targets appear to be inconsistent in that if expenditure is no more than the budget estimates, the revenue targets are unlikely to be attained.

Second, in a situation of demand constraint in the loan market, government capital receipts, as our analysis in the third section shows, do not have a significant effect on aggregate demand eitherway. However, the lower growth in the Reserve Bank of India (RBI) credit to the government along with the new norm for bank advances can, as in 1993–4, have a negative supply side impact on agriculture and small industries.

It is interesting to note that in spite of the cut in the corporate tax, the government expects a 20 per cent increase in collections under this head during 1994–5. Presumably, the government expects a substantial improvement in the performance of the economy in general and that of the corporate sector in particular. This optimism is perhaps based on the expansionary effect budgetary measures are expected to have on private demand. The exemption limit for income tax has been raised; the average income tax is also reduced through adjustment in slabs; the minimum period of holding of units of UTI and mutual fund shares for calculation of long-term capital gains has been cut from three to one year; the exemption limit for gift tax has been raised from Rs 30,000 to Rs 1 lakh; and corporation tax has been reduced by five percentage points. No doubt, all these are expected to raise aggregate demand. But the tax concessions along with transfer through interest payments will, as in 1993–4, provide a further boost to the production of consumer durables and other items of luxury consumption. The only provision in the budget which will contribute directly to the demand for mass consumption goods is the Rs 2,000 crore increase in allotment for rural employment generation (provided there is no leakage from the source). Against this might be set the changeover to the system of *ad valorem* taxes, which, though justified on grounds of providing the much needed buoyancy to the tax system, will have the immediate effect of raising the prices of quite a few goods having large weights in the index of industrial production.

The budget attests to the government's concern regarding the negative growth of capital goods industries in 1993–4 and contains a series of measures to counter this trend. Here also the effect operating directly through the government expenditure is far from expansionary. The government expenditure on capital account is in fact expected to go down by Rs 760 crore in nominal terms or by about 8.5 per cent in real terms.[28] If we include investment expenditure expected to be incurred by public sector undertakings from internal and extra-budgetary sources, the real growth in public sector investment will be near zero. This is of course on the assumption

[28] Financial investment of the government largely reflects budgetary support for public sector investment.

that expenditure on capital account of both the government and public sector enterprises does not (as happened in 1993–4) fall short of the target.

The boost to the domestic capital goods sector is sought to be provided through the following set of measures:

(a) cut in long-term capital gains tax on domestic companies from 40 per cent to 30 per cent;
(b) reduction in corporation tax rates by five percentage points;
(c) extension of modified value-added tax (MODVAT) to capital goods;
(d) decrease in basic customs duty on project imports and general capital goods from 35 per cent to 25 per cent;
(e) reduction in lending rates of banks and financial institutions by one percentage point;
(f) scaling down of import duty on parts of capital goods to 25 per cent from the previous rates ranging from 25 per cent to 35 per cent;
(g) imposition of countervailing duty on imports of capital goods equivalent to the excise duty on domestic capital goods.

Measures (a) to (e) are intended to raise aggregate demand for investment, while (f) and (g) represent devices for preventing the diversion of this demand to imports even when there is no difference between the productivity of domestic capital goods and foreign capital goods.

Our analysis in the third section suggests that the provisions listed above are addressed to the periphery rather than the core of the problem of recession in capital goods industries. The correction of the anomalies in the tax structure via (f) and (g)—anomalies that run contrary to the standard principles of allocative efficiency—was of course long overdue.[29] But simply the prevention of substitution of foreign for domestic capital goods will be of little avail unless there is a significant increase in the aggregate demand for investment. No major improvement on the demand front can be expected from the reduction in institutional lending rates by one percentage point, given the much lower cost of finance from other sources. Provisions relating to the corporation tax and the capital gains tax will help, as in 1993–4, more in generating bullish sentiments in the stock market than in effecting any significant improvement in the climate for investment. Under the package of policies in the budget, growth in demand will primarily be in

[29] However, there is still no import duty on fertilizer projects; the duty on power projects is only 20 per cent; and imports on these two counts do not attract any countervailing duties. Again, there is little appreciation of the principle that even from the viewpoint of allocative efficiency, some subsidy is required for full utilization of existing capacity in capital goods industries, though investment in these industries can be justified only on the basis of their long-run viability (Rakshit, 1986a, 1991).

industries producing goods for upper class consumption and these goods are widely expected to be taken off the negative list of imports in the near future. Public investment in agriculture remains low. There is no move to assure private producers of the future availability of the infrastructural services. In short, long-run policies reflected in the budget cannot but make a rational producer extremely wary of undertaking investment on a large scale at the present juncture.

Long-Run Strategy

The upshot of our analysis is that in the absence of a sound strategy for long-run development of the economy, it will be difficult to avoid stagflationary tendencies in the system. The long-run policy under SAP is fairly clear and simple. There are also important elements in this policy which are eminently sensible and efficiency promoting. However, the policy also has important gaps which need to be recognized and removed for realizing the basic objectives of growth and poverty alleviation.

There are three major policy thrusts under SAP for which the government should be complimented. First, the attempt at the simplification of the tax system and at removal of bureaucratic control and procedural hurdles producers had to face at various stages, cannot but have a salutary effect on the functioning of the economic system. Second, the clear signal given to managers of the public sector enterprises that their job is to make profit and not to promote some non-quantifiable social objectives is essential for healthy growth of these enterprises. Third, the thrust on exports and cost-competitiveness of domestic industries is crucial for long-run viability of the balance-of-payments.

While the overall concern and policy measures on the three counts noted above constitute a welcome departure from the *ad hoc* policies of the earlier decade, some of the steps taken by the government betray an inadequate understanding of some basic economic issues and often go against the implicit model behind SAP itself. We have already referred to the violation of optimality principles arising from the differential duties on capital goods and their components, and from the absence of countervailing duties on imports. While the1994–5 Budget has removed some of these anomalies, others are permitted to persist (fn. 29). What is much more important, the government has not been quite consistent in following the principle of comparative advantage while promoting or discouraging industries.

When consumer goods imports are banned, low customs duties on capital goods (and their components) cannot but have a distortionary effect on the allocation of resources between the two sectors. If the ban on the consumer goods imports is intended to discourage consumption of some non-essentials,[30] the objective would be better served without violation of efficiency criteria by (a) imposing high excise duties on domestically produced luxury goods and (b) allowing imports of these goods with countervailing duties. If the objective is to raise the degree of capacity utilization in consumer durables or other industries in view of the difference between market and shadow prices of imports (Rakshit, 1986a, 1991, 1994), the ban should be supplemented by steps for discouraging investment in these industries. Anyway, the argument applies equally well to capital goods industries. The differential degree of protection to consumer and capital goods industries can be justified only if the former are deemed to enjoy greater dynamic comparative advantage—a hypothesis that cannot apply to all consumer goods industries currently protected, and does not seem to have any solid foundation in empirical findings.

The major flaws in the long-run strategy lie in two areas and there is no serious attempt in the budget to correct these flaws. We have repeatedly emphasized the importance of infrastructural investment and large-scale deployment of resources on selected industries in order to make them internationally competitive within a specified time frame. This requires some allocative planning and close cooperation between the government and the producers, public or private. Second, the government does not seem to have any effective plan for raising agricultural investment and production—a lapse that augers ill for the long-run internal and external balance of the economy.

Removal of the two defects in the government strategy requires, among other things, a significant step-up in the public investment. While the government is not perhaps unaware of this requirement, the stumbling block in this regard appears to consist in the problem of finance and the perception of the government concerning safe limits to fiscal and monetized deficits. Elsewhere we have indicated why the concern of the government should be the revenue rather than the fiscal deficit, and how the policy relating to interest rates, imports, and public investment has led to the fiscal crisis in the Indian economy (Rakshit, 1986a, 1991, 1994). Unfortunately, the process of unlearning the orthodox tenets and of learning from experience appears extremely slow in official quarters and the economy has meanwhile to pay the price in the form of losses in jobs, income, and economic growth.

Conclusion

(a) Poor growth in agriculture and industry in the Indian economy has been accompanied with a substantial increase in the supply of finance,

[30] This amounts to tacit admission of the failure of the direct tax machinery and government expenditure as means of promoting equitable distribution of income.

slow growth in bank advances, inflow of foreign funds, a jump in foreign exchange reserves, and a booming stock market.

(b) The key to the puzzles lies in (i) switch from a regime of credit rationing to a situation of excess supply in the loan market; (ii) the inter-relationship between the demand constraint in the loan market, low investment, and stagnation in agricultural output; (iii) differences in the factors operating in the share market and those affecting investment in fixed capital; and (iv) the way budgetary operations are related to (i), (ii), and (iii).

(c) The government policies under SAP have boosted the demand for consumer durables and contributed to the rise in share prices, but had adverse effects on capital formation in both agriculture and industries.

(d) While measures aimed at simplification of the tax structure, removal of bureaucratic control, generation of profits of public sector undertakings, and promotion of export competitiveness should contribute toward efficiency and viability of the system, there are major flaws in tackling short-run problems and in the long run strategy for development. The flaws consist primarily in the lack of any coherent policy relating to agricultural growth, infrastructural investment, promotion of activities in line with the principle of dynamic comparative advantage, and scale, composition, and financing of the government expenditure.

References

Bernanke, B.S. (1983), 'Nonmonetary Effects of the Financial Crisis in The Propagation of the Great Depression', *American Economic Review*, 73(3), 257–76, June.

Blinder, A.S. (1987), 'Credit Rationing and Effective Supply Failures', *Economic Journal*, 97 (386), 327–52, June.

Government of India (1993), *Economic Survey 1992–3*, New Delhi.

——— (1994), *Economic Survey 1993–4*, New Delhi.

Rakshit, M. (1986), 'Monetary Policy in a Developing Country', *World Institute of Development Economics Research*, Helsinki, mimeo.

——— (1986a), 'On the Inflationary Impact of Budget Deficit', *Economic and Political Weekly*, annual number.

——— (1991), 'The Macroeconomic Adjustment Programme: A Critique', *Economic and Political Weekly*, 26(34), (August 24).

——— (1993), 'Trade and Exchange Rate Policy with a Binding Foreign Exchange Constraint', in P. Bardhan, M. Datta-Chaudhuri, and T. N. Krishnan (eds), *Development and Change: Essays in Honour of K.N. Raj*, Oxford University Press, New Delhi.

——— (1994), 'Issues in Structural Adjustment of the Indian Economy', in Edmar L. Bacha (ed.), *Economics in a Changing World: Development, Trade and Environment*, Macmillan, London.

Reserve Bank of India (1993), *Annual Report 1992–3*, Mumbai.

Stiglitz, J.E. and A.L. Weiss, (1981), 'Credit Rationing in Markets with Imperfect Information', *American Economic Review*, 71(3), 393–410, June.

3

Restoring Fiscal Balance through Legislative Fiat*

If the choice is to be a good one, both the reasoning must be true and desire right; and the desire must pursue the same things that reasoning asserts.

Aristotle, *The Nicomachean Ethics*

The Fiscal Responsibility and Budget Management Bill (FRBMB), proposed by the Ministry of Finance, constitutes a landmark in the history of budgetary operations in India. The main objectives of the bill are by no means new and have figured prominently in successive budgetary statements since 1991. But in recent years the actual figures for the major fiscal indicators fell far short of the targets set in the annual budgets. It is in this context that the Committee on Fiscal Responsibility Legislation was constituted in January 2000 and the Government of India (GOI) is seeking in earnest a speedy enactment of the bill incorporating the Committee's recommendations (GOI, 2000). Our discussion of the bill is organized as follows. The first section summarizes the major provisions and objectives of the bill. In the three subsequent sections we examine how far these provisions are likely to help or hinder in promoting the primary objectives, viz., inter-generational equity, macroeconomic stabilization, and growth. The final section lists the main conclusions of our critique.

Objectives and Provisions of the Bill

The main objectives of the bill are to make budgetary operations sustainable and to further inter-generational equity, macroeconomic stability and economic growth. The 'Statement of Objectives and Reasons' accompanying

* Reprinted from *Economic and Political Weekly*, Vol. 36, No. 23, June 9–June 15, 2001.

the bill draws attention to the fiscal developments that underscore the seriousness of hurdles in securing these objectives.

Erosion of budgetary viability is indicated by the steep growth in interest payments on government liabilities in relation to its expenditure and revenue.[1] Second, heavy reliance on borrowing for meeting government expenditure, it is emphasized, has had an adverse impact on inter-generational equity. Third, attainment of macroeconomic stability has become difficult in the face of constraints on 'the central government's manoeuvrability in fiscal management' due to 'huge public debt and interest burden'. Finally, while large debt service obligations have stood in the way of government investment, hardening of interest rates due to high fiscal deficit has discouraged private investment. Both these factors, it is suggested, must have had negative implications for economic growth.

While the case for fiscal correction thus appears quite open and shut, the need for self-imposed limits, through a separate legislation,[2] is perceived to arise from two sources. First, given the fact that considerable slippage from the fiscal targets, as set in the annual budgets, has become quite routine, enactment of the bill is expected 'to provide a legal and institutional framework *for keeping the attention of policymakers and the general public sharply focused* on the need to bring down the fiscal deficit, contain the growth of public debt and stabilizing debt as a proportion of GDP over the medium term. Secondly, while this enactment will not be one of the crisis-induced measures, the enactment of FRBMB now is likely to be seen (by domestic and international investors) *as a demonstration of the country's resolve to maintaining macroeconomic balance and avoiding recurrence of any crisis* induced by fiscal imbalance.' (GOI, 2000, italics added).

Major Features

In order to make the budgetary process transparent and force the ministry of finance to do its homework in all earnestness, along with the annual budget the central government is to place before the parliament (a) the Medium-term Fiscal Policy Statement; (b) the Fiscal Policy Strategy Statement; and (c) the Macroeconomic Framework Statement. The first statement shall set forth 'a three-year rolling target for prescribed fiscal indicators with specification of underlying assumptions'. The second is to lay down, for the ensuing years, the central government's fiscal priorities, and give an

[1] 'The interest payments constitute about one-third of the central government's total expenditure and pre-empt nearly half of its total revenue' (GOI, 2000a).

[2] Remembering that the budgetary provisions themselves are passed by the parliament.

account, among other things, of the 'rationale for any major deviation in fiscal measures pertaining to taxation'. The third will presumably provide the analytical underpinning behind the first two statements.

Revenue Deficit, Fiscal Deficit, and Monetized Deficit

The operative and most important part of the legislation lies in its enunciation of the fiscal management principles and setting up of medium-term targets for what are considered the key fiscal parameters. The fiscal management principles consist in elimination of revenue deficit and fiscal deficit and building up of 'adequate revenue surplus'. Over the period 2001–6, the central government is required to reduce revenue deficit by at least one-half per cent of GDP in each financial year and bring the deficit down to zero by the end of the five-year period. Thereafter, the government shall build revenue surpluses and utilize the 'amount for discharging liabilities in excess of assets'.

In respect of fiscal deficit also, its annual reduction as a ratio of the corresponding year's GDP is fixed at one-half per cent or more over 2001–6 and within the period the overall fiscal deficit for a financial year has to be brought down to 2 per cent or less of the estimated gross domestic product.

In view of the close similarity between government borrowing and guarantee for loans contracted by public sector enterprises or other bodies, the bill places on upper limit on extension of such guarantee to one-half per cent of GDP in any financial year.

Provisions relating to revenue deficit and fiscal deficit imply that the debt–GDP ratio will register a fairly rapid decline over the five-year period. Beyond this period, elimination of fiscal deficit, building up of revenue surplus, and its use for retiring government bonds or liabilities would continue to impart a downward trend to this ratio. In fact, the bill sets a quantitative target for the debt–GDP ratio over a ten-year time horizon: the central government is called upon to ensure that, within the period from April 1, 2001 to March 31, 2010, 'the total liabilities (including external debt at current exchange rate) at the end of financial year (2009–10) do not exceed 50 per cent of the estimated gross domestic product for that year'.

One of the most noteworthy features of the bill—a feature that would have a substantial bearing on the conduct of macroeconomic policy in India—is the legal framework instituted in granting virtual autonomy to the Reserve Bank from the Ministry of Finance. From the financial year beginning on April 1, 2004, the central government is barred from making primary issues to the Reserve Bank. This will leave the Reserve Bank free to conduct open-market operations on the basis of the emerging monetary trends. However, the bill permits the central government to borrow from the Reserve Bank to meet *temporary* 'excess cash disbursement over cash receipts during any financial year in accordance with the agreements that may be entered into by the Government with the Reserve Bank'.

Transparency

We have already noted how the annual finance bill is required to be presented along with three statements regarding the macroeconomic framework forming the basis of the budget: the fiscal policy strategy for the ensuing year; and medium-term policy goals, specifying the underlying assumptions. This requirement should go a long way (a) in forcing the government to make public its own reading of the short- and medium-term trends of the economy and to explain the rationale of the measures proposed to be implemented; and hence (b) in promoting informed discussion on the merits of the fiscal stance taken by the Ministry of Finance. There are also other provisions in the bill that seek to make the budgetary process transparent. While placing the budget before the parliament the central government is to disclose in an accompanying statement all matters that have important fiscal implications, current or future. More specifically, the statement has to include information regarding changes in accounting standards, policies, and practices of the government and to give figures for its contingent liabilities (created through guarantees) as also for claims and commitments, 'including revenue demand raised but not realized and liabilities in respects of major works and contracts'. Such disclosure together with the three statements mentioned above would, it is expected, considerably reduce the scope for obfuscation on the part of the Ministry of Finance and provide a big boost to the confidence of domestic and international investors.

Compliance

Mere enactment of the bill, it is not very difficult to appreciate, will be of little help in guaranteeing fiscal rectitude or attaining the targets set. The annual budget itself, let us remember, is a piece of parliamentary legislation, but this has not prevented significant departure of the actual fiscal or revenue deficits from their budgetary estimates. The bill under review seeks to plug this loophole through two sets of provisions. The Medium-term Fiscal Policy Statement and the Fiscal Policy Strategy Statement are over time expected to maintain public focus on fiscal slippages and keep the government on its toes by the need to (a) explain why and how its presumptions and strategies went wrong and (b) give an account of the fiscal strategy proposed to be adopted for preventing such slippages.

From an operational viewpoint the corrective measures slated for implementation during the financial year are likely to be much more effective.

First, the bill requires the finance minister to place before the parliament quarterly reviews of government receipts and expenditure in relation to the budget. Second and most important for meeting the annual targets, in case of a revenue shortfall or excess of expenditure over prespecified levels, the government is to effect a proportionate reduction in all items of expenses except for the 'charged' expenditure. Finally, the finance minister has to explain before the parliament the reasons for non-fulfilment of obligations, if any, and the remedial measures the government proposes to take.

The various provisions of the bill leave little doubt regarding the government's resolve to bind itself to a hard budget constraint and to take stringent measures for fiscal correction. Indeed, FRBMB does not permit any room for government discretion in respect of deficit reduction, except on grounds of 'national security or natural calamities of national dimension'. It is also quite clear that the programme chalked out in the bill, when implemented, will have a far-reaching effect on the Indian economy. Hence arises the need to assess the efficacy of the programme in attaining the major economic goals. Since the bill is explicitly intended to promote inter-generational equity, macroeconomic stability, and growth, we propose to discuss in the next three sections how far the provisions of the bill are in fact in consonance with these objectives.

Promoting Inter-generational Equity

In the context of persistently large reliance on borrowed funds for meeting government expenditure, 'The issue of inter-generational equity', the bill emphasizes, 'has...to be addressed without delay'. However, a perusal of the bill and the committee's report suggests that there is a somewhat inadequate appreciation of the issues concerning inter-generational equity on the part of the Ministry of Finance and its think-tank. The result has been that while some provisions under the FRBMB constitute an instance of doing the right thing for the wrong reason, there are others which are against promotion of the professed goal. To see why, we need to go into some basics.

Budgetary Impact on Present and Future Generations

The first of these basics pertains to the incidence of the current budgetary exercise on the present and future generations and is relatively unambiguous. The present (future) generation gains or loses through the budget only to the extent there is an increase or decrease in its level of consumption. Given this perspective, it is not very difficult to discern an important asymmetry between the effects of taxes and government borrowing. By reducing disposable income and hence consumption, taxes impose a burden on the present generation. However, borrowing does not have a similar impact on the future generation, the reason being that people paying taxes for servicing public debt and those receiving interest incomes from the government, both belong to the same generation. To be sure, taxes paid and interests received vary significantly across different individuals; however, such divergences have implications for intra-, *not* inter-generational distribution of income.[3] Similar arguments suggest that provision of public goods and services benefits members of the present generation, while increases in the economy's productive capacity through capital expenditure of the government confer benefits on future generations.

The framers of the bill have gone seriously astray when they seek to apportion the incidence of taxes, borrowing and government expenditure between different generations. Bemoaning the long history of fiscal profligacy in India the bill notes: 'The situation has deteriorated to such an extent that out of every three rupee expended by the Central Government, about two rupees come from its own resources and one rupee from the borrowed funds. Thus, the incidence of two-thirds of the Central Government's expenditure falls on the present generation and one-third on the future generations'. However, as our analysis suggests, the current budgetary exercise has an adverse impact on the welfare of subsequent generations only to the extent it reduces the availability of goods and services in the future. This reduction occurs in case the fiscal policies effect a cut in current investment, since the economy's future productive capacity will then be less.

When there is full employment of resources, an increase in the government's current expenditure, financed through taxes, leaves the distribution between current and future (potential) consumption of the economy more or less unaffected. When the extra expenditure is on interest or other transfer payments, private disposable income and hence private consumption remain unchanged, and so do aggregate investment and public consumption.[4] In the case of other categories of (tax-financed) current expenditure, there is a substitution of public for private consumption,[5] but there is no

[3] This is not say that there is no burden of public debt whatsoever apart from its distributional impact. Such burden arises not from the level of taxes as such, but from their distortionary impact that reduces the maximum attainable GDP out of a given quantum of non-human and human resources.

[4] Ignoring the impact of income redistribution on the overall private propensity to consume.

[5] Such a shift does not constitute a burden on the present generation unless the amount of public goods provided by the government is already above the optimum level (Rakshit, 2000; Samuelson, 1954).

(significant) change in current capital accumulation.[6] The same line of reasoning suggests that when the government takes recourse to borrowing in order to finance its current expenses, consumption goes up at the expense of investment so that there is a diminution in the economy's future output potential.

The results relating to the inter-generational impact of the government budget need substantial revision when the economy operates at less than the full employment level. In this case debt-financed government consumption expenditure need not be at the expense of investment. Indeed, such expenditure, through its salubrious impact on capacity utilization and profits, helps in promoting investment and, hence, in enhancing the welfare of both the present and future generations.[7]

Quite clearly, FRBMB's basic premise—that the proportion of taxes and borrowing in the government budget indicates their relative incidence on the present and future generations—is quite misconceived: the premise holds neither under full employment conditions, nor when the economy is burdened with excess capacity.

Since the objective of inter-generational equity is basically a long-term one, let us focus on government policies required for promotion of this objective, assuming that the economy enjoys full employment of its resources. It is not very difficult to see that the optimum policy package for this purpose depends not only on the incidence of budgetary measures noted above, but also on the notion of what constitutes inter-generational equity—the second basic to which we now turn.

Inter-generational Equity: Orthodox Approach

The textbook view in respect of budgetary rules for attaining inter-generational equity is based on the liberal principle that (as in other spheres, here also) government policies should be dictated by private preferences alone. These preferences are captured in individuals' inter-temporal utility functions, which, together with interest rates and other variables, govern the community's propensity to save. Under this approach the optimal scale

[6] Strictly speaking, there would be some tendency for investment to decline, given full employment of resources. A unit increase in tax collections and the corresponding decline in private disposable income cause a fall in the household consumption, but by less than unity. The implication is that, tax-financed government consumption tends to reduce, to some extent, aggregate investment and saving in an economy. In this case the 'burden' of taxes on the present generation is negative!

[7] As we shall presently see, it is for this reason that in countries with legislative codes concerning fiscal targets, the government is permitted to take recourse to an increase in debt financing in times of depression.

and composition of government expenditure and its modes of financing are governed by the following rules:

(a) The levels of government consumption and investment are such that their (social) marginal returns equal those on private consumption and investment, respectively.[8]
(b) The government consumption and transfer payments are financed by revenue receipts, while costs of public investments are met from borrowed funds.

The first rule ensures allocative efficiency of resource use in consumption and investment. The second, known as the golden rule, is intended to promote inter-generational equity. On the face of it, the golden rule appears eminently sensible. Remembering that the benefits of the government's revenue and capital expenditure accrue to the present and future generations, respectively, the rule ensures that the cost borne by the present generation exactly matches its gains from the budgetary exercise. The implication is that while public investment financed through taxes implies a forced transfer from the present to future generations, debt-financed government consumption, through a decline in capital accumulation, effects a cut in the availability of goods and services in the future. No wonder, the rule has found such universal acceptability among economists who prefer the government's fiscal stance to be neutral.

A Neo-liberal Approach

An important implication of the orthodox approach is that the entire saving is undertaken by households through operation of market forces, and that the government's role is confined to optimal division of investible resources between the private and the public sector.[9] However, as in the case of *intra*-generational income distribution, in respect of inter-generational distribution also the market solution may be seriously biased so that the government

[8] The case for government absorption of resources rests on the fact that *up to a point* (a) provision of public goods at the expense of household consumption adds to the community's welfare (given the amount of consumption by households and the government taken together) and (b) substitution of government for private investment at the margin increases the productivity of overall capital accumulation.

[9] It may easily be shown that when the government follows rules (a) and (b), the saving (and investment) ratio of the community is unique and not amenable to variation through changes in the scale and composition of the budget. The proposition is easily established. Consider an equilibrium configuration where (a) and (b) are satisfied. From this situation, any reduction in (tax-financed) government consumption must be accompanied by a fall in private consumption (to preserve equality between the marginal social utility from the two categories of consumption) and hence by an increase in the level of

needs to take a positive rather than a neutral fiscal stance in order to promote inter-generational equity. Before identifying the major sources of bias in the market solution and the corrective steps the government needs to take for their removal, we need to start with the notion of inter-generational equity itself.

The simplest and what may appear a reasonable approach to the problem is to look at it from the viewpoint of an impartial observer, oblivious of the generation he belongs to. Under this approach, while deciding on the optimal saving ratio or on any other matter having an important bearing on inter-temporal availability of goods and services, the government should truly be neutral and put *equal* weights to the welfare of all generations. Under this approach the market solution will be considered inequitable when consumers care little for the well-being of future generations. Indeed, the bias arises even when in the utility function of an individual the discount factor is the same for his own (future) consumption and that for his descendants.[10] Apart from the inability to visualize one's future needs and tastes, the logic behind the time preference of an individual lies in the risk of death and the perception that capacity to derive enjoyment from most consumables diminishes with age. The relevance of these factors for consumption at some future date differs radically between the present and later generations. Discounting, if any, is thus required to be related not to the date of future consumption, but to the age of the consumer on that date. Hence arises the case for public intervention for raising the community's saving ratio, when individuals' utility functions are characterized by discounting of consumption on the part of future generations.

---

capital accumulation. But this raises the marginal utility on (reduced) consumption and lowers returns on (the enhanced level of) investment at the margin so that households (remembering that their disposable income are also now larger) are induced to consume more, contrary to what the government wants to achieve. Similar inconsistency follows from the government's attempt to change the level of debt-financed public investment. Hence the result that under the budgetary principles considered above preferences of the present generation alone matter in determining the division of full-employment output between consumption and capital accumulation.

[10] Note that when individuals' utility function is of this nature, the Ricardian equivalence holds (Barro, 1974) and the golden rule becomes irrelevant. It does not matter whether the government expenditure, irrespective of its nature, is tax or debt financed, since individuals, while formulating their consumption and saving plans, take the government's inter-temporal budget constraint into account so that any substitution of tax by borrowing, is neutralized by a corresponding rise in the private propensity to save. However, the two key conditions of the model—the first relating to the inter-temporal utility function and the second to perfectly competitive capital market—hold neither for developed nor for developing economies.

The natural question that arises at this stage is: Will not such an approach go against the principle of democracy and representative government? How can a government, as the representative of the present generation, try to force its members to reduce consumption below their preferred level? The answer lies in the duality of individual 'preferences'. Somebody may be interested in only his own consumption and not care for the well-being of future generations. But as a rational individual he should be capable of putting himself in other people's shoes and be inclined to view the government policy of treating all generations on an equal footing as eminently fair and reasonable. Even individuals who are prone to promote their own interests irrespective of injuries inflicted on others in the process, generally welcome legislations that curb such activities.

While the approach suggested above thus seems reasonable enough, we must recognize that it also involves two major problems, one implementational, the other conceptual. First, under this approach the optimal saving ratio in any period depends on the return on investment and the government's view regarding the appropriate marginal rate of substitution between consumption of the present and future generations—something for which the market provides no signal whatsoever and which leaves room for considerable disagreement.[11] However, these difficulties are no more serious than the ones the government encounters in framing policies for an equitable (intra-generational) distribution of income. In both the cases, the solution cannot but be rough and ready.

The second problem lies with some policy implications of the approach, which seem to go against the commonly accepted economic goals of a nation. Treatment of all generations on an equal footing implies that in an economy with growing per capita income, the government should put less emphasis on capital accumulation at the expense of current consumption. Indeed, when the major part of productivity improvements of an economy arises from disembodied technical progress or accumulated experience over time, the optimal saving ratio, it appears, should be negative in view of the fact that even with zero net savings, the later generations will be better off

[11] The optimality condition consists in the equality between the marginal rate of transformation of the present into future consumption (through accumulation of capital) and the marginal rate of substitution between inter-generational consumption. Treating all generations on an equal footing implies that, with zero marginal productivity of investment, consumption of all generations should be the same. With positive return on investment, the optimal saving ratio will be higher, the slower the rate at which the marginal utility (of any generation) is deemed to fall with a rise in (its) consumption level. Note in this connection that market interest rates may reveal inter-temporal preferences of individual consumers, but are no guide to the appropriate marginal rate of substitution between inter-generational consumption.

than the earlier ones.[12] Even when technological progress is not entirely disembodied and capital accumulation plays a key role in promoting economic growth, the present approach seems to militate against widely advocated policies for raising saving ratios in countries such as India from their present levels of 22 to 23 per cent. It may plausibly be argued that in the context of the country's extremely low per capita income as of now, the saving ratio is already too high and there is little justification for a further cut-back in the community's current consumption in order to enable the posterity to enjoy standards of living way above that of the present generation. Indeed, inter-generational equity considerations seem to suggest a cut-back rather than a step-up in the country's overall saving ratio.

Note that in the case of India practically the entire saving of the economy is accounted for by the private sector. Private saving is in fact much higher in quite a few other developing countries as well. The reasons for such high savings may be traced to altruism or readiness on the part of parents in close-knit families to undergo severe privations in order to enable their children and descendants to escape the poverty trap and enjoy a radical improvement in the quality of living. This is especially so after the development process has set in and people have become aware of the possibilities of rapid advancement in family fortunes through accumulation of assets, including education and training. In this case there is obviously no justification for a cut-back in the saving ratio. With children's well-being entering with large weights in parents' utility function, voluntary savings, however large, do not indicate undue sacrifice on the part of the present generation. The implication is that, while deciding on the optimal saving ratio, the government should give equal weights to the welfare levels of all generations, taking into account the utility an individual derives from his progeny's (expected) welfare.[13]

However, the saving ratio derived from the rule enunciated above will generally be considered sub-optimal by development economists, and we for our part are inclined to share this view. But how can one justify public policies for stepping up the saving rate when current consumption is abysmally low and individuals themselves already attach high weights to welfare

[12] This will certainly be true for a stationary population. The problem is trickier when population changes over time since the notion of inter-generational equity itself then becomes more complex.

[13] But what if the progeny feel terribly bad about the privations their parents or grandparents had to suffer? Should the government decisions be influenced by this consideration also? There is no simple answer to the question. Though few seem to lose their sleep pondering over the hardship undergone by their parents or forefathers, the problem of whether the government should try to correct for such uni-directional sympathy or altruism still remains.

of their descendants? In support of such policies, one may perhaps adopt a Hegel-type approach and treat welfare of the nation as a whole as something not dependent entirely on welfare of its members individually. Under this approach promotion of a country's advancement in all spheres—material, scientific, and cultural—is often considered as a categorical imperative, irrespective of private preferences of individual economic agents, present or yet-to-be-born. But the concept of a community's welfare function, not based on preferences of its members, may be considered too authoritarian and is unlikely to find favour with the large majority of social scientists. What then can be the plausible grounds behind the widespread perception that a poor nation should follow the East Asian example and try to short-circuit the development process through a significant step-up in its saving and investment?

There are two sets of factors which suggest why (a) rapid economic growth involving considerable sacrifice on the part of the present generation may be in consonance with individual preferences and (b) state intervention is called for in order to attain the community's optimum saving ratio. Individuals, it is widely observed, derive considerable satisfaction from their country's standing in the community of nations in terms of per capita income, human development index, GDP growth,[14] or in science, technology, culture, sports, and other fields. In other words, people are prepared to sacrifice for raising not only their own and their children's consumption in the narrow sense, but for the nation's rapid advancement as well. The problem, however, is that an individual considers, and rightly so, his own decisions incapable of changing the course of the economy currently or in the future, and hence does not feel inclined, in the absence of any coordinated plan with the rest of the community, to save on national considerations or on grounds of human progress in general. Hence the isolation paradox, the shortfall of the market determined saving from its 'optimum' level (in conformity with individual preferences), and the crucial role the state has to play in attaining the optimum.

Inter-generational Equity under FRBMB

Our foray into approaches to inter-generational equity has been prompted by the fact that among the objectives of the bill such equity receives top priority and the FRBMB provisions are supposed to promote this objective.

[14] Not only a high level of per capita income, but a high GDP growth also improves a country's image. Note also that the higher the level of per capital income, the larger the support the State can provide for excellence in science, technology, culture, and other fields.

Unfortunately, neither the Statement accompanying the bill nor the report of the Committee on the Fiscal Responsibility Legislation reflects an adequate appreciation of the major issues relating to optimal saving and the role of the state in this regard.

A perusal of the bill and the Committee's report suggests that the golden rule is regarded as the ideal for promoting inter-generational equity. However, contrary to what one would expect from such protestations, the provisions of the bill do not in fact conform to the golden rule.

Note first that while the bill enjoins the government to eliminate revenue deficit and bring down fiscal deficit to 2 per cent or less by the financial year ending on March 31, 2006, in the long run the government is 'to eliminate the revenue deficit and fiscal deficit and to build up adequate revenue surplus… and utilise such amount for discharging liabilities in excess of assets'. Quite clearly, these targets go against the golden rule, in as much as a revenue surplus with a zero fiscal deficit implies use of budgetary instruments for raising investment, directly or indirectly,[15] at the expense of current consumption. If, in the context of ineffective tax administration, a revenue surplus is needed to reduce over time the distortionary effects of high taxes or to compensate the future generation for the past fiscal profligacy, the surplus should be used to finance investment projects having the highest rate of return, not necessarily for reducing public liabilities.

A much more serious violation of the golden rule arises from adherence to the age old accounting practice under which some important items of government expenditure are treated as current, even though they benefit the future rather than the present generation. The most important of these items are education, health, grant for supporting (public or private sector) R&D, and costs incurred[16] in connection with setting up institutions for improvement in the working of the economic system. Since these types of expenses are considered crucial for long-term development of a country, putting them on the same footing as other items of revenue expenditure cannot but produce gross distortions in budgetary measures, focussed as they would be on meeting the fiscal targets. Similar is the case for subsidies and tax concessions for boosting investment. These have a negative impact on the government's revenue balance, as conventionally measured, but help in raising the community's future production potential. Hence arises

[15] Directly, when the surplus is used for public investment; and indirectly, when part of the public debt is paid off and the increase in the economy's aggregate saving (associated with the revenue surplus) raises private investment through a lowering of the interest rate (remembering that the economy is assumed to enjoy full employment).

[16] Other than the building cost which is included under the capital account of the government budget.

further scope for bias under the current practice of classifying budgetary items, when the government follows the FRBMB provisions.

Third, the golden rule implies zero public sector saving, and such saving consists of the revenue surpluses of the Union and state governments plus undistributed profits of public sector enterprises.[17] In India, until recently, undistributed profits of public sector enterprises more than neutralized the combined revenue deficits of the Centre and the states.[18] Hence, the government policies, one may argue, are already tilted in favour of future generations, given the none-too-insignificant expenses on human resource development (HRD) by the Union government and the states taken together. On this ground, further increases in public sector savings by way revenue surplus or undistributed profits of government enterprises cannot but be considered highly discriminatory by proponents of the golden rule.

Interestingly enough, conceptual inadequacies, resulting in an inadvertent flouting of the golden rule, has had a positive fallout: FRBMB's focus on generation of revenue surplus is, as we have seen in the previous subsection, eminently justified from the viewpoint of inter-generational equity and provides an example of two wrongs tending to cancel each other out. However, in economics, common sense is no substitute for conceptual clarity. Its absence has been far from inconsequential in the present case and prevented framers of the bill from providing an effective guide-line for fiscal restructuring. Our examination of issues relating to inter-generational equity indicates how the proposed legislation is seriously marred in respect of both its commissions and omissions.

The principal raison d'etre of public savings, we have noted, lies in rapid upliftment of the human development index along with advancement of the country in areas people value highly, but feel incapable of affecting in their individual capacity. Practically all will like to see (a) elimination of hunger and deprivation on an enduring basis; (b) future generations have much improved, and equality of, opportunities for full development of their potential; and (c) their country make rapid strides in uplifting the quality of life of its people. Not only is there no reflection of these concerns in the FRBMB, but quite a few of its provisions seem positively harmful, remembering that most of these objectives require a significant step-up in

[17] Recall that under the golden rule public investment is undertaken through borrowing, not generation of a revenue surplus or undistributed profits of public sector undertakings.

[18] Until 1998–9 public sector savings were always positive. In 1998–9 and 1999–2000 the aggregate revenue deficits of the government were larger than underdistributed profits of PSUs with the result that the public sector's contribution to national savings became negative.

agricultural investment and social sector expenditure. As we shall elaborate in our discussion in the fourth section on the consequences of the FRBMB for income distribution and growth, provisions of the bill regarding revenue surplus, fiscal deficit, compliance of budgetary targets, all militate against adoption of measures that are essential for furthering both growth and inter-generational equity.

Finally, the way the government needs to address the problem in the light of our analysis. The first and the most important is the significant increase in the government expenditure in the sectors identified above. Second, what is relevant in this context is overall public sector saving, so that targets for the Centre's revenue surplus should be set taking into account savings (or dissavings) of the state governments and undistributed profits of public sector undertakings.

Third, fiscal targets are required to be related to the economy's full employment output levels and should not stand in the way of expansionary policies in times of recession. The reason, to recapitulate, is that such policies provide a free lunch, promoting as they do welfare of both the present and future generations.

Fourth, given the distortionary effects of taxes, especially in countries like India, moderate reliance on monetized deficit promotes both efficiency and inter-generational equity. The reason is fairly simple. A higher proportion of government borrowing from the central bank poses a smaller burden on future generations as the problem of servicing public debt is reduced.[19]

Finally, the target for public sector saving should not, as far as possible, be linked to that of public sector investment, remembering that while the first is designed to bridge the gap between the socially optimum and private saving, allocation of investment between the two sectors needs to be based on a different set of considerations, viz., the relative social rates of return on the two types of investment. Our analysis in the present section underlines the need for assigning appropriate weights to *long-term* social objectives while estimating (the relevant) returns on some investment project. Given the prevailing human development index of the country, the government, it is quite clear, has to rely on borrowing on a none-too-insignificant scale for financing its investment in priority areas, despite the slated increase in its revenue surplus. Unfortunately, the FRBMB targets and provisions, as we shall presently see, go against this requirement, even though the bill is supposed to seriously address the problem of inter-generational equity.

[19] See Rakshit (2000) for a discussion of monetized deficit and a second-best fiscal programme for attaining the basic objectives, when the government cannot raise the tax–GDP ratio without creating serious distortions.

Macrostabilization sans Fiscal Policy

One of the major objectives of fiscal policy is to steer the economy close to its full-employment growth path without serious inflationary pressure. The targets for fiscal and revenue deficits in FRBMB have however been set without any reference to the operation of cyclical or other factors which may create a gap between the full-employment and actual output levels. Under the proposed legislation the government is permitted, as we have seen, to run deficits above the stipulated targets only on grounds of national security or natural calamity of a 'national dimension'. In the absence of these two factors, the government is required to effect a cut-back in its non-'charged' items of expenses whenever revenue shortfall or excess expenditure threatens to make the revenue or the fiscal deficit exceed their targetted levels.

Indeed, not only will FRBMB prevent the government from ironing out fluctuations to which all economies are prone, but the provision noted above cannot but raise the amplitude of cycles or reinforce recessionary tendencies, once they emerge in the system.[20] Consider, for example, the case where the economy experiences a contraction in output due to demand deficiency, whatever be its source. The resulting decline in tax collections below their pre-specified target will, under the FRBMB provision, force the government to reduce its (non-charged) expenditure and hence to trigger off through the (negative) multiplier process a cumulative fall in output and employment.[21] It is for this reason that in countries with legislative norms for fiscal targets, the targets are generally required to be met over the course of a business cycle, not each year separately. This provides sufficient room for manoeuvrability to the government for purposes of macrostabilization without endangering long-term fiscal viability. The budget deficits in times of depression may then be balanced through generation of a surplus during the booming phase of the trade cycle.[22] Such anti-cyclical fiscal policies, we have already noted, do not stand in the way of attaining the goal of intergenerational equity.

[20] In technical terms, under FRBMB the government's fiscal stance is not even neutral, but *pro-cyclical*.

[21] FRBMB does not, however, prevent the government from taking anti-inflationary measures through generation of a budget surplus, remembering that the targets relating to deficits are for their maximum, not minimum levels.

[22] The German constitution bars debt-financed revenue expenditure by the government, but provides an escape clause: in the case of 'macroeonomic disequilibrium' borrowing is permitted to exceed public investment. Under the British Code of Fiscal Stability, the government can borrow in excess of its capital expenditure in any particular year so long as the golden rule is fulfilled over the course of the business cycle.

Separation of Power and Responsibility?

Absence of any escape clause in the FRBMB, enabling the government to close the economy's output gap, is difficult to appreciate, especially since macrostability is stated to be an important objective of the bill. The explanation of this omission is perhaps that under the roles assigned to the Ministry of Finance and the Reserve Bank, the framers of the bill do not envisage the need for *fiscal* measures for mitigating cyclical tendencies in the Indian economy. With the bar on the government's *direct* borrowing from the central bank after March 31, 2004, the Reserve Bank will be free to conduct open-market operations or adopt other measures solely for purposes of macrostabilization. Maintenance of full employment with a low inflation rate will, it thus appears, be the responsibility of the Reserve Bank alone, while fiscal policies are to be designed to provide the optimum quantity of public goods and to promote growth along with intra- and inter-generational equity.

The crucial question that arises in this context is the following: Can monetary policy alone preserve macroeconomic balance in a country like India? Note first that in a market-driven economy without quantitative restrictions on credit or on trans-border capital flows, the central bank, *a la* Mundell–Fleming results, can control money supply (and hence the domestic interest rate) or the exchange rate, but not both. Maintenance of full employment will thus require a fully flexible exchange rate for balance-of-payments equilibrium. Indeed, under this scenario the fiscal policy is quite ineffective in influencing aggregate demand since the impact of any expansionary (contractionary) measure adopted by the government will be neutralized by a fall (rise) in the trade balance as the currency appreciates along with a rise in interest rates. Separation of the roles of fiscal and monetary authorities thus appears to be in tune with the textbook theorems on open-economy macroeconomics.

However, several factors stand in the way of the central bank's ability to restore or preserve macroeconomic balance. Some of these factors operate in most countries and are fairly well recognized. However, others, though no less if not more important for developing countries such as India, tend generally to be lost sight of. Economists have for long been aware of the time lag with which monetary policy works and the consequent problem the central bank faces in steering the economy close to its full-employment growth path.[23] Again, the experience of Japan has reminded economists of the strong

[23] Because of such lags a monetary squeeze at the height of booms and a cheap money policy in times of depression may, orthodox monetarists headed by Friedman suggest, tend to magnify rather than reduce the amplitude of business cycles. The problem

likelihood of low interest-elasticity of aggregate demand following a severe meltdown in a country's commodity and financial markets[24]—a factor which deprives traditional monetary instruments much of their cutting edge.

What is no less significant in the present-day world, the central bank cannot leave the exchange rate entirely at the mercy of market forces. Given the ease with which the market for foreign exchange is dominated by short-term expectations, very often of a self-fulfilling nature, a system of pure float cannot but be characterized by sharp fluctuations in exchange rates, especially of developing economies whose foreign currency markets tend to be quite thin. As recent experiences show, when a country's balance-of-payments is severely rocked by external developments, the central bank has to take prompt, corrective actions to prevent extreme volatility in exchange rate movements.

What if the central bank sticks to the policy of a free float through thick and thin, and focuses on internal balance alone? That exchange rate volatility plays havoc with smooth operation of world trade and commerce has long been emphasized in the literature on international economics. The East Asian experience has also brought to light how a free fall in a country's exchange rate may cause serious disruptions in both real and financial sectors and create hurdles in maintaining internal balance. When a country's firms or banks are indebted to the rest of the world, a severe enough depreciation can turn them bankrupt, especially when international financial markets are driven by short-term expectations and herd behaviour. Such bankruptcies in their turn tend to erode investors' and consumers' confidence, produce a systemic crisis in the financial system, and trigger off a cumulative, contractionary process.[25] It is to prevent such developments that central banks including the Reserve Bank have very often found it necessary not only to intervene in the foreign currency market, but also to adopt restrictive monetary policy in order to ward off speculative attacks and stabilize the exchange rate around its long-term equilibrium level. The upshot of our analysis is that, given the past experience and especially the fact that the (market-driven) volatility of the exchange rate is much greater in developing than developed countries, it is difficult to see how the Reserve Bank will be able to maintain full employment without being supported by anti-cyclical fiscal measures.

---

encountering the central bank is compounded by two types of uncertainty, one concerning the phasing of the cycle, the other relating to variability of the time lag with which monetary measures impact the economy.

[24] See Rakshit (1999).

[25] See Rakshit (2002) in this connection.

Structural Issues in Macrostabilization

Apart from the factors noted above, there are structural features of developing countries which make monetary policy relatively ineffective in dealing with the problems of their macroeconomic imbalance and underutilization of resources. One of these features is financial dualism,[26] manifested in the exclusion of large groups of producers and investors from the formal credit market. Though there is some link between the formal and informal financial markets, the link is quite weak and injection or withdrawal of liquidity by the Reserve Bank does not produce a significant impact on the supply of credit in the unorganized sector. This seriously impairs the efficacy of monetary instruments in effecting desired changes in the level of effective demand.

Recent experiences in India have underlined the importance of a different kind of dualism within the formal sector itself. Given the prudential norms required to be observed by banks and other financial institutions, *and* high risk aversion on the part of households whose savings account for the overwhelming part of the economy's investible funds, easy money policy generally results in an increase in demand mostly for government securities[27] rather than for financial instruments supplied by private producers. Except in times of speculative bubbles[28] most producers in the formal sector cannot raise funds through equity issues and this in its turn makes them ineligible for accessing the formal credit market even if they want to invest in a viable project.

The above considerations suggest that in the absence of an economy-wide, integrated financial system, an easy money policy may fail to provide the required boost to aggregate demand even when the overall propensity to invest is not too low. The way out under these conditions is an expansionary fiscal policy which produces an immediate impact on the level of aggregate demand and sets in motion a multiplier process encompassing both the real and the financial sector.[29]

Again, the macroeconomic behaviour of countries like India is influenced considerably by agriculture-industry interaction or imbalances within the

[26] We have examined the macroeconomics of financial dualism in some detail elsewhere (Rakshit, 1982).

[27] It is interesting to note that contrary to the general expectations, reductions in SLR have not caused a decline in bank holding of the government securities or increased the flow of credit to the commercial sector. SLR has in fact become quite inoperative, with banks holding government securities far in excess of the SLR requirement.

[28] These bubbles and the scams associated therewith have played a significant part in making the share market quite ineffective for efficient allocation of investable funds.

[29] See Rakshit (1997).

commodity producing sector itself. Developing country macroeconomics has emphasized how a crop failure or limited agricultural production can stand in the way of full capacity utilization in the industrial sector.[30] Expansionary monetary policy in such cases will be of little avail since (a) industrial investment cannot be revived in the face of food price inflation and low profitability; (b) the credit delivery facility for long-term private investment in agriculture is woefully inadequate; and (c) the development of inflationary pressure can play havoc with the macrostabilization programme. Note that imports of foodgrains or buffer stock operations can curb inflation, but are likely to be quite inadequate in raising the employment level, especially in rural areas. While trying to raise the availability of foodgrains, the government also needs to implement food-for-work or similar schemes which absorb labour on the one hand and raise demand for non-agricultural goods on the other.

One can give other instances where direct government intervention is required in order to correct for macroeconomic imbalances and permit the economy to attain its production potential. Some of the measures designed for this purpose are also necessary, as we shall see, for promoting economic growth. Suffice it to say that since monetary policy on its own has been found wanting in preserving both internal and external balance even in countries where financial markets are deep and well integrated and the commodity producing sector is free from serious bottlenecks and characterized by considerable mobility of resources, placing the entire burden of macrostabilization on the central bank may be viewed, not without some justice, as an act of gross irresponsibility!

Income Distribution and Growth under FRBMB

A fiscal programme is ultimately to be judged by the extent to which it helps, directly or indirectly, in attaining the objectives of growth with equitable distribution of income. From this viewpoint, the target for securing a positive revenue balance within a stipulated period is certainly a step in the right direction, in as much as it will help in promotion of growth as also inter-generational equity. However, there are reasons to believe that even if the Ministry of Finance strictly abides by all the provisions set forth in FRBMB, the economy may not enjoy high growth, rapid improvement in its human development index, or an equitable (intra-generational) distribution of income. Apprehension in this regard arises partly from the priorities of the bill and partly because of some of its major omissions.

[30] See Taylor (1983), Rakshit (1982), and Dutt (2001).

Consider the basic problems confronting the policymakers in India. Low per capita income, widespread poverty, illiteracy and malnutrition, poor health services and sanitation, and absence of any social security system for the vast majority of the population, all these continue to condemn India to the lowest rung of the world league table. The macroeconomic scenario in the recent years has also displayed some disquieting trends of which the most important are slowdown in the growth rate in both industry and agriculture and a rise in the incidence of unemployment, with increases in the labour force running ahead of that in employment. Closely related with these trends are the decline during the 1990s in the economy's aggregate saving and investment ratios and in the rate of capital formation in agriculture, the social sector and infrastructural services.

Elsewhere (Rakshit, 2000) we have discussed in some detail the need for fiscal intervention on a substantial scale for arresting the slide of the economy and for attaining the primary goals of public policy. Attainment of these objectives, we have emphasized, requires not only a substantial step-up of public investment in crucial areas such as agriculture, HRD, and infrastructure, but also time-bound programmes directed toward raising, on a permanent basis, capability and incomes of the disadvantaged groups. Generation of a revenue surplus would, to be sure, enable the government to spend more on capital formation without adding to the fiscal deficit. However, under the provisions of the act neither is public investment likely to be adequate, not its composition be conducive to promotion of the basic goals. Let us explain why and how.

FRBMB specifies targets for scaling down revenue and fiscal deficits, without imposing any restriction on how the reduction is to be brought about. While trying to reduce fiscal deficits during the 1990s (not always successfully), the government cut its expenditure on the social sector and investment in other crucial areas.[31] Such counterproductive fiscal adjustment is not ruled out, in fact may well be more pronounced, under the proposed legislation. Note first that when budgetary trends during a year suggest a slippage in the fiscal targets, the government is required to effect a proportionate reduction in all its non-charged items of expenditure, and these include in the main those types of expenditure which contribute most to growth and removal of poverty, illiteracy, malnutrition, and other endemic ills.

Second, since social sector expenditure will continue to be treated as current, not capital, a time-bound programme for generation of a revenue

[31] One plus point of the FRBMB is its insistence on reduction of revenue deficit—something which was missing in the budgetary stance during the 1990s. For an early critique of this omission see Rakshit (1991).

surplus may force the government to economize its expenditure in this area in order to attain the stipulated targets.

Third, there are provisions in the bill which are likely to make government investment grossly sub-optimal. Over the period 2001–6 both the revenue and the fiscal deficit are scheduled to be cut each year by one-half per cent or more of the year's estimated GDP. The implication is that there would be no increase in the government's capital expenditure during this period,[32] contrary to our assessment of the economy's short- and medium-term requirement. From the financial year beginning on April 1, 2006, the revenue surplus is slated to be positive and this may enable the government to raise investment without adding to the fiscal deficit. However, under FRBMB between 2006 and 2011 the government is required to (a) eliminate fiscal deficit;[33] (b) bring down the ratio of government liabilities to GDP[34] to 50 per cent or less; and (c) utilize the revenue surplus 'for discharging liabilities in excess of assets'. These requirements taken together cannot but depress government investment below its current level (as a ratio of GDP) which is already sub-optimal.

It is difficult to see the economic logic behind the programme of eliminating fiscal deficit and using the revenue surplus for retiring public debt. We have already indicated why public investment in infrastructure needs substantial enhancement for crowding in private investment in both agriculture and other sectors. The major hurdle to such enhancement consists in (a) uneconomic user charges for goods and services provided by the government and (b) large externalities characterizing the government investment in crucial areas, coupled with inefficiency of the tax machinery.[35] However, with the FRBMB requirement for a zero or positive revenue balance, there appears to be no economic justification for putting a brake on public investment with a relatively high *social* rate of return. Legislative targets relating to the revenue balance should automatically act as a brake on unsustainable public investment, since in order to meet the targets the government will then be forced to raise its earnings from the projects directly or to increase the quantum of tax collections.

[32] Ignoring disinvestment in public sector enterprises. Indeed, in the 2001–02 budget, the government expenditure in some crucial areas is made dependent on realization of disinvestment proceeds to the tune of Rs 12,000 crore. Linking the two items of the government budget underlines the distortionary impact of the FRBMB on the scale and composition of the budget.

[33] Which is slated to be about 2 per cent of GDP in the year 2005–06.

[34] Which stood at 59.3 per cent at end 2000–01.

[35] Externalities do not favour charging the beneficiaries of public investment. This would not pose any fiscal problem were it possible to raise taxes in order to recoup the cost incurred by the government.

The political economy of fiscal management since the early 1990s suggests, however, that for high growth along with rapid elimination of the major ills plaguing the Indian economy, it may not be enough to lay down targets for the revenue balance and leave it to the government to choose the fiscal deficit it considers appropriate. The reason is that (a) the same amount of deficit can come about through a wide variety of scale and composition of the government budget, having radically different consequences for the primary objectives and (b) given the close connection between the fiscal deficit and revenue balances over time, the government may continue to opt for scaling down urgently needed expenditure rather than raise taxes and rationalize prices of publicly provided goods and services.

In the context of the government's responsibility relating to growth and human resource development, the FRBMB could have fixed targets for expenditure in some critical areas with the provision that in case these targets (along with that of the revenue balance) are not met, the government must reduce its administrative expenses[36] and impose Kargil- or Gujrat-type taxes in order to make up for the shortfall: widespread disability or morbidity due to illiteracy, malnutrition, or absence of health services, though familiar for long, are no less serious than the emergencies for which the surcharges were levied. At the same time it is also necessary to reduce wastage and plug leakages in the government's expenditure programmes. Unfortunately, the FRBMB does not fix any targets for the tax–GDP ratio or public expenditure in priority areas and it does not contain any clause for raising the cost-effectiveness of government expenditure[37]—omissions that could seriously distort the fiscal stance and provide the government with another pretext for not focussing on its primary responsibilities.

Summary and Conclusion

The FRBMB attests to the seriousness with which the government seeks to tackle the problems of revenue and fiscal deficits and the high ratio of public debt to gross domestic product. The primary objectives of the bill are promotion of inter-generational equity, macroeconomic stabilization and growth. With these goals in view, the FRBMB lays down a time-bound programme of cutting back revenue deficits and generation of revenue surpluses; elimination of fiscal deficit; and a ten percentage point reduction in the debt–GDP

[36] Involving perhaps a (progressive) cut in salaries and perquisites of the government personnel including the ministers.

[37] It may be made mandatory for the government to take corrective measures following the reports of the Comptroller and Auditor General of India and penalize the concerned officials for negligence and dereliction of duty.

ratio. For ensuring that the government adheres to this programme, the bill provides for corrective measures that are to be automatically undertaken once the actual deficits show signs of exceeding their targeted values in any year. One can be reasonably certain regarding the effectiveness of FRBMB, when implemented, to bring down the three crucial ratios from their current magnitudes. At the same time, the bill should go a long way in making the budgetary process transparent and promoting an informed debate, remembering that the government is required to lay on the table all its cards relating to its own perception of the emerging economic trends and the macroeconomic framework behind formulation of short- and medium-term policies.

There can, however, be serious doubts on how far FRBMB will be of help in attaining the primary objectives, as distinguished from the intermediate targets of reducing deficits and debt. Though generation of revenue surpluses is certainly a move in the right direction, conceptual confusion and weak analytical framework seem to have made some of the bill's provisions inappropriate and resulted in omissions of measures badly needed for furthering the basic goals.

Fixation of budgetary targets with reference to actual rather than full-employment GDP not only tends to enlarge the magnitude of cyclical fluctuations but is also not in consonance with the principle of inter-generational equity. Hence arises the need for permitting anti-cyclical variations in revenue and fiscal deficits, especially since in a country like India monetary policy alone is generally incapable of maintaining external balance along with full employment of resources.

Second, our analysis suggests that public saving promotes inter-generational equity primarily since, along with growth in the country's per capita income, people value highly rapid elimination of poverty and illiteracy, scientific and cultural advancement, improvements in health and quality of life. Unfortunately, FRBMB provisions can pose obstacles to attainment of these objectives. In a bid to meet the targets for reducing revenue deficits or generating revenue surpluses, the government may be tempted to scale down expenditure on education, health and other social services, entering as they now do the current rather than the capital account of the budget.

Third, the targets for reduction of fiscal deficits and the programme for using revenue surpluses in order to retire part of the public debt will prevent any increase in the government investment over the next decade. Indeed, since the targets are for minimum reductions in deficits, and since in case of prospective slippages from the targets all non-charged expenses are slated to be reduced proportionately, the declining trend in government investment witnessed during the 1990s is unlikely to be reversed under the FRBMB regime.

Fourth, under the bill the die is heavily loaded against investments in not only human resource development, but also infrastructure, the reason being that in view of their large externalities, a major part of the return on such investments does not directly contribute to the government coffers. One of the major omissions of the FRBMB thus consists in the absence of any targets for time-bound, minimum improvements in these areas which are crucial for both equity and rapid economic growth.

Finally, the bill does not seriously address the problem of financing public expenditure. In the context of the decline in the tax–GDP ratio during the 1990s, targets for increases in this ratio should have been accorded top priority under the proposed legislation. Not only is there no such target under the FRBMB, but the omission is compounded by the bar on relying on monetized deficit to finance government expenditure, current or capital. While it is essential to make effective use of the considerable scope for improvements in tax administration and collections, we need to recognize that it is next to impossible to devise a non-distortionary system of taxes and hence to avoid an increase in the tax–GDP ratio from becoming counterproductive beyond some level. Under these conditions borrowing from the central bank on a moderate scale for financing government investment has an important role to play in promoting the basic objectives and minimizing the adverse effects of debt and deficits.

References

Barro, R.J. (1974), 'Are Government Bonds Net Wealth?', *Journal of Political Economy*, 82(6), 1095–1117, November.

Dutt, A.K. (2001), 'Demand and Wage-Goods Constraints in Agriculture–Industry Interaction in Less-Developed Countries: A Theoretical Analysis', in A. Bose, D. Ray, and A. Sarkar (eds), *Contemporary Macroeconomics*, Oxford University Press, New Delhi.

Government of India (2000), *Report of the Committee on Fiscal Responsibility Legislation*, Ministry of Finance.

——— (2000a), *The Fiscal Responsibility and Budget Management Bill,* Ministry of Finance (Bill No. 220 of 2000).

Rakshit, M. (1982), *The Labour Surplus Economy*, Macmillan, Delhi and Humanities Press, New Jersey.

——— (1991), 'The Macroeconomic Adjustment Programme: A Critique', *Economic and Political Weekly*, 26(34), August.

——— (1997), 'Money, Credit and Government Finance in a Developing Economy', in A. Bose, M. Rakshit, and A. Sinha (eds), *Issues in Economic Theory and Public Policy*, Oxford University Press, New Delhi.

——— (1999), 'Economic Crisis in Japan: Analytical and Policy Issues', *Money & Finance*, 9, 46–73, April–June.

——— (2000), 'On Correcting Fiscal Imbalances in the Indian Economy: Some Perspectives', *Money & Finance*, 2(2), 19–58, July–September.

——— (2002), *The East Asian Currency Crisis*, Oxford University Press, New Delhi.

Samuelson, P.A. (1954), 'The Pure Theory of Public Expenditure', *Review of Economics and Statistics*, 36(4), 387–89, November.

Taylor, L. (1983), *Structuralist Macroeconomics*, Basic Books, New York.

4

Some Public Economics of Food Subsidy and Buffer Stock Operations*

Embarrassment of Riches

One of the most paradoxical features of the Indian economy in recent years has been the persistence of poverty amidst plenty. While widespread hunger and disability due to malnutrition continue to plague a substantial section of the community, the government is at a loss at deciding:

(a) what to do with the huge foodstocks being carried by the Food Corporation of India (FCI) and
(b) how to avoid their further accumulation in future.[1]

Before trying to resolve the puzzle and suggest appropriate policies in this regard, it is useful to summarize the main features of the paradoxical developments and identify the issues involved.

The behaviour of India's food economy is directly and crucially affected by three sets of government's policy instruments, viz., the minimum support price (MSP), the quantity of foodgrains supplied under rationing, and the issue price at which this quantity is released. In times of harvesting, the FCI stands ready to buy any amount of wheat or rice offered to it at the stipulated MSP. The support price is announced each year well in advance of the sowing season and intended to insure farmers against market risk and ensure a 'remunerative price' for their produce.[2] The amount of foodgrains released to support rationing under the public distribution system

* Reprinted from *Money & Finance*, Vol. 2, Nos 4–5, January–June, 2001.

[1] See Government of India (2001), pp. 93–7.

[2] Note that MSP would be inoperative were it less than the free market price during the harvesting season. But this has not happened and the reason lies partly in the rising trend of the MSP set by the government.

(PDS) is (more or less) uniform throughout the year. Until 1997 the issue prices of wheat and rice sold through PDS were the same for all consumers irrespective of their incomes, and fell short of the FCI's economic costs consisting of the minimum support price and costs on account of transportation, handling, and storage of foodgrains. Since the food subsidy provided under PDS should ideally benefit only the lower income groups, since June, 1997 the government has adopted a two-tier pricing structure with the introduction of the Targeted Public Distribution System (TPDS). Under this system the issue price of foodgrains for the below poverty line (BPL) families is (as of now) fixed at 50 per cent of FCI's economic costs, while the price for the above poverty line (APL) families covers the entire economic cost.

Apart from protecting farmers' interests (through a remunerative MSP) and ensuring a minimum level of food intake of all consumers, FCI is also responsible for carrying stocks for purposes of food security and smooth operation of the public distribution system. Since procurement is undertaken during harvesting seasons and hence is lumpy, but the quantities released under rationing are uniform throughout the year, the amount of FCI stocks required to be maintained for public distribution would vary over the year. FCI is also supposed to undertake open-market sale of foodgrains through PDS and this together with the supply under rationing is intended to moderate seasonality of foodgrains prices. Last but not the least, FCI is entrusted with the responsibility of holding 'buffer stocks' in order to guard against food shortage in some years due to crop failure. Taking into account the seasonality of agricultural production and the need for food security, the government fixes quarter-wise norms for some minimum foodgrains stock that FCI has to maintain. In case of any shortfall of the actual stock from its stipulated minimum, the gap is sought to be bridged through imports or larger procurement through a hike in the minimum support price.

Over the last decade the government has been facing increasing difficulties in pursuing the food policy outlined above. First, not only have the actual stocks carried by FCI been persistently way above their minimum norms, but the gap has also been showing a sharply rising trend in recent years. In January 1998 the actual stock of foodgrains with FCI was 18.3 million tonnes compared with the minimum norm of 15.4 million tonnes fixed for that month. The minimum norm for January in the next three years was raised to 16.8 million tonnes, but the actual stocks jumped successively to 24.4, 31.4, and 45.7 million tonnes with the result that the excess stock now amounts to around 30 million tonnes. Maintenance of such huge stocks has added substantially to the government's food subsidy bill as

FCI has to incur mounting interest charges along with costs on account of storage, wastage, and quality deterioration.[3]

Second, the rise in MSP over the years has raised the economic cost of providing foodgrains through PDS and, hence, the subsidy the government has to provide to FCI. Between 1992–3 and 1999–2000 the annual average increases in MSP for wheat and rice were 10.8 per cent and 10.0 per cent, respectively, compared to an annual increase of 7.2 per cent in the wholesale price index (WPI) (Government of India, 2001). Indeed, in recent years the minimum support prices were higher than their open-market counterparts during the harvesting season with the result that there was a large diversion of market surplus of foodgrains from private traders to the FCI. This is perceived to be a major reason for FCI's excessive accumulation of food stocks and the consequent rise in food subsidy.

Third, the problem has been compounded by the poor offtake of foodgrains from the public distribution system, especially after introduction of the two-tier system of pricing (for APL and BPL families) in 1997. Over the period 1997–2000, the allocation of foodgrains under PDS was 70.19 million tonnes, but the offtake amounted to only 51.62 million tonnes (Government of India, 2001). Data available up to December 2000 suggest that the (percentage-wise) shortfall of offtake from allocation widened significantly in 2000–1 compared with that in earlier years. An important reason behind this development is that prices fixed for APL families are often not less than open-market prices so that there is little incentive for these families to buy foodgrains from the public distribution system.

An interesting point to note regarding the behaviour of the food economy is that during 1997–2001 a rise in procurement, poor offtake from PDS, and the quantum jump in FCI stocks took place even while food production did not record any significant increase and the country was a net exporter of foodgrains in each of the four years. It is in this context that the Ministry of Finance has summed up its own reading of the situation:

> So far, Government's food policy framework has been evolved against the background of inadequate or uncertain supply situation. ... It was an effective and reasonably successful policy. However, the situation has now reversed and the country is faced with a large volume of surplus food stock. (Government of India, 2001, p. 94)

[3] Thus the CAG (Comptroller and Auditor General of India) report (Government of India, 2000) notes that the interest charge component of buffer stocks rose from Rs 36.7 per quintal in 1992–3 to Rs 85.99 per quintal in 1998–9. This rise along with the enormous increase in the stocks carried by FCI now accounts for a substantial part of food subsidy.

The emerging scenario calls for a discussion of two sets of policy issues. The first concerns the short-term problem of how best to utilize the surplus stock. The second is more complex and relates to the need, if any, for fundamental changes in the food policy the government has been pursuing so far. Here we will focus only on the first set of issues which admit of straightforward resolution in terms of fairly simple analytical constructs.[4]

Government Policies for Reduction of Excess Food Stocks

The main policy alternatives that the government seems to have seriously considered for scaling down FCI's foodgrains stocks are:

(a) open-market sale (OMS);
(b) increase in BPL quotas; and
(c) exports.

Out of the three, the government has revealed its preference for (b) and (c), especially the last one, though the first option has not been explicitly ruled out. The Antyodaya Anna Yojana, launched in December 2000, is slated to cover 10 million poor families and each family is to receive every month 25 kg of foodgrains at a price of Rs 2 and Rs 3 per kg, for wheat and rice, respectively.[5] The annual allocation under this scheme is estimated at 3 million tonnes, involving a subsidy of Rs 2315 crore. The government has also decided to release 2 and 5 million tonnes of wheat[6] in 2000–1 and 2001–2, respectively, for purposes of exports. Until May 31, 2001 exports are to be routed only through public agencies such as the State Trading Corporation (STC) and the export price is fixed at the level charged from BPL families.[7] From June 1, 2001 onward private traders will also be allowed to export and the price is to be determined through open tender.

The Policy Riddles

The short-term policies adopted for reducing buffer stocks would seem highly perplexing at first sight. The government has already announced enhanced MSP for wheat and rice for the next agricultural year and no significant new measure relating to PDS (other than the Antyodaya Yojana)

[4] Postscript: for an analysis of the second set of issues see Rakshit (2002, 2003).

[5] These prices are less than half of the current prices for BPL quotas.

[6] There is also a scheme for exporting rice, but the amount involved appears to be quite marginal.

[7] Until March 31, 2001 the export price was the same as the BPL price, viz., Rs 4150 per tonne. In response to a public outcry, the government has raised the price for exports between April 1 to May 31, 2001 to Rs 4300 per tonne.

is on the anvil. The widening gap between FCI's yearly procurement and disbursal of foodgrains may thus be expected to continue in the foreseeable future, other things remaining the same. Under this scenario the net cost of carrying excess stocks is extremely high to the government. While the future expected price the FCI can obtain on these stocks is near zero,[8] they involve significant interest and storage costs. Hence, any cut-back in excess stocks even with no addition to FCI's current revenue would have a positive impact on the government's budgetary balance.

Note, however, that the policies announced so far are aimed at additional sales of a little over 2 million tonnes in 2000–1 and 8 million tonnes in 2001–2, compared with an excess stock of more than 30 million tonnes in mid–March 2001. Hence arises the following riddles:

(a) Why does not the government try to dispose of the entire amount of excess stock (remembering that carrying them adds to the budgetary problems and involves wastage of resources)?

(b) Second, why is the government relying more on export than on domestic disbursement, even though the export price is about one-half of the domestic open-market price?

The solution to the puzzles lies in the government's policy objectives and its reading of the current domestic and international economic situation. The measures adopted as of now relate exclusively to disposal of food stocks in the foreign or domestic markets and the official policy statements suggest that the government does not deem it necessary to change policies in other spheres in order to tackle the problem of excess stocks. This perception, implying what economists call a partial equilibrium approach,[9] seems to have played a crucial role in formulation of the programme on the part of the government. The primary goal of the programme, it is also quite clear, is reduction of budget deficit with some concession to the need for poverty alleviation, so long as it (the concession) does not entail any significant increase in food subsidy. In order to evaluate the government's policy package let us examine, using a partial equilibrium framework, how alternative ways and scales of reduction in food stocks affect the budgetary balance and other important variables in the system.

[8] Carrying excess stocks indefinitely implies that these stocks do not add to FCI's total revenue or to anybody's welfare at any point of time.

[9] The approach consists in examining the behaviour of a particular sector on the assumption that demand and supply conditions in the rest of the economy remain the same or their change is not large enough to produce a perceptible feedback on the sector concerned.

Case 1: Open-market sales (OMS)

Consider first the impact of OMS through the public distribution system. Given the price inelastic demand for foodgrains, the result will be a fall in FCI's revenue and an enlargement of budget deficit.[10] Indeed, if the government tries to dispose of a major part of excess stocks through such sales, the open-market price is likely to go below the BPL or even the Antyodaya prices, making the rationing system redundant and leading to a quantum jump in the food-subsidy bill.[11]

So far as the non-government sector is concerned, it is easy to identify two types of effect of large-scale sales in the open market. First, there will be a sharp decline, at least in the short run, in the incidence of poverty and malnutrition. Second, OMS, through changes in relative prices, will also have an impact on the rest of the economy.

There is no evidence that while choosing among policy alternatives the government has estimated or taken cognisance of their impact on the non-agricultural sector, though even a partial equilibrium approach warrants such an exercise.[12] Let us also ignore such impact for the moment and try to appreciate the reason behind the rejection of OMS as a means of reducing food stocks. The reason, it may appear from above, lies in the government's overwhelming urge to reduce budget deficit—an urge that has won hands down over the objective of poverty alleviation. The more charitable interpretation is that reduction in budget deficit is considered essential for growth and a permanent solution to the problem of poverty, and open-market sales seriously jeopardize attainment of these goals. Let us suspend for a while our judgement on merits of this view and focus on short-term consequences of the policies being pursued.

There is an important reason why OMS on a large scale may raise food subsidy manyfold, but do not produce any significant impact on the

[10] As we show in Appendix 4.1, the increase in budget deficit is not due to the gap between FCI's 'economic cost' and the 'sale price', but to the fall in total revenue (on account of inelastic demand). Strictly speaking, if saving in interest-cum-storage costs per unit of sale exceeds the (negative) marginal revenue, open market sale reduces budget deficit—a highly improbable outcome under the prevailing conditions.

[11] Reduction of food stocks through open market sales requires a cut-back in APL, BPL, and Antyodaya prices as and when the open market price tends to fall below them. Otherwise there will be no net decrease in excess stocks held by FCI. As of now, APL prices are not lower than those in the free market so that any attempt at reducing food stocks through open market sales has to be backed up by a reduction in APL prices.

[12] It is only when one takes into account the feedback on agriculture itself due to this impact and the final outcome resulting from interaction among sectors that the analysis becomes 'general'. In the next section we use a simplified, general equilibrium framework for drawing some policy conclusions.

incidence of hunger and malnutrition. When FCI tries to dispose of its surplus stock in the domestic market, it will be difficult to prevent the major part of the amount sold finding its way, directly or indirectly, in the stocks held by private traders. The reason is that as the price consumers are willing to pay tends to nosedive below the MSP fixed for the next harvesting season, traders will find it profitable to add to their stocks in anticipation of higher prices in the future.[13] Under competitive conditions the open market price at the time FCI releases its stock should approximate MSP less the cost of carrying stocks until the next harvesting season. In the process consumers gain little, the amount procured registers a quantum jump and so does the level of food subsidy. In other words open market sale on its own aggravates rather than solves the problem of excess stocks held by FCI.

Case 2: Enhanced allocation for BPL families

Economic Survey (Government of India, 2001) toys with the idea of a substantial increase in the BPL quota in order to reduce excess stocks—a scheme that the government has not opted for, though a limited quantity of foodgrains is to be released under the Antyodaya Yojana. Since the impact of the Antyodaya Yojana is not *qualitatively* different from that of enhanced allocation for BPL families, it is not necessary to examine the two schemes separately.

Compared with the open-market sales, this scheme will undoubtedly have a much greater impact on poverty alleviation, provided that BPL families have been properly identified (and the additional allocation actually reaches them). So far as budgetary balances are concerned, note that even in this case there will be a tendency for open-market prices to go down as the poor consume less from the open market or may even turn sellers if the additional quota is large enough.[14] However, in this case the impact on budgetary balances will be unambiguously better than that under OMS, the reason being that the increase in real income of BPL families associated with the additional quota raises the aggregate demand for foodgrains, moderates the fall in their open-market prices, and, hence, reduces FCI's revenue loss due to additional allocation. Indeed, as we show in Part A of Appendix 4.1, compared with the baseline case (where FCI carries excess stocks indefinitely) there will be a fall in food subsidy provided the

[13] Given the limited administrative capability of the government, stock piling on the part of traders will be next to impossible to prevent.

[14] An increase in quota implies an additional income amounting to the increase in the quantity times the difference between the open-market prices and the BPL prices. Since only a part of the additional income will be spent on food, the net demand in the open-market cannot but fall.

price-elasticity of demand is not too small and the fall in the open-market demand of BPL families is not too large.[15]

What about the role of traders under the current scheme? Note first that unlike in Case 1, in this case the poor will benefit despite the fact that traders' activities tend to raise open market prices: traders can after all add to their stocks only if BPL families reduce their demand for food; but even then trading moderates the fall in the open-market prices and does not raise them. So the poor still benefit, though there is some reduction in the extent of their gain.[16] Indeed, if the additional allocation to BPL families equals the whole of the excess stock, trading can boost income and welfare of the poor as they turn net sellers in the market and reap the benefit of a higher price!

When traders can be prevented from dealing in stocks released through the PDS, allocation to BPL families, we have seen, is superior to OMS (through fair price shops) on grounds of both equity and reduction of budget deficit. However, when seepage from the PDS to traders' stocks is difficult to avoid, the choice between cases 1 and 2 is not that clear cut. The latter is still superior from the viewpoint of poverty alleviation, but may entail larger budget deficit when the quantity released is substantial. We have explained why OMS with private trading raises the amount of procurement and hence stands in the way of a cut-back in FCI's excess stocks and in food subsidy. Note that the gains on account of higher prices due to trading accrue to FCI under Case 1[17] and to BPL families in Case 2 when the amount released is large enough to make them sellers in the open market. Again, since consumption is larger in Case 2 than in Case 1, the former involves a smaller increase in procurement. Quite clearly, since large BPL allocations raise net sales by poor families and hence the food subsidy bill, from the viewpoint of improving budgetary balances, Case 2 scores over Case 1 for relatively small allocations, but not for large enough ones. In the context of the priority the government attaches to reduction of

[15] It may be useful in this context to indicate the flaws in the *Economic Survey's* estimate (Government of India, 2001) of additional food subsidy due to Antyodaya Yojana. The amount mentioned constitutes the quantity to be released (3 million tonnes) times the gap between FCI's economic cost and the Antyodaya price. There is thus a presumption that the beneficiary families will not reduce their demand from the open market—a presumption that is at variance with the theory of consumer behaviour. Again, for reasons already noted the 'economic cost' is of no relevance here in evaluating the policy option.

[16] The reason is that their purchase from the open market is at a higher price than what would obtain in the absence of addition to traders' stock. Because of the MSP, traders' activities, let us recall, raise the quantum of procurement and the open-market price of foodgrains.

[17] Provided FCI adjusts the issue price to clear the market.

budget deficit, it is thus not difficult to explain why only a modest amount is earmarked for the Antoyodaya scheme.[18]

Case 3: Export of foodgrains

In contrast to the two alternatives considered above, export of excess stocks does not contribute toward poverty alleviation, but has an unambiguously positive impact on budgetary balances. Exports do not reduce FCI revenue from the domestic market so that the budget subsidy is reduced by earnings from exports plus reduction in the cost involved in carrying the stocks. Note also that this alternative, unlike the earlier two, does not raise the amount of FCI's procurement in times of harvesting. No wonder, the government has opted for exports for purposes of reducing food stocks even though the export price is about one-half of FCI's 'economic cost'.[19]

The natural question to ask at this stage is: why does not the government try to eliminate the entire amount of excess stock through this route? Part of the answer lies in WTO rules which do not permit export subsidy, though there is some ambiguity regarding whether exports at prices below FCI's economic cost as well as domestic free-market prices violate the rules.[20] The more important reason behind limiting the disposal of FCI stocks through this route lies in imperfectly elastic demand for Indian exports in the world foodgrains market. This is particularly true in respect of rice, the international market for which is rather thin, and even at moderate quantities of export the demand turns inelastic and marginal revenue negative. The reason behind the negligible export of rice is thus not difficult to appreciate. The situation is better in the world wheat market; but here also additional sales beyond a point reduce export earnings and impair rather than improve

[18] Note that low prices charged under this scheme should also have a favourable impact on food consumption (because of enlarged real income) and hence moderate the increase in future procurement.

[19] As we have shown in Part A of Appendix 4.1, the 'economic cost' has no significance in choosing policy options relating to excess stocks. What is relevant is FCI's marginal return from carrying stocks, and this, our analysis suggests, is negative as of now. Note also that, from the viewpoint of budgetary objectives it makes sense to export rather than raise BPL quotas even though the two prices are the same, since the latter leads to a decline in FCI's revenue from non-BPL sales in the domestic market.

[20] In order to get round this problem the government has adopted the system of selling FCI stocks to private exporters through tender. If exports are undertaken by private traders and their purchase is through competitive bidding, WTO rules are presumably not violated, though there is no difference between the effects of exports by public and private agencies so long as the quantity is the same! The equivalence arises from the fact that private traders are forced to export the amount procured from FCI, and not permitted to sell it in the domestic market, which they would undoubtedly like to do under the prevailing price differences.

budgetary balances. Even the third mode, it transpires, can play only a limited role in solving the problem of FCI's excess stocks.

Optimal Policy Package

We are now in a position to indicate the optimum mix of the three measures discussed above. Under the partial equilibrium approach adopted in this context, the policy instruments are designed for furthering only two objectives, viz., (a) reduction of budget deficit and (b) poverty alleviation. Our analysis suggests that enhancement of the BPL quotas is better than open-market sales from the viewpoint of (b). The conclusion holds in respect of (a) also so long as the amount involved is not too large. Exports do not contribute toward (b), but are superior to the two other options for purposes of reducing budget deficit. Under this situation the optimal policy involves a combination of export and increase in the BPL quotas, the ratio between the two being determined by (among other things) relative weights attached to (a) and (b).

In order to appreciate the nature of the optimum mix, consider first what the government needs to do for effecting the maximum cut in the budget deficit. For this purpose the optimum levels of export and (additional) BPL allocations are determined independently of each other. As we show in Part A of Appendix 4.1, the budget deficit is minimized when FCI's marginal revenue from both exports and BPL sales equals the opportunity cost of carrying stocks.

A few interesting features of this solution[21] are worth taking stock of. First, since storage charges make this opportunity cost negative, additional exports and BPL allocations contribute to the budgetary balance even if they reduce FCI's revenue at the margin.[22] Second, the optimal programme for minimizing budget deficit also reduces the incidence of poverty to a certain extent, the reason being that for small increases in the BPL quotas, FCI's revenue reduction on account of a fall in the open-market prices is more than outweighed by the BPL price.[23] Third, minimization involves (in this particular instance) destruction of a part, perhaps a substantial part, of excess stocks, given their positive carrying cost. Economic logic suggests that giving away this part to the poor raises budget deficit because of the fall in FCI's revenue due to such disposal. No wonder, the subject has earned the sobriquet, 'the dismal science'![24]

[21] To the problem of minimizing budget deficit.

[22] So long as the fall in total revenue does not exceed the marginal carrying cost.

[23] So that FCI's marginal revenue is positive.

[24] As we shall presently see, such notoriety is due in main to inappropriate economic analysis for drawing policy conclusions.

Consider now the nature of the optimum policy package corresponding to the objectives the government wants to promote. Any increase (or reduction) in export from the level given in the above solution reduces FCI earnings without any alleviation in poverty. Additional BPL quotas, on the other hand, improves the lot of the poor, but raises budget deficit. Since the government attaches some weight, however modest, to poverty alleviation, at the optimal mix the quantity of export is the same, but allocation for BPL families will be more compared with the earlier exercise. Quite clearly, the optimum BPL quotas will be larger, if reduction of poverty is more highly valued, and the elasticity of food demand, especially of the poor, with respect to changes in income and price is higher.[25]

We have tried to provide, what seems to us, the most plausible explanation of the chosen policy package, characterized by (a) an absence of OMS; (b) a modest allocation under the Antyodaya scheme, and (c) exports that are larger than the Antyodya quota, but still leave FCI with surplus stocks of mountainous proportions. There are two policy puzzles which have not yet been resolved. First, why has not the government destroyed the excess stock? Second, what about gifts to sub-Saharan or other countries facing acute food shortage and famine conditions?

The answer to the questions may be sought in two types of considerations that influence government policies. First, under FCI's accounting procedure stocks are valued without taking into account the fact that their sale price may become near zero. The procedure results in gross underestimation of FCI losses and, hence, in a corresponding fall in the amount the government has to provide by way of food subsidy. This suits the government interested in reducing *current budgetary deficits*, although it involves piling up much larger losses for the future.

The second consideration involves electoral logic. In the presence of high incidence of poverty in the country itself, few governments can afford to appear so callous as to destroy foodstocks or make large-scale gifts to other nations;[26] but carrying excess stocks is likely to be considered not too reprehensible in view of the expectation that they will be put to some good use sometimes in the future.

Government Policies Reconsidered

As emphasized in the preceding section, the programme being followed for the disposal of FCI's excess stocks is derived from a partial equilibrium

[25] So that the fall in FCI's revenue due to increases in quotas is smaller.

[26] Note that the hue and cry raised against the government decision to export wheat at the BPL price led to the revision of the export price at a slightly higher level—a move that is perhaps sub-optimal from the viewpoint of the government's twin objectives.

framework. Such an approach is, however, quite inappropriate in the current context since, given the importance of the food sector in the Indian economy, not only do happenings in this sector produce a considerable impact on the rest of the economy, but there is also a significant feed-back from the non-agricultural sector to the market for foodgrains.[27]

There are two main reasons why neglect of sectoral interdependence may lead to choice of a wrong set of policies in the case under investigation. First, some of the policies, which do not *directly* relate to the food market, may be rejected out of hand, even though a general equilibrium approach may vindicate their superiority. Second, conclusions regarding the *quantitative* impact of some policy differ, often substantially, under the partial and general equilibrium analyses, though the results regarding the sign or qualitative nature of the effects are generally the same. The implication is that, for any given set of policy instruments considered by the government, the trade-offs among the objectives from the most efficient combinations of these instruments[28] will not be the same under the two analyses. When the government considers the pros and cons of policy instruments, the package chosen on the basis of partial equilibrium approach will thus generally be sub-optimal.

A General Equilibrium Framework: Some Preliminaries

A general equilibrium analysis, if it is too general, does not serve any purpose for drawing policy conclusions. The art of building a useful general equilibrium framework for analysing a particular problem consists in ignoring peripheral elements and focussing on the major sectors and interlinkages among them. Again, since the effects of any policy depend on both the nature of sectoral interdependence and the initial state of the economy, it is necessary to take into account the main features of the prevailing economic situation. Apart from the demand and supply conditions in the foodgrains market

[27] In non-technical terms, changes in food prices and quantities sold affect the demand and supply conditions in markets for other goods. The resulting change in non-agricultural output and prices in its turn produces what economists call a feedback effect on the foodgrains market itself. While partial equilibrium analysis abstracts from such effects, a general equilibrium framework is designed to examine how the initial impulse (in this case the policy initiative) changes the major economic variables, taking into account the interdependence among and adjustments in all sectors of the economy.

[28] Consider exports and BPL quotas for promoting the objectives of budgetary balance and poverty alleviation. A combination of the two instruments is said to be efficient when there is no other combination which reduces poverty without raising budgetary deficit or vice versa. Given an efficient policy combination and the associated values of the two objectives, a trade-off between them indicates the minimum sacrifice of one objective necessary for a unit increase in the other objective.

discussed in the previous section, the other characteristics of the economy relevant for our exercise are the following.

The first and the most important is recessionary conditions and excess capacity in industries along with considerable unemployment in most sectors of the economy.

Second, trends in domestic production and import of capital goods suggest a severe decline in the country's rate of investment. The decline may be traced partly to weakening demand for consumer goods, but the more important reason seems to lie in poor infrastructural facilities in both rural and urban areas.

Third, except in the case of petro-products, whose prices are administered and linked (though imperfectly) to import prices, inflation in prices of other goods remains quite modest.

Finally, the country's foreign exchange reserves are fairly comfortable, non-petroleum imports have declined, but export performance has been reasonably satisfactory.

Apart from factoring in the above features in our analytical framework, we also need to consider a larger set of variables and objectives relevant for choosing policy instruments. In the second section the choice has been on the basis of domestic consumption of food, especially by the poor, and reduction of budget deficit. However, since policies for reducing food stocks affect, as we shall see, employment, output, and other variables[29] through inter-dependence among sectors, the number of intermediate objectives[30] will now be larger than in the earlier exercise. Let us briefly examine how broadening of the analytical framework modifies the result for the three instruments discussed in the second section.

Exports

The first thing to note regarding the general equilibrium impact of foodgrains export is that the textbook-type foreign trade multiplier, indicating the increase in gross domestic product from a unit increase in export proceeds, does not operate in the case under consideration. The reason is

[29] There are two reasons why these variables do not figure in our partial equilibrium analysis. First, effects on the rest of the economy are abstracted from. Second, there are changes in the FCI stocks and consumption of food, but production of foodgrains is assumed to depend only on MSP. The revised approach will continue to be marked by the second feature, though not the first.

[30] An intermediate objective is one which contributes to some primary objective. Thus reduction in budget deficit is an intermediate objective since it is considered important for stability and growth of the economy. Poverty reduction and a more equitable income distribution are ends in themselves and hence are primary goals.

that agricultural production and income are not directly related to FCI exports; nor do such exports automatically generate extra demand for industrial or other goods. The effects of the policy measure on the rest of the economy can operate through two routes, both of which involve the policy stance of the Reserve Bank.

First, depletion of the FCI stock releases locked-up funds in the banking system, and this can produce an expansionary impact through financing of additional investment.[31] However, the effect depends on the Reserve Bank policy of permitting the quantity of non-food credit to rise—something which cannot be rationalized. A reduction in the food stocks by itself, when there is no additional release in the domestic market, does not justify additional non-food credit.[32] Again, recent behaviour of the Indian economy suggests that additional reserves at the disposal of banks is unlikely to have a major effect on private investment—a phenomenon whose significance for the problem at hand we shall presently discuss. Suffice it to say for the moment, while choosing among alternative ways of reducing FCI stocks, we need not consider the *direct* monetary impact on the rest of the economy, since not only are such effects common to all measures, but they would in all probability be quite unimportant in the current context.

The foreign currency market constitutes the second route through which foodgrains exports can impact the economy. Here also the result depends on the Reserve Bank's policy response. If the Reserve Bank keeps its hands off the foreign exchange market, additional export earnings, through an appreciation of the rupee, will tend to produce a negative impact on the trade balance and hence on output and employment in the non-agricultural sector. This also reduces FCI sales in the domestic market so that the fall in stocks will be less than the volume of foodgrains exports. In order to ward off such negative consequences, the Reserve Bank can add additional export earnings to its foreign exchange reserves and sterilize the resulting increase in reserve money through sale of securities.[33]

[31] Notice once again the difference between the textbook and the present case. When the additional investment equals the amount of foodgrains released, national income accounts show zero net investment, decumulation of foodstocks being balanced by the investment undertaken through new bank loans, so that readers familiar with elementary macroeconomic analysis would not expect any increase in output or employment. However, unlike the textbook case, here the new investment has a net income generating effect, the reason being that disinvestment by way of a decline in FCI stocks does not reduce the demand faced by producers of agricultural goods.

[32] If such credit is deemed desirable, the Reserve Bank can inject more liquidity even if there is no change in the FCI stocks. In our alternative approach we shall examine the role the Reserve Bank can play along with other policies.

[33] Once again, non-sterilization does not seem relevant in the present context.

To summarize, under the most plausible scenario, the effects of foodgrains export will in the main be (a) a reduction in budget deficit and (b) an increase in the country's foreign exchange reserves.

Open-Market Sale (OMS)

Using the partial equilibrium analysis, we have discussed how OMS leads to a reduction in prices of foodgrains and raises budget deficit (in view of low price elasticity of food demand). In our general equilibrium analysis, we shall ignore the impact of budget deficit on the rest of the economy since it depends on the mode of financing the deficit and, hence, on the policy stance of the Reserve Bank.[34] So far as the effect of reduction in food prices on the rest of the economy is concerned, it is unambiguously expansionary and operates in three ways. First, the income effect associated with a decline in food prices raises the consumption demand for industrial and other goods. Second, higher capacity utilization in industries and moderation of cost inflation[35] may also raise investment demand to a certain extent.[36] Third, the initial expansion in non-agricultural output and employment (due to a decline in food prices) will be magnified by the multiplier effect,[37] as the rise in income sets an expansionary process in motion with further increases in demand, production, and so on.

Expansion in non-agricultural income and employment will in its turn tend to raise demand for agricultural goods. The general equilibrium framework permits us to examine how different sectors of the economy interact in the process of adjustment to the initial policy shocks and to characterize the nature of the final equilibrium when the adjustment process

[34] If the deficit is financed through market borrowing, there will be some contractionary effect due to an increase in interest rate. Monetized financing on the other hand has an expansionary effect. We shall assume that the government finances the additional deficit through sale of bonds to the Reserve Bank, while the Reserve Bank does not permit any further increase in money supply through an appropriate upward revision of CRR. Such policies neutralize the impact of budget deficit as such on the interest rate and private sector credit.

[35] This is due primarily to moderation of wage increases, since absorption of rice and wheat (especially rice) in India's food processing industries is fairly low.

[36] Note that, given the minimum supply price, a reduction in food prices does not produce a significant fall in investment demand in the agricultural sector.

[37] Strictly speaking, the initial impact on the non-agricultural sector comes from (a) an increased consumption demand due to the income effect, and (b) additional investment demand resulting from cost reduction. The multiplier operates on the sum of these two impulses and depends on (i) the marginal propensity to consume non-agricultural goods out of income originating in this sector, plus (ii) the additional investment induced by a unit increase in capacity utilization, less (iii) the amount of additional consumption-cum-investment demand that leaks out in the form of imports.

has fully worked itself out. Assuming that the Reserve Bank pursues an accommodating monetary policy,[38] the (general) equilibrium impact of OMS will exhibit the following features.

First, the non-agricultural output and employment rise along with a reduction in open-market prices of the foodgrains. The reduction in food prices is less than what has been suggested in the second section, since the increase in income in the rest of the economy raises the demand for foodgrains. The important thing to note in this connection is that in equilibrium expansion of the non-agricultural sector moderates the magnitude of price fall in the agricultural market, but cannot eliminate the negative impact altogether. Similarly, the rise in non-agricultural income is less than what is indicated by the (sectoral) multiplier[39] analysis in view of the fact that food prices recover to some extent and crowd out some of the expansionary effect.

Second, there is an increase in budget deficit but in this respect also the negative impact on the revenue balance is less (than is suggested by the partial equilibrium approach), as (a) moderation of fall in food prices reduces the extent of decline in FCI earnings and (b) the increase in non-agricultural output adds to the government's revenue receipts.

Third, both lowering of food prices and expansion of non-agricultural employment reduce the incidence of poverty. It is, however, not clear whether this reduction is more or less than the impact from adjustments in the food market alone. Moderation of the fall in prices of foodgrains adversely affects BPL families, but the increase in non-agricultural employment should help in reducing poverty.

Fourth, the effect of OMS operating through the external sector depends on how the Reserve Bank responds to the tendency for trade deficit to rise following an increase in non-agricultural output and employment. If the Reserve Bank tries to keep the exchange rate unchanged, foreign currency reserves fall and the widening of the import–export gap moderates the rise in gross domestic product. In the absence of any intervention by the Reserve Bank forex reserves do not change, nor will there be any impact, *through the external sector,* on domestic output and employment[40] because market forces will effect enough depreciation to keep the trade deficit unaffected.

[38] i.e., permits the supply of money and credit to adjust in response to changes in demand at the prevailing interest rates.

[39] See Taylor (1983) and Rakshit (1982).

[40] Strictly speaking, we also need to assume that international investors do not want to change their exposure in the Indian financial market. Note that while an increase in GDP promotes investors' confidence and hence tends to raise capital inflows, depreciation may have an opposite effect as it could produce an adverse balance-sheet impact and undermine expectations.

Increase in BPL allocation

In respect of food prices and non-agricultural output and employment, the impact of enlarged BPL quotas is similar to that of OMS, but there can be considerable quantitative differences in the effects of the two policies. Since the major benefit of BPL allocations accrues to poorer families whose income and price elasticities of food demand are larger (than that of the affluent), the decline in food prices under the present case will be lower. Again, the marginal propensity to consume *non-agricultural goods* of BPL families is generally lower than its average for the community as a whole.[41] A smaller fall in food prices in the open market and redistribution of income in favour of poorer families should thus moderate the expansionary impact on the non-agricultural sector.

So far as the external sector is concerned, given the Reserve Bank's policy stance, here also the effects are qualitatively the same, but smaller in magnitudes than those under OMS. With the exchange rate kept unchanged, the increase in trade deficit and fall in foreign currency reserves are smaller, and so is the extent of depreciation when there is no intervention in the foreign exchange market.

We have discussed in the second section how an enhancement of BPL allocations scores over OMS from the viewpoint of poverty reduction. When we take the sectoral interdependence into account, the conclusion is not so unambiguous *a priori*. Against the greater benefits accruing to the poor through larger quantities of rationing, there is now a smaller increase in non-farm output and employment. Our own assessment is that the policy still dominates OMS since (a) under the current conditions properly targeted food subsidies have a much more significant impact on poverty reduction than untargeted ones;[42] and (b) the increase in non-agricultural employment operating through a fall in open-market food prices is unlikely to be very large, remembering that the greater part of the additional demand comes from the relatively well-off and, hence, is mostly for consumer durables and other capital- or import-intensive products.

Finally for the budgetary consequences of the policy under consideration. Using a partial equilibrium approach we have found that up to a point an increase in BPL quotas reduces the budget deficit, but for large enough increases, the deficit tends to go up. In view of expansion of non-agricultural income (and rise in imports), the extent of fall in budget deficit is larger or

[41] Despite the fact that the marginal propensity to consume is higher for poorer families.

[42] It is, however, a moot point whether identification of BPL families is satisfactory or seriously biased because of inadequate coverage, inefficiency, corruption, and political considerations.

the rise in deficit smaller (for a given amount of additional allocation) than what is suggested under the partial equilibrium analysis. It is also not very difficult to see that the maximum decline in budget deficit occurs at a larger allocation for BPL families.

TABLE 4.1
Effects of Exports, Open-Market Sales (OMS), and Increase in BPL Quotas (with unchanged exchange rate and interest rate)

Policies	GDP	Poverty	Budget Deficit	Forex Reserves	Price Level
1. Export	0	0	–	+	0
2. OMS	++	–	++	–	–
3. BPL Allocation	+	–	–, +	–	–

Notes: 1. 0 = unchanged; + = rise; – = falls; –, + = first falls and then rises.
2. Number of plus or minus signs across a column indicate the relative ranking of the three policies in terms of their impact on the concerned variable.

Table 4.1 summarizes the results regarding the (general equilibrium) impact of the three policies.[43] Our analysis suggests that BPL allocation dominates from the viewpoint of poverty eradication and exports from that of reducing budget deficit and accumulating foreign exchange reserves, but the option of OMS cannot be rejected out of hand since its impact on output and employment is the largest. However, this does not mean that the optimal policy package should contain all the three measures, with their weights being determined by the relative importance attached to the various objectives. The reason is that we are yet to consider, in the context of the current economic scenario, what we regard as the most efficient set of instruments for tackling the problem of excess food stocks.

An Alternative Macro-theoretic Approach

Even if we take into account the interdependence among various sectors of the economy, it will be difficult, with the three policy instruments considered in the previous section, to dispose of the entire amount of FCI's excess stocks without a crash in foodgrains prices and adding significantly to the government's budget deficit. What is much more important, the expansionary

[43] We have also indicated the effects on the price level. This effect is dominated by movement in agricultural prices, since other prices are mostly fixed on a cost plus basis and the fixed exchange rate ensures that prices of imports do not change. We have chosen not to include the price level as a separate policy objective, since price level changes are important to the extent they affect the first four variables. Note also that, with no changes in non-food prices, the fall in the price level does not affect exports.

effects of the policies (even of OMS) are likely to fall far short of the requirement; nor do the measures go to the heart of the macroeconomic including fiscal problems bedevilling the Indian economy in recent years. In our search for an effective solution to the problems, we need to keep the following, fairly elementary but basic, considerations in view.

First, in the context of large-scale underutilization of both capital and labour, there is *no cost, from the economy's viewpoint*, of an increase in consumption and investment, public or private.[44] The implication is that if an expansionary fiscal policy raises consumption and investment, the economy enjoys a free lunch irrespective of whether there is an increase in budget deficit or not. The present generation gains through an enhancement of public or private consumption,[45] but this gain is not at the expense of future generations, given the existence of excess capacity. To the extent the government raises its capital expenditure or private capital formation takes place because of higher capacity utilization or other factors, future generations benefit in view of the increase in the economy's production potential.

Second, while discussing the budgetary implications of alternative policies for reducing FCI's excess stocks, it is important to distinguish between the revenue deficit and government borrowing for purposes of investment. The reason is that unlike the first type of deficit, the second is accompanied with an increase in the economy's productive capacity and in the revenue potential of the government, directly or indirectly (Rakshit, 2000), so that adverse consequences of servicing public debt[46] do not arise in this case.

Third, the basic problems of the Indian economy, we have emphasized elsewhere (Rakshit, 2000), consists in relatively low rates of investment and persistence of poverty, illiteracy, and ill health on a wide scale. The solution to these problems lies in stepping up public investment in physical infrastructure as well as investment in human resource development by way of a drive toward universal elementary education and extension of basic health services throughout the country. Such policies not only crowd in private investment through improvements in infrastructural services and quality of the labour force, but also should go a long way in providing a lasting solution to the endemic problems of poverty and morbidity.

[44] Except for the import component of such expenditure.

[45] In case the expansionary policy is in the form of additional public investment, the gain accrues through an increase in private consumption.

[46] Public debt does not impose a burden on future generations directly since its servicing involves only a transfer among members of the same generation. The adverse effect arises partly by way of increased (intra-generational) inequality that such transfers lead to, and partly through distortions in resource use on account of taxes required to service interest charges. What public investment does is to reduce if not totally obviate the need for additional tax-cum-transfer schemes for servicing debt. See Rakshit (2000).

Finally, subsidies are generally an inefficient mode of solving the problems of poverty in view of (a) the difficulty of proper targeting; and (b) the fact that apart from creating vested interests they fail to raise, or enhance utilization of, the poor's income earning assets including the labour power. Hence, along with extension of health and educational facilities for raising their long-term earning potential, the poor can be served best in the short run through provision of gainful employment opportunities, directly or indirectly.

Keeping the above considerations in view, we examine two types of policies for disposal of FCI's excess stocks. The first set of policies is growth oriented, consisting of public investment in key infrastructural and social sectors, and these may not have a significant, immediate impact on the incidence of poverty. The poor benefit under these policies through an *overall* increase in employment opportunities in the short (as also the long) run, and through an improvement in their health and educational status and in productivity of their physical assets.[47] The second set of policies is for purposes of relieving distress in draught-hit and poverty-stricken areas. While both sets of instruments may enter the optimum policy package, before deciding on the extent of reliance on these measures, we need first to examine their impact on the relevant economic variables.

Investment in Infrastructure

We first discuss the economic and budgetary consequences of infrastructural investment taking the prevailing features of the Indian economy into account. Apart from raising the country's production and growth potential, the policy helps to curb industrial deceleration, generate employment, and permit the FCI to reduce its excess stocks.[48] As in earlier exercises we assume the Reserve Bank to keep unchanged the interest and exchange rates,[49] and take non-agricultural prices to be fixed on a cost-plus basis. However, unlike in the earlier cases here we take the FCI to adjust its sales to demand at the prevailing open-market prices of foodgrains.[50] Given the existence of excess capacity and unemployment, fixity of food prices and the exchange rate ensures that other prices also remain unaffected in the face of an increase in demand.

The first thing to note regarding the (short-term) expansionary impact of public investment is that, additional output and employment are generated only in the non-agricultural sector since the increase in food demand is

[47] Examples of such policies are extension of irrigation facilities, soil conservation, bunding and linking villages with the rest of the country.

[48] See Part B of Appendix 4.1 for derivation of the results in terms of a simple model.

[49] We shall presently discuss the problem of keeping the exchange rate fixed.

[50] Which are currently close to minimum support prices.

met from FCI's excess stocks and neither the minimum support price nor agricultural input prices change. The increase in non-agricultural GDP, as we show in Part B of Appendix 4.1, will in fact be a multiple of the additional capital expenditure by the government. The reason is similar to that operating in the Keynesian multiplier. In the present case the value of the multiplier is higher when the crowding-in effect on private investment is larger; and out of the non-agricultural income a greater fraction is spent on industrial goods and services and a smaller fraction on imports.

Since in the short-run the poor benefit from the policy primarily through employment generation, increases in GDP can be taken as a good proxy for the extent of poverty alleviation public investment will result in. The effect also depends on the composition of the investment package. However, the two-way classification of public investment we have adopted should capture the major elements of the problems and enable us to suggest the nature of the trade-offs among alternative investment programmes.

So far as the budgetary effects are concerned, the most important thing to note is that there is an unambiguous decline in the revenue deficit. The fall in revenue deficit arises on two counts. First, an expansion of income raises the government's revenue receipts, the magnitude of which varies positively with the value of the (sectoral) multiplier and the marginal rate of non-agricultural tax. Second, the food subsidy is reduced as the rise in the demand for food permits FCI to reduce excess stocks and bring down its losses. What is perhaps most important, unlike exports and BPL allocations, the impact of the present policy on revenue balances does not turn negative beyond a certain point. Indeed, a large enough increase in public investment can eliminate the excess stock altogether and provide in the process a boost to output, employment, growth, and revenue receipts of the government. Lest the reader regards increased public investment as the panacea for India's current economic ills, let us consider other effects of the policy which can be viewed, rightly or wrongly, as seriously circumscribing the scope for its use on a large scale.

Fiscal Deficit

The most important reason behind the government's reluctance to increase capital expenditure lies in its bugbear of raising fiscal deficit. Suspending our judgement regarding the economic rationale of such fear, let us see how this deficit is affected by the expansionary fiscal programme. The first thing to note in this regard is that in view of the fall in revenue deficit resulting from an increase in public investment, the increase in fiscal deficit, if any, will be less than the additional capital expenditure the government undertakes.

Second, when significant crowding-in effect on private investment and high propensity to consume make the value of the multiplier large *and* FCI's cost saving per unit decline in foodgrains stock is substantial, the policy may lower rather than raise fiscal deficit, with the fall in revenue deficit outweighing the increase in public investment expenditure.[51]

Third, even if the absolute value of the fiscal deficit rises, its proportion as a ratio of GDP is almost certain to decline.[52] In view of the universal (though largely unwarranted) concern in India for the fiscal deficit ratio, some explanation may perhaps be in order at this stage.

Consider the effects of the policy on the four components of fiscal deficit as ratios of GDP, viz., the government's capital expenditure, public consumption, transfers including interest payments, and revenue receipts (which appear with a negative sign). Out of the four, a change in only the first component may add to the fiscal deficit ratio, since with no change in agricultural income the proportional increase in GDP may turn out to be less than that in the public investment. But in the context of the significantly large share of non-agriculture in the GDP and of the crowding-in effect of infrastructural investment, even this ratio can register a decline.[53] So far as the other ratios are concerned, not only do they move in the right direction, but their changes, as shown in Part B of Appendix 4.1, produce a much larger impact on the fiscal deficit than that of the first component, the reason being that the ratio of the government's capital expenditure to GDP is now significantly less than that of transfers, revenue receipts, and fiscal deficit.[54] Under the current economic scenario there is thus little doubt that the policy of enhanced public investment in priority areas cannot be faulted even on grounds of 'fiscal prudence', however defined. Only when the government's capital expenditure becomes relatively large and the expansionary impact on non-agricultural income quite moderate, is it possible, though not probable, for the ratio of fiscal deficit to rise. But even in this case, there is no reason for not going in for an expansion in public investment so long as there are unemployed resources. This involves larger government borrowing no doubt, but such borrowing does not have any adverse effect in the short run,[55] nor does it store up problems for the future

[51] As we show in Part B of Appendix 4.1, a large multiplier on its own is not enough to ensure a positive impact on fiscal deficit; FCI's cost saving or crowding-in effect also needs to be large enough.

[52] See Part B of Appendix 4.1 for details.

[53] We have already indicated the possibility of an absolute fall in fiscal deficit.

[54] For the Union and state governments taken together.

[55] While crowding out through operation of real factors is ruled out by excess capacity, the financial crowding out can be avoided through an accommodating monetary policy.

in view of the increased production potential of the economy, especially when the Reserve Bank provides the necessary finance (Rakshit, 2000).

External Balance

Apart from the non-agricultural capacity constraint, the only serious obstacle to the policy of eliminating FCI's excess stocks may arise from deterioration in external balances. An expansion in gross domestic product leads to an increase in trade deficit when the Reserve Bank does not allow the exchange rate to depreciate by intervening in the foreign currency market. Given the comfortable foreign exchange position as of now, there should not up to a point be any difficulty in raising public investment. But a fall in foreign exchange reserves below some critical level may invite a speculative attack against the rupee and trigger off a financial turmoil. However, such a fallout of public sector investment does not appear very likely because of three reasons. First, the marginal propensity to import of the Indian economy is still fairly small so that the government investment in infrastructure and human resource development, the import content of which is generally low,[56] will not cause a serious erosion in the country's foreign exchange reserves. Second, a gradual and moderate depreciation of the rupee can be relied upon to contain the trade deficit, enlarge the domestic expansionary effect[57] and improve further the government's revenue and fiscal balances. Third and the most important for the problem under consideration, the rise in capacity utilization and current profits along with imporved prospects of infrastructural and labour services should induce foreign capital inflow, especially FDI. This not only solves the short-term problem due to a trade deficit, but is also likely to provide a boost to total factor productivity and long-term competitiveness of India's exports.

Food-for-work Programme (FFP)

The only fly in the ointment suggested above is existence of poverty in some pockets which may be difficult to alleviate through investment projects based on the (direct-cum-indirect) marginal returns criterion.[58] Such consideration justifies food-for-work or similar programmes, though even in these cases it is necessary to ensure that the project is temporary or designed to effect an enduring increase in the income earning ability of the targeted groups. Let us, however, focus on only the short-term consequences of FFPs

[56] Remembering that the major part of imports consists of petroleum products.

[57] Note that the enlarged expansionary effect due to depreciation can moderate the extent of rise in trade deficit, but cannot lower it.

[58] That does not include relief from hunger itself as yielding a very high return.

and see how they differ from those of public investment examined in the previous sub-section.

The major difference between the two types of investment projects may be traced to their impact in the first round. Projects for poverty reduction have a larger (direct) wage–cost component; the lion's share of these wages is spent on food, while only a small part is spent on non-agricultural goods; leakages by way of imports occur only from the non-wage component of the project cost; and out of the total income generated in the first round the direct wage income does not contribute anything to tax revenue. Given these features of the programmes, it is not very difficult to appreciate how they differ from other types of public investment in their impact on the rest of the economy.[59]

Given the fact that the overwhelming part of income received by the indigent is spent on food rather than non-agricultural goods, the aggregate income-generation effect under FFP will be less than that under other public investment projects. Only in the unlikely case of marginal imports from non-farm income exceeding the marginal propensity to consume industrial goods and services out of this income will the result be the reverse. However, there is no such ambiguity in respect of the relative effects on tax revenue. The increase is less under FFP than in the case of other projects. The reason lies in the fact that the wage component of FFP escapes the tax net and that a significant part of this component goes out of the (non-agricultural) income stream through additional consumption of food.

Like other public investment projects, FFPs also contribute to a decline in foodgrains stocks and hence to a reduction in food subsidy. However, contrary to common intuition, the reduction can be less under FFP because of its low multiplier effect, especially if the marginal propensity to consume food out of non-agricultural income is not too low. Thus while FFP reduce the revenue deficit and may even improve the government's fiscal balance, conclusions regarding the relative efficacy of the two types of policies in raising budgetary balances is not quite clear cut. The impact on external balance is less ambiguous: the factors which tend to lower the multiplier effect of FFPs compared with other projects also ensure that the trade deficit and hence loss of foreign currency reserves will tend to be less under the former. However, even in this case the result may be the opposite if the effect of infrastructural investment, operating through FDI and FII, is strong enough.

Conclusion

Our analysis suggests that neither open-market sales, nor enhancement of BPL quotas should figure in an optimal policy mix for reducing FCI's

[59] See Part B of Appendix 4.1 for derivation of the results.

excess stocks: the two policies are inferior to public investment and/or FFPs from the viewpoint of poverty reduction, tackling industrial recession, long-term growth, and improvement in budgetary balances. For the same amount of reduction in food stocks, people in dire poverty will tend to gain more under FFPs than other public investment projects; but objectives like GDP growth and reduction in revenue and fiscal deficits generally tilt the balance in favour of the latter.

So far as the choice between public investment in priority areas and FFPs is concerned, given the magnitude of stocks lying with the FCI and the expected amount of procurement in the current year, there is in fact scope for going in for both types of investment. In drought-hit areas and localities with large concentration of poor families, there is a strong case for implementing food-for-work programmes, especially since apprehensions in official circles regarding their adverse impact on budgetary balances are, as we have shown, quite unfounded. Our analysis also suggests that the major component of the optimal package will consist of investments for improvement in infrastructural facilities, in the knowledge base and in quality of the labour force. These policies, we have emphasized, can not only tackle the problem of industrial recession and contribute toward budgetary viability, but also raise economic growth, total factor productivity, and export competitiveness.

Indeed, the most important conclusion of our exercise is that, instead of creating a 'problem', FCI's 'excess' stocks provide a golden opportunity for promoting the primary objectives of public policy, viz., growth, poverty eradication, and rapid improvement in the country's human development index. The official perception that the aggregate supply of food in India is in excess of her requirement (Government of India, 2001) is based in fact on an extremely superficial reading of the country's economic conditions. The per capita net availability of cereals and pulses was lower in 1998–2000 than in the 1980s and early 1990s. Obviously, it is the large–scale unemployment and low purchasing power of a major section of consumers that account for the poor offtake from the public distribution system and accumulation of FCI stocks. While formulating public policies there is thus no economic logic for taking the prevailing supply-demand conditions as the norm. Our analysis indicates how the 'excess supply' of food is likely to disappear when the government implements a combination of FFPs and other investment programmes.

The only serious obstacle to the policy can arise not on the budgetary or 'financial front', but due to inadequate capacity of the non-agricultural sector to provide gainful employment to the labour force[60] or to external

[60] See Rakshit (1982) in this connection.

sector imbalances.[61] Though as of now there is an output gap in the non-agricultural sector, creaking infrastructural services seriously limit the potential output and labour absorptive capacity of major parts of this sector. Under these conditions, larger weights need to be placed on those investment projects which draw less on infrastructural inputs. Such considerations will tend to favour food-for-work and other labour-intensive projects. So far as the external imbalances are concerned, part of the solution lies in permitting the rupee to depreciate mildly. Presence of this obstacle also apparently makes FFPs more attractive. However, considerations of capital inflows induced by investments in infrastructure and human resource development make them more effective in easing the foreign exchange constraint. Finally, if this constraint does constitute a serious problem in raising public investment and reducing FCI stocks, export of foodgrains may be required to support the other parts of the optimal policy package.

To sum up, concern for budget deficit in disposing of the country's (so-called) food surplus through FFPs along with public investments in education, health, and physical infrastructure appears totally misplaced at the current juncture. The concern, our analysis shows, reflects quite inadequate appreciation of macroeconomic linkages in a developing country like India and provides yet another instance of how in economics common sense may turn out to be nonsense.

References

Government of India (2000), Comptroller and Auditor General of India, *Report on Ministry of Food and Consumer Affairs*.

——— (2001), Ministry of Finance, *Economic Survey 2000–01*.

Rakshit, M. (1982), *The Labour Surplus Economy: A Neo-Keynesian Approach*, Macmillan, Delhi and Humanities Press, New Jersey.

——— (ed.) (1989) *Studies in the Macroeconomics of Developing Countries*, Oxford University Press, New Delhi.

——— (2000), 'On Correcting Fiscal Imbalances in the Indian Economy: Some Perspectives', *Money & Finance*, 2(2), 19–58, July–September.

——— (2002), 'Food Policy in India: Some Longer Term Issues', *Money & Finance*, 2(9–10), 52–71, April–September.

——— (2003), 'Some Analytics of Medium and Long Term Food Policy', *Economic and Political Weekly*, 38(18), 1777–94, 3 May.

Taylor, L. (1983), *Structuralist Macroeconomics*, Basic Books, New York.

[61] To be more accurate, it is only in the presence of these two obstacles that significant budgetary or financial problems arise.

Appendix 4.1

Part A: Understanding the Government's Choice among Open-market Sales, Increase in BPL Quotas, and Exports

In order to examine the choice among the three policies for reducing FCI's excess stocks, consider first the baseline case where FCI does not try to reduce its excess stocks. Under the present conditions, it is quite reasonable to assume that the expected future revenue from holding the excess stocks is zero, but FCI will have to incur costs on account of storage of the stock.

Open-market Sales

Given the fact that open-market prices are close to the APL ones, we ignore the distinction between the two and consider only two types of domestic sales,[62] open market and BPL. Under the partial equilibrium approach, the open-market price, p, is then given by the relation:

$$p = p(S, Q, p_b), \qquad -p_1 > -p_2, \tag{A.1}$$

where S is the total open-market sales; Q is the total BPL quota; and p_b is the BPL price.

Elementary considerations suggest that partial derivatives of p with respect to changes in all the three arguments are negative;[63] and that compared with Q, an increase in S will have a larger absolute impact on p.

FCI's total revenue, R (ignoring exports), is given by

$$R = p(.)S + p_b Q, \tag{A.2}$$

while the total cost C is given by

$$C = F + \delta T,$$

[62] Note that if open-market sales go up, APL prices will accordingly have to be reduced for effecting the targeted reduction in stocks. Hence the clubbing of the two types of sales.

[63] $\partial p/\partial p_b < 0$ because a rise in BPL prices reduces the real income of the poor and hence their demand from the open market.

where F is the fixed cost (consisting of the total cost of purchasing foodgrains); T is the total stock carried over the unit period; and δ is the cost per unit of storage.

The impact of OMS on FCI's financial position is indicated in Figure A4.1, taking Q and p_b to equal the prevailing BPL quota Q_0 and price $\bar{p}_b$, respectively. PP indicates open-market prices at different levels of S and MR_{OMS} the corresponding marginal revenues.

Given Q_0 and $\bar{p}_b$, the profit-maximizing or loss-minimizing value of S is S^*. The actual sale is taken to be at a point like S_0. Though considerations of reduction in budget deficit suggest a cut-back in OMS by S^*S_0, such a move may perhaps be politically unacceptable.

Consider now the effect of changes in Q. Marginal revenue from an increase in Q is obtained from *Eq.* (A.2):

$$\frac{\partial R}{\partial Q} = p_b + S\frac{\partial p}{\partial Q} < p_b. \qquad \text{(A.3)}$$

Note that the absolute value of $\partial p/\partial Q$ depends upon the extent to which an increase in p reduces BPL families' food demand from the open market. Since this fall is likely to be quite small until Q is large enough, at the existing Q ($=Q_0$) and S_0, $\partial R/\partial Q$ is taken to be positive.

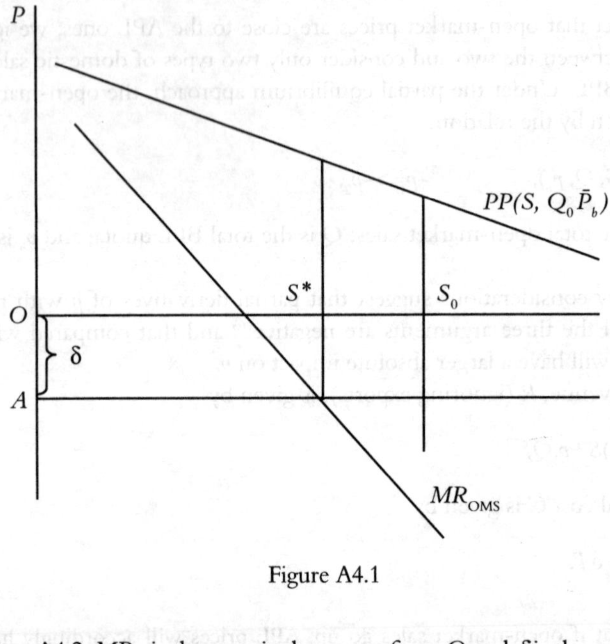

Figure A4.1

In Figure A4.2, MR_Q is the marginal revenue from Q and δ is the cost per unit of storage. If an increase in BPL quotas is the only option exercised for minimizing FCI losses, the optimum increase in Q will be Q_0Q^*. (This involves a fall in the open-market price, but this is taken into account while deriving MR_Q.)

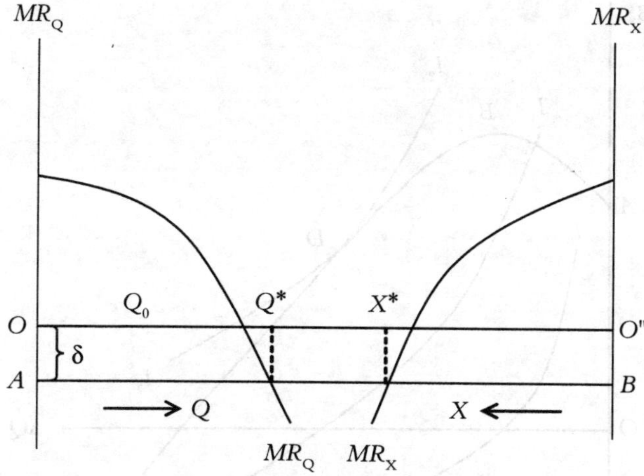

Figure A4.2

As we have already pointed out, since OMS is inferior to increases in BPL quotas from the viewpoint of poverty reduction and since the former also involves a rise in the food subsidies, it will not enter the optimal policy package. In order to see how far exports will be relied upon, assume that (a) FCI's excess stocks amount to Q_0O'' (Figure A4.2); and (b) the initial amount of export is zero. With a less-than-infinitly-elastic export demand, FCI's marginal revenue from exports is negatively sloped and becomes negative beyond some point. In Figure A4.2, FCI's losses are minimized when addition to Q is Q_0Q^*, exports are $O''X^*$, and Q^*X^* amount of stock is destroyed—a kind of solution that appears to capture the current situation better than the one where MR_Q and MR_X intersect above *AB* and the entire amount of Q_0O'' can be profitably used through an increase in BPL quotas or exports.

Since apart from reduction in the budget deficit, poverty alleviation is also an objective the government wants to promote, the loss minimizing combination of Q and *X*, given in Figure A4.2, will not be the optimum policy package. In order to indicate the nature of this package, take the increase in the BPL quota, ΔQ, as the proxy for the extent of poverty reduction. In Figure A4.3, the government's preferences are reflected in indifference curves like I_0I_0, I_1I_1, each showing combinations of the increase in budget surplus, Δ*BS*, and ΔQ which yield the same value of the objective function. The maximum possible value of Δ*BS* corresponding to different quantities of ΔQ, obtained from Figure A4.2, is given by the curve ABC.

Figure A4.2 also suggests why the curve *ABC* rises initially and then becomes negatively sloped. It is quite clear that at the optimum combination the budget deficit is not minimized. In fact the objective function of the government may yield a set of indifference curves such that the optimum combination occurs at a point like *D*. This, however, does not appear to be the case in India.

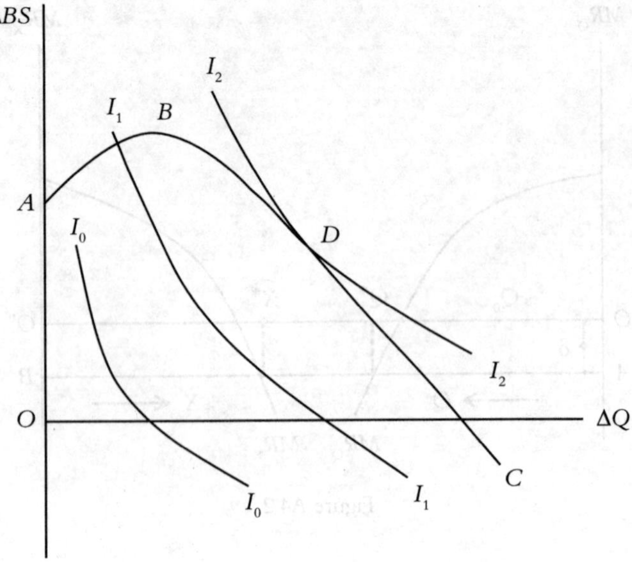

Figure A4.3

Note: Point A corresponds to $O''X^*$ amount of export with $Q = Q_0$ in Figure A4.2; point B to $O''X^*$ and Q_0Q^* amounts of X and ΔQ, respectively.

Part B: Public Investment and Food-For-Work Programmes

Some Short-term Consequences

While assessing the short-run macroeconomic consequences of public investment programmes, we assume that (a) FCI meets the additional food demand at the prevailing price; (b) the Reserve Bank keeps the interest rate and the exchange rate fixed; and (c) the non-agricultural sector is characterized by mark-up pricing, excess capacity, and unemployment. Our analysis is based on the by now familiar two-sector analytical framework for developing countries.[64] However, the three assumptions ensure that prices of non-agricultural goods and hence the terms-of-trade between the two sectors remain unchanged. Without any loss of generality its value is put at unity. Since at the fixed minimum support price, agricultural production and income are unaffected by changes in non-agricultural output, we need to focus only on this sector for examining the macroeconomic effects of public policy.

[64] See Taylor (1983), Rakshit (1982, 1989).

1. Public Investment

Given our assumptions, and ignoring agricultural inputs entering industrial production, the equilibrium in the non-agricultural sector is easily specified:

$$Y = C_2[Y - T(Y)] + C_{a2}(\bar{A}) + I_g + I_p(.) + G + X(.) - M(Y, \bar{A}), \tag{B.1}$$

where Y is the non-agricultural output; C_2 is the consumption of Y by income earners from Y sector; A is the agricultural income, assumed to be fixed; T is the taxes less subsidy from Y sector; C_{a2} is the demand for Y from the agricultural sector; I_g is the government investment demand for Y; I_p is the private investment demand for Y; G is the government consumption of Y; X is the export of Y; and M is the import of Y.

The exchange rate, being constant, has been suppressed in X and M functions so that not only C_{a2} but X also does not respond to changes in the public investment. For the moment we also specify I_p to be dependent only on the interest rate so that the income-generation effect of a change in I_g looks identical to what students learn in elementary macroeconomics (even though in the present case the multiplier is sectoral, not for the economy as a whole):

$$\gamma_1 \left(\equiv \frac{dY}{dI_g} \right) = \frac{1}{\Delta}, \tag{B.2}$$

where γ_1 = Y-sector government investment multiplier;[65]

$$\Delta = 1 - c_2(1 - t) + m; c_2 = C'_2(.); t = T'(Y); m = \frac{\partial M}{\partial Y}.$$

The effect of an increase in public investment on the government revenue, r_1, is then given by

$$r_1 \left(\equiv \frac{dT}{dI_g} \right) = \frac{t}{\Delta}. \tag{B.3}$$

In order to find out the effect on the food subsidy bill note that the depletion of FCI stocks under the first policy, denoted by D_1, is given by FCI's additional sale of foodgrains:

$$D_1 = c_1(1 - t) / \Delta, \tag{B.4}$$

where c_1 = marginal propensity to consume food by non-agricultural income earners. The economic interpretation of *Eq.* (B.4) is fairly simple, remembering that

[65] The subscripts 1 and 2 attached to γ indicate the two types of policies, viz., public investment (in general) and food-for-work projects.

$(1\text{-}t)/\Delta$ is nothing but the additional disposable income in the non-agricultural sector. FCI's loss reduction and, hence, fall in government subsidy under the first policy, S_1, is then immediate:

$$S_1=(1+\delta)D_1, \quad \text{(B.5)}$$

where δ is FCI's cost saving per unit of stock reduction.[66]

The change in the revenue balance of the government, rb_1, is obtained from (B.3) and (B.5):

$$\begin{aligned} rb_1 &= r_1+S_1 \\ &= [t+(1+\delta)c_1(1-t)]/\Delta \end{aligned} \quad \text{(B.6)}$$

The increase in public investment has, it is clear, an unambiguously positive impact on the revenue balance of the government.

The change in fiscal deficit due to a unit increase in the government's capital expenditure, fd_1, is

$$\begin{aligned} fd_1 &= 1-rb_1 \\ &= [\{(1-t)(1-c_1-c_2)+m\}-\delta c_1(1-t)]/\Delta. \end{aligned} \quad \text{(B.7)}$$

The expression within the second brackets on the right-hand side of (Eq. B.7) is nothing but the marginal non-agricultural saving out of post-tax income plus marginal propensity to import and should be positive. The other expression on the numerator indicates FCI's cost saving due to stock depletion following the rise in non-agricultural income (by one unit).

For plausible values of the variables entering (Eq. B.7), the fiscal deficit, it is not difficult to see, increases due to additional government investment; but the increase will be less than the extra expenditure incurred by the government. Though it is not inconceivable for fd_1 to be negative, the result may be treated as a theoretical curiosum. However, if increased capacity utilization (associated with a rise in Y) and prospects of *future* improvements in infrastructural facilities on account of the government's capital expenditure exert a positive influence on private investment, a fall in fiscal deficit is quite probable.

Let us use a simple private investment function incorporating the two effects just noted:

$$I_p = I_p(Y, I_g) \quad \text{(B.8)}$$

Using (Eq. B.8) in (Eq. B.1), the change in fiscal deficit due to a unit increase in government expenditure, fd_{1a}, is found to be

$$fd_{1a} = [\{(1-t)(1-c_1-c_2)+m-i\}-tn-\delta c_1(1-t)]/(\Delta-i), \quad \text{(B.7a)}$$

where $i = \partial I_p/\partial Y$ and $n = \partial I_p/\partial I_g$. Quite clearly, the probability of a decline in fiscal deficit is much greater in this case in view of the larger expansionary effects and higher tax collections.

[66] Recall that the price of foodgrains is set at 1 by choice of units.

Finally, the fall in foreign exchange reserves, fx_1, operating through variations in imports is given by

$$fx_1 = m/\Delta. \tag{B.9}$$

Fiscal Deficit as a Ratio of GDP

Since the government is concerned more with the magnitude of the fiscal deficit as a proportion of gross domestic product, it is useful to examine how an increase in public investment affects this ratio. Fiscal deficit, FD, is defined as

$$\text{FD} = I_g + G + T_r - R, \tag{B.10}$$

where T_r is the transfers including subsidy and R is the government revenue. Dividing throughout by GDP and differentiating, we get

$$\frac{d}{dI_g}\left(\frac{\text{FD}}{\text{GDP}}\right) = \frac{1}{\text{GDP}} + \frac{T_r}{\text{GDP}}\cdot\frac{1}{T_r}\cdot\frac{dT_r}{dI_g} - \frac{R}{\text{GDP}}\cdot\frac{1}{R}\cdot\frac{dR}{dI_g} - \frac{FD}{\text{GDP}}\cdot\frac{1}{GDP}\cdot\frac{d\text{GDP}}{dI_g} \tag{B.11}$$

Multiplying by the change in I_g, dI_g, it is easy to see that:

$$\text{sign}\left|\frac{d}{dI_g}\left(\frac{\text{FD}}{\text{GDP}}\right).dI_g\right| = \text{sign}\left|\left[\frac{1}{\text{GDP}} + \frac{T_r}{\text{GDP}}\cdot\frac{I_g}{T_r}\cdot\frac{dT_r}{dI_g} - \frac{R}{\text{GDP}}\cdot\frac{I_g}{R}\cdot\frac{dR}{dI_g} - \frac{FD}{\text{GDP}}\cdot\frac{I_g}{GDP}\cdot\frac{d(\text{GDP})}{dI_g}\right].dIg\right| \tag{B.12}$$

Note that out of the four terms on the right-hand side of (Eq. B.12), except for the first, all others are unambiguously negative. To appreciate how FD/GDP ratio changes when the *absolute* value of the fiscal deficit does not fall, consider the effect of a 1 per cent increase in I_g. Let GDP also increase by 1 per cent, but government revenue and subsidy remain unchanged. In this case though the level of fiscal deficit goes up, its ratio to GDP, as may be verified from (Eq. B.12), registers a decline in view of the fact that as of now the government investment to GDP ratio is less than the fiscal deficit. Indeed, even if GDP does not go up in the same proportion as I_g, FD/GDP is almost certain to decline, remembering that (a) the overwhelming part of tax collections comes from the non-agricultural, rather than the farm sector;[67] (b) the share of tax in GDP is three times that of public investment; and (c) food subsidy also registers a fall (i.e., T_r goes down).

Objectives and Constraints

Consider the case where the amount of excess stocks with FCI is E, the output gap is y^f, and the difference between the current level of foreign exchange reserves and

[67] So that elasticity of tax collections with respect to an increase in I_g will tend to be large.

the optimum required for maintaining external balance is x. Using the relations in the present model, the additional public investment, dI_g, required for eliminating FCI's excess stocks is given by[68]

$$dI_g = E.\frac{\Delta}{c_1(1-t)}. \tag{B.13}$$

However, the programme founders on the rock of Y-sector capacity constraint if

$$y_1 \times dI_g > y^f, \tag{B.14}$$

that is

$$\frac{E}{c_1(1-t)} > y^f;$$

or create external imbalance if

$$m.\frac{E}{c_1(1-t)} > x. \tag{B.15}$$

It will take us too far afield to chart out courses of action in case Eq. (B. 14) or Eq. (B. 15) holds, though we have indicated in the text the way in which composition of investment or the exchange rate policy may be modified under these conditions.

2. *Food-for-work Programme*

We can still use, with some modifications, the model used in the first section in order to examine the second type of public investment, viz., food-for-work projects. The main difference between the impact of the two types of investment occurs in the first round of income generation. Although a unit increase in government expenditure in FFP causes an equivalent rise in Y, no taxes accrue to the government from the wage component of FFP. Again, the major part of wages received by workers in these projects is spent on food, and only a small fraction on Y. Hence, out of the unit increase in the first round income,

$$\text{additional expenditure on food} = c_{1p}w + c_1(1-t)(1-w), \tag{B.16}$$

where c_{1p} is the the indigent's marginal propensity to consume food[69] and w is the the proportion of labour-cost in FFP.

Similar considerations suggest that out of the first round increase in income, the additional demand for Y is given by

$$Y = c_{2p}w + c_2(1-t)(1-w) - m(1-w), \tag{B.17}$$

[68] Remembering that Eq. (B.4) gives the depletion of FCI stocks per unit of I_g.

[69] Note that c_1 is the marginal propensity to consume (MPC) of all income earners in the Y sector and is a weighted average of MPCs of different income groups.

where c_{2p} is the poor's marginal propensity to consume Y. The derivation of the change in non-agricultural income, y_2, is then fairly straightforward:

$$y_2 = 1+[c_{2p}w+\{c_2(1\text{-}t)\text{-}m\}(1\text{-}w)]/\Delta. \tag{B.18}$$

The effects on the other variables are given by

$$r_2 = t[(1\text{-}w)+(y_2\text{-}1)] = t(y_2\text{-}w), \tag{B.19}$$

$$D_2 = c_{1p}w+c_1(1\text{-}t)(y_2\text{-}w), \tag{B.20}$$

$$S_2 = (1+\delta)D_2, \tag{B.21}$$

$$rb_2 = r_2+S_2, \tag{B.22}$$

$$fd_2 = 1\text{-}rb_2, \tag{B.23}$$

$$fx_2 = m(y_2\text{-}w), \tag{B.24}$$

where the notations have the same meaning as in earlier equations, and a variable with subscript 2 refers to its equilibrium value following a unit increase in the second type of investment (FFP).

Note that there is no qualitative difference in the effects of the two policies. The difference in the expansionary impact of the two measures is easily obtained from Eqs. (B.2) and (B.18):

$$y_1 - y_2 = \frac{1}{\Delta}w[c_2(1-t)-(c_{2p}+m)], \tag{B.25}$$

where the expression within the third brackets denotes how the demand for Y will change if in FFP there is a unit increase in material cost at the expense of the wage bill. Since c_{2p} is likely to be negligible and the value of m is quite small, y_1 is larger than y_2.

We leave it to the reader to verify that tax collections are always larger under the first policy and so is the increase in trade deficit when $y_1>y_2$. The first policy is also likely to be better from the viewpoint of a reduction in revenue and fiscal deficits, though in these cases, larger consumption demand for food on the part of the poor creates some ambiguity, especially if w is large.

5

Perspectives on Correcting Fiscal Imbalances in the Indian Economy*

Introduction

By common consent, the most serious weakness of the Indian macroeconomy in recent years has consisted in the continuing and growing imbalances in the fiscal sphere. This view is also reiterated by the Eleventh Finance Commission (Government of India, 2000) which, under its terms of reference, has recommended a programme of fiscal adjustment and restructuring over the period 2000–5. It is thus an opportune moment to take a fresh look at the nature of the fiscal problems confronting the Indian economy and initiate a fruitful debate on the basic issues and policy options, especially since some of the widespread and popular perceptions in this regard do not seem to be based on sound economic reasoning or a close scrutiny of the empirical evidence.

In order to motivate the discussion it is useful first to recapitulate the commonly perceived areas of fiscal imbalance that the government has been trying to rectify since the mid-1980s, especially after the adoption of the economic reforms programme in 1991. At the time when the programme was introduced the most important troubles were identified to be large fiscal and monetized deficits and the growing debt–GDP ratio. A related area of concern was the proportion of the economy's resources appropriated by the public sector and there was a general feeling that a downsizing of the government should form an important plank of any fiscal restructuring programme.

Over the last decade the government has been successful, perhaps too successful, in bringing down monetized deficit (see Table 5.1) so that this issue no longer figures prominently in discussions on budgetary policies. In other

* Reprinted from *Money & Finance*, Vol. 2, No. 2, July–September 2000.

TABLE 5.1

Fiscal Profile of the Indian Economy (figures, unless specified otherwise, are as percentage of GDP)

	1990–1	1991–2	1992–3	1993–4	1994–5	1995–6	1996–7	1997–8	1998–9	1999–2000
Revenue receipts	19.7	20.7	20.3	18.0	18.5	18.4	18.1	17.9	16.2	17.8
of which										
Interest, profit, and dividend receipts	1.3	1.8	1.6	1.5	1.3	1.2	1.4	1.4	1.4	
Revenue expenditure	24.2	24.2	23.6	22.3	22.1	21.6	21.7	22.0	23.2	23.2
of which										
Interest payments	4.7	5.0	5.2	5.0	5.2	5.0	5.1	5.1	5.2	5.7
Social sector expenditure	7.7	7.5	7.3	7.2	7.1	7.1	6.8	7.1	7.3	5.1
Capital receipt	8.7	8.4	7.0	7.7	8.9	6.7	5.6	8.1	9.3	8.5
Fiscal deficit	10.0	7.4	7.4	8.3	7.1	6.6	6.4	7.3	8.9	9.9
Primary deficit	5.3	2.4	2.3	3.3	1.9	1.6	1.3	2.2	3.7	4.2
Monetized deficit	2.8	0.8	0.6	0.1	0.2	1.7	0.2	0.7	1.0	–0.2
Public debt[1]	65.5	64.5	64.1	65.4	63.3	61.5	60.0	62.1	62.0	65.1
Public debt held by RBI	16.6	15.2	13.9	11.6	10.0	10.3	9.1	8.9	8.7	7.7
Interest cost of government borrowing (per cent)[2]		8.8	9.2	9.5	9.3	9.2	9.7	9.5	9.9	
Incremental return on government capital disbursement (per cent)[3]		11.8	6.3	5.6	4.1	3.9	5.1	4.7	4.9	
Memo Item										
Nominal GDP (growth rate)	15.7	14.5	15.4	14.4	17.9	15.0	13.9	9.8	13.7	

Sources: Government of India (2000), Reserve Bank of India (2000, 2000a, 2000b).

Notes: Figures are for Central and state governments taken together.

[1] Public debt includes internal and external debt and other liabilities. Other liabilities comprise small savings scheme, PFs, and Reserve Funds and Deposits.

[2] Interest cost of government borrowing of a year = Interest payment of the current year/public debt at the end of the previous year.

[3] Incremental return on government capital disbursement = Change in interest, dividend, and profits as % of cumulative capital disbursement, both from 1990–1 till the year concerned.

areas the record of the government is far from satisfactory and has drawn flak from practically all quarters including the International Monetary Fund (IMF), the World Bank, and the Eleventh Finance Commission (EFC). An important part of the Commission's report is accordingly devoted to formulating a fiscal correction programme under which, among other things, between 1999–2000 and 2004–5 the fiscal deficit (as a percentage of gross domestic product) is to be brought down[1] from 9.83 per cent to 6.5 per cent, and the debt–GDP ratio from 65.82 per cent to 55 per cent or less.[2]

Before commenting on any fiscal reforms programme or offering suggestion in this regard, it is necessary to have a clear idea regarding why and how the current fiscal scenario is worrisome and badly requires corrective steps. Second, it is also important to consider the economic implications of alternative modes of fiscal adjustment so that we are in a position to judge how far they benefit the society at large. The need for going into these basics may be illustrated by the problem one encounters in answering a few obvious questions that arise in this connection. Why, for example, should a 65 per cent debt–GDP ratio be considered too high, remembering that instances abound when some countries often had debt–GDP ratios exceeding 100 per cent, without any apparent clogging of their economic wheels? If public debt does constitute a burden, why should it not be brought down to zero within the shortest possible period? Why target for a fiscal deficit of (say) 6.5 per cent, no more, no less?

In any given situation it is no doubt extremely difficult to assign numerical values to fiscal targets due to informational problems and uncertainty regarding the future course of events impacting on the economy. However, while some element of subjective judgement or hunch is unavoidable in any policy decision, it is imperative to be fully conversant with the major factors and considerations on the basis of which policies should 'ideally' be framed. Hence, our foray into some elementary economics while discussing the modalities of fiscal restructuring for the Indian economy.

The discussion in the present chapter is organized as follows. There is a widespread belief that the fiscal stance of the government in recent years is unsustainable: not only is the debt–GDP ratio uncomfortably high, but the government's accumulation of financial liability due to large, continuing fiscal deficit poses a serious threat to both the solvency of the Treasury

[1] Unless mentioned otherwise, figures relating to fiscal deficit and other variables refer to those of the Union and state governments taken together.

[2] We should add that the Finance Commission does not explicitly specify the length of time over which the target for the debt–GDP ratio is to be reached, though it is possible to work this out from other fiscal targets and the Commission's assumptions relating to GDP growth and other trends.

and viability of the economy. In the context of such concerns, in the second section we go into the economic implications of public debt and fiscal deficit, and examine the problem of sustainability of debt-financed government expenditure. In the third section we will focus on issues relating to optimality. Even if the fiscal stance is sustainable, it can be grossly sub-optimal and leave plenty of room for correction. Keeping this consideration in view, we discuss in this section some general principles with special reference to the norms for deciding on the scale and composition of government expenditure and modes of its financing. The fourth section assesses the Indian fiscal scenario and offers some guidelines, drawing on the discussion in the earlier two sections. The final section summarizes the main conclusions.

On the Economic Impact and Sustainability of Debt and Deficit

Sustainability of the fiscal stance is a long-term problem and concerns the way in which budgetary viability may get eroded over time due to financing of government expenditure through borrowing. Fiscal deficit represents the scale of such financing and accumulation of public debt over the year. While examining the sustainability issue we need to consider three inter-related sets of questions. The first is the old one regarding the burden of public debt. The second concerns the problem of whether continuing fiscal deficit leads to an explosion of the debt–GDP ratio. Third, even if there is no such explosion, it is important to examine whether or how debt financing itself[3] has any deleterious impact on the economic system.

Burden of Public Debt

From a purely accounting viewpoint public debt,[4] economists emphasize, do not constitute any net liability of the economy as a whole, since financial assets held by the rest of the economy exactly offset government debt. By the same logic, however large may be the interest payments on public debt, they are nothing but transfers and do not constitute any net diminution in the community's command over goods and services available for consumption or investment. Why do we then worry about the size of the public debt or the interest liability thereon?

One reason is that when interest payments are very large, transfers to holders of government securities from the rest of the community can have

[3] As distinguished from the existence of a large public debt.

[4] So long as it is not externally held. In the present chapter we do not go into the problem of external debt, since it raises a different set of issues.

an adverse impact on income distribution. Second, given the rates and structure of taxes, larger interest payments imply a higher ratio of private disposable income to the gross domestic product. This can seriously distort the pattern of domestic absorption, as private consumption tends to rise at the expense of capital accumulation and provision of public goods and services. The distortionary impact on the economy's use of available goods and services is also likely to be strengthened by the operation of the wealth effect (on household consumption), since holders of government securities generally regard them as part of their assets.[5]

The adverse consequences of large public debt mentioned above can, one may argue, be avoided through appropriate tax-transfer schemes. However, these schemes themselves cause substantial distortion and misallocation of resources. Indeed, with or without public debt, the limited ability of the Treasury to raise revenue without producing large distortions very often makes the government face a Hobson's choice: either it refrains from implementing some urgently required welfare enhancing schemes, or it is forced to borrow in order to finance the programmes. But does not such financing store up troubles for the future when interest obligations of the government may assume enormous proportions? Herein arises the question of sustainability: given the proportion of GDP the government can collect by way of taxes without creating too much distortions, can it take recourse to borrowing for meeting part of public consumption expenditure as also for interest payments on the growing public debt?

Canonical Views on Sustainability

Before providing an answer to the question in the Indian context, it is useful to summarize the canonical views in this regard:[6]

(a) For any given tax–GDP ratio, financing part of public consumption expenditure[7] through borrowing is sustainable so long as the interest rate on government borrowing is less than the GDP growth rate. When this condition is satisfied, public debt, revenue deficit, and interest payments rise over time; however, their values as ratios of

[5] The effect will not operate if households, *a la* the Ricardian equivalence theory, are 'rational', take into account the future tax liabilities or cut-back in provision of public goods and services on account of interest payments on public debt and put the consumption of their descendents on the same footing as that of their own—conditions which are unlikely to be satisfied in full. See Barro (1974) in this connection.

[6] See Appendix 5.1 for details of the canonical model and some of its extensions.

[7] Public consumption is that part of revenue expenditure of the government which involves use of real resources such as labour or material. Hence, interest payments and subsidies do not constitute public consumption.

the gross domestic product stabilize in the long run, and do not go on increasing indefinitely.

(b) Lowering of tax rates or enhancement of debt-financed government consumption raises the long-run values of the debt–GDP and other ratios, but do not alter the sustainability result.

(c) Under the canonical scenario one need not worry about the government's inability to provide some essential public services on account of a high ratio of interest payments to tax collections, associated with a large public debt. In this scenario not only are interest payments made through borrowing without any cut-back in public consumption, but the problem of the government's 'inability' to incur such expenditure without raising taxes does not arise so long as the sustainability condition holds.

Some Caveats and Extensions of the Canonical Framework

An important problem with the canonical model is that it assumes the interest rate and the growth rate to remain unaffected irrespective of the government's fiscal stance—an assumption that is hard to reconcile with our discussion of the burden of public debt. Given the tax–GDP ratio, larger interest payment on public debt implies a higher ratio of private disposable income to the gross domestic product. This (together with a larger wealth effect associated with a higher debt–GDP ratio) tends to raise household consumption. Maintenance of public consumption expenditure under these circumstances would then raise interest rates, reduce investment and, hence, the growth rate of the economy.[8] It is thus not very difficult to see how a public consumption–GDP ratio larger than some critical value becomes non-viable without an increase in the tax–GDP ratio. Though the general principles for locating the critical value are fairly straightforward,[9] in any actual situation the estimate cannot but be rough and ready and leave substantial scope for disagreement among economists.

[8] An increase in private consumption need not have an adverse impact on growth when the economy has excess capacity. In Appendix 5.1 the canonical results are drawn on the assumption of full employment of resources. It is true that long-run growth in the neo-classical model is independent of saving or investment ratios; but the result holds only in the very long-run. In the intermediate run, spanning a period of up to twenty to thirty years, changes in the investment ratio will have a considerable impact on the economy's growth rate. Note also that the new growth theories have re-established the (Harrod–Domar) positive association between higher growth and higher investment ratios even in the long run.

[9] Given the relevant set of information, one may work out how an increase in the ratio of debt-financed public consumption to GDP affects the interest rate and the growth rate, and hence locate the value of the ratio at which the former exceeds the latter.

Apart from the impact of tax–GDP and public consumption–GDP ratios, it is necessary to recognize other factors having an important bearing on the sustainability issue[10]—factors which are not dealt with in the canonical model. An implicit assumption of the canonical approach is that the base of taxation is GDP, not earnings of private agents. A more reasonable assumption appears to be that it is the ratio of tax collections to total private 'income', irrespective of whether it is by way of factor earnings or transfers, that the government finds difficult to raise without producing serious distortions. Under this assumption debt financing is far less problematic, since sustainability now requires the growth rate to exceed the *post-tax* interest rate. In this case the burden of public debt will also be lighter than what has been suggested in our earlier discussion.

Central Bank Holding of Government Securities

In many countries, including India, public debt refers to all financial liabilities of the government, irrespective of to whom they are owed. While examining the sustainability and the related issues, government securities held by the central bank should not, however, be included in public debt: the central bank is after all an organ of the state so that there is no government liability corresponding to bonds held by the central bank; nor does the interest paid thereon stand on the same footing as those paid on private holdings of government securities.[11] Such a perspective appears necessary for judging the Indian fiscal scenario since not only is the proportion of 'public debt' held by the Reserve Bank not insignificant, but this proportion has undergone considerable changes over time. The scale and temporal behaviour of the official figures for public debt may thus give a wrong impression regarding sustainability of debt financing and other related issues.

Liabilities and Assets

Perhaps the most important difficulty of the canonical approach for assessing fiscal programmes in countries like India arises from neglect of the asset side of the government's balance sheet.[12] Let us consider first how conditions

[10] As also the optimality issue, as we shall discuss in the next section.

[11] Recall that public debt creates difficulties primarily through its impact on private consumption and distortions due to taxes and transfers, required for its servicing. These effects do not arise unless the expenditure programme of the central bank is not in consonance with the objectives the government seeks to promote. For examining the debt-related issues one has in fact to consider the consolidated accounts and balance sheets of all parts of the state sector, including public undertakings.

[12] This neglect is, however, in accord with the assumption that government expenditure is entirely on consumption or transfers.

relating to sustainability of debt financing are affected when the government borrows in order to meet capital expenditure and interest payments, but not for provision of public goods and services.[13] Given the other assumptions of the canonical model, sustainability now requires the growth rate to be higher than the (post-tax) interest rate less the return on assets being accumulated by the government—a much less onerous condition than the canonical one.[14] It is also easy to see that compared with the canonical case loan financing of public investment will be associated with a lower debt–GDP ratio, a higher growth, and a lighter burden of public debt.

When the government borrows for meeting not only capital, but part of consumption expenditure also,[15] it is necessary to take into account the relative importance of the two categories of debt-financed expenditure. To see why, assume that the aggregate debt-financed government consumption-cum-capital expenditure is fixed as a ratio of the gross domestic product. The larger the proportion of this expenditure for purposes of accumulation of assets, the higher will tend to be the growth rate of the economy.[16] Again, the cost of government borrowing (relevant for sustainability) will in the long run be a weighted average of (a) the (post-tax) interest rate and (b) the (post-tax) interest rate less the return on government investment, the weights being the fractions of debt-financed government expenditure on public consumption and investment, respectively. The implication is that, for any given amount of government borrowing for meeting its non-interest expenses, a larger proportion spent on investment will tend to promote budgetary viability through higher growth and lower (net) interest on the public debt.

Government Borrowing: Crowding-out and Crowding-in Effects

Our analysis has so far been based on the presumption that government borrowing, irrespective of its purpose, tends to raise interest rates and hence

[13] The implication is that the government's revenue deficit equals interest payments.

[14] In this connection it is important to distinguish between the sustainability condition and the requirement that the *net* asset of the government, given by the discounted sum of all future revenue receipts less that of revenue expenses of the government, must not be negative. Note that in the canonical model, the net asset position of the government is negative, but the fiscal stance may well be sustainable. Similarly, the government's net asset is negative when the return on public investment is not enough to meet interest charges, but debt-financing of such investment is likely to be sustainable.

[15] In addition to loans for interest payments.

[16] Note that even when there is some crowding out effect of government borrowing on private investment, the effect will not generally be one-to-one, as we shall presently see. Be that as it may, the relevant point here is that the aggregate investment in the economy will be larger when government absorption takes the form of investment rather than public consumption.

to crowd-out private investment. However, if the economy operates with excess capacity, debt-financed government expenditure, it is well known, may generate a crowding-in rather than a crowding-out effect. The boost to aggregate demand, capacity utilization, and profits due to expansionary fiscal measures are likely to raise not only the current gross domestic product, but also private investment and the long-term growth potential of the economy.[17]

What about the interest-rate effect? Note first that crowding-in can materialize despite an increase in interest rates. Second, as we shall see in a few moments, the interest-rate effect is crucially dependent on the type of government borrowing.[18] Third and perhaps the most important, the popular perception regarding the crowding-out process is based on an extremely narrow view of the financial market and ignores the increasingly important role being played by the stock market, mutual or pension funds, and innovation of financial instruments. When an expansionary fiscal policy improves investors' sentiments, there will generally be an increase in the supply of funds to the private sector despite debt financing by the government.[19] So long as the economy has excess capacity, an increase in the government expenditure supported by borrowing may thus raise private capital formation along with household consumption expenditure.

Once the economy has attained full employment, any increase in government consumption or investment, no matter how it is financed, will necessarily reduce private absorption. The usual conclusions in this respect are:

(a) Both private consumption and investment will decline.
(b) The greater the reliance on debt financing, the larger will be the fall in private investment.[20]
(c) Even with 100 per cent debt financing, the fall in private capital accumulation will be smaller than the additional investment expenditure by the government.

[17] Indeed, the salubrious effects of an increase in government expenditure will then be more pronounced with debt financing compared with tax financing.

[18] Thus government expenditure financed through credit from the central bank may well reduce the rate of interest. In this case the crowding-in effect is indubitable.

[19] The basic point to note here is that when asset holders find shares or other financial instruments more attractive compared with bank deposits, there will be an increase in the flow of funds outside the banking sector, *without any decrease in the supply of aggregate bank finance*. See Rakshit (1997) for a theory of the flow of funds within and outside the banking system.

[20] Even under tax financing, investment tends to fall with an increase in the interest rates (remembering that taxes reduce both consumption and private saving). Since borrowing per se does not reduce consumption, in this case the rise in interest rates is steeper and the fall in private investment larger.

However, these conclusions abstract from the impact of changes in composition of the government expenditure or in the modes of borrowing. The government expenditure for extension and improvement of infrastructural facilities, education, health services, law and order, etc. tends to raise prospective profits in the future and the aggregate demand for investment by firms. We thus need to distinguish between government disbursements which promote private investment demand and those which do not.[21]

So far as modes of government borrowing are concerned, consider first the two polar cases. Instruments such as the SLR requirement, to the extent they act as effective constraints, produce a one-to-one financial crowding out. At the other extreme, monetized deficit raises aggregate flow of finance, within and outside the banking sector, by a multiple of the deficit. In this case there is financial crowding-in, rather than crowding-out. In between the two instruments stand various types of government borrowing some of which tend to raise, others lower, the availability of finance to the private sector.[22]

Our analysis does not suggest that debt-financed government expenditure (under full-employment conditions) necessarily crowds in private investment when the budgetary exercise raises firms' investment demand and there is increased availability of finance to the private sector. The reason is that, given the level of full-employment output, crowding-in requires a fall in household consumption in excess of the incremental consumption or capital expenditure by the government.[23] This can come about only when the price rise, due to increased demand supported by enhanced availability of funds effects a sufficient cut-back in private consumption—an outcome that is neither guaranteed nor devoid of its flip side. What is unambiguous is that, both composition of government expenditure and modes of borrowing have an important bearing on the question relating to crowding-in and crowding-out effects.

Fiscal Deficit: Disabusing some Common Notions

While discussing the sustainability of a budgetary stance we have not referred to fiscal deficit, the centre of attention of all finance ministers and economists. The perceptive reader must have realized that this was not an

[21] Or which tend to depress the private propensity to invest.

[22] See Rakshit (1997) for a discussion on these issues.

[23] Note that compared with public consumption or investment, government disbursements by way of transfer and subsidies are more likely to promote private investment when they raise investment demand and there is a financial crowding-in.

oversight. Our earlier analysis indicates why fiscal deficit is not a very useful concept for judging the short- and long-run impact of the budget and, hence, of the sustainability of debt-financed government expenditure. However, in view of the extensive (mis)use of the concept in practically all discussions on fiscal reforms, it appears necessary to clarify our position even at the risk of labouring the obvious.[24]

Fiscal deficit, as defined in India, is the gap between the aggregate government expenditure and the sum of revenue receipts, proceeds from disinvestment in public sector undertakings, recovery of past loans, and other non-debt creating receipts. The basic difficulty with the concept, it is not very difficult to appreciate, arises from clubbings of various items of government expenditure and of receipts which do not have the same implications for sustainability[25] of a budgetary programme.

Many Faces of Government Borrowing

Consider first the problems associated with clubbing all categories of government borrowing under the sobriquet 'fiscal deficit'. We have already discussed why government securities held by the central bank should not be regarded as a part of public debt, and how monetized deficit produces a financial crowding-in effect. Indeed, apart from the fact that monetized financing of the government expenditure does not add to the future interest burden of the government, in a growing economy such financing (called seignorage) upto a point also produces no inflationary impact either.[26] The effects of alternative modes of government borrowing from the public can also differ significantly, as we have emphasized in the previous sub-section. No wonder then that, fiscal deficit, comprising all kinds of government borrowing over a year, does not on its own indicate the extent or even the sign of financial crowding out.

Disinvestment for Budgetary Nirvana

Much more misleading is the treatment of disinvestment in public sector undertakings (PSUs) and recovery of loans on the same footing as tax collections. Note first that when the government sells PSU shares in the stock market or recovers past loans, there should, other things remaining the same, be some pressure in the financial market—a pressure which in the aggregate

[24] Also relevant in this connection is Rakshit (1991).

[25] Or for optimality, as may be seen from our discussion in the next section.

[26] The reason is fairly simple. In a growing economy the demand for real balances and, hence, for reserve money (in real terms) rise over time. This creates scope for some *non-inflationary* monetized financing of government expenditure.

need not be less than that created by an identical amount of government borrowing from the public.[27] The crowding-in or crowding-out effect of financing government expenditure through unloading of shares or loan recovery on the one hand and market borrowing on the other may not thus be very different.

Second, unlike tax collections, non-debt creating receipts like disinvestment proceeds reduce future earnings of the government by way of interests and dividends. From the viewpoint of budgetary viability there can thus be little doubt that reduction of fiscal deficit through disinvestment cannot but be worse than tax financing.[28] Indeed, a cut-back in fiscal deficit through disinvestment may well erode rather than promote the long-run viability of the budget, since (a) the government's borrowing rate of interest is lower than that of private agents and (b) private asset holders tend to be risk averse.[29] This is not to deny that there can be a number of instances where disinvestment—backed by changes in management, incentives, and work environment in the undertakings—contributes toward budgetary viability. It is quite possible that the boost to expected profitability and, hence, the prices of the shares are then high enough to offset the impact associated with the higher borrowing rate of, and risk premium demanded by, private investors.[30] However, the first-best solution even in this case consists in adoption of measures for promoting profitability, without disinvestment.

[27] Disinvestment and recovery of loans constitute flow of finance from the rest of the economy to the government; so does government borrowing from the public.

[28] To take a simple example, let r be the interest on public debt, i the interest on loans advanced by the government and d the expected average rate of return on the current market value of shares proposed to be sold. In this case r-d, r-i, and r, respectively indicate the net impact on future revenue earnings per year following a unit reduction in fiscal deficit through disinvestment, recovery of loans, and tax or non-tax revenue.

[29] To see why, let d be the expected annual dividend per share, r the government's borrowing rate of interest, $r'(>r)$ the interest rate for private agents and π the risk premium for holding shares (instead of bonds). The sale price per share is then approximated by $d/(r'+\pi)$ which, when used to cut fiscal deficit, saves the government $d{\cdot}r/(r'+\pi)$ in terms of interest payments per year. Note however that, with $r'+\pi>r$, the fall in the government's future annual revenue due to disinvestment per se, viz., d, is higher than the saving in interest payments. Hence, the erosion of budgetary viability.

[30] Let disinvestment and the accompanying measures raise the dividend per share of the company from d to d^*. Following the argument of the previous footnote, under the disinvestment package the government gets $d^*/(r + \pi)$ per share which, when used to cut fiscal deficit, reduces the government's interest payments per annum by $r{\cdot}d^*/(r'+\pi)$. Since the government loses d per annum by selling one share, the disinvestment package will promote budgetary viability only if $r{\cdot}d^*>(r'+\pi)d$.

Indeed, from the viewpoint of budgetary viability, market borrowing may be a better alternative to disinvestment even when the increase in profitability under the best possible reorganization without disinvestment is less than what reorganization with disinvestment can permit.[31] It is only when political and bureaucratic interference, lying at the root of poor performance of PSUs, cannot be removed without disinvestment, should the government opt for this second-best measure for promoting sustainability.

The issues related to government disinvestment in PSUs are in fact broader and closely concern the political economy of efficient use and allocation of nation's resources. But these issues are not brought to the fore when the focus is on disinvestment as a means of reducing fiscal deficit; nor does there seem an adequate appreciation of the fact that even for promoting the narrower objective of improvement in the government's balance sheet, the measure may turn out to counterproductive.

Government Expenditure

We have already examined how different types of government expenditure—public consumption, investment and transfer—have quite different implications for future receipts of the government. For examining the sustainability of a fiscal stance it is thus necessary to consider the composition of the government expenditure, not simply its aggregate. This need is all the more urgent, as we shall see in the next section, for formulating an optimum, and not simply a sustainable, budgetary programme.

Budgetary Objectives and Instruments

The root of the sustainability problem, as already emphasized, may be traced to the difficulty the government encounters in collecting enough taxes for promoting its basic social and economic objectives. In order to examine the best way of resolving the problem, given the basic goals of public policy, it is useful to recapitulate first the nature of the optimum budgetary programme when the tax constraint is not operative. Second, we then have to examine how the textbook programme needs to be modified in the presence of the constraint faced by the government.

[31] Consider the example in the previous footnote. If the measures other than disinvestment raise the rate of dividend to d^*, by not disinvesting, the government earns d^* per share, which is larger than the saving in interest payments through disinvestment, viz., $r \cdot d^*/(r' + \pi)$. It may easily be shown that if the accompanying measures without disinvestment raises the dividend rate to $\hat{d}$, lying between d and d^*, it is better not to disinvest so long as $\hat{d} > r \cdot d^*/(r' + \pi)$.

Budgetary Rules sans Tax Constraint

For discussing the budgetary rules when the tax constraint is not operative, consider first the intermediate objectives[32] of public policies. These objectives are:

(a) optimum distribution of full employment output between consumption and investment;
(b) optimum balance between household and public consumption;
(c) optimum division of investment between the public and the private sector; and
(d) an equitable (post tax-transfer) distribution of income.

The first involves issues relating to inter-temporal and inter-generational distribution of consumption. We ignore the problem for the moment and assume that in this matter the government is guided entirely by the time preference (or its absence) of private economic agents.[33] The budgetary implications of the other objectives may be summarized as follows:

(a) An equitable distribution of income implies an optimum tax-transfer scheme. We put this first since estimation of marginal benefits from private and public consumption or investment under the ideal situation presumes an equitable distribution.[34]
(b) Government expenditures on administration, defence, maintenance of law and order and provision of other public goods are to be fixed at the level where their social benefit at the margin equals the marginal benefit from private consumption[35] (Samuelson, 1954).
(c) The equi-marginal principle should also apply in the division of aggregate investment between the public and the private sector. However, this principle refers to the social, not private, return. Thus while

[32] Apart from the objective of full employment of resources, which we ignore here, the ultimate goal is promotion of social welfare for which the intermediate targets constitute the means.

[33] The implication is that in any period, given the full-employment output and the (desired) distribution of income, the private propensity to save is taken to be the optimum.

[34] Note that when the distribution is ideal and private agents are taken to be the best judge of their own welfare, except in the case of externalities there is no need for differential investment or consumption taxes (e.g., those on tobacco).

[35] The basic economic rationale of government's use of resources in this connection lies in non-excludability in provision of public services and non-rivalry of consumers in the use of these goods. Thus benefits enjoyed by a person from a peaceful law and order situation does not reduce the extent of such benefits to the person's neighbours. Nor is it possible in a locality to permit only a select few to enjoy such benefits and exclude others.

estimating the return on investment, positive or negative externalities have to be taken into account and appropriate taxes or subsidies to be levied for securing the optimal composition and level of private investment. For public investment the relevant return needs to include all future incremental gains to the economy irrespective of whether they contribute anything to government coffers.

(d) All government consumption expenditure and transfer payments[36] are to be met from revenue receipts of the government, while public investment and net government support to private investment should be financed through borrowing. The textbook principles thus enjoin the government to target for a zero 'revenue deficit' and a fiscal deficit no more, no less, than the optimum level of public investment expenditure plus net subsidy on private investment.[37]

Before we examine how the above results are modified on account of constraints faced by the government, a few observations appear to be in order.

First, the budgetary programme chalked out above does not create any sustainability problem: even when public investment in roads, improvement in environment, or setting up broadcasting facilities does not yield any direct return to the Treasury, (non-distortionary) taxes permit the government to service interest payments on borrowings on account of such investment.

Second, given the optimal level of incremental reserve money and total investible funds, monetized deficit implies an equivalent decrease in financial resources available to the private sector. Hence, for framing an optimal budgetary programme the monetized and non-monetized borrowing of the government should be put on the same footing, both having the same opportunity cost from the viewpoint of the society as a whole.

Third, government support to human resource development, R&D, etc. should be treated as capital expenditure and financed by borrowing, not taxation.[38]

[36] Other than the excess of subsidy over taxes on private investment.

[37] The reason is that financing current expenditure through borrowing or capital expenditure through taxes distorts the society's choice between the current and future consumption. Note also that an item of expenditure is treated as capital when its benefits accrue in subsequent periods, not currently. Hence, that part of investment subsidy which is not met through taxation of investment should be treated at par with the conventional capital expenditure of the government for deciding on the mode of financing.

[38] It is interesting to note that the Union government has made essentially the same point before the Eleventh Finance Commission.

Second-best Budgetary Programmes

High economic costs of tax collections[39] in developing countries require considerable modifications in the principles enunciated above, especially when the government is already saddled with large interest obligations on public debt.[40] The problem in this context lies in devising the most effective means of promoting the basic objectives, given the tax constraint and the current committed expenditure of the government such as interest payments. The revised programme, it is not very difficult to see, will (compared with the first-best optimum) display a tilt in favour of those budgetary measures which tend to (a) raise future revenue of the government, (b) lighten the burden of interest obligations over time, and (c) reduce the current or future need for government expenditure for promoting the primary goals. Quite clearly, the revisions in fiscal policy will depend not only on the degree of severity of the tax constraint, but also on the relative weights attached to these goals. In order to discuss the nature of revisions in the composition and scale of the budget, it is useful to examine the type of budgetary measures which helps in easing the inter-temporal budget constraint and promotes the main objectives of public policy.

Faced with the revenue constraint, it is tempting for the government to scale down all types of expenditure as far as possible in order to contain growth of public debt and future interest liabilities. Since in the short run it is difficult to reduce interest payments as also wages and salaries, expenditure adjustment under the revenue constraint generally takes the form of cut-backs in government's capital expenditure, subsidies, and allocations for social and other sectors which do not form part of the government's committed expenditure. Such an adjustment may appear eminently sensible: distortionary effects of taxes reduce after all the net marginal (social) benefits of all types of government expenditure.[41] However, scaling down government expenditure, with across-the-board cut-backs in different

[39] To the extent tax reforms and better administration can reduce these costs, the economy can move closer to the first-best solution. Our focus in this sub-section is, however, on the nature of the budgetary programme, given the tax constraint in force.

[40] There are other problems such as inefficiency of government administration and enterprises that bedevil developing economies like India. Administrative reforms and public sector reforms should no doubt form an important part of fiscal correction; but so long as taxes are not distortionary, inefficiency in other spheres changes the scale and composition of the optimum budget, but not the principles laid down for its formulation.

[41] So that the second-best optimum levels of all items of government expenditure may be expected to be smaller than their first-best counterparts. It may also seem reasonable to start with the adjustable items in the short run and then try to reduce others over time.

items, may not in fact be optimum. Indeed, even the revised level of government spending in the short run need not necessarily be smaller than in the first-best solution. The reason, as we shall see, is that revisions in the expenditure and financing programmes are to be decided on simultaneously, taking into account their impact on easing the inter-temporal budget constraint and the consequent promotion of the primary goals of public policy.

Non-tax Sources of Government Revenue

Let us consider first the alternative sources of non-tax finance and examine their implications for the inter-temporal budget constraint and basic objectives.

Monetized Deficit

We have already indicated how monetized deficit or seignorage can, within limits, promote budgetary viability, but does not have any special role in the ideal situation. When the tax constraint does not permit the government to implement the first-best expenditure programme, borrowing from the central bank constitutes the most effective means of easing the constraint and moving closer to the first-best solution. Indeed, when the tax constraint is severe and the government is burdened with a large committed expenditure, maximizing the seignorage generally constitutes an optimum policy, provided the inflation associated therewith does not seriously distort the economic system.[42] However, since even the maximum amount of resources the government can extract through monetized deficit is unlikely to be large enough to ease the budget constraint significantly, further adjustments on the financing side are called for.

Borrowing from the Public

Governments in practically all developing countries have often appropriated funds from the financial sector at below market interest rates through instruments like the SLR. Though such instruments are inefficient or distortionary under the first-best scenario, in the case under consideration, up to a point their use should be welfare enhancing. Borrowing at below market interest rates constitutes, it is true, taxation of financial saving and

[42] In a growing economy inflation does not occur until monetized deficit goes beyond some point. After this point (until the seignorage reaches the maximum level) one has to consider the distortionary effects of inflation on the one hand and gains due to easing of the budget constraint on the other.

may induce savers to switch from financial to real assets. However, given the fact that the problem of distributing the saving between physical and financial assets does not arise for the vast majority of economic agents,[43] the distortionary effect by way of substitution between the two types of assets is likely to be minor. The main problem with borrowing through SLR and similar devices arises from the increased cost of financial intermediation and its impact on production and private investment. It is these effects which limit the amount of such borrowing under the optimum budgetary programme.

Restructuring Government Expenditure

Considerations of the tax constraint suggest that, other things remaining the same, the revision in the government's expenditure programme will be along the following lines.

First, compared with the first-best solution, more emphasis will be put on capital expenditures than on public consumption. The reason is that such a shift improves the future revenue collection of the government,[44] eases the inter-temporal budget constraint, and contributes to promotion of social objectives.

Second, similar considerations tilt the balance in favour of those items of public investment whose returns directly accrue to the Treasury, and against capital disbursements that have positive externalities.[45]

Third, the second-best optimum will be characterized by exercise of some degree of monopoly power[46] up to a point, even though these measures are inefficient under the first-best situation.

Fourth, while large externalities militate against public sector investment,[47] the fact that it is easier to tax income generated through public enterprises and that their entire profits contribute toward relaxing the government's budget constraint tend to favour investment in the public at the expense of the private sector.

[43] These agents' optimum pattern of asset holding displays a corner solution, to use economists' jargon.

[44] Because of an increase in the GDP growth.

[45] The implication, we emphasize, is not total exclusion of such items of investment, but only their smaller scale compared with the ideal situation where these externalities do not produce any tax constraint.

[46] By public or private enterprises. In the case of private enterprises, the government will appropriate the surplus by way of license fees, auctions or other devices.

[47] Since investments having large externalities or producing public goods add less to the government's future revenue than those yielding direct returns, given the problem of taxing incomes generated elsewhere.

Income Inequality and Poverty

The steps considered above are designed to raise future revenue or reduce the interest burden of the government so that provision of public goods, expenditure for reducing income inequality and poverty, and government support to economic growth can move closer to their optimum levels. Under the revised programme, these steps will be supplemented by measures that reduce the need for current and future expenditure of the government to promote social objectives.

In developing countries most of these measures will be directed toward bringing down both current and future pre-tax-transfer income inequality and poverty, given the prohibitive cost of redistributing purchasing power from the richer to the poorer sections of the society. All empirical studies suggest that the incidence of poverty at the national as also the regional level is closely dependent on agricultural production, prices of foodgrains, employment, primary education, and health. In the context of this relationship, we may distinguish between two sets of measures for reducing the need for direct government intervention aimed at improving income distribution and reducing poverty, the first designed to tackle the short-term, the second the long-term problem.

Food and fertilizer subsidy along with credit facilities to farmers tend to raise production and reduce prices of foodgrains;[48] suitably designed employment guarantee schemes ensure means of subsistence to the indigent groups of society; and supply of potable drinking water along with health services in rural areas[49] moderates the incidence of disease and disability. All these measures help reducing current poverty and expenses incurred thereon and thus partake of the characteristic of the government's revenue expenditure from the viewpoint of its objective of poverty elimination.[50] The longer term solution to the problem lies in the investment in agriculture, development of infrastructure in the rural areas, setting up of microcredit agencies, and rapid expansion of primary education and basic health services.

In order to appreciate how or to what extent these constitute a departure from the ideal programme, a few observations appear to be in order.

[48] Note that we are not considering here public distribution system which requires direct government intervention in distribution of foodgrains.

[49] We are referring to the current supply of water and health services, not setting up of health centres or installation of new tubewells.

[50] The distinction between current and capital expenditure should in principle be based on whether the expenditure enhances current or future well-being. Note that to the extent current expenditure on employment schemes or health services contributes toward future production or improvement of income distribution, part of the expenditure should be treated as capital disbursement.

First, the current and capital expenditure for poverty elimination are larger here than what is suggested under the first-best solution.[51] For example, there is now near unanimity among economists regarding the crucial role of education, health, research and development (R&D), and a well-functioning financial system in promoting economic growth. Under the revised programme, we may note, allocation of public funds under these heads will be somewhat different from what is optimal in the ideal situation. There is a smaller allocation for higher education and other areas which do not directly benefit the poor and more for primary education, supply of potable drinking water, provision of health services in rural and distressed areas, research related to agriculture and mass communicable diseases, and extension of micro-credit facilities.

Second, larger expenditure on agriculture and other items mentioned above violates the first-best principles of allocative efficiency and involves some loss of GDP.[52] But given the enormous informational and implementation difficulties of tax-transfer schemes, it is not difficult to appreciate the need for special steps[53] to reduce income inequality and poverty by tackling the problem at its source, viz., the process of income and employment generation.

Third, while drawing up the fiscal programme for poverty elimination, it is important to weigh the relative efficacy of current expenditure such as subsidies on food or agricultural inputs, and of capital expenditure on irrigation, power supply in rural areas, or primary education. Given the inter-temporal budget constraint faced by the government, the litmus test of efficacy of a poverty programme consists in the extent to which it leads over time to growth of income earning assets and capability of the

[51] Recall that under this solution no capital expenditure is involved for meeting income distributional objectives and the entire amount of current expenditure takes the form of income transfer and is financed through taxes.

[52] The extent of 'inefficiency' or loss of output is not however as large as it may appear at first sight. As students of welfare economics are told at the very beginning, the relative prices characterizing conditions of allocative efficiency and all that are by no means sacrosanct and depend on the initial distribution of income earning assets, both tangible and intangible. In the first-best solution the relative prices correspond to an equitable income distribution—a far cry from any actual situation. Again, some of the measures under the revised programme also go against the principle of allocating domestic resources on the basis of border prices of goods (*a la* the theory of comparative advantage), and thus reduce the community's potential levels of consumption and investment. However, unless there is an easy means of income redistribution, 'maximization' at border prices may leave untouched, if not aggravate, the problem of poverty.

[53] This is not to suggest that the special steps actually taken in countries like India have been optimal.

disadvantaged, and hence reduces the need for special steps like agricultural subsidy that are otherwise distortionary.

Fiscal Malady in India: Diagnoses and Remedies

Since all observers including the Eleventh Finance Commission regard India's on-going budgetary stance as unsustainable, we first take a critical look at the behaviour of the relevant variables in recent years, and try to identify the positive developments as also the major blemishes in the fiscal system. This provides the necessary backdrop for discussing both the sustainability problem and the efficacy of alternative programmes of fiscal correction.

Sustainability of Fiscal Stance

Table 5.2 summarizes the time profile of the most important indices of the health of India's fiscal system during the 1990s. At first sight, the behaviour of the usual indicators does not seem to suggest that there was a marked deterioration in the fiscal health of the country during the reference period. The public debt–GDP ratio did not show any rising trend; in fact, but for the rise over the later part of the period, the trend would have been distinctly downward. Behaviour of the fiscal deficit (as a ratio of GDP) was also similar, registering a rapid decline in the earlier phase and rising in the last three years. What may appear decisive, the crucial condition for sustainability of debt financing, viz., the growth rate of the economy exceeding the interest cost of government borrowing, is also satisfied. While the interest rate on government borrowing was less than 10 per cent throughout,[54] the average GDP growth (in nominal) terms was about 14 per cent per annum.[55]

Despite having reservations regarding the efficacy of the budgetary programme being followed by the government, one may thus be tempted to dismiss fiscal sustainability as a non-issue for the Indian economy. However, the dismissal is perhaps too hasty, based as it is on neglect of some important negative developments. First, as is evident from Table 5.2, since 1996-7 while the public debt and fiscal deficit ratios have shown a rising trend, the GDP growth rate in relation to the interest rates has tended to

[54] Ours is an overestimate, since, because of non-availability of the required data, new Treasury Bills issued but retired within the year, do not form part of the denominator, but interest paid thereon is included in the numerator.

[55] For checking on the sustainability condition, we need to consider either the nominal values of the interest rate and the growth rate or their real values. Note also that what is relevant for sustainability is the average values over a considerable period of time, not over say five or ten years.

TABLE 5.2

Indicators of Fiscal Sustainability—1990–2000 (figures, unless specified otherwise, are as percentage of GDP)

	1990–1	1991–2	1992–3	1993–4	1994–5	1995–6	1996–7	1997–8	1998–9	1999–2000
Public debt	65.5	64.5	64.1	65.4	63.3	61.5	60.0	62.1	62.0	65.1
Fiscal deficit	10.0	7.4	7.4	8.3	7.1	6.6	6.4	7.3	8.9	9.9
Nominal GDP growth rate	15.7	14.5	15.4	14.4	17.9	15.0	13.9	9.8	13.7	
Interest cost of government borrowing		8.8	9.2	9.5	9.3	9.2	9.7	9.5	9.9	
Growth–interest differential		5.7	6.2	4.9	8.6	5.8	4.3	0.3	3.8	
Public liability[1]	48.9	49.2	50.2	53.8	53.3	51.2	50.9	53.2	53.4	57.4
Incremental financial liability (IFL)[2]	10.8	9.5	8.5	9.1	8.5	7.3	7.1	8.0	9.6	
Fiscal gap[3]	8.0	8.7	7.9	9.0	8.3	5.6	6.9	7.3	8.6	
Revenue deficit	4.5	3.6	3.4	4.2	3.7	3.2	3.6	4.1	6.3	6.7
Capital expenditure	6.4	5.9	5.1	4.8	4.9	4.1	3.6	3.9	3.9	
Capital expenditure as percentage of IFL	58.8	62.6	60.5	53.0	56.9	55.9	49.8	48.4	40.4	
Net interest cost of government borrowing[4]		5.2	5.4	6.5	7.0	7.0	7.1	7.3	8.0	
Growth–net interest cost differential		9.3	10.0	7.9	10.9	8.0	6.8	2.6	5.7	
Non-interest revenue receipt[5]	18.5	18.9	18.7	16.5	17.2	17.2	16.7	16.5	14.8	
Primary gap[6]	3.3	3.6	2.7	3.9	3.1	0.6	1.8	2.2	3.4	

Sources: Government of India (2000), Reserve Bank of India (2000, 2000a, 2000b).

Notes: [1] Refers to public debt and other liabilities net of public debt held by RBI.

[2] Incremental financial liability = capital disbursement + revenue deficit.

[3] Fiscal gap = incremental financial liability – monetized deficit.

[4] Net interest cost of government borrowing = Weight of capital expenditure × (interest cost – interest return) + weight of revenue deficit × interest cost.

[5] This is the difference between revenue receipts and interest, profit, and dividend receipts.

[6] Primary gap = fiscal gap – interest payments.

move in the opposite direction. It is this reversal of the trend that has caused apprehension in many a quarter regarding the sustainability of mounting debt and deficit.

Indeed, a scrutiny of the more relevant indicators of, and factors contributing to, sustainability of debt financing[56] reveals a much more unhealthy trend on the fiscal front than what is suggested by the behaviour of public debt, fiscal deficit, or even the (overall) growth–interest differential. As we have already noted, the relevant indicator of the burden of government's indebtedness is public debt less the RBI holding of government securities, or what we call public liability (PL). Unlike the (public) debt–GDP ratio, the proportion of PL to the gross domestic product showed a steeply rising trend during the 1990s, with the ratio registering an increase of nearly nine percentage points between the beginning and the end of the decade (Table 5.2). The counterpart of this trend was the decline in public debt held by the Reserve Bank (as a ratio of GDP), from 16.6 per cent in 1990–1 to 7.7 per cent in 1999–2000. Thus the stability of the debt–GDP ratio during the 1990s is somewhat misleading in judging the sustainability of the budgetary stance or the change required therein.

An indicator closely related to the above is what we call the fiscal gap, which is nothing but the government's incremental financial liability[57] (IFL) less monetized deficit. The fiscal gap (FG) thus represents the yearly increase in the government debt to the rest of the economy plus reduction in its financial assets, and hence constitutes, as we have already argued in the second section, a better measure than fiscal deficit of the government's incremental debt burden arising from current budgetary measures. As Table 5.2 shows, during 1990–5 fiscal deficit recorded a significant decline, but FG showed a mildly upward trend. Thus contrary to the widely held belief, the first phase of the reforms programme did not contribute to the fiscal health of the economy. Government expenditure (as a ratio of GDP) did decline during this period (Table 5.1), but with its focus on reduction of fiscal and monetized deficits in the face of a decline in revenue receipts, the government apparently lost sight of the troubles it was piling up for the future. There was some fall in FG during 1995–7, but its subsequent increase at a fairly steep rate constitutes a serious weakness of the budgetary programme pursued in recent years.

What about the uses of funds borrowed by the government—a question the answer to which is of crucial importance in assessing the viability of the

[56] As discussed in the second section.

[57] IFL is nothing but fiscal deficit plus non-debt creating capital receipts. We have discussed in the second section why such receipts are required to be taken into account for examining sustainability.

fiscal stance? As we have emphasized in the second section, other things remaining the same, the greater will be the erosion of fiscal viability, the larger the proportion of total borrowing used for bridging the revenue deficit and the smaller the fraction devoted to capital expenditure. A look at the relative importance of the two uses of borrowings[58] leaves little doubt regarding the unhealthy trend in India's fiscal system during the 1990s: over this period while revenue deficit (as a ratio of GDP) went up by 2.2 percentage points, capital expenditure was reduced by about 2.7 percentage points (Table 5.2). There are wider implications of this sharp change in the government's fiscal stance to which we shall presently turn; but let us first indicate its impact on sustainability.

A larger proportion of capital expenditure in relation to revenue deficit reduces the net interest cost of the government borrowing. This cost, as already discussed in the second section, is nothing but the weighted average of (a) the borrowing rate and (b) this rate less the (gross) return on government investment, the weights being the ratios of revenue deficit and capital expenditure respectively (to their total). On the basis of the budgetary figures for the Union and state governments taken together we have estimated the government's borrowing rate, incremental return on its capital expenditure, and, hence, net interest cost of government borrowing[59] (Table 5.2). It is this net interest cost which is more relevant than the government's borrowing rate for examining the sustainability of the on-going fiscal stance. According to our estimate throughout the 1990s the net interest cost of debt financing showed an uninterrupted rising trend, the rise amounting to more than 2.5 percentage points between 1991–2 and 1998–9. Part of the increase was accounted for by the fall in the return on government's capital expenditure, but the major reason, especially during the later part of the period, lay in changes in relative weights of the two uses of borrowing, as revenue deficits mounted even while capital disbursements were on their downward course.[60]

For examining sustainability we need to compare the GDP growth and the net interest cost of government borrowing, or the growth-net interest cost differential. During the reference period this differential came down

[58] Borrowings here include monetized deficit and non-debt creating capital receipts.

[59] Due to data limitations we have not taken into account interest on borrowing from the public (other than the RBI) separately. But this does not affect our main conclusions.

[60] Note that there was no significant upward trend in the government's borrowing rate so that this was not very important behind the rising net interest cost of debt financing. Abstraction from RBI financing, which came down sharply over the reference period, makes the time trend of the estimated net cost of government borrowing less steep; but the conclusion regarding the impact of changes in the relative importance of revenue deficit and capital expenditure is not affected thereby.

sharply,[61] especially after 1995–6, lending credence to the common refrain that the budgetary correction programme of the government has gone awry in recent years. However, despite the downward trend of the differential, the GDP growth has remained above the net cost of government borrowing. One may also argue that even if the declining trend in capital expenditure in relation to revenue deficit continues unabated, the net cost of borrowing can at most reach the interest rate, which still falls short of the economy's growth rate.

Such optimism concerning the country's fiscal sustainability needs to be moderated in light of two major disquieting trends.[62] First, a positive growth–interest differential as a sufficient condition for sustainability presumes a constant tax–GDP ratio. In the Indian context, the relevant ratio is that between revenue receipts less earnings from government assets[63] and the gross domestic product, or what we call non-interest revenue–GDP ratio (NIRR). This ratio has shown a distinctly downward trend and registered a fall of about 3.5 percentage points during the 1990s (Table 5.2). Remembering that even with a positive growth–interest differential, a falling NIRR tends to raise over time the debt–GDP ratio and interest burden on public debt, the declining trend in the government's non-interest revenue must be regarded as a negative development from the viewpoint of budgetary viability.

The second disquieting trend relates to the behaviour of what we call 'primary gap', that is, the difference between the fiscal gap and interest payments of the government. This is nothing but the increase in the government's liability to the public (excluding the Reserve Bank) due to its current budgetary exercise,[64] and determines (along with other factors) the future course of the government's debt burden:[65] other things remaining the same, the burden will rise over time with an increase in the primary gap–GDP ratio. As Table 5.2 shows, this ratio also recorded a steep rise during the second half of the 1990s and suggests that sustainability of debt financing is not guaranteed unless the trend is arrested, if not reversed.

It is not very difficult to form an overall assessment on the basis of Table 5.2 that shows how the main indicators relating to sustainability of debt

[61] Short-run changes in the differential may be due to operation of cyclical factors and should not be given undue importance. Thus in 1991–2 (and also partly in 1994–5), the large growth–net interest cost differential was due primarily to spurt in inflation. What is relevant for sustainability is the long-term trend of the differential.

[62] Apart from the problem regarding the prospective growth rate to which we turn in the next sub-section. See fn. 55 in this connection.

[63] Note that we take into account returns on government assets while estimating the net interest cost of government borrowing.

[64] Not to past borrowings.

[65] See Appendix 5.1.

financing changed during the 1990s. There is little doubt that despite, or because of, the reforms measures initiated since 1991, practically all indicators show a deteriorating health of India's fiscal system. The negative developments on the fiscal front, though worrisome, do not nevertheless suggest that the economy is being inexorably pushed to an internal debt trap. Much more important is the question whether the current fiscal stance, even if sustainable, helps in promoting the basic social and economic objectives, and if not, how best to alter the policy stance.

Fiscal Correction for Promotion of Economic and Social Objectives

In order to judge whether or to what extent budgetary policies have helped or hindered attainment of primary objectives such as growth and equity, it is useful to consider first the performance of the economy and identify the positive or negative role of the government in the outcome. On the basis of the behaviour of the two most important macro variables, viz., GDP growth and inflation, one may feel reasonably optimistic regarding the outlook of the Indian economy (Table 5.3). After an initial setback in the first few years since the reforms programme was initiated, the GDP growth picked up and averaged more than 6.5 per cent per annum during 1994–2000. The higher GDP growth in this period was also accompanied with a lower inflation rate than in the earlier years. This happy conjunction of the two most important macroeconomic trends, many an observer feels, augers well for the country's economic performance in the new millennium.

A closer look at Table 5.3 suggests, however, that the macroeconomic scenario is not that picture perfect. Not only did the average GDP growth over 1997–2000 fall short of the average during the earlier three years, but the performance of both the industrial and agricultural sectors has been quite lackluster. The last four years of the decade saw a distinct deceleration of industrial growth—a trend also confirmed by the current year's data so far. The average agricultural growth over the decade remained low, and what is no less worrisome, showed sharp year-to-year fluctuations. The relatively high GDP growth in recent years has in fact been driven by growth of services. But it is a moot point whether the tertiary sector growth can be maintained in the absence of growth in the other two sectors and an adequate back-up by way of investment in required fields.[66]

[66] Note that services are either intermediate inputs or consumption items. In the absence of an adequate growth elsewhere in the economy, the tertiary sector cannot but be hit, sooner or later, by a demand constraint, remembering that export of services constitutes a small fraction of the total. Again, to the extent production of services requires inputs from other sectors, there will be supply constraint due to slowdown in the growth of productive capacity in the rest of the economy.

TABLE 5.3

Macroeconomic Indicators of India—1990–1 to 1999–2000 (figures, unless specified otherwise, are as percentage of GDP)

	1990–1	1991–2	1992–3	1993–4	1994–5	1995–6	1996–7	1997–8	1998–9	1999–2000
GDP growth rate	5.4	0.8	5.3	6.0	7.0	7.3	7.5	5.0	6.8	6.4
Agricultural growth rate	4.2	–2.0	5.8	3.6	5.3	–0.4	8.8	–1.1	6.5	1.3
Industrial growth rate	7.0	–1.7	4.4	6.9	9.3	12.5	6.6	5.6	4.5	7.8
Inflation rate	10.3	13.7	10.1	8.4	10.9	7.7	6.4	4.8	5.9	3.3
Food price inflation	11.9	20.2	12.3	4.9	9.9	7.4	11.8	3.4	12.7	3.8
Government consumption expenditure (GFCE)	11.5	11.3	11.1	11.2	10.6	10.7	10.6	11.5		
Investment	27.7	23.4	23.9	23.1	26.1	27.2	24.6	26.2	23.4	
Public	10.4	10.0	10.3	8.2	8.8	7.6	6.9	7.2	6.6	
Private sector	16.1	13.9	14.6	13.0	14.8	18.8	17.1	16.9	15.2	
of which										
Household	11.5	9.4	9.3	7.3	7.9	9.6	9.3	8.3		
Private corporate	4.6	4.5	5.3	5.7	6.9	9.2	7.7	8.7		
Investment in agriculture	2.2	2.2	2.2	1.8	2.0	2.0	1.9	2.0		
Investment in infrastructure	5.9	6.1	6.3	5.8	5.1	5.0	4.8	4.8		
Investment growth rate	12.2	–11.0	12.4	–2.7	19.9	19.6	–1.3	7.7	–21.5	
Saving	24.3	22.9	22.0	22.5	25.0	25.5	23.3	24.7	22.3	
Household	20.5	17.7	17.7	18.4	19.8	18.5	17.1	19.0	18.5	
Private corporate	2.8	3.2	2.8	3.5	3.5	5.0	4.5	4.3	3.8	
Public sector	1.0	1.9	1.5	0.6	1.7	2.0	1.7	1.4	0.0	
of which										
Public sector undertakings	5.5	5.5	4.9	4.8	5.4	5.2	5.3	5.5	6.3	

Sources: Government of India (2000a), Reserve Bank of India (2000, 2000a).

There were other developments in the economy which cast doubts on the possibilities of robust growth in the absence of major policy initiatives. The most important of these negative developments was the fall in investment and saving ratios, especially since 1995–6 (Table 5.3). Remembering that the East and South East Asian economies have been saving and investing 35–45 per cent of their gross domestic product almost from the beginning of their attempts at industrialization, and that raising the domestic investment and saving ratios from around 25 per cent to at least 30 per cent was the avowed target of the government in the early 1990s, the fall in the two crucial macro variables by two percentage points cannot but be regarded as a major failure of government policies pursued over the previous decade.

The failure is also reflected in the composition of investment and sources of saving. Note first that despite the perceptible rise in per capita income during the 1990s, household saving as a ratio of GDP showed a significant fall over the period. Saving in the private corporate sector did register an increase; but not only has its upward trend been reversed since 1995 and the increase quite insufficient to arrest the downward drift of private saving,[67] but the corporates' contribution in this respect has also not been commensurate with the increase in their share in the economy's total capital stock.[68] Nor does the record of the public sector appear quite commendable: it did manage to raise its saving ratio by one percentage point over 1990–6, but since then the ratio has come down sharply and the sector ended up with zero saving in 1998–9.

A Tale of Private Profligacy and Public Thrift

In order to suggest corrective measures on the fiscal front, it is important to locate the major factors behind the dismal behaviour of the economy's saving ratio. The first point to appreciate in this connection is that, contrary to popular perception, it was private, not pubic, profligacy that lay at the root of the trouble. The government consumption[69] ratio, unlike that in the private sector, did not go up in the reference period. In fact, over the 1980s, this ratio went up by more than two percentage points, but showed some slide, albeit marginal, during the last decade.

[67] Consisting of household and private corporate saving.

[68] Note that while both household and public capital accumulation came down sharply over the reference period, investment in the private corporate sector as a proportion of GDP increased by more than four percentage points (Table 5.3).

[69] This refers to revenue expenditure of the government less transfer payments such as interest and subsidies—items that do not involve absorption of goods and services by the government.

The explanation of the declining trend in aggregate saving seems to lie in two sets of factors. First, over the 1990s the tax–GDP ratio came down by more than 3.5 percentage points; government transfer payments by way of interest and subsidies mounted; and out of interest payments, by far the largest item in government's revenue expenditure, an increasing fraction was accruing to the private sector, as monetized deficits came down sharply and the government liability to private agents went up by nine percentage points. The result was a whopping six percentage points increase in the ratio of the household disposable income to the gross domestic product. Such an increase could not but produce a fall in the aggregate saving, remembering that the private marginal propensity to consume is quite substantial and much larger than that of the government. Thus, while public consumption was not responsible for the downward drift of the saving ratio, the fiscal policies pursued by the government played an important role in inducing the drift.

No less important behind the negative trend in savings was the increasing profligacy of households during the 1990s, something which stands in sharp contrast to their behaviour in earlier periods. An increase in household disposable income (at the expense of the government) reduces aggregate saving in the economy; however, under normal conditions household saving *as a ratio of GDP* should rise.[70] The fall of the ratio implies that for every additional rupee households received from the government by way of transfer, they spent more than one rupee on consumption! This pattern of household behaviour stands in sharp contrast to the experience in the 1980s: over the period 1981–90, thanks to an increase in the tax–GDP ratio from 15.1 to 17.5 and the government's heavy reliance on monetized deficit to meet the budgetary gap, household disposable income–GDP ratio came down from 81.6 per cent to 79.7 per cent; but even so, household saving as a proportion of the gross domestic product recorded an increase of 4.5 percentage points. Over 1990–9, on the other hand, the ratio came down from 20.5 to 18.5 per cent although the disposable income–GDP ratio rose steeply, from 80.2 per cent to 85.7 per cent. There was thus a sharp reversal of the earlier trend of household saving and a quantum jump in the private propensity to consume during the 1990s. It will take us too far afield to go into the reasons for the jump or to examine to what extent it was induced by the government policies themselves.[71] However, the fact remains that in the context of such changes in consumer behaviour, budgetary policies, through their

[70] The reason is that both the marginal propensity to consume and save are positive fractions.

[71] The hypothesis, that the reforms measures, by promoting 'consumerism', were responsible for private profligacy, may have some validity, but is extremely difficult to verify.

impact on private disposable income, played a major role in driving down the overall saving ratio, instead of raising it to the targeted level.

The 1980s and the 1990s were marked by contrasting behaviour of public saving as well, but in the opposite direction than that of private saving. During the period 1981–90, the public sector saving declined by nearly three percentage points even though there was a rise in the tax–GDP ratio.[72] During the 1990s the government on the whole became much more thrifty, especially over 1990–8.[73] Despite the fall in the tax–GDP ratio and mounting transfers to the private sector, the period was characterized by an upward trend in the public sector saving.

For both analytical and prescriptive purposes it is useful in this regard to consider separately contributions of the two parts of the public sector, viz., Government Administration (and Defence) and PSUs.[74] Even though public consumption did not go up during the 1990s, the fall in the revenue ratio and substantial transfer payments resulted in large negative savings of Government Administration, as reflected in the growing revenue deficits. It was this, rather than the poor performance of PSUs, that accounted for the government's failure to provide a push to the aggregate saving ratio. Indeed, the PSU savings (as a proportional of GDP), after a dip in 1992–3 and 1994–5, have been showing a mildly upward trend since then (Table 5.3), and this, in the context of substantial decline in public sector investment during the reference period, should be regarded as a positive development in operation of this sector, though there is no doubt ample scope for its improvement.

Investment and Public Policy

The decline in the aggregate capital formation as a proportion of the gross domestic product does not tell the full story of disquieting trends and the government's policy failure in this crucial area. One of the major blemishes of the Indian economy during the 1990s consisted in extremely large year-to-year fluctuations in the growth rate of investment (Table 5.3). Such fluctuations not only heighten the risk producers face, but also reflect the following:

(a) lack of stable economic (including policy) environment under which investments can be undertaken on the basis of their long-term returns;

[72] As we have noted elsewhere (Rakshit, 1994), public sector consumption played a no mean role in driving aggregate demand and growth during the 1980s.

[73] i.e., if we exclude the year 1998–9.

[74] Whose accounts do not form part of the government budget.

(b) coordination failure in decision making; and
(c) failure of anti-cyclical fiscal and monetary policies.

These deficiencies are inter-related and largely attributable to the government policies, or their absence, during the period under consideration. An important reason behind the government's inability to iron out fluctuations and ensure sustained growth in investment and industrial production was its focus on fiscal and monetized deficit, ignoring the fact that what matters for sustainability and allocative efficiency of the budgetary stance is (among other things) the ratios of the relevant variables to full employment rather than actual GDP. Failure of the government to steer the economy close to its full employment growth path implies that private investment can neither be robust nor steady.

The problem on the investment front has been compounded by the on-going and prospective bottlenecks in infrastructural services—a deficiency to which many a commentator has drawn attention. The cut-back in the government's capital expenditure has taken a heavy toll of investment in infrastructural facilities; also, the private sector has not stepped in to fill the void left by the state. The result has been a decline in infrastructural investment, with its ratio to gross domestic product coming down by 1.5 percentage points over 1993–8 (Table 5.3).

Investment in Human Resource Development and Poverty Alleviation

In the context of the huge shortfall of India's indices relating to education and health from those of high performing emerging economies including China, everybody bemoans the low and stagnant social sector expenditure of the government during the last decade (Table 5.3), and emphasizes the need for a substantial step-up of public investment in this area, if the country is to enjoy a growth rate of 7 per cent or more on a sustained basis. However, when it comes to suggesting specific steps, there appears to be quite inadequate appreciation of the urgency of the matter: while 'desirability' of a cut-back in government support to higher education and research has become almost an article of faith in most quarters, the Eleventh Finance Commission has recommended a mere 0.43 percentage point increase for primary education and a 0.61 percentage point rise for the entire social sector between 1999–2000 and 2004–5—increases which are bound to keep the country lag far behind others in human resource development.

Inadequate investment in primary education and health services will also postpone, as noted in the third section, a lasting resolution of the problems of income inequality and poverty. We have already drawn attention to the sharp fluctuations in agricultural growth around a fairly low average during the 1990s (Table 5.3). This along with large swings in food price inflation constitutes a major factor behind slow eradication of poverty and its periodic intensity.[75] The source of this trouble is not difficult to trace. The basic reason lies in the slowdown in the capital accumulation in agriculture. This slowdown started in fact from the 1980s and throughout the next decade investment in the sector remained abysmally low. The most important factor behind this development was the reversal in government policies. As public sector investment was gradually being reduced from the mid-1980s, a disproportionate burden of adjustment fell on the agricultural sector. Given the widely observed crowding-in effect of the public on private investment in this sector, it is no wonder that the aggregate capital accumulation in agriculture showed a declining trend and the performance of the sector, providing livelihood for the vast majority of the country's population and determining the incidence of poverty, continues to remain a major source of worry.

Expenditure Priorities and Financing

Before offering our suggestions for fiscal restructuring, it is useful to recapitulate the major policy implications of the foregoing analysis. In light of the experience of the Indian economy over the last decade, we have identified the need for:

(a) arresting the slide in aggregate saving and investment, and for their rapid increase;
(b) stepping up investment in infrastructure and human resource development in order to remove bottlenecks impeding production and capital accumulation in the rest of the economy;
(c) tackling the problems of mass illiteracy and lack of adequate health services in rural areas on an emergency basis; and
(d) raising capital accumulation in agriculture and avoiding large year-to-year variations in foodgrains production and prices.

While there is a fair measure of unanimity concerning the needs suggested above, there can be a good deal of disagreement regarding the best way of meeting these needs and the budgetary measures required in this context. Let us first turn to the least controversial of the measures which the fiscal authorities can implement without much difficulty.

[75] We do not go into the inconclusive debate regarding whether or to what extent poverty fell during the 1990s. The important point to note in this connection is that the incidence of poverty can vary widely from one year to another: in years of high agricultural production and low food prices, the poverty ratio goes down; but the opposite happens in the event of a harvest failure and high food price inflation.

Preventing Cyclical Swings and Promoting Growth

One can hardly overemphasize the importance of anti-cyclical fiscal (and monetary) policies for both full utilization of resources and promotion of investment and growth. However, in the context of sluggish demand producing a sharp deceleration of industrial growth from 1996–7 (Table 5.3), we need to examine whether there are in fact some serious obstacles which have prevented the government in pursing these policies.

Elementary economic logic suggests that, given the underutilization of resources, by increasing its own expenditure, the government also promotes private consumption and investment and helps the economy attain a higher growth trajectory. It is the bugbear of fiscal deficit, it seems, that has held the government back in following an expansionary fiscal programme, even when there is considerable slack in the economy. In terms of our earlier analysis it is not difficult to see how ill-founded the fear is.

First, the increase in fiscal deficit will be significantly less than the rise in the government expenditure, as the gross domestic product goes up by a multiple of additional government expenditure and the resulting increase in revenue receipts helps meeting part of extra expenses. Second, to the extent government expenditure is on revenue yielding assets and stimulates future growth, current public borrowing need not create future budgetary problems. Third, in the presence of underutilized resources, monetized financing of government expenditure will generally be non-inflationary; such financing does not raise future debt burden or budgetary difficulties for the exchequer.

Elimination of output gap[76] will enable the government to further economic and social objectives without storing up troubles for the future; but even with no underutilization of resources, significant changes in the scale and structure of the budget are necessary for removing major impediments to higher growth and elimination of mass poverty.

Expenditure Reforms

Our diagnosis of the ills afflicting the Indian economy calls for substantial increases in the government expenditure in quite a few areas. However, since public absorption of resources implies their withdrawal from other uses,[77] the nature of restructuring the budget will depend significantly on the efficacy or cost effectiveness of government expenditure[78] in meeting

[76] Given by the difference between the full employment and actual output.

[77] Remember, we are considering the reforms measures when there is no slack in the economy.

[78] In relation to the marginal benefits of using the resources elsewhere.

the desired goals. It is the widely held belief regarding the inefficiency and wastage in government's use of resources that makes many an analyst view enhancement of public expenditure with disfavour. Such belief is also one of the main reasons why tax payers may feel little compunction while trying to avoid and evade their dues to the exchequer; such acts of 'avoision' are not regarded as too reprehensible by the general public. Reducing wastage in the government expenditure constitutes, to be sure, an important aspect of fiscal correction, but for the present we do not propose to go into these issues while offering our suggestions for expenditure reforms.[79]

Consider first the role fiscal policy can play in boosting the level of aggregate capital accumulation in the economy. We have emphasized how and why such a boost requires a substantial step-up in investment in both physical infrastructure and human resource development. Everybody recognizes that primary education and basic health services are to be provided by the government and that there is an urgent need for a substantial increase in the public expenditure in these areas. In respect of higher education and research there is, it must be recognized, scope for private sector participation. However, given large externalities and significant private risk associated with investment in education and research, the cut-back in government expenditure on these items during the 1990s appears short-sighted.

So far as physical infrastructure is concerned, it is useful to distinguish between three categories of services. First, in cases such as roads, bridges, flood control, canal irrigation, and gathering and providing items of information that have important uses for the vast majority of the population, it is not very difficult to see that such investment has to be undertaken by the government: the scale of private provisioning of these services, even when possible, will be grossly inadequate and distortionary.[80]

Second, both the private and public sector can undertake electricity generation, transport, and other activities where externalities are relatively unimportant and beneficiaries can be easily identified and charged for use of

[79] While drawing up the government's expenditure programme, the relative efficacy of private and public use of resources in promoting social and economic goals is no doubt to be taken into account. However, it is by no means clear that government inefficiency justifies lowering of all types of government expenditure. For meeting urgent needs such as law and order, prevention of epidemics, promotion of literacy, or avoidance of mass starvation and death, larger allocations are required when nothing can be done to reduce the leakage. Quite clearly, as far as possible, expenditure programmes need to contain built-in safeguards against wastages.

[80] Thus private production may be sustained through tolls for use of roads and bridges, or through charges for access to information; but the resulting investment and production in these areas will not only be quite sub-optimal, but the pattern of resources used for providing the services will also be inefficient.

services. The only rider here is that private investment is these areas is guided by long-term expectations of future demand, which in its turn depends on how other activities grow in the future. In view of such coordination problems the government has generally to take an active role in promotion of such investment either directly or through provision of facilities which, while attracting private investment, do not lead to serious distortions or inefficiencies.[81]

Third, for schemes like extension of railways, electricity, telecommunications, or other services in some large areas (especially depressed ones), it is possible to levy user charges; but in many of these cases, even when some investment passes the benefit–cost test (for evaluation of large projects), private producers may not be able to break even, or their profits fail to reflect net gains from the investment.[82] Such cases require public support to investment projects, though whether the support should assume the form of direct public investment or of (non-distortionary) inducements to private producers depends on the specifics of the project under consideration.

A back-of-the-envelope calculation suggests that if over the next five to six years the investment ratio is to rise from the current rate of about 23.5 per cent to 30–31 per cent, the major increase has to be in infrastructure, and the government's financial support in this area needs to go up by three to four percentage points. This figure needs to be raised by around one to two percentage points when we bring in the special role of public sector investment in agriculture for a lasting solution to the problem of poverty. Add to that a minimum of 2.5 percentage point increase in education and health, and the additional government expenditure for meeting the objectives of growth and long-term poverty alleviation comes to around seven percentage points.

What about the scope for economy in government expenditure in other fields? Public consumption as a ratio of gross domestic product did not go up during the 1990s. However, the ratio recorded a more than two percentage point increase in the 1980s and its subsequent stability needs to be judged against the fact that in the process of liberalization many administrative

[81] The implication is that the government should avoid schemes such as guaranteed returns on capital which tend to produce gross inefficiencies in both investment and production.

[82] This may be true even when the gain is purely economic, rather than income-distributional or social. The reason is that through pricing, producers appropriate only the marginal gain multiplied by the quantity bought, so that users are left with substantial net surpluses when the project is fairly large. This is why extension of railway lines or electricity to some area raises house rents and land prices in the locality, even though railway fares or electricity charges are fixed entirely on the basis of profitability considerations.

activities of the government became redundant or lost their earlier importance. There is thus scope for at least a two percentage point cut-back in public administration without any loss of efficiency.

So far as subsidies are concerned, we have already indicated why their prolonged continuation constitutes a mark of inefficacy of the system in securing the objectives of growth and equity. Except in some exceptional cases,[83] public investment in selected areas (such as agriculture and backward area development) appears a much more effective means of promoting these objectives than provision of subsidies in various forms.[84] Phased elimination of these items of expenditure should, on the basis of figures for 1998–9, save the government's revenue disbursement by about 0.5 percentage point.

Considerable scope for expenditure reduction, though in the medium and the long run, lies in the sphere of interest payments. However, the process is closely related to not only the size of the gap between the government expenditure and total revenue receipts, but also how the gap is financed.

Financing of Government Expenditure

The perception that the heart of the fiscal matter lies in the tax machinery is amply supported by the Indian experience over the 1990s. The declining

[83] We have suggested above how public support may be required to induce private investment in some infrastructural projects.

[84] The most controversial in this respect are subsidies on food and fertilizer. There are several factors that need consideration here. First, it is often argued, for example, by the Planning Commission, that water and fertilizer subsidies have resulted in degradation of the soil and fertility. However, this impact is due primarily to farmers' lack of knowledge or absence of telescopic faculty solution to which lies more in spread of information or awareness than in withdrawal of subsidy. Second, textbook principles do suggest that all input subsidies constitute inefficient means of raising production. The recommended mode for the purpose is output subsidy along with easy availability of all inputs, including credit, at market prices. But devising an effective output subsidy is by no means simple in countries like India. Thus subsidy on marketed output neither meets the condition for allocative efficiency, nor is it defensible on distributional grounds, since the scheme leaves out small and marginal farmers producing primarily for self consumption. Third, while input subsidies may raise production, contain food price inflation and help small farmers to some extent, apart from allocative inefficiency, one has to take into account the opportunity cost of the government expenditure on these heads. Compared with public investment in agriculture and rural development, the government expenditure on subsidies may appear less efficient in promoting growth and alleviating poverty. However, in an overall restructuring, it is not clear whether or to what extent they are to be reduced immediately, when judged against a variety of government expenditure which are not only inefficient, but have also a negative impact on income distribution.

trend in the household and aggregate saving ratio, the mounting public debt, and the difficulty of sustaining public investment having large externalities and of expenditure for poverty alleviation, all these may be traced to the government's inability to mop up purchasing power from the private sector. Both for attaining targets relating to aggregate investment and saving and for enabling the government to discharge its other functions effectively, one can hardly overemphasize the need for raising tax collections. The government will be better able to invest in public goods and infrastructure having widespread external effects, the more efficient it is in collecting taxes from the general public. Second, a decline in the tax–GDP ratio tends to raise households' permanent income (and wealth), as there is a jump in expected future disposable income. This not only reduces aggregate saving in the economy (given the differential between the public and household propensity to save), but tends to lower current household saving as well. This perhaps was the main factor behind the household saving paradox noted in the third section and adds to the importance of reversing the trend in the tax–GDP ratio. Remembering that the tax–GDP ratio fell by nearly 3.5 percentage points between 1989–90 and 1999–2000, and that there has been a significant increase in the household purchasing power in the meanwhile, an increase in the ratio by four percentage points during the current quinquennium and by seven percentage points over the present decade should be feasible and go a long way in reversing the trend in the aggregate saving ratio and easing the government's inter-temporal budget constraint.

Apart from taxation, the other important factor constraining the government's ability to further the basic objectives has been the low and negative returns on public investment in electricity, irrigation, and other infrastructural areas. While there is considerable scope for cost cutting in many of these cases, it is also important for the government to earn competitive rates of returns by levying appropriate user changes, where the beneficiaries can be clearly identified. Indeed, to the extent the government is faced with the tax constraint, even some monopoly returns are justified in some cases, remembering that the additional revenue to the government can be employed for raising growth and reducing poverty. However, the first-best alternative in these cases, as we have seen, is competitive pricing and using taxes in order to further distributional objectives. Be that as it may, most observers feel that, in the context of low user charges for most publicly provided private goods, it should not be difficult for the government to raise non-tax revenue by one percentage point over the next five years.

The increase in tax and non-tax revenue by five percentage points should enable the government to finance the lion's share of additional expenditure under the suggested programme. Indeed, since the enhancements in public absorption are primarily on capital account, the additional receipts will, on the basis of figures for 1999–2000, enable the government to reduce revenue deficits by six percentage points. The cut-back will, in fact, amount to a highly respectable 8.5 percentage points if, following the suggestion in the second section, the government's social sector expenditure is treated as capital accumulation. However, for reducing the interest burden on public debt, raising aggregate saving to above 30 per cent, easing the future budget constraint, and moving towards the first-best alternative, further fiscal restructuring aimed at economizing the cost of government borrowing is of crucial importance.

We have already explained why the government reliance on the monetized deficit is, within limits, one of the simplest and most effective means of reducing public expenditure when the cost of additional tax collection is prohibitive. Given the fact that monetized deficit was below 1 per cent of GDP over 1996–2000 and that its safe limit is about 2.5 per cent, there can be a one percentage point increase in this source of financing without putting too much constraint on the Reserve Bank in its conduct of the monetary policy.[85]

Second, the government should reduce reliance on tax-free, high-interest borrowing instruments such as Public Provident Fund (PPF), NSCs, etc. These modes of financing have raised the interest burden on the public debt and the associated increase in the government transfer payments has, we have seen, only served to reduce aggregate saving in the economy without promoting distributional objectives.[86]

Finally, given the inter-temporal budget constraint, moderate reliance on government borrowing from financial institutions at below market interest rates through requirements such as the SLR[87] also constitutes a part of the second-best programme, provided such borrowing does not put too onerous a burden on the financial sector. Our perception is that requiring banks to hold 20 per cent of their unencumbered deposits[88] in government securities

[85] This policy relates to the management of external balance, not macrostabilization, because we are considering a budgetary programme with no output gap.

[86] Apart from the fact that the benefits of these high cost borrowings accrue mostly to income tax payers who form a tiny part of total population, we need to consider the opportunity cost in terms of foregone public investment aimed at poverty alleviation. We have also argued elsewhere (Rakshit, 1991) that these financial instruments do not promote even private saving, since they affect primarily the *allocation* of saving between different financial assets, rather than their total.

[87] Note that the SLR requirement implies a mode of taxation only to the extent bank holding of SLR bonds is in excess of what otherwise would have been held. In India this requirement is no longer an indirect means of taxation, since over the last six to seven years the bank holding of SLR securities has exceeded their stipulated minimum.

[88] With corresponding changes in the ratios for other financial institutions.

at 200 basis points below the market rate will not stand in the way of efficient financial intermediation: remembering that the operation of the financial institutions depends crucially on the investment demand, economic environment, and growth, the SLR as a part of the fiscal reforms programme suggested above should promote rather than impair the health of the country's financial system.

Given the fact that the government's interest obligations currently amount to nearly 6 per cent of the GDP, discontinuance of high cost borrowing and turning SLR into an effective instrument should improve the revenue balance of the government by 0.5 to 1.0 percentage point.

Fiscal Restructuring: An Overview

Let us summarize the arithmetic of fiscal restructuring proposed here and indicate how it agrees with and differs from that recommended by the Eleventh Finance Commission (EFC). The changes in the major budgetary items suggested under the EFC and our adjustment programmes are reproduced in Table 5.4. A cursory look at the table shows that there is no disagreement between the two schemes regarding the directions in which the main fiscal parameters are required to be changed.[89] In fact, the extent of scaling down of revenue deficit suggested by the EFC and us are also almost the same. However, a close scrutiny of the table suggests considerable differences in the magnitude of fiscal correction under the two programmes for various items in the revenue and capital budget of the government.

The suggestion in the present chapter concerning the overall revenue deficit is quite close to that under the EFC scheme, but the cut-back in the revenue expenditure is significantly less and the slated receipts substantially larger under our proposal. We have also put much more emphasis on the social sector and suggested steeper cuts in other items of revenue expenditure: the increase in social sector expenditure amounts to 2.5 percentage points in our proposal compared with 0.61 percentage points recommended by the EFC, while the cuts in government administration, interest payments, and subsidies under the two programmes, total 3.5 and 1.76 percentage points, respectively.

The most important difference between our and the EFC programme lies in the relative weights attached to increases in saving and capital accumulation, both human and physical. This is reflected first in the substantial gap between adjustments in what we call 'current deficit' under the two sets of proposals. The current deficit is nothing but the revenue deficit less social sector expenditure, and constitutes a much better index of

[89] Since for quite a few items the figures under the EFC programme are not available, it is difficult to say whether the agreement extends to all major fiscal variables.

TABLE 5.4
Fiscal Restructuring Programme
(changes as percentage of full-employment GDP)

	Our Suggestions	Eleventh Finance Commission's Recommendations
Revenue expenditure	–1.0	–2.37
of which		
Social sector	2.5	0.61
Government adminstration	–2.0	NA
Interest payments	–1.0	NA
Subsidies	–0.5	NA
Revenue receipts	5.0	3.39
of which		
Tax revenue	4.0	2.64
Non-tax revenue	1.0	0.75
Revenue deficit (conventional)	–6.0	–5.77
Current deficit (Revenue deficit less social sector expenditure)	–8.5	–6.38
Capital expenditure (conventional)	4.5	2.44
of which		
Infrastructure (excluding agriculture)	3.5	NA
Agriculture	1.0	NA
Government investment (including social sector expenditure)	7.0	3.05
Government borrowing (Fiscal deficit[1])	–1.5	–3.33
of which		
Monetized deficit	1.0	NA
Fiscal gap[2]	–2.5	NA

Source: Government of India, (2000).
Notes: [1] Ignoring disinvestment.
[2] Fiscal gap = government borrowing – monetized deficit.

government's dissaving due to budgetary operations. In view of our emphasis on the human resource development and the need for promotion of aggregate saving in the economy, as against the EFC figure of 6.38, we have suggested a cut-back in current deficit to the tune of 8.5 percentage points.

Second, the government's (conventionally defined) capital expenditure under our programme is slated to go up by 4.5 and that under the EFC's by 2.44 percentage points. Much larger is the difference in respect of total investment including social sector expenditure: against the 3.05 percentage point increase suggested by the Commission, the increase in our scheme amounts to 7.0 percentage points.

Even though the revenue and current deficits are to fall significantly in our programme, the proposed increases in capital accumulation permit only a 1.5 percentage point fall in government borrowing,[90] compared with the much larger cut-back at 3.33 percentage points suggested by the EFC. However, in our adjustment programme, the 'fiscal gap', the more relevant indicator of debt financing, is slated to record a not inconsequential 2.5 percentage point decline.

Compared with the restructuring recommended by the EFC, our proposals, it seems, are much more drastic in respect of expenditure and taxes, but more moderate regarding fiscal deficit. In the absence of information regarding the estimation procedure behind the Commission's figures, it is difficult to assess the relative efficacy of and implementation problems associated with the two schemes. While there are bound to be differences among economists offering policy prescriptions under a given situation, our plea is that in putting forth the suggestions we have tried to take into account the needs of the economy and the feasibility of the programme in light of macroeconomic and budgetary trends over the last two decades.

Conclusion

(a) For a given tax–GDP ratio, sustainability of debt financing depends, *a la* Domar, on whether or not the growth rate of the economy is higher than the government's borrowing rate of interest. Behind the Domar condition, however, lie the more primitive factors such as scale of government borrowing for financing public absorption; proportion of consumption and investment in the aggregate expenditure on goods and services by the government; the return on the government's capital expenditure; the extent of monetized deficit; and the patterns of government borrowing from the public. These factors affect sustainability through their impact on the growth rate and/or the net cost of government borrowing.

(b) Fiscal deficit is a hybrid concept and not of much significance for judging sustainability of debt financing or the efficacy of the government's budgetary programme for furthering the basic objectives of public policy.

[90] Since we have not considered disinvestment, standing as it does on a completely different footing from that for ordinary capital receipts, government borrowing would be the same as fiscal deficit, properly defined. In order to make the two figures comparable, we have also ignored disinvestment proceeds implicit in the EFC figures for fiscal adjustment.

(c) In the context of large, pre-existing public debt and the tax constraint faced by the government, not only can the problem of sustainability become quite serious, but the textbook rules regarding the optimal scale and pattern of government expenditure and their modes of financing also require major modifications. The second-best budgetary programme under the constraint will be characterized by reliance, within limits, on monetized deficit and borrowing through instruments such as SLR; greater emphasis on government investment, especially those generating direct returns; and short- as also long-term measures aimed at reduction of pre-tax-transfer income inequality and poverty.

(d) Though the Indian scenario does not as yet suggest that the country is heading toward an internal debt trap, there were quite a few disquieting developments during the 1990s on both the macroeconomic and the fiscal front. The most important of these were decline and stagnation of aggregate investment and saving; low agricultural growth along with sharp year-to-year fluctuations in foodgrains price inflation and output growth; deceleration of industrial growth during the second half of the decade; decline in the tax–GDP ratio; fall in the public investment; and rise in the revenue deficit.

(e) So far as the expenditure side of the budget is concerned, the adjustment programme suggested here includes substantial increases in the government expenditure on investment, especially in agriculture and infrastructural facilities; roll-back of public consumption expenditure to the level obtaining in the early 1980s; a decline in subsidies that affect current rather than future production and income distribution; and a considerable increase in social sector expenditure in general and primary education and health services in particular. On the financing side, we have suggested restoration of the tax–GDP ratio to its late 1980s' level; greater reliance on monetized deficit than in the 1990s; termination of high cost instruments of government borrowings; and moderate deployment of instruments such as the SLR.

References

Barro, R.J. (1974), 'Are Government Bonds Net Wealth?', *Journal of Political Economy*, 82(6), 1095–1117, November.

Domar, E.D. (1944), 'The "Burden of the Debt" and the National Income', *American Economic Review*, 34(4), 798–827, December.

Government of India (2000), *Report of the Eleventh Finance Commission (2000–05)*, New Delhi.

——— (2000a), *Economic Survey 1999–2000*, Ministry of Finance, New Delhi.

Rakshit, M. (1991), 'The Macroeconomic Adjustment Programme: A Critique', *Economic and Political Weekly*, 26(34), (August 24).

——— (1994), 'Issues in Structural Adjustment of the Indian Economy', in Edmar L. Bacha (ed.), *Economics in a Changing World: Development, Trade and Environment*, Macmillan, London.

——— (1997), 'Money, Credit and Government Finances in a Developing Economy', published in A. Bose, M. Rakshit, and A. Sinha (eds), *Issues in Economic Theory and Public Policy*, Oxford University Press, New Delhi.

Reserve Bank of India (2000), *Handbook of Statistics on the Indian Economy 2000*, Mumbai.

——— (2000a), *Report on Currency and Finance 1998–9*, Mumbai.

——— (2000b), *Annual Report 1999–2000*, Mumbai.

Samuelson, P.A. (1954), 'The Pure Theory of Public Expenditure', *Review of Economics and Statistics*, 36(4), 387–9, November.

Appendix 5.1

Sustainability of Public Debt—The Canonical Model

The Domar results (Domar, 1944) related to sustainability of public debt may be demonstrated in terms of a fairly simple model. Assume that over time the interest rate, r, remains unchanged and gross domestic product, Y, grows at a constant proportional rate g:

$$Y = Y_0 e^{gt}. \tag{A.1}$$

Let the public consumption expenditure as a ratio of Y be c; the government revenue (net of subsidies) as a proportion of GDP be h; there be no government expenditure (financial or real) on capital account; and the government keep c and h unchanged over time. Assume further that the entire excess of aggregate government expenditure (including interest payments) over revenue is financed by borrowing from the public. Hence, increase in public debt, P, per unit of time is given by

dP/dt = (Public consumption expenditure - government revenue less subsidies) + interest payments on pre-existing public debt

$$\text{or } \frac{dP}{dt} = (c-h)Y + rP$$

$$= (c-h)Y_0 e^{gt} + rP. \quad \text{[from Eq. (A.1)]} \tag{A.2}$$

The solution to the differential equation (A.2) is fairly standard and yields the time path of public debt, given the fiscal stance of the government:

$$P = P_0 e^{rt} + \frac{c-h}{g-r} Y_0 [e^{gt} - e^{rt}], \tag{A.3}$$

where P_0 and Y_0 denote the initial levels of P and Y, respectively. Relations (A.1) and (A.3) immediately yield the behaviour of the debt–GDP ratio, p, over time:

$$\frac{P}{Y} \equiv p = \frac{P_0}{Y_0} e^{(r-g)t} + \frac{c-h}{g-r}[1 - e^{(r-g)t}]. \tag{A.4}$$

It is thus clear that whether or not continuous debt financing is sustainable depends crucially on the relative values of r and g.

Quite clearly, when $r > g$, the debt–GDP ratio p rises without any limit and the budgetary stance becomes non-viable in the long run. Indeed, even if the government finances all its consumption expenditure through revenue (so that $c = h$), any public debt inherited from the past will make budgetary operations unsustainable, with p rising without any limit. The only means of ensuring viability of the budget in such a case consists in a crash programme of paying off public debt by generating a revenue surplus over a specified period and not permitting c to exceed h thereafter.

To be more precise, assume that $r > g$ and the initial debt–GDP ratio is positive. In order to see what happens to p over time if the government henceforth generates a primary surplus (with $h > c$) per unit of time, it is useful to rearrange Eq. (A.4) slightly:

$$p = \left(p_0 - \frac{h-c}{r-g} \right) e^{(r-g)t} + \frac{h-c}{r-g}. \tag{A.4a}$$

It is thus obvious that with $(h\text{-}c)/(r\text{-}g) > p_0$, public debt would be eliminated within a finite period, the length of which will be negatively related to the excess of $(h\text{-}c)/(r\text{-}g)$ over p_0. If the government continues to have a primary surplus beyond that period, its claim on the private sector as a ratio of GDP will rise without limit,[91] something which also cannot be sustained over time.

To see what happens when $r = g$, consider first the limit of p at any t as $r \rightarrow g$. From Eq. (A.4), the limit is given by

$$\lim_{r \to g}(p) = \frac{P_0}{Y_0} + (c-h)t, \tag{A.5}$$

where the second term on the right-hand side corresponds to the second term on the right-hand side of Eq. (A.4) and is obtained by using L'Hopital's rule.[92] Thus even in this case borrowing for purposes of financing government consumption is unsustainable, though pre-existing debts do not erode viability of government finances so long as c does not exceed h.

Only when $r < g$, is a continuous excess of c over h sustainable. In this case, the long-run value of the debt–GDP ratio, p^*, is

$$p^* \equiv \lim_{t \to \infty}(p) = (c-h)/(g-r). \tag{A.6}$$

The long-term values of the ratio of revenue deficit to GDP and of interest payments as a proportion of government revenue are then given by

$$\alpha^* \equiv \lim_{t \to \infty}\left(\frac{\text{Revenue Deficit}}{\text{GDP}} \right) = \lim_{t \to \infty}\left[\frac{(c-h)Y + rP}{Y} \right]$$

$$= gp^* = g\frac{c-h}{g-r}; \tag{A.7}$$

[91] However, if $(h\text{-}c)$ is fixed at $p_0(r\text{-}g)$, the debt–GDP ratio is stabilized at $(h\text{-}c)/(r\text{-}g)$.

[92] Which is $\lim_{x \to x^*} [f(x)/g(x)] = \lim_{x \to x^*} [f'(x)/g'(x)]$.

$$\beta^* \equiv \lim_{t\to\infty}\left(\frac{\text{Interest Payments}}{\text{Revenue}}\right) = \frac{r}{h}p^* = \frac{r}{h}\cdot\frac{c-h}{g-r}. \tag{A.8}$$

The main conclusions of the canonical model may be summed up as follows:

(a) With $r < g$, the initial size of the public debt, the scale of government expenditure, tax–GDP ratio, etc. do not affect the viability of the debt-financed public consumption.

(b) Given r and g, the government can choose only two out of the five possible long-term fiscal targets, c, h, p^*, α^* and β^*. Indeed, given P_0 and Y_0, once the government chooses the time paths of any two out of the five ratios, the values of the other three ratios over time are uniquely fixed.[93]

(c) The choice relating to c and h (or any other pair) has to be made on the basis of the relative benefits and costs of alternative fiscal stances. Under the canonical approach the main objectives of public policy are taken to be (i) provision of optimum amounts of public goods and (ii) equitable distribution of income.[94] Were there no distortionary effects of taxes and transfers, the government could choose optimum values of public consumption, transfers, and taxes independently to attain the objectives. However, in view of the costs associated with large-scale taxes and transfers, the government is faced with the problem of choosing the three instruments taking these costs into account. The implication is that the targets for c, v (gross tax as a ratio of GDP), and n (transfers as a ratio of GDP)[95] should not be set independently, but are to be obtained as a solution to a constrained optimization problem.

(d) Once the optimal targets for c, v, and n are set, the values of p^*, α^*, and β^* are uniquely fixed and these do not have any further operational significance.

[93] In the model we have assumed that the government chooses to fix c and h.

[94] Remembering that the growth rate is exogenous to the system.

[95] And hence for c and $h(= v - n)$.

6

Some Analytics and Empirics of Fiscal Restructuring in India*

Introduction

In compliance with the new terms of reference set by the government, the Twelfth Finance Commission (TFC), like its predecessor, has advanced a plan for restructuring public finances for 'restoring budgetary balance, achieving macroeconomic stability and debt reduction along with equitable growth' (Government of India, 2004). TFC recognizes that such a plan should be based on 'a broad analytical framework' that takes into account the interrelationship between the size and composition of government expenditure, modes of its financing, growth, inflation, interest rate and external balance. TFC's analysis starts with a three-fold distinction between (a) full-employment levels of output; (b) 'potential' or trend levels of output; and (c) actual levels of output. Since structural rigidities can 'keep the economy below full-employment on a long-term basis' and macroeconomic stability implies that the economy operates close to full-employment with inflation below an 'acceptable' rate, while framing fiscal policies it is important to examine (a) whether in a year there is a gap (called the 'output gap') between the potential and actual output; and (b) whether over time the potential output remains persistently below full-employment output levels. The first situation calls for demand management through expansionary or contractionary fiscal policy. In the second case, the fiscal policy should be designed for removal of structural constraints in order to 'bring potential output closer to full-employment levels'.

Since the manner of financing government expenditure in general and fiscal deficit in particular affects macrostabilization and growth, for suggesting fiscal restructuring TFC deems it necessary to distinguish between two

* Reprinted from *Economic and Political Weekly*, Vol. 40, No. 31, July 30–Aug 5, 2005.

components of fiscal deficit, 'a structural or long-term component and a cyclical component reflecting deviation from the long-run average'. The deleterious impact of fiscal deficit presumably arises from its structural part,[1] not from its cyclical component, since 'it may be used to stabilize fluctuations around the trend rate of growth'. With a Reserve Bank estimate (Reserve Bank of India, 2003) of structural fiscal deficit at about 10 per cent of GDP compared with the cyclical deficit ranging between 0.12 and minus 0.21 per cent,[2] TFC has to look no further for identifying the villain of the piece in India's macroeconomic scenario.

Debt Financing, Saving, and Growth

TFC's focus on the fiscal deficit arises from the fact that its 'fiscal reform strategy centers on growth' which in its turn is negatively impacted by the fiscal deficit. The growth debilitating effect of the deficit is explained in terms of a causal link running from the fiscal deficit to the economy's aggregate saving and hence to investment and growth, remembering that a higher fiscal deficit implies faster accumulation of public debt, larger interest payments, and higher revenue deficit or government dissaving. For empirical support of its thesis in the Indian context, TFC first highlights the 'deleterious effects of government dissavings on growth' with a review of the long-term profile of growth along with that of overall and sectoral saving-investment rates. In particular, attention is drawn to four main features relating to changes in some crucial macro indicators between the mid-1990s[3] and 2000–3: (a) fall in average GDP growth from 7.5 per cent to 4.7 per cent; (b) decline in public sector saving by a whooping 4.1 percentage points; (c) fall in overall and public sector investment rates by 2.2 and 1.9 percentage points respectively; and (d) decline in current account deficit (indicating the excess of domestic investment over domestic saving) from 1.4 to -0.2 percentage points.

Second, the fall in public sector saving during the period mentioned above, according to TFC, is intrinsically linked to growing fiscal imbalances as indicated by the time profile of various measures of budgetary deficits. Thus between 1995–6 and 1999–2003 revenue deficit, fiscal deficit and primary deficit registered a sharp rise, from 3.2 per cent, 6.3 per cent, and 1.1 per cent to (an average of) 6.7 per cent, 9.5 per cent, and 3.7 per cent, respectively.

[1] Though TFC does not explicitly state the analytical or policy significance of the structural deficit.

[2] The latter implies a surplus.

[3] Covering the years 1994–7.

Third, the TFC draws pointed attention to the deteriorating quality and structural changes in government finances that had had adverse consequences for budgetary viability, growth, and other primary objectives of public policy. Thus between the two periods 1987–90 and 1999–2002 interest payments as a ratio of revenue receipts went up from 21.0 per cent to 34.0 per cent implying that the government had to rely more and more on borrowing for discharging its basic responsibility such as administration and defence. In fact, with the ratio of revenue to fiscal deficit going up from 34 per cent to 68 per cent between the two periods, there was a doubling of the share of government borrowing not used for creation of assets, and a cumulative increase in the level of public debt.

The rapidly deteriorating trends in finances of the government and its burgeoning liabilities prompt the Commission to go into issues relating to the sustainability of debt financing. Particularly disturbing according to TFC has been the acceleration of public debt since the mid-1990s, reflected in a jump in the debt–GDP ratio from 56.3 per cent in 1995–6 to 81 per cent in 2004–5. While it is difficult to provide a categorical answer to the questions concerning sustainability[4] of debt financing in India, there can be little doubt regarding the urgent need for restructuring public finances with a view to promoting growth and enabling the government to effect an enduring improvement in the country's social services and infrastructural facilities.

TFC Programme of Fiscal Restructuring

Since for the government 'borrowing is often the easier option than raising revenues', TFC, in light of the experience of Euro economies and the UK, advances a restructuring programme whose essential ingredients are setting targets for revenue and fiscal deficits (for both the Centre and the states). The targets are fixed by taking into account 'an underlying growth scenario along with levels of interest rates and other macroeconomic parameters'. This scenario provides the basis of estimating the debt dynamics in terms of the primary deficit ratio and the growth–interest differential.

Under the Fiscal Responsibility and Budget Management Act (FRBMA) the targets for the revenue and fiscal deficit of the Centre have been fixed at 0 per cent and 3 per cent, respectively. For its part TFC also stipulates that the revenue deficits of the states should be brought down to zero over its reference period 2005–10. So far as the fiscal deficit is concerned, the combined target (for the Centre and the states taken together) to be attained by 2009–10 is set at 6 per cent, compared with 8.9 per cent in 2004–5. This, the Commission thinks, 'would be consistent with the availability of

[4] Which of necessity is a long-term concept.

savings of the household sector in financial assets, which is of the order of 10 per cent, the desirable level of current account deficit, and the requirements of the corporate sector and the non-departmental public sector undertakings'.

Taking the current account deficit to rise from -0.5 per cent in 2004–5 to an 'acceptable level' of 1.5 per cent in 2009–10, and requiring the combined revenue, fiscal, and primary deficits to be reduced from 4.5, 8.9, and 2.8 per cent to 0.0, 6.0, and 1.5 per cent, respectively, over the same period, TFC projects the (aggregate) investment rate and GDP growth to reach 27.5 per cent and 7.0 per cent, respectively; the inflation rate to be 5 per cent; and nominal interest rates to remain at their current level. Given the projected fall in the primary deficit on the one hand and a five percentage point growth-interest differential on the other, the ratio of interest payments to revenue receipts and the debt–GDP ratio—acknowledged as the two principal indicators of fiscal fragility—are targeted to be brought down from 33.7 and 80.8 per cent to 21.6 and 74.5 per cent, respectively, between 2004–5 and 2009–10. The longer-term targets for the two indicators suggested by TFC are 17 per cent and 56 per cent, respectively.

The targets for reduction in deficit, debt, and interest payments are backed by a fairly comprehensive programme for augmenting revenues and restructuring expenditures and debt. The core of this programme lies in (a) an increase in the tax–GDP ratio by two percentage points; (b) keeping primary expenditure as a ratio of GDP unchanged at the 2004–5 level; (c) a step-up in the ratio of government investment to GDP by one percentage point; and (d) inducing states to rein in deficit through market discipline and enactment of legislations similar to the Centre's FRBMA.[5] On the revenue side, especial emphasis is laid on building up a 'non-distortionary and revenue-elastic system of taxation', and imposition of adequate user charges

[5] An important element of TFC's restructuring programme which we do not propose to examine due to space limitation relates to putting the state finances in order. Apart from setting separate revenue and fiscal deficit targets for states, the Commission recommends that henceforth states must borrow from the market if required, and not rely on the Centre as the intermediary. For lightening the heavy debt burden of the states TFC also suggests a carrot-and-stick scheme. Under this scheme all outstanding central loans to the states at end-March 2005 are to be consolidated at an interest rate of 7.5 per cent with a twenty-year repayment period and provision for debt relief linked to states' achievement in reducing revenue deficit. It is stipulated that a state can avail of the benefit under the scheme only if it enacts a fiscal responsibility legislation. The two instruments of exposure to market (in respect of borrowing) and 'self-evaluation' under a fiscal responsibility act should, in the Commission's view, prove effective in restoring the fiscal health of the states and enabling them to effectively discharge their basic responsibilities.

on publicly provided goods for meeting at least the operating expenses in the short run and for full recovery of costs in the long run.

In respect of expenditure restructuring, TFC recommendations include a rise in capital outlay 'focused on infrastructure'; devoting revenue expenditure primarily for provision of public goods and merit goods such as education and health that have large positive externalities; abandonment of the distinction between Plan and non-Plan expenditure[6]; progressively bringing down the ratio of salaries to revenue expenditure net of interest payments and pensions to levels prevalent in 1996–7; and elimination of all hidden subsidies or their substitution by transparent ones where deemed justified. For all government expenditures the Commission lays especial stress on relating them to their 'outcomes' and underlines 'the need to bring back performance budgeting as an integral part of the preparation and evaluation of budgets'.

Macroeconomic Framework behind TFC Recommendations

The fiscal restructuring programme (FRS) recommended by the TFC contains a whole host of sensible suggestions. One could not agree more with the priority the Commission accords to the elimination of revenue deficit; the step-up in infrastructural investment; ensuring outcomes of government outlays; doing away with hidden subsidies; transparency in the budgetary process; and moving toward a non-distortionary and revenue-elastic tax system. The Commission has also been meticulous in preparing the road map for fiscal indicators for both the Centre and the states over the reference period 2005–10. However, though the targets are consistent with macroeconomic accounting, their theoretical and empirical basis is often weak; nor do they always follow from the Commission's own analysis or reading of India's macroeconomic scenario. Since the main deficiencies of the TFC programme can be traced to its inadequate conceptual framework, it useful to indicate first the nature of these inadequacies before examining how far the programme is suitable in the Indian context.

Full-employment Output and Potential Output

Macrostabilization, the overarching objective of FRP, means keeping the economy close to full-employment with a tolerable rate of inflation. In view of the structural constraints operating in countries such as India, for operational reasons TFC's macroeconomic framework starts with a distinction between 'potential' and 'full-employment' levels of output. The former

[6] Since the priority accorded to Plan expenditure at the expense of non-Plan expenditure often leads to poor maintenance of capital assets built up in the earlier Plans.

refers to the trend level of output along its long-term growth path and can lie below the full-employment level because of structural rigidities. Macrostabilization, TFC suggests, is to be 'considered with reference to growth of "potential" or trend levels of output'. The authorities need to take recourse to demand management measures to iron out cyclical variations of actual output around its trend; but for 'bringing potential output closer to full-employment levels public finances should be designed to remove structural constraints such as supply bottlenecks' (Government of India, 2004, p. 53).

The distinction between potential and full-employment output suggested above is not very helpful in analysing the macro behaviour of the economy or for drawing policy conclusions. Consider for example the significance of the concept of potential output. Since potential output is identified as trend levels of output and the trend is obtained from actual output levels (after eliminating cycles around the trend), the 'potential' output in any period need not be the same as the maximum achievable through demand management without making inflation exceed some tolerable rate.[7] This would be so if the economy has been suffering from prolonged demand deficiency as has happened in recent years in Japan, Germany, and India. In such cases the gap between the actual and 'potential' output (as defined by TFC) would be an inappropriate indicator for framing the demand management policies.

Difficulties similar to those considered above arise in the distinction between the structural and cyclical components of fiscal deficit made in a Reserve Bank study[8] (Reserve Bank of India, 2002) and used as input in the TFC exercise. The study estimates the structural fiscal deficit as a ratio of GDP to be 10 per cent and the cyclical deficit to lie between 0.12 and -0.21 per cent. The unwary may interpret the estimates as suggesting that fiscal correction should proceed along conventional lines, with large cut-backs in government expenditure along with a steep increase in taxes. However, if the economy has for quite a while been suffering from inadequate aggregate demand, the estimates of trend output will be lower and that of structural fiscal deficit larger than their values in the absence of such demand

[7] According to mainstream macroeconomics this output level is characterized by non-accelerating inflation and the unemployment rate corresponding to it is defined as the non-accelerating inflation rate of unemployment (NAIRU). Note that the inflation rate at NAIRU is constant, but can be at any level, depending on the growth rate of money supply on the one hand and real GDP growth (due to supply side factors) on the other (assuming the money demand function to remain stable over time).

[8] Following the standard literature and estimation procedure which subsume that the economy hovers around its full-employment growth path.

deficiency.[9] In such cases, the conventional mode of tackling the 'structural' deficit would lower the trend growth further and aggravate fiscal imbalances.

RBI-type estimates for structural and cyclical deficits would make eminent economic sense only in a neo-classical world where (a) wage-price-interest flexibility keeps the economy close to the full-employment (or supply determined) growth path and (b) anti-cyclical fiscal policies themselves have little role in affecting the full-employment growth path. In such an economy for reducing structural fiscal deficit the trend component of government expenditure needs to be reduced or that of its revenue receipts raised. However, the RBI study itself (as well as the Commission) refers to the prevalence of excess capacity (and recessionary conditions) in India since the mid-1990s. Again, the decline in private investment pulling down growth since the mid-1990s was due in no small measure to the failure of the government (a) in ensuring adequate effective demand and (b) in tackling infrastructural bottlenecks faced or anticipated by producers (Rakshit, 2004). Under these conditions the fact that the estimated structural deficits are large and cyclical deficits are small do not suggest that fiscal policy should focus on restraining government expenditure and raising revenue or that the need for aggregate demand management is minor.

Demand and Supply Side Policies

The foregoing observations suggest that for purposes of policy formulation it is important to identify whether output is demand or supply constrained. In mainstream macroeconomics 'full-employment' output is identified as the supply determined output and given by prevailing technology, capital stock and its composition, availability of different types of labour, and the institutional set-up including market structure and regulations in force. Thus, unlike under the TFC definition, infrastructural (like other supply side) bottlenecks limit and their removal raises the full-employment output itself.

For framing demand management and supply side policies the conventional rather than the TFC concept of full-employment[10] appears more

[9] Strictly speaking, fiscal deficit depends on how demand deficiency is removed. In fact, an expansionary fiscal policy, as we have discussed elsewhere (Rakshit, 2005), may be so designed that the government ends up with a fiscal surplus.

[10] There is one operational problem with the TFC definition of full-employment that may be mentioned in this connection. Not only for labour, but also for capital, full-employment does not mean employment lasting twenty-four hours a day for 365 days a year. Thus if real wages paid to labourers for working at night exceed their marginal productivity, keeping machines idle at night is perfectly consistent with 'full-employment' of resources. Nor need infrastructural 'shortage' cause underutilization or idle

useful.[11] Identification of full-employment with supply determined output implies that any departure from it is due to deficient or excess demand. Hence, under this (operationally more useful) definition, the economy is said to have attained full-employment when any further demand driven increase in output will be associated with rising inflationary pressure. From this definition follows the concept of output gap, signifying the difference between full-employment and actual output levels, and indicating the need for expansionary or contractionary policies according as the gap is positive or negative.[12]

The conventional definition of full-employment suggests two types of measures for raising its level and growth. Policies designed to promote capital formation, human resource development, or technological innovation directly raise full-employment output through an increase in the supply of resources or improvement in the technical know-how. These are the factors that are generally considered in the growth theoretic literature. The second set of supply side measures are emphasized by development economists and include setting up of new institutions; legal, administrative, and economic reforms; and direct public intervention—measures intended to promote enterprise and allocative efficiency of resource use.[13]

Compared with demand management policies, supply side measures, it is clear, are much more wide ranging and many of them fall outside the domain of fiscal policy. Among the most important of supply side budgetary policies are generation of revenue surplus, provision of incentives to save, tax reforms, restructuring of government expenditure, and subsidization of education, health, research, or other economic activities that are characterized by large positive externalities.

---

capacity of some capital stock if (a) there are substitution possibilities among inputs or (b) prices of infrastructural goods and services are flexible and market-clearing. Note also that even when both (a) and (b) holds, there may be a strong case, as we shall discuss, for focussing on infrastructural investment for raising the full-employment growth path.

[11] Though even the conventional concept, as we shall presently discuss, requires some modification in the Indian context.

[12] Neo-classical economists explain the negative output gap, that is, excess of actual over full-employment output, in terms of misperception of labourers regarding their real wages: lacking adequate information relating to price movements, they often regard an increase in money wages (due to aggregate demand pressure) as reflecting an increase in real wages

[13] What about public investment in infrastructure? To the extent there is an increase in aggregate capital stock it belongs to the first type of supply side policy. When the policy consists in reallocation of investment for removal of bottlenecks, it is of the second type.

Apart from differences in their impact, there is another important distinction between the demand and supply side measures that is worth taking note of. In the presence of an output gap, fiscal expansion provides a 'free lunch' with zero marginal opportunity cost of resource use: an increase in the government's current or capital expenditure can go hand in hand with a rise in private consumption or investment.[14] But because of full-employment of resources or frictions operating in the process of structural adjustment, supply side measures involve some cost somewhere: generation of revenue surplus requires a reduction in public consumption or private disposable income;[15] restructuring of government investment expenditure raises production in some sectors at the cost of that in others; reforms (e.g., reduction in input subsidies) which are efficiency enhancing and help raising the full-employment output level generally hurt certain groups of economic agents temporarily or even permanently.[16] Framing supply side measures including fiscal restructuring programmes thus requires much more careful scrutiny of their benefits in relation to costs than policies for demand management.

A Developing Economy Perspective

The distinction between the demand and supply side policies made above does not mean that there is no link between them or that they may be drawn up independently of each other. This is especially so for a country such as India where because of structural factors demand and supply side constraints may operate simultaneously in different sectors of the economy. Development economists have drawn attention to the fact that while agricultural output is mainly supply determined, demand deficiency may limit production in industries or services (Bose, 1989; Rakshit, 1982, 1989; Taylor, 1983). Such coexistence is fairly common within the non-agricultural sector as well: power cuts, clogging of transport, or shortage of specific inputs may cause supply constraint in some areas or sectors even while output in others is limited by demand.

What is no less important to note is that operation of supply constraints in some sectors often aggravates the problem of demand deficiency in others: a monsoon failure tends to reduce non-agricultural output; output

[14] Since operation of the multiplier raises household disposable income as also capacity utilization and profits of private enterprises.

[15] Because of larger tax or non-tax revenue of the government.

[16] This perception led to the development of an important branch of welfare economics centring round the pros and cons of the compensation criterion. The idea of providing a safety net for workers hurt in the process of structural adjustment may be traced to this literature.

losses due to power cuts may reduce demand for goods whose production is not supply constrained.[17] Unfortunately, in its macroeconomic framework TFC does not take cognisance of intertwining of some of the major demand and supply side factors operating in India with the result that its fiscal restructuring programme becomes less than satisfactory. Let us indicate the most important policy implications of these factors.

Consider first infrastructural bottlenecks, removal of which has been accorded top priority by all Indian economists as well as the TFC. The bottlenecks are no doubt a supply side factor; however, as the Indian experience suggests, they also tend to depress private investment and reduce aggregate demand. Such linkages suggest that demand management policies in India would have to be different from those followed in the United States or the UK, and require dovetailing into long-term programmes of economic transformation and growth. Thus when there is an output gap, the government should not follow a policy of the digging-holes-and-filling-them-up variety, or even of a reduction in taxes or an increase in revenue expenditure, but go in for large-scale investment in infrastructure. Again, when there is an excess demand and inflationary pressure, the government should avoid scaling down its long-term investment programme and rely on other contractionary fiscal measures along with a monetary squeeze. In fact, since returns on investments for removing supply side bottlenecks are higher than those on private capital accumulation at the margin, not only restructuring of public expenditures in favour of such capital outlays, but also a reduction in private consumption and investment in order to maintain these outlays should form an important plank of an anti-inflationary fiscal policy.

Second, demand management policies are often required to be specific to shocks or constraints causing underutilized capacity. Although agriculture now accounts for less than 25 per cent of India's GDP, agricultural production affects significantly demand for non-agricultural goods and services.[18] A monsoon failure not only reduces agricultural income, but causes demand deficiency[19] in the rest of the economy as well. Though the general price level tends to rise under these conditions, a contractionary policy would only add to the problem of excess capacity without much impact on the price front. For tackling such twin problems of inflation and demand deficiency, it is necessary to adopt expansionary measures by way of relief operations, public works, etc., along with release of foodgrains in the open

[17] May be because their producers do not use much power, or have their own power generators, or are located in other areas.

[18] Including demand for fertilizer, pesticides, transport, and trade.

[19] A deficiency that is magnified by the multiplier operating in the non-agricultural sector (Rakshit, 1982; Taylor, 1983).

market. Oil price shocks also tend to raise prices on the one hand and create demand deficiency on the other and require heterodox demand–supply management policies.

Finally, the need for taking into account the demand side impact of fiscal restructuring or efficiency enhancing programmes cannot be overemphasized. Cuts in customs duties balanced by taxes on consumption, elimination of subsidies on fertilizer and other inputs, and raising user charges on publicly provided goods and services, tend to promote allocative efficiency, but may cause demand deficiency and have a negative impact on growth in the short and medium run. In fact, an exclusive focus on reduction of revenue and fiscal deficits[20] without any regard to their demand and supply side consequences has been a major factor behind the prolonged slack, growth slowdown *as also* fiscal stress in the Indian economy.

Growth, Debt Dynamics, and Fiscal Restructuring

Though TFC takes cognisance of the output gap and mentions the need for demand management policies when required, its 'fiscal reform strategy centres on growth' of supply determined output. TFC does not set forth a fully spelt out macroeconomic model on which its strategies are based. However, its analysis of factors affecting growth and their relation with fiscal variables runs in terms of two sets of causal links. The first chain of causation goes from saving to investment to growth; the second from fiscal deficit to accumulation of debt, increase in the government's interest outgo, rise in revenue deficit (reflecting government dissaving), fall in aggregate investment, and slowdown in growth.[21] In terms of the second set of links the Commission explains the sharp build up of public debt since the late 1990s, goes into the possibility of its being unsustainable and provides a road map of bringing down revenue and fiscal deficits and raising saving, investment and growth during 2005–10.

Saving as an Engine of Growth

TFC's focus on saving as the ultimate determinant of growth is in the neoclassical tradition and presumes that the economy stays close to its full-employment growth path. This is somewhat odd. Though the Commission itself recognizes recessionary trends since the mid-1990s, it seeks to ascribe the slowdown in growth in this period to rising government revenue

[20] What we elsewhere called 'fiscal fetishism' (Rakshit, 2004).

[21] Fiscal deficit and other variables are expressed as proportions of GDP so that the chain running from fiscal deficit to investment culminates in a fall in the growth rate, though there may be an increase in the absolute level of GDP.

deficits pulling down aggregate saving; it does not appreciate that the fiscal mess was due in no small measure to the sharp fall in growth in public sector investment in general and infrastructural investment in particular (Rakshit, 2004). The important point to note in this connection is that in a demand-deficient economy, it is the investment that drives saving (and growth), not the other way round: In such an economy attempts to save more (say through a cutback in the government's revenue expenditure along with an increase in taxes) end up with a fall in income as well as in aggregate saving and investment.[22]

Neglect of the nature of the saving–investment relationship operating in the presence of an output gap has led the Commission astray in its analysis of sectoral savings behaviour as well. The increase in the government's revenue expenditure, especially following the pay revision, was no doubt an important factor raising government dissaving, but it also helped generate demand and raise household disposable income and saving. This is not to justify the extraordinary pay hike. Had the government stepped up capital expenditure, the resulting demand magnified by the multiplier and the crowding-in effect would have raised income, tax collections, and profits of both public and private sector companies and hence all the three categories of saving, public, private corporate, and household.

Even in a full-employment economy causation need not run from saving to investment. An improvement in investment prospects induces companies to retain a larger share of profits rather than distributing them as dividends. An increase in investment tends to raise the share of profits (and hence saving) even if the Keynes (Treatise)-Kaldor-Kalecki result—'Workers spend what they earn and capitalists earn what they spend'—requires some modification. Finally, as the experience of the United States, Ireland, Germany, and Japan suggests, with increasing integration of domestic and international capital markets, creation of opportunities of profitable investment is more important than trying to boost saving for stepping up economic growth. A congenial investment climate has sucked in foreign saving in fuelling the United States and Irish economic growth, but in view of inadequate incentives to invest, relatively high savings in Japan and Germany have not been translated into even modest growth in the recent decade.

Our discussion of macroeconomic linkages in India also indicates how saving can be promoted through well-designed investment projects. TFC recommendation for an increase in infrastructural investment as a part of fiscal restructuring is well taken. But there is a presumption that such an increase can take place only at the expense of other types of investment unless the

[22] When private investment is positively related to profits and capacity utilization.

revenue deficit is reduced first. In many areas, especially in the remoter parts of the countryside, labour as well as local resources remains unutilized because of lack of marketing facilities, road transport, or supply of working capital. These are no doubt supply side bottlenecks, but direct investments or financial support for their removal leads to utilization of hitherto unemployed resources and an increase in the pool of aggregate saving—something which would not materialize unless the additional investment takes such specific forms.[23] In view of widespread existence of such potential sources of saving in India, for purposes of policy formulation, it is necessary to consider the two-way connection between investment and saving.

Apart from problems with the unidirectional causal link catalogued above, TFC's treatment of support to R&D as well as education, health, and other social sector expenditures as consumption rather than investment weakens both its analytical framework and fiscal restructuring programme. The exclusion is particularly unfortunate since (a) TFC's 'core strategy of fiscal restructuring' is said to centre 'on raising the trend rate of growth'; and (b) new growth theories and empirical research on factors behind the Solow residual have brought out the enormous importance of these investments relatively to that of accumulation of physical capital as determinants of long-term growth. TFC does suggest that the government should, along with provision of basic public goods such as administration and defence, spend more on education and health in view of their positive externalities; but such expenditures are still considered items of revenue, not capital outlay. This is likely to make the restructuring programme sub-optimal, remembering the requirement that revenue deficits of both the Centre and states are to be brought down to zero during the reference period.

Debt Dynamics and Fiscal Restructuring

TFC's focus on reduction of revenue and fiscal deficit as a key element of fiscal correction is backed by considerations of debt dynamics, showing how the temporal behaviour of the debt–GDP ratio (b) is related to primary deficit[24]–GDP ratio (p). The debt–GDP ratio at the end of the period t (b_t) may be written as

$$b_t = p_t + b_{t-1}(1+i_t)/(1+g_t). \qquad (6.1)$$

[23] As earlier development economists have argued, the saving potential from additional income generated through use of hitherto unutilized or underutilized resources can be quite significant. Strong empirical support for this hypothesis is provided by the experience of Grameen Bank and many a micro-finance scheme.

[24] Primary deficit is defined as fiscal deficit less interest payments and refers to that part of the increase in debt which is attributable to the *current year's* budgetary operations (interest payments being committed expenditure on account of past borrowings).

This relation splits b_t into two parts: (a) the primary deficit ratio and (b) interest payments plus previous period's debt[25] as a ratio of current GDP.[26] From Eq. (6.1) follows the change in b_t over b_{t-1}:

$$b_t - b_{t-1} = p_t - b_{t-1}[(g_t - i_t)/(1+g_t)]. \tag{6.1a}$$

This yields the result that debt financing of any primary deficit (as a fraction of GDP) is sustainable (i.e., *b* remains bounded) when in the long run *g* exceeds *i* (Domar, 1944).[27] Unlike many analysts examining the sustainability of India's debt financing, TFC recognizes that *i* and *g* are endogenous and affected by fiscal measures;[28] but even so, its use of Eq. (6.1a) for empirical and policy-oriented analysis is not generally happy.

While discussing the sharp rise in the debt–GDP ratio during 1996–2003, TFC, following Eq. (6.1a), estimates 'the contribution of cumulated primary deficits and that of the differential between growth and interest'; notes how 'the excess of growth over interest could not absorb any part of the impact of cumulated primary deficits, the benefit in the first three years being negated by the opposite effect in the latter three years'; and concludes,

> The entire increase therefore was due to an accumulation of primary deficits, which remained unabsoibed by any excess of growth over interest rates. (Government of India, 2004, p. 65)

The problem, however, is that decomposition of the change in the debt–GDP ratio into two parts, as shown in Eq. (6.1a), follows from *definitions* of the variables involved, so that the relation is an *identity* devoid of any causal significance. Only when Eq. (6.1a) is supplemented by a model specifying the links between primary deficit, interest rates, and growth,[29] can it become substantive. In the absence of such a model, TFC's constitutes a tautological exercise,[30] providing no clue to why the growth–interest differential was positive in the first half of the period but negative in the second,

[25] Which gives debt at the end of t were primary deficit in t zero.

[26] Note that the GDP in *t* equals GDP in *t*–1 times $(1+g_t)$. Hence, the second term on the right-hand side of Eq. (6.1).

[27] The Domar result is based on a differential equation version of 6.1a.

[28] Nor does TFC commit the fairly common fallacy of mixing up solvency and sustainability conditions. On the significance and relevance of the two sets of conditions see Rakshit (2005).

[29] Thus one (though implausible) specification may be that the government controls the primary deficit ratio, but growth and interest rates are exogenously given.

[30] It is like decomposing GDP between consumption and investment or between wage and non-wage income, and 'explaining' GDP growth in terms of growth of the two components, without any specification of their determinants.

even though primary deficits remained positive throughout. Again, had the government tried to reduce the primary deficit through additional cut-backs in investment expenditure, aggregate demand and GDP growth, our earlier analysis suggests, would have plummeted further and the fiscal position could have become worse.

For analysing the effects of fiscal policy on the debt–GDP ratio under full-employment conditions, it is useful to distinguish among three categories of primary revenue expenditure, viz., social sector expenditure, other government consumption expenditures and subsidies-cum-transfers (other than interest payments). While the first, unlike the second, constitutes part of human capital formation and hence has implications for growth and future revenue receipts, the third also differs from the second in that it raises private sector disposable income and hence its consumption and saving. Quite clearly, the composition of primary revenue expenditure is not neutral for growth or evolution of the debt–GDP ratio. The composition matters for non-debt creating receipts as well since the nature and consequences of their four major components—taxes, non-tax revenues (like dividends and interest), seignorage (or net central bank credit to the government) and disinvestment proceeds—differ significantly. The second component reflects revenue from past investments and its time path could be quite different from that of the tax revenue. A reallocation in favour of PSU investments, for example, tends to raise the dividends–GDP ratio even while the tax ratio may stagnate. Seignorage, though absent in budgetary accounts, is similar to other revenues in that it does not involve any future interest burden.[31] Disinvestment reduces the need for current borrowing, but through its negative impact on future revenue can worsen the longer term debt scenario (Rakshit, 2000, 2005).

TFC makes no mention of seignorage or of implications of disinvestment for debt dynamics. Though growth-promoting effects of government investment (but not of social sector expenditure) are recognized, sustainability of debt financing of such outlays is summarily dismissed on the ground that the return on them 'is negligible' and 'even the more indirect return through higher growth to match the growing interest liabilities has not been forthcoming' (Government of India, 2005, p. 68). Since issues relating to infrastructural finance loom large in any fiscal restructuring programme and their analysis by the august body seems far from satisfactory, it may be useful to go into some basics in this regard.

[31] Interest payments on government borrowings from the central bank come back to the fisc by way of dividend from the bank. That is why seniorage is in fact treated as part of revenue in all standard discussions of debt dynamics (though TFC has in line with the mainstream Indian tradition included seignorage in fiscal deficit).

Debt Financing of Public Investment

The weakness in TFC's analysis arises from a lack of distinction between demand and supply side effects of public investments and an adequate appreciation of how the effects operate in a demand-deficient and full-employment economy. In the presence of an output gap, an increase in public investment raises income by a multiple of the amount spent so that the government's revenue receipts also go up. If public sector investment stimulates private investment due to an increase in the capacity utilization and profits and to prospects of larger supply of infrastructural facilities in the future, the increase in revenue may exceed the additional government expenditure (Rakshit, 2005): by spending more the government has effected a fall in fiscal deficit! Even if the additional revenue falls short of additional investment, reliance on seignorage[32] to meet the gap strengthens government finances: with zero net interest on seignorage, *any* positive return on investment reduces future revenue deficits.

Now consider a scenario where the economy suffers from prolonged demand deficiency; government investment declines over time; seignorage comes down sharply and is increasingly substituted by borrowing from the public; and interest rates on past debts incurred during the expansionary phase of the economy are relatively high. In such a scenario, a demand-driven deceleration of growth pushes down the tax–GDP ratio and returns on government investments. Interest rates also tend to come down along with growth; however, in view of the preponderance of past borrowings in the stock of public debt, the *average* rate of interest on debt remains much higher than the rate on *current* borrowings.[33] Under such a scenario an unwary observer may regard public investment as unjustified because of its low return, and conclude [on the basis of a mechanical application of Eq. (6.1a)] that in view of the negative growth–interest differential debt financing of government investment is unsustainable. This is precisely what TFC does while examining the pros and cons of sustainability of fiscal deficit incurred for purposes of investment.

Unlike in a demand-deficient economy public investment under full-employment does not constitute a free lunch, its opportunity cost being the foregone private investment (or household or public consumption). When social marginal productivity of government investment is higher than that

[32] Which does not lead to inflation (i.e., a continuing rise in prices) under conditions of demand deficiency.

[33] Note that TFC considers the average interest rate on debt, not even the borrowing rate during the period under review, not to speak of the (zero) cost of borrowing from the Reserve Bank.

of private investment, optimality requires reallocation of investible resources in favour of the former. However, because of the difficulty or costs of capturing the marginal productivity through user charges or taxes, debt financing may prove problematic.

When costs of raising taxes are high, seignorage can be a better option than not only borrowing, but even taxation (beyond some stage). Unlike taxes, seignorage does not raise the community's saving;[34] but the marginal cost of taxation can be prohibitive beyond a point and make seignorage an optimal budgetary instrument. Again, seignorage is superior to borrowing since the latter involves a reduction in the future saving potential (because of the interest outgo) or costs of additional taxation. Finally, remembering that the maximum seignorage may be small in relation to the 'needed' investment expenditure, supplementing seignorage with debt financing is likely to be optimal since (a) an increase in GDP growth enlarges the scope of future seignorage (both the zero-inflation and the maximum seignorage being positively related to the growth rate); and (b) the marginal costs of tax collections tend to be lower at higher levels of GDP. Sans any of these optimality considerations, TFC's remarks on financing government investment would strike the reader as somewhat cavalier.

Different Faces of Public Debt

Since public debt is considered an unmixed evil, the fiscal restructuring programme of TFC is ultimately directed toward bringing the debt–GDP ratio down to some tolerable level (though it is not clear why the longer-term goal is not a *zero* debt–GDP ratio). The concept of public debt used by TFC is, however, unsatisfactory and constitutes an important source of weakness in its analysis and policy conclusions. The first problem in this regard relates to the inclusion of the RBI holding of government securities as part of public debt. Interest payments on these securities do not accrue to the private sector or add to its disposable income, but come back to the Treasury in the form of RBI dividends. Hence, for analytical purposes, especially for examining the debt dynamics and implications of alternative modes of financing government expenditure, the RBI holdings of government securities should not be included in the public debt. Had the Commission followed the dictates of economic logic in this regard, it would have found an important source of fiscal stress in the Indian economy. Not only has the net RBI credit to the government (especially as a proportion of total government borrowing) been declining since the early 1990s, in recent years the net credit has become negative. Thus the increase in the debt–GDP ratio

[34] Ignoring the impact of inflation tax.

over the 1990s as conventionally measured provides an underestimate of the increase in the burden of public debt. In sharp contrast to the position in the early 1990s, the share of government securities held by the Reserve Bank is now near zero.

One fallout of the foregoing development has been that practically all interest payments of the government have increasingly swelled private sector disposable income and the widening of revenue deficits proved difficult to contain. Clubbing of the RBI with other creditors of the government has prevented TFC to identify a major reason behind the rise in household saving and government dissaving and to realize that the two phenomena are in fact closely related. (The fall in the tax–GDP ratio has also produced a similar effect on the composition of aggregate saving.) Neglect of this factor has had an important bearing on the fiscal restructuring exercise: though elimination of the government's revenue deficit in order to raise aggregate saving and growth constitutes the core of the programme, TFC makes no mention of the composition of the government's interest outgo and its policy relevance.

The second problem with TFC's concept of public debt lies in the exclusion of market stabilization bonds (MSBs). The main reason behind the negative net RBI credit to the government and exhaustion of its stock of GOI securities has been sterilization of large inflows of foreign funds. With the RBI stock of GOI bonds nearing zero, the government and the Reserve Bank have adopted the Market Stabilization Scheme (MSS) under which for sterilization purposes RBI (on behalf of the government) sells MSBs, but their proceeds, kept in a separate account, cannot be used to meet the government expenditure. However, as interest-bearing assets, the MSBs are completely at par with other government securities held by the public. Even so TFC excludes these bonds from public debt, the reason adduced being that cash balances from MSB proceeds constitute government assets! Such a perception of government assets defies all economic logic[35] and has led the Commission astray in more ways than one. Since the government's cash balances with the central bank are immaterial for consequences relating to the burden of public debt, the TFC treatment of MSBs leads to an underestimation of the government's liabilities and interest burden.[36] TFC has also failed to spot the considerable quasi-fiscal costs the government is bearing on account of large-scale substitution of US/EU government bonds for GOI

[35] It would make much more economic sense to exclude debt which had been contracted for asset creation. But then one would have to consolidate the balance sheet of the entire public sector.

[36] Which the Ministry of Finance seems to be aware of (Government of India, 2005), though it has no idea of how to tackle the problem.

securities in the Reserve Bank's portfolio (Rakshit, 2003). More generally, there is an inadequate appreciation of the link between the fiscal, monetary, and exchange rate policies. This was no doubt outside the Commission's domain, but the link is integral in the presence of large capital inflows and outflows and needs to be taken into account while formulating a fiscal restructuring programme.

An Approach to Fiscal Restructuring

An important and positive aspect of TFC's fiscal restructuring programme is the focus on growth through removal of budgetary imbalances, redirection of government expenditure, and reforms such as transparency, elimination of hidden subsidies, and performance budgeting that would improve efficacy of the budget as an instrument of public policy. The core of the programme lies in the quantitative targets set for all major fiscal indicators like the fiscal deficit, revenue deficit, tax and non-tax revenue, public debt, etc. as ratios of GDP.[37] The targets set and the projected macroeconomic indicators (e.g., aggregate saving, investment and current account deficits as ratios of GDP) are consistent with macroeconomic accounting rules. However, several important issues remain unresolved in this connection.

First, what are the instruments for attaining the targets? The question assumes significance since the government has some direct control over nominal expenditure, its composition and amount of borrowing; it can also vary the rates and structure of taxes or revise user charges; but tax and non-tax revenue receipts, GDP, inflation, and interest rate are determined through working of the entire macroeconomic system. The Commission presumes the growth and the inflation rate to be 7.0 per cent and 5.0 per cent, respectively, and the nominal interest rate to remain at the current level; but the basis for the presumption is not clear. The only clue to the Commission's thinking in this regard is to be found in its description of the 'core reform scenario' during 2005-10. Through elimination of revenue deficit, the Commission expects the aggregate saving ratio to rise from 24.0 per cent to 26.0 per cent between 2004–5 and 2009–10. With an expected increase in the current account deficit from -0.5 per cent to 1.5 per cent, the economy's aggregate investment would rise from 24.5 per cent to 27.5 per cent and the GDP growth from 6.5 per cent to 7.0 per cent. But this scenario leaves unaddressed how the aggregate saving, investment, and current account deficits are attained, remembering that these depend not only on the instruments used by the government, but also the behaviour

[37] Only in the case of interest the target is for total interest payment as a ratio of total revenue.

of the household and corporate sectors and of international investors. Nor does the Commission make it clear whether the economy would be demand or supply driven, though there seems to be a presumption that the projection is for full-employment growth, derived on the basis of the expected investment (saving[38]?) rate and the incremental capital–output ratio. Since the Commission does not specify the fiscal measures required to ensure and maintain full-employment, or induce the projected savings and investments on the part of the private sector, it is difficult to take its projections more seriously than those churned out by the Eleventh Finance Commission.

The second set of issues relates to the optimality of the restructuring programme, assuming that the economy will operate with full-employment and the government will be able to meet the fiscal targets. Optimality considerations, as our discussion in the second section suggests, require weighing the costs and benefits at the margin of raising the government's capital and primary revenue expenditures, tax and non-tax revenue including seignorage, and borrowing from the public and external sources. On the basis of these considerations, it is not clear why the targets set by the Commission should be regarded as optimum. Why, for example, should the government strive merely for a zero revenue balance, not for a surplus, so that the growth rate could exceed 7 per cent? One response may be to invoke the golden rule which enjoins upon the government to borrow only for meeting capital expenditure since market-determined saving is optimal: it reflects the community's time preference including the preference relating to inter-generational consumption.

However, no development economist seriously regards the saving rate driven solely by market forces as optimum for countries like India; nor is there any evidence that TFC itself thinks so. Hence, the more reasonable response would be to suggest that bringing down the revenue deficit to zero will involve a substantial increase in tax and non-tax revenue[39] so that the marginal social cost of further increases in tax collections (or a reduction in primary revenue expenditures) would tend to exceed the marginal benefit from extra saving resulting therefrom. The revenue deficit target might

[38] The incremental capital–output ratio estimated on the basis of growth and investment rates in 2004–5 is 3.77 compared with 3.91 for 2009–10. The ratio estimated on the basis of saving (rather than investment) rate is 3.7 in both the years. Since there is no mention of any factor causing the incremental capital–output ratio (ICOR) to rise in the process of fiscal restructuring, the Commission has presumably (and wrongly) used the saving rate and its estimate of ICOR for 2004–5 in arriving at the expected growth rate in 2009–10.

[39] And containing the increase in primary revenue expenditure to 0.9 percentage point.

indeed have been based on such a cost-benefit calculus (though there is no reference to this type of exercise in the report). But then neglect of seniorage as a source of revenue, especially when it is zero inflation, violates the optimality condition relating to financing of government expenditure. In a full-employment economy seignorage revenue (unlike taxes) does not immediately add significantly to the domestic saving.[40] However, through a reduction in interest outgo, it tends to raise the revenue surplus, bring down the debt–GDP ratio (for the same level of primary expenditure) and effect a permanent increase in the community's aggregate saving (and investment) without an increase in (distortionary) costs of taxation.

The significance of the impact of seignorage on the debt–GDP ratio and the revenue balance may be illustrated with a simple numerical example adhering to the TFC approach to debt dynamics and to the TFC assumption (purely for illustrative purposes) that the nominal GDP growth and the interest rate remain stable at 12 per cent and 6 per cent, respectively. With a conservative estimate of seniorage that would not raise inflation above 5 per cent at 1.5 per cent of GDP, tapping this source of revenue will over time bring down the debt–GDP ratio by 28 percentage points and raise revenue surplus by 1.68 percentage points—an increase not to be sneezed at when judged against the TFC targets relating to tax and debt–GDP ratios. Factor in the growth-promoting effects of the rise in revenue surplus and, hence, the added scope for seignorage, and the total neglect of this source of revenue would appear to lie in ideological orthodoxy, not analytical-cum-empirical reasoning.

We have already drawn attention to the way in which treating the social sector outgo as revenue expenditure tends to cause sub-optimal allocation of resources between government expenditures on physical investment, human resources development and consumption expenditure. This in fact seems to be so in TFC's restructuring programme. With a 2.9 percentage point increase in revenue and a 1.6 percentage point fall in interest payments, revenue deficit is slated to be reduced to zero along with an increase in the government capital expenditure by 1.0 percentage point. However, the primary revenue expenditure wherein social sector outgoes are included is targeted to fall by 0.1 percentage point. Given the abysmal state of public health and education services in India and their enormous significance for equity, quality of life and growth potential, absence of any quantitative target for social sector expenditure (backed by a transparent cost–benefit calculus)

[40] To the extent seignorage is inflationary private consumption is reduced and saving is raised through the wealth effect or because of 'inflation tax'. In the Indian context, seignorage involving substitution of GOI for US government securities will immediately affect both the revenue balance and the national income.

must be considered a major deficiency of TFC's agenda for 'multi dimensional' reforms aimed at 'equitable growth'.

So far as infrastructure is concerned, investment in this sector does constitute a focus of TFC recommendations. However, out of the projected 3.0 percentage point increase in domestic capital formation, government investment accounts for 1.0 percentage point. Considering the huge shortfall of infrastructural facilities bedevilling the Indian economy, TFC's targeted allocation for this sector appears grossly sub-optimal: under the restructuring programme, the marginal productivity of investment in infrastructure will continue to remain significantly higher than that of capital accumulation in other areas. In view of the importance of the subject, the nature of the optimal investment programme required for removal of supply bottlenecks may be illustrated with a simple example.

Suppose that there are only two types of capital stock (K), infrastructural (K_n) and other (K_0). Assume further that the production function is neoclassical and that given the wage rate, the optimum ratio of K_n to K_0, say r, is r^*, the optimum being characterized by the equality of the (social) marginal productivity of K_n and K_0. The presence of large-scale infrastructural bottlenecks implies that actual r falls far short of r^*. Under an optimal investment programme, the entire capital formation would take place in the infrastructural sector until r has attained r^*. Only then should investments in the two sectors as proportions of their respective capital stocks be the same so that r^* remains unchanged over time. The programme may have to be modified because of the rising cost of capital accumulation in particular sectors and of mobilizing private savings by the government. But the constrained optimization programme would also generally be characterized by a relatively high share of infrastructural investment in the earlier phase and its decline over time[41] toward the longer term optimal level $r^*/(1+r^*)$.

Finally for some counterproductive aspects of target setting. Given the large imponderables in the economic system, the government may, despite its best efforts, fail to attain all the targets. Under these conditions it may focus on attaining the easier ones at the cost of others even though they may be more important. Hence arises the need for prioritization of targets. To be more concrete, suppose the government faces a trade-off between targets for interest payments on public debt on the one hand and those for infrastructural investment or social sector expenditure[42] on the other. In the

[41] That TFC targets are not based on any optimality considerations is corroborated by the fact that despite wide differences in the endowment of infrastructural and social sector capital stocks across states, the revenue and fiscal deficit targets set for them are identical.

[42] Though TFC, as we have seen, does not set any target for this expenditure.

absence of any guidelines the government may try to attain the former at the cost of the latter and seriously damage the long-term prospects of the economy. Indeed, if TFC's presumptions regarding the behaviour of private economic agents, the international scenario and growth or inflation rate prove wrong, all the targets cannot be attained simultaneously. Hence arises the need for focussing on those which are directly related to full-employment, growth, and equity: as the Indian experience suggests, mechanical attempts at attaining budgetary targets create an environment where primary objectives are often lost sight of. The importance of our observation arises from the fact that (a) there is generally no unique policy package for attaining fiscal targets, especially when the targets are expressed as ratios; and (b) the optimum policy package and the corresponding fiscal targets will differ when there are unforeseen changes or major shocks in the domestic or the international economy.

Conclusion

TFC's focus on growth as a key element of its fiscal reform strategy is well taken. Also eminently sensible are its recommendations for performance budgeting; doing away with the distinction between Plan and non-Plan expenditure; and transparency including elimination of all hidden subsidies. However, the major weakness of the strategy consists of not dovetailing demand management policies in a developmental programme; ignoring the saving–generating impact of investment in an economy where the rural and informal sectors are characterized by considerable underutilization of resources even while the formal sector may not have much slack; treating education, health, and other social sector expenditures as current; and absence of optimality considerations in respect of allocation of expenditures and of alternative modes of their financing, taking into account their short- and longer-term effects on growth, equity, and government finances.

A fiscal restructuring programme and the accompanying macro indicators drawn up on the basis of a well-formulated growth-theoretic framework would differ from the one suggested by TFC in the following important respects. First, given the initial overall output gap and investment-saving potential in the informal sector, growth in the first one or two years, driven by (policy induced) demand, should be much higher than in subsequent years. In the second phase, growth will largely be supply determined and cannot but slowdown after its initial burst. In the third phase (extending beyond 2010), as aggregate saving and investment rates rise, structural imbalances (including shortage of infrastructural facilities and skilled labour force) are removed, and labour and other resources are shifted from low to high productivity areas, growth rate should go up and remain high for quite a while before decelerating when the economy matures (and technological innovations become the major driver of per capita GDP growth). So far as the fiscal targets are concerned, in the initial phases infrastructural and social sector investments (including expenditure on rural reconstruction) as ratios of aggregate investment should be higher, reliance on seignorage and borrowing from the public greater, and government consumption as ratio of GDP smaller than in the later phases of adjustment.

From an operational viewpoint, the restructuring programme could gain in effectiveness if the authorities are required to focus on primary instruments of fiscal policy, for example, changes over time in government expenditure and its composition; in structure and rates of taxes; and in monetized deficit and borrowing from the public. Given the initial situation, expectations relating to the evolution of exogenous factors, and demand and supply side impact multipliers of the primary instruments,[43] choice of their optimal set[44] yields a corresponding set of targets for fiscal indicators, such as, primary or fiscal deficit ratios. The implication is that choosing the fiscal targets without any reference to primary instruments for attaining them would generally be counterproductive.

Our analysis also underlines the danger of setting detailed annual targets for fiscal correction. Even if the targets are derived from an optimality exercise whose underlying assumptions are broadly correct, in view of unforeseen contingencies and shocks, trying to meet the annual targets may do more harm than good. That is why, in countries like the UK, the government's revenue budget is required to be balanced over a trade cycle, not every year. Since agricultural cycles are much more important in India than business cycles, requiring (say) the four-to-five year moving average of revenue deficits to be contained within a band seems more sensible. Similarly, since the optimum division of investible resources between the government and other sectors can change due to a whole host of unforeseen developments on both the domestic and the international front, the UK practice of borrowing only for purposes of investment also appears superior to setting a rigid target for fiscal deficit. After all, if the medium run revenue deficit is required to be near zero, there is an automatic check on unremunerative investment financed through borrowing.

[43] Estimated from a well-specified macroeconometric model.

[44] Based on their short and longer run consequences for the economy and the Treasury on the one hand and the basic goals of public policy on the other.

References

Bose, A. (1989), 'Short Period Equilibrium in a Less Developed Economy', in M. Rakshit (ed.), *Studies in the Macroeconomics of Developing Countries*, Oxford University Press, New Delhi.

Domar, E.D. (1944), 'The "Burden of the Debt" and the National Income', *American Economic Review*, 34(4), 798–827, (December).

Government of India (2004), *Report of the Twelfth Finance Commission (2005–10)*, New Delhi.

——— (2005), *Statements laid before the Parliament as required under the Fiscal Responsibility and Budget Management Act, 2003*, New Delhi.

Rakshit, M. (1982), *The Labour Surplus Economy,* Macmillan, Delhi.

——— (1989), 'Underdevelopment of Commodity, Credit and Land Markets: Some Macroeconomic Implications', in M. Rakshit (ed.), *Studies in the Macroeconomics of Developing Countries,* Oxford University Press, New Delhi.

——— (2000), 'On Correcting Fiscal Imbalances in the Indian Economy: Some Perspectives', *Money & Finance*, 2(2), 19–58, (July-September).

——— (2003), 'External Capital Flows and Foreign Exchange Reserves: Some Macroeconomic Implications and Policy Issues', *Money and Finance*, 2(13–14), 63–95, (April-September).

——— (2004), 'Some Macroeconomics of India's Reform Experience', in K. Basu (ed.), *India's Emerging Economy: Performance and Prospects in the 1990s and Beyond*, MIT Press, Cambridge, Mass.

——— (2005), 'Budget Deficit: Sustainability, Solvency and Optimality', in A. Bagchi (ed.), *Readings in Public Finance*, Oxford University Press, New Delhi.

Reserve Bank of India (2003), *Report on Currency and Finance, 2001–2*, Mumbai.

Taylor, L. (1983), *Structuralist Macroeconomics*, Basic Books, New York.

7

External Capital Flows and Foreign Exchange Reserves*

Macroeconomic Implications and Policy Issues

Introduction

India's balance-of-payments position has undergone a sea change since late June 1991 when, with foreign currency reserves totalling only two weeks' import cover, the country was on the brink of reneging on its international debt obligations. During the 1990s not only did India weather with aplomb a series of financial storms raging in a number of emerging market economies, but she was also able to attract considerable capital inflows, build up huge reserves, and maintain 'orderly development' in the foreign exchange market. However, as is to be expected in our profession, a few doubting Thomases continue to see some darker sides in the bright scenario on the external front. Improvements in current account balance, inflows of external finance, and accretion of foreign currency reserves have been most marked since the mid-1990s. But this is also the period when the country's growth rate has decelerated and the budget deficit widened considerably. In the context of interdependence among major macroeconomic variables, it is important to examine (a) if or how the domestic and external developments of the economy are linked; (b) whether the policies pursued by monetary and fiscal authorities have been 'optimal'; and (c) the scope for improvements in macroeconomic measures including those directly impinging on the balance-of-payments.

Before undertaking an analytical-cum-prescriptive exercise, we highlight in the second section the policy stance pertaining to the external sector and take stock of the positive and negative developments during the post

* Reprinted from *Money & Finance*, Vol. 2, Nos 13–14, April–September 2003.

reforms era, especially since the mid-1990s. For a deeper understanding of developments in this period, we discuss in the third section the interlinkages among and the implications of capital inflows, domestic investment, the current account deficit, and accretion of foreign exchange reserves. This prepares the ground for a critical evaluation of the on-going macromanagement in the fourth section and for suggesting our own policy package in the fifth section. The final section summarizes the findings and conclusions of the paper.

External Sector Developments During the 1990s

Though some limited moves toward trade liberalization were initiated from the mid-1980s, it was the 1990–1 payments crisis that caused a major break in the government's overall economic strategy in general and external sector policies in particular.[1] The immediate response to the crisis was adoption of emergency measures such as securing financial assistance from international bodies like the IMF, issue of India Development Bonds (IDB) and institution of immunity schemes for residents bringing back funds from abroad.[2] As a pre-requisite for tapping these sources of finance, the rupee was devalued by 18 per cent[3] in the first week of July 1991 and a two-tier exchange rate system (with an official and a market-driven rate) was introduced.[4] These measures aided with a severe fiscal and import squeeze enabled the government to tide over the payments crisis, raise foreign exchange reserves to a fairly decent $5.6 billion by March 1992,

[1] As we have observed elsewhere (Rakshit, 2004), both the major breaks in India's post-independence policy stance, viz., adoption of the 'new' agricultural strategy in the late 1960s and initiation of economic reforms from 1991, were due in no small measure to the loss of face of the country's leaders before the international community: it was no coincidence that the first break followed Indira Gandhi's (putative) indignity while seeking US food aid under the PL480 Programme, and the second, the humiliating need to airlift gold to the Bank of England as a security against loans.

[2] Over the period June 1991–March 1992 while aggregate financial assistance from the IMF, the World Bank, and Asian Development Bank (ADB) was a little over $3.1 billion, funds garnered through IDB, immunity schemes, and loans against gold (from the Bank of England) amounted to $1.61, $0.7, and $0.6 billion, respectively (Government of India, 1993).

[3] Given the payments problems faced by the country, the IMF would not have extended loans without devaluation and the immunity schemes would not have been attractive enough. The success of the IDB issue was also crucially dependent upon positive signals from the IMF.

[4] Under this system exporters had to surrender a part of their foreign currency earnings at the official rate, but could sell the rest to prospective importers at the market rate. This enabled the government to finance petroleum and other bulk imports at a subsidized rate.

and considerably restore the confidence of international investors. It was however felt that for long-term balance-of-payments viability and for making international transactions a potent instrument of economic growth, radical changes in both trade and exchange rate regimes were called for.

Already from the mid-1980s the climate of opinion was veering toward trade liberalization and this became the dominant view in the wake of the payments crisis. The first step towards external sector liberalization consisted in removal of most quantitative restrictions on trade, their replacement with tariffs, and a significant lowering of import duties over a relatively short period. The two-tier exchange rate system was soon abandoned and the rupee became current account convertible by August 1994, implying that (except for a few items) there was no exchange control on trade in goods and services.[5]

In view of both the 1991 payments problems and the series of currency crises many a Latin American country had to endure since the late 1970s, it was felt in the government circles that trade liberalization was not enough to ensure balance-of-payments viability of the country. The major issues in this context were examined by a high-level committee (HLC) whose recommendations formed the basis of the country's external sector policy stance since the early 1990s (Reserve Bank of India, 1993).

The policy stance consists in avoiding misalignment of the exchange rate; containing external debt–GDP ratio within prudential limits; reduction in short-term loans; encouraging non-debt capital inflows; maintenance of adequate foreign exchange reserves; and keeping the current account deficit at a sustainable level, in line with the country's absorptive capacity.

Trade, Exchange Rate, and Current Account Deficits

Table 7.1 attests to the success of the authorities in attaining the policy objectives. Since the payments crisis, the Indian economy has become much more open: between 1990–1 and 2001–2, merchandise trade and total trade in goods and services as ratios of GDP increased from 14.6 and 19.4 per cent to 21.3 and 33.2 per cent, respectively. Particularly impressive was the performance of invisible receipts (including remittances and software exports) and invisible balances whose ratios to GDP over the reference period rose from 2.4 and -0.1 per cent to 7.4 and 2.9 per cent, respectively. The result was that despite an upward trend in merchandise trade deficit, the deficit on the current account balance was contained at around 1.0 per cent of GDP and the balance turned into a surplus in the last two years (Table 7.1).

[5] A few quantitative restrictions, mostly on consumer durables and security-related items, still remained.

TABLE 7.1

A Profile of India's External Sector, 1990–2003

	1990–1	1991–2	1992–3	1993–4	1994–5	1995–6	1996–7	1997–8	1998–9	1999–2000	2000–1	2001–2	2002–3
1 Nominal exchange rate (Index)#	67.2	52.51	43.46	44.69	43.37	39.73	38.97	40.01	36.34	35.46	35.54	35.75	37.31
2 Real effective exchange rate (Index)#	75.58	64.2	57.08	61.59	66.04	63.62	63.81	67.02	63.44	63.29	66.53	68.43	72.93
(% of GDP)													
3 Total trade (goods & services)	19.42	21.28	23.57	25.25	27.34	29.92	30.03	30.13	30.02	31.43	35.05	33.17	
4 Total invisibles	4.79	6.53	6.63	7.21	7.88	8.46	8.47	8.90	10.24	10.63	12.43	11.87	
a. Invisible receipts	2.36	3.59	3.61	4.13	4.82	5.00	5.56	5.66	6.23	6.79	7.50	7.40	
b. Invisible payments	2.43	2.94	3.02	3.07	3.06	3.45	2.91	3.24	4.01	3.84	4.93	4.47	
5 Merchandise trade	14.64	14.75	16.94	18.04	19.46	21.47	21.56	21.23	19.78	20.80	22.62	21.30	
a. Exports	5.83	6.88	7.32	8.28	8.33	9.13	8.86	8.72	8.30	8.40	9.76	9.34	
b. Imports	8.81	7.87	9.62	9.76	11.13	12.34	12.70	12.51	11.48	12.40	12.86	11.97	
6 Current account balance	–3.05	–0.34	–1.71	–0.42	–1.05	–1.65	–1.19	–1.37	–0.96	–1.05	–0.54	0.29	0.74*
a. Invisible balance	–0.08	0.65	0.60	1.06	1.76	1.55	2.65	2.43	2.22	2.94	2.56	2.92	
b. Merchandise trade balance	–2.98	–0.99	–2.30	–1.48	–2.81	–3.20	–3.84	–3.80	–3.19	–3.99	–3.11	–2.63	
7 Capital account balance	2.27	1.46	1.59	3.54	2.84	1.31	2.96	2.47	2.01	2.48	1.86	1.99	2.57*
(Items 8, 9, and 10 are in USDM)													
8 Total debt (end-March data)	83801	85285	90023	92695	99008	93730	93470	93531	96886	98263	101132	98489	NA
9 Capital account balance	7188	3777	2936	9695	9156	4689	11412	10011	8260	11100	9023	9545	13300
10 Net non–debt inflows	103	133	557	4235	4807	4805	6153	5390	2412	5191	4588	5286	2296*

(Table 7.1 Contd.)

(Table 7.1 Contd.)

	1990–1	1991–2	1992–3	1993–4	1994–5	1995–6	1996–7	1997–8	1998–9	1999–2000	2000–1	2001–2	2002–3
10a Non–debt inflows as % of capital account balance	1.43	3.52	18.97	43.68	52.50	102.47	53.92	53.84	29.20	46.77	50.85	55.38	23.54*
a1. FDI	97	129	315	586	1314	2144	2821	3557	2462	2155	2339	3905	2857
a2. FPI	6	4	244	3567	3824	2748	3312	1828	–61	3026	2760	2020	986
10b Loans	7085	3644	2379	5460	4349	–116	5259	4621	5848	5909	4435	4259	7456*
(% of GDP)													
10 Total debt	28.66	38.72	37.51	33.80	30.78	27.00	24.55	24.27	23.62	22.13	22.42	20.93	
11 Short–term debt as % of total debt	10.30	8.20	7.10	3.90	4.30	5.20	7.20	5.40	4.40	4.00	3.59	2.79	
(USDM at end March)													
12 Foreign exchange reserves	5834	9220	9832	19254	25186	21687	26423	29369	32490	38036	42281	54106	74805

* refers to April–December data;

\# refers to base 1985 =100,36 country bilateral weights.

Source: Reserve Bank of India (2003a), Government of India (2003).

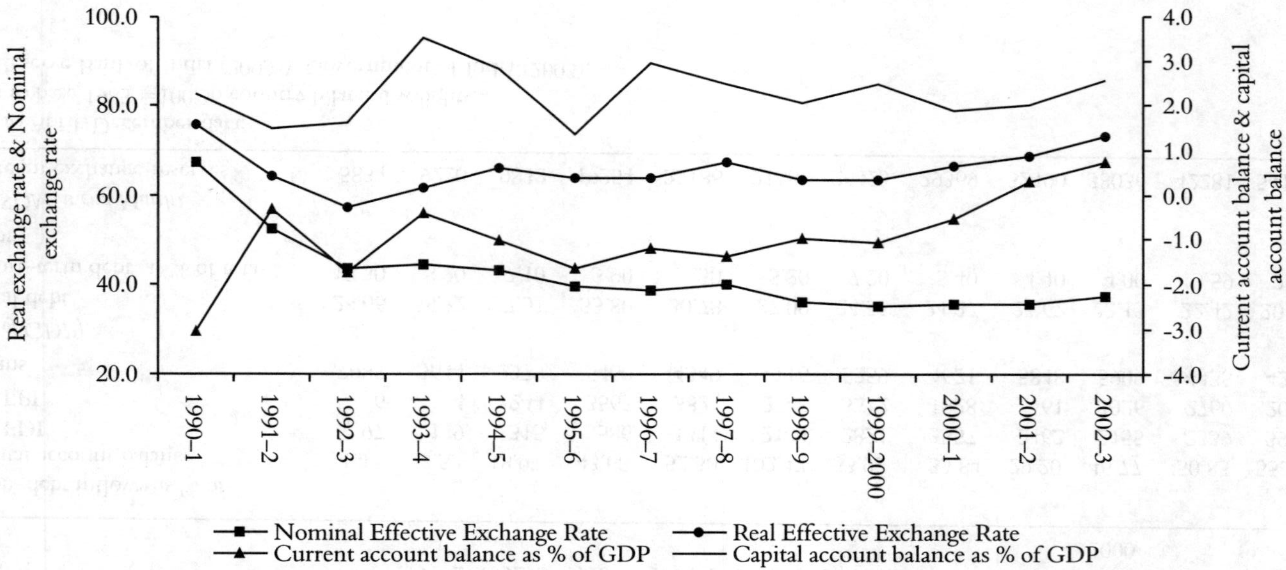

FIGURE 7.1: Some External Sector Indicators.

Source: Table 7.1.

A flexible exchange rate policy and avoidance of large and persistent over- or under-valuation of the rupee were important factors behind the country's modest trade deficit. Since August 1994 (when the rupee became fully current account convertible) the real effective exchange rate[6] (REER) has remained remarkably stable (Table 7.1 and Figure 7.1) despite the fact that the period saw serious currency turmoils in different parts of the world. For avoiding sharp exchange rate fluctuations and keeping current account deficits within sustainable limits, the Reserve Bank during this period relied on a number of policy instruments.

Under the flexible exchange rate regime in force, regulation of capital flows formed an important target of the RBI measures. For this purpose rules governing capital account transactions were often changed in response to major external or domestic developments, even while the overall trend was toward relaxation of capital controls. Interest rate changes were also often used to deter unduly large capital inflows or outflows.[7] In order to prevent sharp swings in the exchange rate and keep it close to its long-term equilibrium value, the Reserve Bank regularly intervened in the foreign exchange market mopping up or adding to the market supply of foreign currency, as and when required. In most instances, especially in recent years, market intervention took the form of Reserve Bank purchases of foreign currency. However, since this generally tends to raise money supply[8] and make the real exchange rate appreciate (through increases in the price level), the Reserve Bank has very often 'sterilized' increases in its foreign currency holding through open-market sale of securities.[9] A judicious combination of policies outlined above played a decisive role during the 1990s in ensuring 'orderly behaviour' of the exchange rate, increases in the trade–GDP ratio, and relatively small current account deficits.

[6] If there is only one foreign nation with which the country trades, its real exchange rate is the nominal exchange rate times the ratio of foreign to domestic price levels. For each trading partner there is thus one real exchange rate. The REER is nothing but the weighted average of all the real exchange rates, the weights being the respective shares of different foreign nations in the country's total trade.

[7] Thus the RBI's dear money policy following the outbreak of the East Asian crisis was designed to discourage capital outflows and prevent contagion.

[8] Purchases of foreign currency by the Reserve Bank raise the supply of reserve money by an equivalent amount and this in its turn enlarges the supply of broad money through the money-multiplier process. Thus if the purchase of foreign currency is worth Rs 1000 crore and the value of the money multiplier is 3.5, the broad money rises by Rs 3500 crore in equilibrium.

[9] Thus in the example of the preceding footnote, if the Reserve Bank sells government securities worth Rs 1000 crore, the reserve money, and hence, the broad money remain unchanged.

Viability of Balance-of-Payments

Perhaps the single-most policy objective of the Reserve Bank during the reforms era has been guarding against the payments crisis or raising the economy's (external) shock absorptive capacity. We have already noted how, in consonance with the conventional wisdom, current account deficits were kept at a low level for promoting balance-of-payments viability.[10] No less important has been the transformation effected in the country's composition of capital inflows and the external balance-sheet position. In the post-reforms period, India attracted substantial quantities of external capital both in absolute terms and as percentages of GDP; but what was more important, non-debt inflows[11] came to account for a major source of foreign funds (Table 7.1). The period 1990–2003 saw an increase in the total external debt from \$83.8 billion to \$101.13 billion; but the debt–GDP and debt-service ratios, the more important indicators of the burden of debt, came down from 38.7 and 30.2 per cent in the crisis year (1991–2) to 20.9 and 14.1 per cent, respectively, in 2001–2. Much more significant was the fall in short-term debt, the villain of the piece in many a currency crisis in recent decades. The ratio of short-term loans to GDP and to total debt registered a decline from 2.9 and 10.3 per cent in 1990–1 to 0.6 and 2.8 per cent, respectively, in end-March 2002. Finally, in light of inadequate foreign exchange reserves triggering off currency crisis in a number of emerging market economies, the Reserve Bank has deemed it prudent, especially over the last six years, to accumulate substantial foreign exchange reserves (Table 7.1). Indeed, judged by the amount of reserves in relation to imports, short-term debt and non-debt liabilities, and by the other usual criteria,[12] India's external shock absorptive capacity has improved dramatically in recent years (Table 7.2) and the country now ranks among the top group of developing economies in terms of the ability to counter speculative attacks on her currency (Reserve Bank of India, 2003).

Some Sources of Discomfort

India's spectacular performance on the external front has not unfortunately been matched by her macroeconomic record in some crucial areas. After a

[10] Large and persistent current account deficits are widely regarded as a major factor behind a currency crisis. See, however, Rakshit (2002), Chapter 5.

[11] Recognized as much more stable and far less injurious to a country's balance-of-payments viability than loans, especially short-term ones.

[12] We have not considered here the criterion relating to the strength of the domestic banking system. However, judged in terms of capital adequacy, non-performing assets, and other indicators, this criterion also attests to the country's balance-of-payments viability.

TABLE 7.2
Some Indicators of Balance-of-Payments Viability

	1990–1	1991–2	1992–3	1993–4	1994–5	1995–6	1996–7	1997–8	1998–9	1999–2000	2000–1	2001–2	2002–3
1 Total debt to GDP	28.70	38.70	37.50	33.80	30.80	27.00	24.50	24.30	23.60	22.10	22.40	20.90	
2 Short–term debt to GDP	2.90	3.16	2.65	1.32	1.33	1.40	1.77	1.31	1.04	0.90	0.80	0.60	
3 Debt-service ratio	35.30	30.20	27.50	25.40	26.20	24.30	21.20	19.00	17.80	16.20	17.30	14.10	
4 Debt to current receipts	323.04	307.13	319.20	272.62	233.46	187.55	168.30	158.73	161.29	144.82	127.46	122.31	
5 Liability sevice ratio	35.60	NA	NA	NA	NA	24.70	NA	NA	NA	17.00	18.30	15.30	
6 Import cover of reserves (in months)	2.70	5.60	5.10	8.60	8.50	6.10	6.60	6.90	8.20	8.20	8.6	11.3	13.7
7 Short–term debt to foreign exchange reserves	146.50	76.68	64.48	18.84	16.95	23.20	25.46	17.18	13.15	10.30	8.60	5.10	
8 Non–debt liabilities and short–term debt to reserves	148.20	79.24	72.57	44.54	57.00	92.30	105.35	107.41	102.10	99.90	100.80	88.40	
9 Short–term debt and non–debt reversible liabilities to reserves	146.60	76.79	67.07	38.68	47.30	71.10	77.32	70.08	60.78	59.00	58.50	48.10	
Memo items													
10 Total forex reserves to GDP	2.0	3.7	4.1	7.0	7.9	6.3	6.9	7.6	7.9	8.6	9.4	11.5	14.51

Source: Reserve Bank of India (2003, 2003a).

spurt of robust GDP growth during 1992–7, there was a sharp deceleration of the growth rate in the next six-year period (Table 7.3). Particularly disconcerting was the performance of agriculture and industries. For three consecutive years from 1992–3, agriculture recorded high growth, averaging 5.1 per cent per annum; but during the next eight years the growth rate showed sharp year-to-year fluctuations and its average plummeted to a dismal 0.2 per cent. Industrial growth, with an average of 7.8 per cent, was characterized by a rising trend between 1992–3 and 1995–6; however the trend from 1995–6 onward has been distinctly negative (Table 7.3). The slowdown, as is to be expected, was accompanied with increased excess capacity[13] and dampened propensity to invest.

That the year 1995–6 (and not 1997–8) marked the dividing line between the accelerating and decelerating phases of the Indian economy in the post-liberalization period is also strongly suggested by the behaviour of saving and capital accumulation. The investment and saving ratios, which showed a significantly upward trend from the crisis year 1991–2 up to 1995–6, came down by nearly 1.4 and 3.0 percentage points, respectively, during 1996–2002. This is a far cry from the expectation in the early phase of the reforms that, by the end of the millennium, the country's investment and saving ratios would touch if not exceed 30 per cent, and the growth rate would rival China's.

Current Account Balance and Domestic Developments

Interestingly enough the decelerating phase of the economy has also been characterized by substantial improvements in the country's current account balances and the foreign exchange reserves position (Table 7.3, Figure 7.2). One may thus wonder how far the domestic and external sector developments are related or have affected one another. Note however that except for reserves accretion, which by and large can be taken to reflect the Reserve Bank's policy stance, the other macro variables are joint outcomes of a number of factors including the monetary, fiscal, and exchange rate policies. We have examined elsewhere (Rakshit, 2004) the major forces governing India's macroeconomic performance in the post-reforms period. Here we propose to discuss, in the context of recent economic trends, the rationale behind targeting of the current account balance, capital inflows, and reserves accretions, and to identify areas where a modification or redesigning of policies is called for.

[13] Capacity utilization in manufacturing came down from 90.6 per cent to 75.7 per cent between 1990–5 and 1995–2000 (Reserve Bank of India, 2003). There are strong grounds for believing that the figure for the latter period is in fact an overestimate (Rakshit, 2004).

TABLE 7.3
A Macroeconomic Profile of India

	1990–1	1991–2	1992–3	1993–4	1994–5	1995–6	1996–7	1997–8	1998–9	1999–2000	2000–1	2001–2	2002–3
1 GDP growth	5.60	1.30	5.10	5.90	7.30	7.30	7.80	4.80	6.50	6.10	4.40	5.60	4.40
2 Industrial growth	6.76	–1.22	4.09	5.20	10.20	11.60	7.10	4.30	3.70	4.80	6.60	3.30	6.10
3 Investment growth	13.72	–12.32	9.28	5.83	22.92	11.10	–1.00	7.70	0.70	20.30	–1.40	3.00	NA
4 Investment as % of GDP	26.30	22.60	23.60	23.10	26.00	26.90	24.50	24.60	22.60	25.20	24.00	23.70	NA
5 Saving as % of GDP	23.10	22.00	21.80	22.50	24.80	25.10	23.20	23.10	21.50	24.10	23.40	24.00	NA
6 Current account balance as % of GDP	–3.05	–0.34	–1.71	–0.42	–1.05	–1.65	–1.19	–1.37	–0.96	–1.05	–0.54	0.29	0.74
7 Capital account balance as % of GDP	2.27	1.46	1.59	3.54	2.84	1.31	2.96	2.47	2.01	2.48	1.86	1.99	2.57
8 Reserves accretion as % of GDP	–0.40	1.43	0.33	3.18	1.44	–0.82	1.52	0.94	0.95	1.38	1.31	2.46	3.35

Source: Reserve Bank of India (2003a), Government of India (2003).

Note: Items 6, 7, and 8 (for 2002–3) are for the period of April–Dec. 2003; GDP is also adjusted for estimating the ratios.

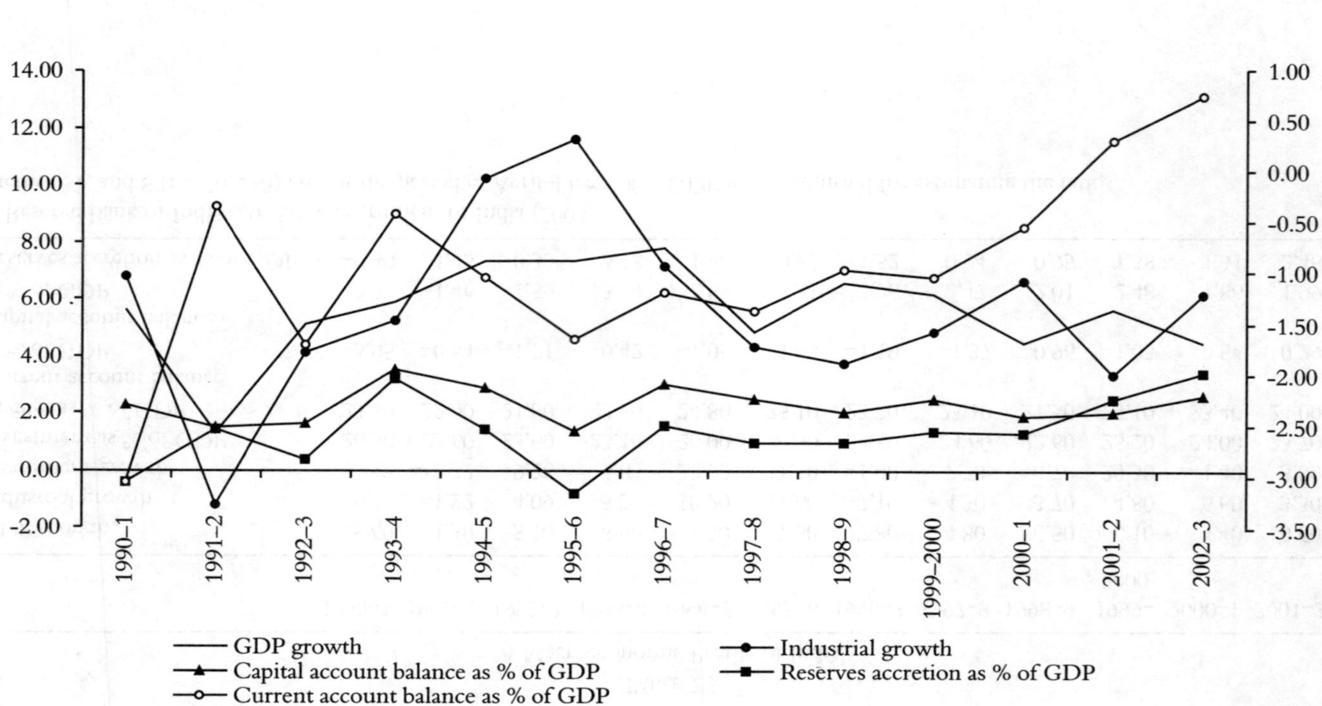

FIGURE 7.2: Time Profile of some Macroeconomic Indicators (current account balance is measured on the right-hand-side Y-axis.)
Source: Table 7.3.

To a development economist the economic scenario since the mid-1990s, with declining saving on the one hand and improvements in current account balances on the other, cannot but seem highly enigmatic. In order to step up its pace of economic development, a poor country is presumed to require net foreign capital inflow in order to raise domestic investment above its level of saving (see Box 7.1). This makes economic sense for both

Box 7.1

Foreign Capital and Economic Development

Because of enormous difficulty a poor country faces in raising its saving, development economists advocate reliance on foreign capital for stepping up investment and growth. The relation between domestic capital accumulation and borrowing from abroad may be appreciated from the following version of national income analysis:

$$Y=C+I+(X-M), \qquad (7.1)$$

$$I-S=(M-X)=\text{CAD}, \qquad (7.1a)$$

where Y is the national income; C the consumption[1]; I the investment[2]; X= exports of goods and services[3]; M = imports of goods and services; $S(=Y-C)$ = saving; and CAD=the current account deficit. Equation 7.1a shows that an excess of investment over saving is financed through borrowing from abroad (to meet the shortfall of export earnings from expenditure on imports).

It was customary for early development economists to indicate, in terms of this relation and the relation between investment and increase in productive capacity, how foreign capital inflow could raise economic growth. Expressing I, S, etc. as proportions of Y and noting that a unit of investment raises productive capacity by the reciprocal of the incremental capital–output ratio, v, the following relations are easy to establish:[4]

$$g=\frac{i}{v} \qquad (7.2)$$

$$g=\frac{1}{v}\,(s+s^f), \qquad (7.2a)$$

where g is the growth rate of Y; $i=I/Y$; v the incremental capital–output ratio; $s=S/Y$; and $s^f=CAD/Y$. The reason for using the symbol s^f for CAD/Y is that this shows foreign saving (as a proportion of Y) used for financing domestic capital accumulation. The implication of Eqs. (7.2) and (7.2a) is apparently that the larger the current account deficit or foreign capital inflow, the higher the growth of the domestic economy.

(Box 7.1 Contd.)

(Box 7.1 Contd.)

Before one draws such a conclusion, several caveats are in order. First, the relations show the supply side impact of capital accumulation with full employment of resources; they do not constitute a complete macroeconomic model indicating the determinants of investment, saving, and growth. Second (and related to the first), an increase in capital inflows may reduce domestic saving or even investment, and hence need not be growth promoting.[5] Third, even with full employment of resources and an equivalent increase in domestic investment, foreign capital may produce a negative impact if the marginal cost of borrowing is relatively high, complementary resources such as skilled labour and infrastructural facilities are scarce in the domestic market, or the country's terms-of-trade are expected to deteriorate.[6] Finally, depending upon the policy initiatives and working of the macroeconomy, both the magnitudes and signs of gross capital inflows can be different from CAD.

[1] Household and government taken together.

[2] Private plus public sector investment.

[3] Including remittances.

[4] The relation ignores for simplicity the difference between domestic product and national product.

[5] See the third section 'Capital Inflow, Investment, and Reserves Accretion: Some Analytics'.

[6] The reason is that even with no fall in the physical productivity of capital, a deterioration of the country's terms of trade raises the debt-servicing cost. The problem is compounded when the country's exports are confined to a few goods and their share in world trade is not insignificant.

developing countries and advanced nations (supplying loans), the reason being that returns on investment are generally higher in capital-scarce economies.[14] Thus the implication of the 1995–2003 Indian experience is that, not only did the country rely less on foreign finance even while her own saving was on a decline, but of late she has started lending her meagre resources to support increases in consumption and investment in the United States and European Union! One cannot help feeling that there is something seriously amiss with the macroeconomic policies being pursued over the last seven years or so.

[14] See Rakshit (2001) for a discussion of how international capital flows can benefit all countries and how they may also cause serious disruptions. On the need for foreign capital even when domestic saving is not small, see Chenery and Bruno (1962), Chenery and Strout (1966), and Obstfeld and Rogoff (1996).

That the combination of low investment and current account surplus suggests some policy failure has not gone completely unnoticed in official circles. Not only has there been a relaxation of controls on corporates securing foreign funds for their domestic operations, but both the Union and State governments have been using and seeking loans from the World Bank, Asian Development Bank, and foreign governments or other agencies for financing of infrastructural investment. However, the use of foreign capital to augment domestic investment under the present scenario goes against elementary economic logic and entails substantial, avoidable cost to the country. Since most discussions on these issues as well as the government's policy pronouncements reflect inadequate appreciation of this logic, it may be useful to summarize some 'do's and don'ts' in respect of reliance on external finance for executing domestic investment projects.

Capital Inflow, Investment, and Reserves Accretion: Some Analytics[15]

When development economists recommend borrowing from abroad to step up capital accumulation and growth, the presumption is that domestic resources are fully employed. However, when there is an output gap[16] (as there has been for quite some time in India) the opportunity cost to the economy of raising investment through increased use of domestic resources is zero,[17] but the use of foreign capital involves cost of its servicing in the future.

Capital Inflows without Central Bank Intervention

The cost of capital inflows in a demand-deficient economy are in general much larger than the burden imposed through their future servicing. In order to appreciate these costs, ignore first the need for reserves accretion and assume that the central bank does not intervene in the currency market. Capital inflows then cause an appreciation of the domestic currency, raise the trade deficit, and enlarge the output gap through operation of the foreign trade multiplier.[18] With no change in other transactions on capital

[15] Readers not interested in theoretical underpinning of our assessment and policy conclusions may skip the section.

[16] This is nothing but the gap between the full-employment (or full-capacity) output and actual gross domestic product of the economy.

[17] Though not to the investor, since he has to pay for use of labour or other resources required for investment.

[18] When imports exceed exports, GDP tends to fall by a multiple of the trade deficit through the initial fall in domestic demand getting magnified by the decline in output, consumption and investment in subsequent rounds of income generation. Note that

account, in equilibrium the fall in GDP then must be enough to raise the domestic investment-saving gap (which equals the current account deficit) by the incremental capital inflow.

The most important element of the cost is thus the decline in current output, amounting to a multiple of the inflow. Second, operation of the (negative) foreign trade multiplier effects a reduction in domestic capital accumulation as well, remembering that investment propensity is dampened by an increase in excess capacity or the output gap.[19] Thus contrary to popular perception,[20] the economy's investment and hence the future production potential are reduced through foreign capital inflows! Finally, the inflows (while reducing current income and investment) raise the economy's external liabilities and the burden of their future servicing.

Relevance of the foregoing results for judging the macroeconomic effects of external sector policies can hardly be overemphasized. In view of the significant differential between domestic and foreign interest rates, some corporates have sought and been granted permission to borrow from abroad [or issue global depositary receipt (GDR)] for purposes of retiring rupee debt or funding domestic operations. Again, the Union and state governments have been using loans from the World Bank, Asian Development Bank (ADB), and other international agencies for financing infrastructural investments. Our analysis suggests that when companies substitute foreign borrowing for domestic borrowing (with no increase in their net investments), the economy cannot escape the three types of costs listed above.[21] Thus while such substitution is eminently sensible for individual corporates, its macroeconomic impact is unambiguously negative. Similar are the effects of foreign portfolio investment (FPI) and even of foreign direct investment (FDI) when it is not directly related to an increase in domestic capital accumulation.[22]

---

the trade multiplier operates on a change in the import–export gap due to changes in factors other than income. In the present case, it is the currency appreciation which triggers off the (negative) foreign trade multiplier.

[19] When investment is positively related to capacity utilization, the value of the foreign trade multiplier tends to be larger. In this case capital inflows have larger negative effects on GDP, investment, and saving.

[20] The wrong perception seems to be shared even by the Ministry of Finance (Government of India, 2003), which cites increased capital inflows (apart from other things) as indicators of a rise in domestic investment!

[21] viz., a fall in aggregate investment and GDP on the one hand and an increase in foreign liability on the other.

[22] Which will generally be the case when a multinational takes controlling interest in some domestic company. However, there are technology transfers and other benefits of FDI which we shall presently take note of in the context of our discussion of optimal capital inflows and their composition.

What if external funds are used to finance some investment which otherwise would not be undertaken (as is presumably the case with some government infrastructural projects)? In this case the increase in the domestic propensity to invest is exactly the same as capital inflows so that the equilibrium GDP remains unaffected: the negative impact of trade deficit is balanced by the positive impact of investment.[23] The implication is that the country's additional liability to the rest of the world is matched by an increase in the capital stock, and there is no fall in the domestic income. Note however that, given the zero opportunity cost of unemployed resources, additional trade deficits or imports are not necessary for raising domestic investment, that is, external financing of the project has needlessly raised the economy's cost of future debt servicing—a perception which seems to be lacking both among the laity and in official circles. Indeed, even if the external loan is a zero-interest loan (and used directly for raising investment expenditure), it still entails substantial costs to the economy on account of repayment obligations.[24] Only in the case of an outright grant is there no cost to the economy, *provided it is used for additional investment*. The following policy conclusion thus seems fairly robust: From a macroeconomic viewpoint, government policies in a demand-deficient situation should try to ensure that the economy's expenditure on capital accumulation is met through domestic, not foreign, finance.

Capital Inflows and Central Bank Intervention

The cost of capital inflows considered above presumes no intervention on the part of the central bank. When the central bank mops up the inflows without undertaking sterilization,[25] the exchange rate remains unaffected in the first round: additional supply of foreign funds is offset by extra demand by the central bank. However, the increase in money supply associated with unsterilized intervention tends to raise aggregate demand, gross domestic product, and hence trade deficit. If there is no further intervention in the currency market and transactions on the country's capital account remain unchanged, the exchange rate depreciation eliminates the incipient trade

[23] Check that demand for domestically produced goods and services remains the same. It is as *if* the additional investment project is undertaken entirely through imported goods and services.

[24] Thus if a zero-interest loan of Rs 1,000 crore is used for building a national highway and the loan has to be repaid in ten equal yearly instalments starting from one year after the loan is obtained, the present value of the cost to the economy with, say, a 5 per cent discount rate is as much as Rs 772.12 crore, that is, more than 77 per cent of the loan.

[25] i.e., without any open-market sale of securities to keep money supply unaffected.

deficit so that under the new equilibrium the economy enjoys a higher level of income; but despite the capital inflow, current account deficit, reflecting the increase in the country's net indebtedness to the rest of the world, remains unaltered.

Does capital inflow then have a salubrious effect even in a situation of demand deficiency? As the perceptive reader must have realized, the answer is an emphatic 'no'. The reason is that exactly the same increase in GDP without any enlargement of current account deficit could have been achieved had the Reserve Bank raised domestic money supply by an equivalent amount through an open-market purchase of securities: the rise in domestic demand (due to the expansionary monetary policy) drives down the exchange rate to keep the current account balance unchanged in equilibrium. Note further that in the example of non-sterilized intervention, the current account balance and, hence, the country's net external liability position remain unchanged since the capital inflow is exactly matched by an increase in the central bank's foreign currency reserves. However, as we shall discuss later, in view of the interest outgo on foreign loans exceeding returns on foreign currency reserves, the country's net benefits from the capital inflow are negative.[26]

It is also easy to see that when reserves accretion is fully sterilized, not only the current account balance, but GDP and the exchange rate also remain unaffected, remembering that in this case there is no expansionary effect operating through an increase in money supply. Here also, because of the returns differential noted above, capital inflows reduce national income—something which is not reflected in the country's asset–liability position vis-à-vis the rest of the world.

It is thus fairly clear that unless there is some urgent reason for increasing the central bank's foreign exchange reserves, capital inflows are costly for an economy facing demand deficiency. Hence arises the need for going into some economics of holding or adding to foreign exchange reserves, especially since over the last two years the RBI reserves have nearly doubled, jumping from $42.3 billion at end-March 2001 to more than $81 billion in mid-June 2003.

Uses and Abuses of Foreign Exchange Reserves

The most important reason for a central bank's holding of foreign exchange reserves lies in non-synchronization of the country's receipts from and payments to the rest of the world. In the absence of adequate reserves, payments for imports or on other counts, as and when they become due, may become difficult. The country may thus be starved of timely imports,

[26] Assuming that reserves are not sub-optimal—an issue we shall presently discuss.

which can cause serious disruptions in the domestic economy.[27] When the exchange rate is market determined, non-synchronization is likely to cause wild swings in the rate, which in its turn negatively impacts the country's trading.[28] Hence arises the need for holding reserves even in a flexible exchange rate regime so that the central bank can prevent sharp, short-term changes in the rate, not warranted by the country's long-term fundamentals.

Quite clearly, the economic rationale for reserves holding in the above case is similar to that for transactions demand for money balances. Where this is the only ground for holding foreign exchange reserves, their most important determinants would be the volume of imports, the degree of volatility of exports and imports, and the opportunity cost of holding reserves at the margin.[29] Though the last two factors tend to differ from one country to another, most central banks have found an import cover of three to four months adequate for smooth settlement of transactions on current account.

However, in the wake of a succession of currency crises during the last decade, central banks of emerging market economies have become aware of the volatility of international capital flows and the danger of self-fulfilling speculative attacks on their currencies. Forestalling such attacks requires that investors have enough confidence in the country's ability to withstand capital outflows without significant devaluation or depreciation of the currency. If investors expect the value of the currency to fall sharply in the near future, they will rush to exit and make the expectation self-fulfilling (Flood and Marion, 1996; Obstfeld, 1996; Rakshit, 2002). An important means of promoting investors' confidence and averting currency turmoils is holding of large foreign exchange reserves by the central bank: not only can it then repel sporadic, probing forays by speculators to test the currency's strength, but large reserves holding itself acts as a deterrent to the attacks. Here the economic rationale is similar to what prompted commercial banks in the olden days to hold cash balances and liquid assets in order to prevent 'runs' on the part of depositors. Nowadays, thanks to deposit insurance and the central bank acting as the lender of last resort, banks with fundamentally strong balance sheets do not require to hold large low-yielding liquid assets in their portfolio. But since international investors are not covered by insurance and the IMF's role is a far cry from that of a lender of last resort, it is not surprising that emerging market economies including India consider it prudent to accumulate large foreign exchange reserves.

[27] Consider the impact on the Indian economy of a severe cut-back in petroleum imports.

[28] Remembering that even if traders can buy or sell in the forward market to hedge against the risk, the cost of hedging is higher when exchange rate fluctuations are larger.

[29] We shall presently discuss the meaning and determinants of the opportunity cost.

But how large should the reserves be? The question has acquired significance in the context of RBI's substantial and growing reserves, and perception in some quarters that their costs to the economy exceed the benefits. Since the probability of the import–export gap of a country at different points of time in the short or even the medium run can be estimated with a tolerable margin of error, the benefits of reserves holding for current account transactions requirements are not too difficult to quantify. So far as gains accruing from crisis prevention are concerned, there can be little doubt that these are substantial, remembering the extensive damage the currency crises can inflict on emerging market economies.[30] The problem however is that, while with other things remaining the same addition to reserves promotes balance-of-payments viability at the margin, some of these 'other things' are very often crucial in determining a country's vulnerability to external shocks or proneness to currency crisis.

Before coming to consider flows on capital account, let us take a quick look at factors affecting a country's (external) shock absorptive capacity when the exchange rate regime is characterized by full current, but not capital account convertibility.[31] Given the expected degree of non-synchronization of export receipts and import payments, we have already noted how an increase in the reserves–imports ratio reduces the probability of payments default or import bottleneck. However, reserves may prove inadequate and severe balance-of-payments problems surface even without full capital account convertibility.[32] Thus when the exchange rate is fixed and remains persistently overvalued, holding of forex reserves, however large, cannot prevent collapse of the currency sooner or later: persistent over-valuation causes chronic current account deficit which over time leads to a cumulative loss of reserves or piling up of unsustainably large external liabilities. Again, when the volume and nature of foreign debt is such that (a) interest payments eat up a major part of export earnings, (b) short-term loans are large, and (c) there is considerable bunching of maturity dates (of medium- or long-term loans), the country's external payments position becomes vulnerable and its currency a ripe target for speculative attack.

The vulnerability increases manyfold under full capital account convertibility. Apart from the fact that foreign portfolio investments (and short-term

[30] We have estimated elsewhere the GDP loss, inflation, and financial volatility Thailand, Indonesia, Malaysia, Korea, and the Philippines had to suffer from during the East Asian currency crisis (Rakshit, 2002).

[31] Under this regime there are no restrictions on current-account transactions, but capital controls are in force.

[32] Indeed, India's 1991 payments crisis took place when onerous controls on capital transactions were in force.

loans) are volatile and can be withdrawn at a moment's notice, expectations of an impending crisis can then lead to a torrent of domestic capital outflow and make the expectations self-fulfilling. The implication is that, for keeping the probability of a payments crisis[33] below some pre-stipulated level, the required foreign exchange reserves need to be larger when (a) the debt-service ratio is higher; (b) liquid external liabilities consisting of short-term loans and portfolio investments are larger;[34] (c) domestic economic agents are given freer access to the international capital market; and (d) the exchange rate (instead of being flexible) is fixed or targeted to remain within some narrow band. It is for this reason that many countries deem it necessary to cut-back external liabilities (in relation to exports) and impose restrictions on capital movement, especially short-term loans, portfolio investment, and outflow of domestic capital. These controls entail some loss to the economy, but without them the cost of additional foreign exchange reserves required for balance-of-payments viability is generally much larger.

Cost of Reserves Holding

The simplest way of estimating the cost of reserves holding at the margin is to find out the gains the economy enjoys when the central bank takes the best possible combination of measures for reducing its foreign exchange reserves by one unit.[35] This gain depends crucially on whether the economy is operating with or without an output gap. In case there is excess capacity, the best way of reducing foreign exchange reserves by one unit is to pursue an easy money policy[36] such that the increase in trade deficit due to the expansionary effect equals unity. With the additional trade deficit being financed through depletion of reserves, the real exchange rate remains unaffected.[37]

The marginal gain from the reduction in reserves is then affected by three elements. The first and most important is the increase in the gross domestic

[33] Of a given degree of intensity.

[34] Since FDIs are relatively stable and are guided by long-term fundamentals they do not make the payments situation vulnerable.

[35] The reason being that the marginal gain from a unit reduction in reserves equals the marginal cost of reserves accretion.

[36] The presumption here is that the policy can produce the desired expansionary impact—something which may not be true for the Indian economy.

[37] Note that if the central bank sells foreign exchange but does not permit any change in domestic money supply, there is a contractionary effect because of appreciation of the exchange rate. Hence in a demand deficient economy a reduction in foreign exchange reserves needs to be brought about through an expansionary monetary (or fiscal) policy.

product resulting from the policy package.[38] Second, the fall in foreign exchange reserves reduces interest earnings from abroad[39] and hence national income. Note, however, that with the discount rate exceeding the relatively low returns earned on foreign liquid assets of the central bank, the reduction in gain on this account would tend to be small.[40] Third, there is an increase in net profits of the central bank[41] since (a) the interest rate on domestic securities is higher than the return on foreign assets and (b) central bank's purchase of domestic bonds, required to generate a unit increase in trade deficit, is likely to exceed unity.[42] The addition to central bank's profits improves the government's fiscal balance and the (capitalized value of) benefits resulting therefrom must be regarded as part of the gains from reduction in reserves.[43]

Benefits from reduction in reserves when the economy enjoys full employment of resources are somewhat different. Since GDP can no longer be raised through expansionary measures, there are now two major policy options. The first consists in raising domestic absorption, especially investment, through an enlargement of the investment–saving or import–export gap (at full-employment output) and reduction in reserves to meet the gap. An increase in the investment–saving gap (with income remaining unchanged at the full employment level) requires a reduction in the interest rate. Again, an appreciation of the real exchange rate is also necessary for the targeted increase in current account deficit. While the central bank can effect the

[38] Note that an expansionary monetary policy results in an increase in both domestic consumption and investment. Taking GDP as the measure of gain implies equal weights being attached to the two components of domestic absorption.

[39] Note that under the policies considered here there is no corresponding reduction in interest payments to the rest of the world since reserves depletion is due to enlarged current account deficit.

[40] Thus if the discount rate is 8 per cent while the return on foreign exchange reserves is 3 per cent, the present value of the fall in interest receipts from abroad approximates 0.37 from a unit reduction in reserves. But with a 14 per cent marginal propensity to import, the GDP increase required to raise trade deficit by one unit equals 7.14.

[41] The increase in the central bank's profits due to the factors noted here does not constitute additional national income since we have already considered the GDP increase and the fall in interest receipts from abroad.

[42] The reason lies in relatively low interest-sensitivity of investment and small propensity to import. The first implies a large increase in money supply required to cause a given expansionary impact and the second a significant rise in GDP to enlarge trade deficit by one unit.

[43] Though assigning a numerical value to these benefits poses serious estimation problems. Note that we are not considering here fiscal policies that can also effect a decline in reserves. We propose to go into them in the next section.

required appreciation through sale of foreign exchange, changes in interest rates require some adjustment in the domestic market. The adjustment is triggered off by the trade deficit causing an incipient excess supply in the commodity market, which in equilibrium is eliminated through a fall in interest and an increase in the investment–saving gap (under the neoclassical full employment situation). For maintaining price stability and avoiding slack during the process of adjustment, the central bank may neutralize the monetary impact of reserves depletion through purchase of domestic securities. With full employment of resources, these policies have no impact on the current GDP. However, the increase in investment, approximating that in domestic absorption,[44] raises the economy's productive capacity. The gain on this count equals the marginal productivity of (domestic) investment less marginal return on reserves.[45] The second component of the gain arises from fiscal easing consequent upon an increase in central bank profits, given by earnings from additional domestic securities held less fall in incomes from foreign assets.[46]

The second mode of reducing reserves is to pre-pay (high-interest) foreign loans along with an equivalent increase in domestic credit of the central bank.[47] In this case there is no change in the domestic absorption and the gains to the economy consist of (a) interest on foreign loans less reduction in central bank's interest earnings from abroad and (b) benefits from additional profits to the central bank due to (one-to-one) substitution of domestic bonds for foreign currency reserves in its portfolio. Quite clearly, the benefits from the first set of policies will in most cases be greater than from the second since the marginal productivity of investment in a developing economy is generally higher than interest on foreign loans. Hence, while considering alternative uses of foreign exchange reserves under full-employment conditions, except in exceptional circumstances only the first constitutes a serious policy option.

The gains considered above reflect the opportunity cost of reserves accretion at the margin under two situations, one without and the other with full capacity production of the economy. Whether under a given economic configuration the optimal policy package of the central bank involves accumu-

[44] When saving is not very sensitive to interest rate changes.

[45] Reflecting the opportunity cost of use of reserves. Note that since there is no change in the country's gross liability to the rest of the world, interest on foreign loans does not enter in estimation of gains or losses of the policy being examined.

[46] Here also we have to take the present value of the stream of additional future profits and estimate the benefit resulting therefrom.

[47] We did not consider this alternative for an economy with an output gap since it is palpably inferior to the one suggested by us.

lation or running down of reserves[48] depends on the opportunity cost of reserves accretion on the one hand and its benefit through promotion of balance-of-payments viability on the other. Quite clearly, the marginal benefits tend to be greater when reserves holdings are smaller and there is a higher probability of contagion from financial turmoils raging elsewhere. The marginal opportunity cost on the other hand tends to be relatively large when the degree of capacity utilization is small, the gap between the marginal productivity of capital and the borrowing rate from abroad significant, and the revenue constraint prevents the government from providing essential services and supporting development expenditures having considerable crowding-in effects.

External Finance since the mid-1990s: An Assessment

In light of the cost–benefit analysis of the current account deficit, capital inflows, and accretion of reserves in the foregoing section, we are in a position to assess how far the policies relating to management of external finance have been appropriate and suggest some combination of measures which the on-going economic conditions seem to warrant. There can be little doubt that in the wake of the 1991 payments crisis, transition to a system of dirty float[49] and building up of foreign exchange reserves were eminently sensible. So was the focus on reduction of short-term debt and debt–service ratio. As Table 7.2 suggests, by end-March, 1996, the country's external balance sheet was strong enough to withstand considerable shock. This along with the cautious policy concerning capital account convertibility stood the country in good stead in weathering the Asian financial turmoil during 1997–9.

However, with the on set of industrial slowdown from 1996, external sector financial policies have not been adjusted for attaining the objectives of balance-of-payments viability on the one hand and providing stimulus to GDP growth on the other. As we have explained elsewhere (Rakshit, 2004), the major policy failure behind the lacklustre performance of the economy since the mid-1990s lay in the fiscal sphere in general and neglect of public investment in crucial areas in particular; but the 1996 monetary squeeze[50] also seems to have played some role in reinforcing, if not triggering off, the deceleration process. Again, while one may appreciate the need for a

[48] Note that it does not make much sense to talk of marginal gain or loss from reserves accretion without specifying the economic configuration and considering the best possible mode of changing the reserves.

[49] Where the exchange rate is flexible, but the central bank tries to prevent sharp changes in the rate by intervening through the market.

[50] When the flows of both reserve and broad money registered sharp falls.

relatively conservative monetary policy during the East Asian currency crisis (1997–9), external sector policies over the last four years or so, our analysis of the previous section suggests, seem to leave significant room for improvement.

Some Not-so-positive Policy Indicators

We have already commented on the country's low current account deficit in the second half of the 1990s (especially over 1998–2001) turning into positive balances during 2001–3. While a conservative central banker is likely to view these developments with a good deal of satisfaction, they must be judged, as we have emphasized, in the context of the economic slowdown and the declining trend in the country's saving and investment.[51] Current account balances are, to be sure, governed by several factors (both internal and external) many of which lie outside the control of the central bank. However, the behaviour of some key financial variables over the last five or six years suggests that the Reserve Bank's policy stance has not helped in tackling the slowdown or effecting optimal utilization of resources available to the economy.

Consider first the trends in capital inflows and reserves accretion—the two variables which the Reserve Bank can control directly or indirectly. Since 1995–6 the country has enjoyed persistently large capital inflows, but the major part of these have been used for accumulation of reserves (Table 7.1). We have already discussed in the previous section the relatively high opportunity costs of such accumulation, especially when the economy faces demand deficiency, and noted how raising the country's long-term growth potential requires massive investment in infrastructure and the social sector.[52] All available evidence suggests that these costs have exceeded the gains from reserves accretion, especially since 1998. By the third quarter of 1998 the East Asian crisis economies were already on a recovery path (Rakshit, 2002) and all usual indicators attested to the high (external) shock absorptive capacity India had acquired by the end of the year 1998 (Table 7.2). The implication is that at the margin the gains from additional foreign exchange reserves in terms of their contribution to the balance-of-payments viability have been small (relatively to their opportunity cost *under an optimal policy mix*).

[51] The Reserve Bank of India (2003) itself cites demand deficiency as a factor contributing to the recent trends in current account balances. Unfortunately, the Bank (or rather, the authors of the report) does (do) not draw the appropriate policy conclusion in this respect.

[52] As we shall presently discuss, the solution to the problems requires a combination of monetary and other measures.

To be more specific, let us examine some implications of monetary and balance-of-payments developments during 1999–2003. At the beginning of the period, the country, judged in terms of all the usual criteria,[53] had already had 'adequate' foreign exchange reserves (Table 7.2); but even so total reserves nearly doubled during these four years, from $38.0 billion to $74.8 billion[54] (Table 7.1). Note also that during this period the current account deficit as a ratio of GDP averaged only 0.14 per cent, but for net capital inflow[55] the annual average amounted to 1.95 per cent. In other words, net capital inflows totalling more than 1.8 per cent of the country's gross domestic product were being used to lend to the rest of the world, not for supporting higher domestic production or investment.

Given the operation of demand constraint, some back-of-the-envelope estimate of the most important component of the opportunity cost, viz., the short-term marginal impact of reserves changes on the gross domestic product, may be made at this stage. Assuming that the country's marginal and average import propensities are the same, at around 12 per cent to 13 per cent,[56] and that exports are governed by world demand (and the exchange rate), an expansionary policy causing a GDP increase of eight units can be supported by a unit reduction in foreign exchange reserves without any change in the exchange rate.[57] The implication is that the suggested policy package, causing a fall in the Reserve Bank's foreign currency holding equivalent by, say, 0.2 percentage point of GDP,[58] boosts domestic production of goods and services by as much as 1.6 per cent.[59] Add to that the growth in productive capacity that can be effected by the expansionary programmes through increases in investment, and it is not very difficult to appreciate the significant opportunity cost of reserves (as of now) by way of loss in current GDP and in future production potential.

[53] e.g., the ratios of reserves to imports, external debt and short-term external debt.

[54] The trend has continued in the current financial year (2003–4).

[55] Indicated by the net receipt on capital account.

[56] The average import ratio for the two-year period 2001–3.

[57] Note that we have assumed foreign capital inflows to remain unaffected. As we shall presently see, given the rules relating to capital account transactions, the changes in inflows will differ according to whether the expansion is brought about through fiscal or monetary policies. Note also the implicit assumption that the exchange rate is in conformity with the country's long-term fundamentals.

[58] Note that in 2002–3 reserves accretion amounted to as much as 3.4 per cent of GDP.

[59] Assuming that the initial output gap is larger than 1.6 per cent of GDP. The interested reader may work out the extent of reserves depletion required to bridge some given output gap. It is also not very difficult to see that the required amount generally differs for alternative expansionary programmes, remembering that capital inflows may be influenced (apart from the rules in force) by domestic interest rates and, hence, the nature of fiscal stance accompanying the policy package.

The other major element of the opportunity cost is indicated by some features of monetary developments during the reference period—developments that were closely related to capital inflows and reserves accretion (Table 7.4). During 1999–2003 the average reserve money growth—reflecting increases in central bank credit through its power of creating high power money[60]—was a fairly lowly 9.2 per cent per annum.[61] Second, over this period, as a percentage of reserve money stock (outstanding), the net RBI credit to the government and to the commercial sector came down from 49.8 and 5.4 per cent to 32.6 and 0.8 per cent respectively, while the RBI's net foreign exchange assets increased from 59.1 per cent to 91.1 per cent.[62] Much more dramatic was the change in the flow of RBI credit to different sectors. As Table 7.4 illustrates, during this period, there was a steep decline in RBI's domestic credit, especially to the government, while its addition to net foreign exchange reserves (signifying yearly increases in credit to advanced economies) registered a quantum jump.

We have examined elsewhere (Rakshit, 2000, 2004) the macroeconomic and fiscal implications of slowdown in reserve money growth and in net RBI credit to the government. Such slowdown, apart from its aggregate demand-generation effect, also implies, as we have seen, lower seignorage revenue for the government. Ignoring the slowdown in growth of reserve money, let us consider only the change in the composition of RBI credit. As we have noted in the earlier section, the switch in the RBI portfolio in favour of foreign exchange reserves at the expense of credit to the government and the commercial sector involves a loss of revenue of the Reserve Bank and, hence, to the government. A rough and ready calculation (based on the assumption that foreign exchange reserves of $40.0 billion are 'adequate' and the interest differential of domestic and foreign assets of the Reserve Bank is around 4 per cent) suggests that the opportunity cost of 'excess reserves', by way of revenue loss, amounts to about Rs 7,700 crore or 0.31 per cent of the 2002–3 GDP, not an inconsequential figure for a fiscally constrained government.

Some Sub-optimal Policy Alternatives

While accumulation of large foreign exchange reserves in the context of the country's macroeconomic trends over the last seven years or so does not

[60] The other part of the central bank's credit comes largely out of its undistributed profits forming a component of the net non-monetary liability (NNML).

[61] Compared with (for instance) 18.4 per cent over 1992–6 when the economy enjoyed robust growth.

[62] In the context of the 1991 payments crisis the sharp rise in foreign exchange reserves over 1990–4 was quite natural. Between 1994–5 and 1996–7 the accretion rate was fairly modest. But from 1999 onward the rate registered an acceleration.

TABLE 7.4
Monetary Developments

(Rs. crore)

	1990–1	1991–2	1992–3	1993–4	1994–5	1995–6	1996–7	1997–8	1998–9	1999–2000	2000–1	2001–2	2002–3
1 Broad money (M_3) (stock)	265828	317049	364016	431084	527596	599191	696012	821332	980960	1124174	1311583	1500003	17245578
Growth rate	15.10	19.27	14.81	18.42	22.39	13.57	16.16	18.01	19.44	14.60	16.67	14.37	14.97
2 Broad money (M_3) (flow)	34878	51221	46967	67068	96512	71595	96821	125320	159629	143214	187409	188420	224575
Growth rate	–6.89	46.86	–8.31	42.80	43.90	–25.82	35.23	29.43	27.38	–10.28	30.86	0.54	19.19
3 Reserve money (stock)	87779	99505	110779	138672	169283	194457	199985	226402	259286	280555	303311	337970	368931
Growth rate	13.13	13.36	11.33	25.18	22.07	14.87	2.84	13.21	14.52	8.20	8.11	11.43	9.16
4 Reserve money (flow)	10188	11726	11274	27893	30611	25175	5528	26416	32884	21269	22756	34659	30961
Growth rate	–30.38	15.10	–3.85	147.41	9.74	–17.76	–78.04	377.87	24.48	–35.32	6.99	52.31	–10.67
as % of reserve money (stock)													
5 Net RBI credit to the government	98.84	92.72	87.13	69.79	58.43	61.08	60.36	59.02	56.08	49.84	48.31	41.83	32.55
6 RBI credit to the commercial sector	7.22	7.30	5.61	4.65	3.89	3.53	3.12	3.62	4.72	5.44	4.38	1.75	0.83
7 Net foreign exchange assets of RBI	9.09	18.93	20.44	37.08	44.14	38.10	47.41	51.19	53.21	59.13	65.01	78.10	97.10

(Table 7.4 Contd.)

(Table 7.4 Contd.)

	1990–1	1991–2	1992–3	1993–4	1994–5	1995–6	1996–7	1997–8	1998–9	1999–2000	2000–1	2001–2	2002–3
as % of reserve money (flow)													
8 Net RBI credit to the government	144.73	46.97	37.76	0.93	6.96	78.87	34.99	48.89	35.88	–26.27	29.46	–14.86	–68.74
9 RBI credit to the commercial sector	–0.07	7.83	–9.22	0.81	0.48	1.04	–10.99	7.34	12.29	14.31	–8.72	–21.23	–9.31
10 Net foreign exchange assets of RBI	18.80	92.57	33.79	103.16	76.11	–2.49	374.91	79.77	67.10	131.30	137.52	192.72	304.50
Memo Items													
11 Interest rate (PLR)**	14–15	18–20	17–19	14.5–17.5	15.0	16–19	16.2	13.3	13.5	13.6–17.1	14.0	11.5	12.5
12 Inflation rate*	11.81	15.71	11.58	9.63	12.50	8.10	4.60	4.40	5.90	3.30	7.2	3.6	3.4
13 Real rate of interest#	2.69	3.29	6.42	6.37	2.50	9.40	11.60	8.90	7.60	12.05	6.80	7.90	9.1

Source: Reserve Bank of India (2003a).

* Base 1993–4 = 100; ** IDBI PLR; #11–12.

appear appropriate, economists, as is to be expected, do not agree on what constitutes an optimal policy under the circumstances. Before putting down our own prescription, we indicate, by way of clearing the deck, the main problems with some of the alternatives suggested in this connection.[63]

Market-driven Exchange Rate

The simplest way of avoiding reserves accretion is to let the exchange rate find its equilibrium without any intervention by the Reserve Bank. Indeed, it has been argued[64] that, by mopping up the inflow of foreign capital, the Reserve Bank has prevented an appreciation of the real exchange rate and hence a higher growth the country could have enjoyed through an increase in trade deficit permitting enhanced domestic capital accumulation.[65] The most important problem with this approach is that appreciation of the real exchange rate[66] aggravates the problem of demand deficiency[67] so that widening of the current account deficit will be due more to a fall in domestic saving[68] than to a rise in investment. Indeed, if, as is most likely, a GDP fall acts as a damper to capital accumulation, there will be a fall in both investment and saving, though the gap between the two goes up in equilibrium. Thus the policy of letting the exchange rate appreciate causes a substantial loss to the economy.[69]

The second problem concerns the appropriate exchange rate policy. Most economists agree that the rate should be consistent with the economy's long-term fundamentals. Though estimation of this rate is a horrendous task, one or two policy imperatives appear to be in order. A country should not try to depreciate its way out of a demand-constrained situation, remembering that not only does it amount to exporting unemployment,[70] but the policy is likely to cause serious distortions in the country's structure of production and investment.[71] This does not exclude expansionary monetary or

[63] Or being followed by the Reserve Bank.

[64] e.g., in Lal et al. (2003), referred to in Reserve Bank of India (2003).

[65] Over domestic saving, remembering that in the absence of Reserve Bank intervention, the inflow of foreign funds would have caused an equivalent increase in the investment–saving gap.

[66] When the Reserve Bank does not neutralize the impact of capital inflow through accretion of reserves.

[67] Through operation of the foreign trade multiplier.

[68] Due to a fall in income.

[69] While countering the Lal et al. thesis, the Reserve Bank of India (2003) seems to have missed the most serious deficiency of the paper.

[70] And may trigger off competitive beggar-thy-neighbour policies.

[71] i.e., the policy is likely to go against the principle of allocating resources in line with the country's longer-term comparative advantage.

fiscal policy which, with full-employment equilibrium, may be associated with a depreciation or appreciation. Reliance on capital inflow (with an import–export gap) for raising investment becomes necessary, we have already emphasized, when domestic resources are fully employed. As in other spheres of economic policy, here also the criterion boils down to the net benefit of the inflow, governed by its impact on the additional flow of domestic production on the one hand and the cost of debt servicing on the other.

Reduction of External Indebtedness

Part of the country's growing foreign exchange reserves has been used by the government to pay off high-cost foreign debt and plans are afoot for more of such repayments in the near future. The measure may seem eminently sensible. In view of the return on RBI reserves falling significantly short of interest on some categories of the government's foreign debt, an early retirement of the latter raises the gross national product[72] as also the revenue balance of the government. Again, apart from the fact that the country's foreign exchange reserves as of now are more than adequate by all usual criteria, reduction of debt lowers the amount of reserves[73] the RBI needs to hold for ensuring a given degree of balance-of-payments viability.

However, the boost to GNP and government revenue would be much larger, as we shall presently see, if the reserves are utilized to support an expansion that not only secures full utilization of domestic resources, but effects an excess of investment over (full employment) saving at a real exchange rate commensurate with the country's economic fundamentals. The implication is that pre-payment of foreign debt may be justified when, *with full employment of resources*, marginal productivity of domestic investment falls short of the cost of foreign loans at the margin.

Capital Account Liberalization

Flush with foreign funds, the Reserve Bank has started relaxing control on capital account transactions, especially for the residents. These include permission (a) to professionals to hold abroad 100 per cent of their foreign exchange earnings; (b) to residents to hold their earnings from abroad in domestic foreign exchange account; (c) to banks to invest in overseas money and debt instruments; (d) to individuals, corporates, and mutual funds to invest in equities of foreign corporates having at least 10 per cent share holding in a company listed in India; and (e) concerning remittances from

[72] The GNP rises through an increase in net factor incomes from abroad.
[73] Though not by one-for-one.

transfer of asset sales, enhanced forward contract facilities and travel quotas, and hassle-free remittances abroad up to $500.00. These gradual relaxations have led the financial market to expect full capital account convertibility of the rupee in the none-too-distant future.

While the new rules are not expected to raise significantly the outflow of funds on capital account, it is not very difficult to see that these measures do not form an integral part of a programme aimed at boosting domestic production and investment or more efficient utilization of investible resources.

A Framework for Optimal Policy Intervention

The foregoing analysis suggests that asking questions, such as, should the Reserve Bank reduce its holding of foreign exchange reserves, or try to curb inflow of foreign capital, or aim at making the current account balances negative, is not very helpful in framing external sector policies. There are, for one thing, several ways of attaining these intermediate targets and the extent to which they promote the basic objectives depends crucially on (a) the state of the economy and (b) the measures adopted for the purpose. It is also quite clear that in view of close linkages among the commodity, money, and foreign exchange markets, and of the multiplicity of macroeconomic objectives (e.g., full employment, growth, and budgetary-cum-balance-of-payments viability), any single policy measure is bound to be sub-optimal. Hence the need for a package of policies of which those directly related to reserves accretion or the foreign currency market form only a part. Needless to say, while choosing the constituents of the package, we have to take into account the major constraints facing the economy and the effects of alternative policies on the domestic and external sectors.

We have identified elsewhere (Rakshit, 2000, 2004) the major maladies associated with economic slowdown in India since the mid-1990s. These include substantial excess capacity due to demand deficiency or infrastructural bottlenecks[74]; low levels of investment and saving; poor state of education and health services; large revenue deficits; and credit crunch faced by the majority of medium and small enterprises despite the overall easy liquidity position in formal money and capital markets. These features together with our analysis in the last two sections suggest the nature of measures required in the short and medium run.

[74] In view of the heterogeneity of the production structure, both the constraints can operate simultaneously at the macroeconomic, though not at the firm level. The Planning Commission puts the estimate of excess capacity in 2002 at 21 per cent in manufacturing and 8 per cent overall, though it did not quantify underutilization according to its source.

Reduction of interest rates or injection of liquidity is the preferred policy for tackling recessionary trends in the United States and other developed countries. However, given the underdeveloped credit delivery system and structural factors impeding private investment, monetary policy in India as of now can play at best a supplementary part in the policy package. The major thrust has to be in the form of public investment in infrastructure and social services—a thrust which, through decline in excess capacity and expectations of adequate demand, better quality labour and improved infrastructural services, should create a favourable climate for private investment (both domestic and external) and for efficient use of 'excess' reserves (over their 'optimal' level) and foreign capital inflows. If the real exchange rate is targeted to remain more or less the same,[75] the increase in current account deficit (with elimination of the output gap) has to be met through depletion of foreign currency reserves.[76] The expansionary process, it is also pertinent to note, needs to be supported through an increase in money supply in order not to pose obstacles to enlargement of private investment including that in working capital. The implication is that the increase in the Reserve Bank's domestic credit must be larger than the fall in its holding of foreign exchange reserves and this should also contribute toward medium- and long-term budgetary viability.

While an expansion-led depletion in foreign exchange reserves is to form the core of policy initiatives at the current stage, it is unlikely that this alone would constitute the optimum strategy. Consider first the current account deficit likely to be associated with full employment (at the unchanged real exchange rate). The Planning Commission (Government of India, 2002) estimates the overall slack in the economy at the end of the period 2001–2 to be about 8 per cent which, given the investment and production increases in the meantime, suggests that a 15 per cent GDP growth over a year would close the output gap.[77] With a 13 per cent marginal propensity to import this implies an additional import bill of about Rs 74,000 crore. However, if merchandise exports,[78] invisibles, and capital inflows sustain their recent trends, in the medium run the rise in the import bill alone is likely to keep reserves accretion positive, though at a reduced rate.

[75] On the presumption that it is in line with the country's competitive position vis-à-vis the rest of the world. Note, however, that in order to avoid speculative troubles, the target, if any, should not be explicit.

[76] Strictly speaking, this refers to the fall in reserves from the level without any expansionary policy.

[77] Assuming that a 24 per cent investment ratio raises capacity output by around 6 per cent and that the GDP slowdown in 2002–3 has added to the slack by about one percentage point.

[78] An increase in domestic demand may, however, cause a slowdown in export growth.

From a medium-run perspective, apart from capital inflows and reserves accretion the policy package needs to tackle a few more problems. The first relates to the real exchange rate itself. Since 1999–2000 the rate has appreciated significantly, especially vis-à-vis the country's main competitors in the world market. There is thus a general perception that the prevailing exchange rate is overvalued and needs to be brought down. However, this will tend to moderate the increase in current account deficit associated with full capacity output and (unless backed by other measures) keep foreign exchange reserves and their accretions at above-optimum levels in the near future. What is much more important, the policy (of exchange rate depreciation) is likely to go against the Tenth Plan target of raising the investment rate to 32.3 per cent of GDP, of which 2.9 per cent is to be financed from external savings[79] (Government of India, 2002).

This brings us to the problem of fixing intermediate policy targets. When steps have already been taken to eliminate demand deficiency and there is little scope for raising domestic saving further, stepping up growth requires an enlarged current account deficit and, hence, an appreciation of the exchange rate (than what would be required were investment to be financed solely from domestic sources). Hence, the close connection between policies relating to the exchange rate and those concerning the optimal scale of domestic investment and foreign capital inflows. In deciding on these matters the following considerations seem crucial.

The optimal level of current account deficit, it goes without saying, should depend on the prospective yield on domestic investment relative to the cost of foreign finance. Investment in infrastructure, education, and health positively impacts returns on private investment and enlarges the economy's absorptive capacity of foreign capital. However, an increase in current account deficit for financing additional investment raises its cost at the margin through (a) an increase in the marginal cost of executing investment projects[80]; (b) the additional risk perceived by foreign investors; and (c) heightened uncertainty faced by the domestic economy in view of enlarged future debt (or liability) service obligations. It is these considerations which need to be kept in view while fixing targets for current account deficit.

Even at the cost of some repetition, a few points relating to the target should perhaps be emphasized at this stage. First, the target acquires its

[79] These targets are for the terminal year, viz., 2006–7. The average investment and current account deficit rates over the five-year period are 28.4 per cent and 1.6 per cent, respectively.

[80] Which is the main factor limiting scale of investment at the firm level in a closed economy.

significance only when the economy is on its full-employment growth path.[81] Second and related to the first, attainment of the target requires policies both for avoiding demand deficiency and for stimulating sufficient investment by private (including foreign) and public sectors. Third, an increase in the economy's absorption of foreign capital requires an appreciation of the currency. The implication is that at the early stage of adjustment to foreign capital inflows, the real exchange rate (and current account deficit) should be relatively high in a capital poor economy; but as the economy develops, the marginal return on investment falls and the servicing requirement of foreign liabilities grows, the real exchange rate needs to fall in order to reduce the trade and current account deficits (as proportions of gross domestic product). While formulating macroeconomic measures it is thus important to keep in view the major factors governing the optimum trajectory of the intermediate targets such as the exchange rate, current account deficit, saving, and investment.

Finally for measures relating to cross-border capital flows and foreign exchange reserves. Our earlier analysis suggests why full capital account convertibility should not be a serious policy option despite the large and growing reserves at the disposal of the Reserve Bank. Borrowers from emerging economies face a highly imperfect international capital market because of informational gaps and investors' perception of risk. This, along with the higher country risk associated with larger liabilities to the rest of the world,[82] makes the marginal cost of external finance *to the economy* higher than that to an individual borrower,[83] and, hence, calls for controls on capital inflows[84] (Rakshit, 2001, 2002). These controls need not be quantitative, but may take the form of a tax on foreign loans.

Second, when domestic agents are free to invest anywhere in the world, central bank calculations regarding 'adequacy' of foreign exchange reserves can go haywire and the risk of currency crisis, as the Latin American experience suggests, increases manyfold. The reason is fairly simple. If residents of a country expect a sharp depreciation and seek to transfer their assets

[81] It is for this reason that large capital inflows in the midst of excess capacity have not been a positive feature of the Indian economy.

[82] An individual foreign investor is concerned with the risk of increasing his exposure to a particular borrower or country. For the economy as a whole an increase in external liability has a negative impact on international perception of its credit rating. The implication is that borrowing from abroad by an economic agent raises the cost to other borrowers in the economy.

[83] In other words, the average cost of foreign capital to the economy is lower than the marginal cost.

[84] The intervention may be through the market rather than quantitative restrictions.

abroad, it becomes next to impossible to avoid a free fall of the currency along with a severe financial squeeze and trade disruptions. Free access to the international capital market for residents has thus to be ruled out in the foreseeable future.

Third, there is now a general consensus that, among various types of capital inflows for financing current account deficits,[85] short-term loans and portfolio investments, because of their volatility, are the highest-cost. Since the optimum reserves requirement for such liabilities tends to be high, only a relatively small fraction of them can support domestic investment, so that more often than not their net returns tend to be negative. Long-term loans produce less volatility when care is taken to avoid significant bunching of their repayments. However, even such loans are not risk-free and need some regulation, remembering that the fixed payments obligations they entail pose a burden when the country becomes subject to adverse shocks, internal or external.[86] Hence the relative superiority of FDI which is generally governed by long-term prospects and involves sharing of risk (at both the firm and the macro level) on the part of foreign investors. (This is apart from the role of such investments as vehicles for transfer of technical-cum-managerial know-how.) The implication is that with only a small reserves requirement at the margin, the economy can use the lion's share of FDI for financing domestic capital accumulation.

So far as foreign exchange reserves are concerned, the suggested policy package—comprising expansionary measures (for closing the output gap and maintaining full-capacity production over time), curbs on short-term loans and foreign portfolio investment, and regulation of other capital inflows in line with the country's absorptive capacity—should go a long way in widening the investment–saving gap, moderating net capital account balances, and reducing the need for holding large foreign liquid assets. The first two policies should cause a fall in reserves accretion, while the third reflects the need for reducing reserves on the basis of their cost–benefit calculus. However, the policy programmes, intended to affect (the flows of) production, trade, and current and capital account balances, are still likely to leave foreign exchange reserves above their optimum level over the next two to three years, remembering that at end-June 2003 they constituted about 16 per cent of the gross domestic product. Hence arises the problem of dealing with these excess reserves.

[85] Or adding to foreign exchange reserves in case they are sub-optimal.

[86] The observations hold true also for long-term non-resident Indian (NRI) deposits. This is apart from the fact that during the period of economic slowdown they have arguably constituted the most burdensome external liability of the country.

We have already indicated why blanket liberalization of capital transactions by resident Indians cannot be a serious policy option. So far as pre-payment of foreign loans are concerned, there is little doubt that[87] it is better than holding excess reserves. However, the problem here is whether the cost of these loans to the economy is higher than the marginal cost[88] of new long-term external credit including non-resident Indian (NRI) deposits. If not, it is economical for the country to reduce reserves through curbs on current borrowing from abroad instead of premature retirement of old loans.

Over the medium-run, considerations of efficiency and risk management suggest some further policy options, especially when the country's saving ratio has been raised sufficiently and the economy has become relatively open. Domestic enterprises having comparative advantage in certain lines of activity may be encouraged to set-up or acquire production facilities abroad, even while FDI investment is being promoted in the domestic sector. Such two-way capital flows not only raise productivity of resources employed, but constitute an important means of reducing risk.[89] As the economy matures further, one plank of efficient risk management would be to permit relatively large mutual funds or finance companies to hold part of their portfolio in foreign assets. However, at the present stage of the country's development, this does not seem to be a move in the right direction: all available evidence suggests that (a) returns in major international capital market are lower on the average and their variability greater than in India; and (b) domestic financial companies have to undertake considerable expenses before they can acquire the necessary expertise to operate in these markets.

Summary and Conclusion

(a) The post-reforms era has seen a remarkable improvement in India's balance-of-payments position. During this period the current account deficit has been quite low; the real effective exchange rate remained fairly stable; the external debt–GDP ratio as well as the debt-service ratio come down significantly; the country attracted considerable capital inflows; and foreign exchange reserves of the central bank, as ratios of imports, external debt and short-term liabilities, have registered a sharp rise, especially from the mid-1990s.

[87] With full employment of resources and optimal current account deficit.

[88] Which, as we have noted, is generally higher than the interest rate being paid on these deposits.

[89] With diversification of income earning sources of the country. Such diversification also promotes balance-of-payments viability.

(b) However, performance of the domestic economy since 1995–6 has been quite poor, with a deceleration in industrial and agricultural growth, an increase in excess capacity, and a negative trend in investment and saving ratios. Hence arises the question of whether and how the domestic and external sector developments are related to one another and what the macroeconomic policy stance should be in the present context.

(c) Concern has been expressed in some quarters on accretion of huge foreign exchange reserves along with positive current account balances in recent years—something which runs contrary to development economists' advocacy of use of foreign funds for stepping up domestic investment in the early stages of a country's economic development. It is often suggested in this connection that had the Reserve Bank refrained from accumulating foreign exchange reserves, the resulting appreciation of the rupee would have raised current account deficit and, hence, capital accumulation and growth. The problem, however, is that such a policy aggravates the problem of demand deficiency, and the current account deficit would then have widened through domestic saving falling at a faster rate than investment. Exchange rate appreciation by itself in the presence of output gap is thus counterproductive.

(d) Even when the central bank purchases of foreign currency prevent an exchange rate appreciation, an economy with an output gap incurs considerable cost due to capital inflows (unless the country's foreign exchange reserves are initially 'inadequate'). The cost is due to a decline in future national income, avoidable increases in external liabilities, and revenue loss to the government (because of the central bank's lower profits). Even interest-free foreign loans for executing domestic investment projects entail a net loss to the economy. There appears to be quite inadequate appreciation of these losses when the Union and state governments seek loans from the World Bank, ADB, or other external sources for financing infrastructural projects.

(e) In the absence of an economy-wide, well-functioning credit delivery system, for closing the output gap and putting the economy on a high growth trajectory without creating balance-of-payments problems, the Reserve Bank's role as of now can only be supportive. The main thrust has to be in the form of a significant step-up in public investment in infrastructure and social services in order to boost aggregate demand, raise capacity utilization, crowd-in private investment (including FDI), and promote the productivity of resource use. Such an expansionary policy, causing an enlargement of current account deficit with full employment of resources, permits the Reserve Bank to reduce its holding of foreign exchange reserves, extend credit to the government and, hence, raise national income along with an improvement in the budgetary balance.

(f) Apart from measures for securing full employment and keeping current account deficits at their optimum level, regulation of capital movements has to form an integral part of a macroeconomic policy package. Indeed, such regulation along with intervention in the market for foreign currencies is essential to keep reserves accretion and the domestic investment–saving gap in line with their net benefit to the economy. Taking into account the relative volatility, incremental reserves requirement, and impact on productivity of domestic resource use, it is quite clear that short-term loans and foreign portfolio investments need strict control, and for bridging the current account deficit and maintaining adequate reserves, the country should rely primarily on FDI and long-term loans.

References

Chenery, H.B. and M. Bruno (1962), 'Development Alternatives in an Open Economy: The Case of Israel', *Economic Journal*, 72(285), 79–103, March.

Chenery, H.B. and A.M. Strout (1966), 'Foreign Assistance and Economic Development', *American Economic Review*, 56(4), 679–733, September.

Flood, R.P. and N.P. Marion (1996), 'Speculative Attacks: Fundamentals and Self-fulfilling Prophesies', *NBER Working Paper* No. 5789.

Government of India (1993), *Economic Survey 1992–93*, New Delhi.

——— (2002), Planning Commission, *Tenth Five Year Plan 2002–7*, New Delhi.

——— (2003), *Economic Survey 2002–3*, New Delhi.

Lal D., S. Bery, and D.K. Pant (2003), 'The Real Exchange Rate, Fiscal Deficits and Capital Flows: India 1981–2000', *Economic and Political Weekly*, 38(47), 4965–76, November 22.

Obstfeld, M. (1996), 'Models of Currency Crises with Self-Fulfilling Features', *European Economic Review*, 40(3–5), 1037–47, April.

Obstfeld, M. and K. Rogoff (1996), *Foundations of International Macroeconomics*, MIT Press: Cambridge, Massachusetts.

Rakshit, M. (2000), 'On Correcting Fiscal Imbalances in the Indian Economy: Some Perspectives', *Money & Finance*, 2(2), 19–58, July–September.

——— (2001), 'Globalisation of Capital Market: Some Analytical and Policy Issues', in S. Storm and C.W.M. Naastepad (eds), *Globalisation and Economic Development*, Edward Elgar, Cheltenham.

——— (2002), *The East Asian Currency Crisis*, Oxford University Press, New Delhi.

——— (2002a), 'Food Policy in India: Some Longer Term Issues', *Money & Finance*, 2(9–10), 52–71, April-September.

——— (2004), 'Some Macroeconomics of India's Reform Experience', in K. Basu (ed.), *India's Emerging Economy: Performance and Prospects in the 1990s and Beyond*, MIT Press, Cambridge, Massachusetts.

Reserve Bank of India, (1993), *Report of the High-level Committee on Balance of Payments* (Rangarajan Committee Report), Reserve Bank of India, Mumbai.

——— (2003), *Report on Currency and Finance 2001–2*, Mumbai.

——— (2003a), *Handbook of Statistics on the Indian Economy 2002–3*, Mumbai.

8

Using Forex Reserves for Infrastructural Investment*

It is useless to attempt to reason a man out of a thing he was never reasoned into.

Jonathon Swift

Introduction

In the context of large accumulation of foreign exchange reserves[1] and the near universal perception that inadequate infrastructural facilities constitute the most serious impediment to India's economic growth, the Planning Commission has mooted a scheme (to be called PCS hereafter) for utilizing United States dollar (USD) 10 billion worth of forex reserves over the next two years for purposes of investment in infrastructure. Under the scheme, the net Reserve Bank credit to the government is to go up by the rupee equivalent of USD 10 billion; the fund will be routed through special purpose vehicles (SPVs) for implementing identified investment projects; and the Reserve Bank will neutralize the monetary impact of its purchase of government securities through sale of foreign currency.[2] Despite its apparent attractiveness PCS has not found favour with a large number of economists

* The paper is a revised version of a lecture delivered at the Annual Conference of the Indian Econometric Society held at Jadavpur University, Calcutta in January 2005.

[1] Which stood at over USD 140 billion in the second week of April 2005.

[2] The fiscal and monetary outcomes are the same whether the fund accrues to SPVs via the government or the Reserve Bank extends credit to them against government guarantee. There is some doubt whether PCS requires investment agencies to execute projects entirely through imports so that the need for RBI's advancing rupee loans along with sale of foreign currency in the market is obviated. However, such operation does not make economic sense since most infrastructural projects are not very import intensive. (Anyway, the decision regarding the optimal way of executing the projects should

and policymakers. The main reservations expressed in this regard are as follows.[3]

First, raising investment expenditure through monetized deficit, it is claimed, will be inflationary since (a) there is as of now very little slack in the economy and (b) a major part of the expenditure is likely to be on non-tradables.

Second, the scheme goes against the spirit of the Fiscal Responsibility and Budget Management Act[4] (FRBMA) and may make the government postpone taking hard decisions for raising the tax–GDP ratio. Be that as it may, the increase in fiscal deficit it is argued will tend to have a growth-debilitating impact by crowding-out private investment.

Third and partly related to the second, the government is not deemed to be the most efficient entity for productive utilization of foreign exchange reserves. For this purpose it is much better to (a) bring down import duties and (b) encourage private investment in infrastructure through institutional and regulatory reforms.

Fourth, PCS, it is widely felt, is fraught with the danger of undermining the country's balance-of-payments viability. The reason is said to be two-fold. The scheme involves use of short-term finance from abroad for long-term investment. This coupled with the fact that infrastructural projects themselves are not 'foreign exchange earners' may well lead to an East-Asia-type currency crisis.

Our examination of the merits of PCS and the arguments advanced by its opponents is based on two open-economy macro-models, one for a neo-classical full employment and the other for a demand-deficient economy. The formal models and the results obtained therefrom are set forth in Appendix 8.1. Since PCS makes much more sense under full employment, in the second section we discuss first the raison d'étre of the scheme in such an economy and provide a critical appraisal of the main concerns of its opponents. However, despite the pick-up in GDP growth over the last two

---

be left to the investors themselves.) The important point to note here is that an increase in domestic absorption (here infrastructural investment) through trade involves a fall in the current account balance and this can come about through a reduction in exports or a rise in imports irrespective of whether the changes are in exports/imports of consumption or investment goods.

[3] For details see Patnaik (2004), Rao (2004), and Virmani (2004). For a somewhat contrarian, still critical view, see Chandrasekhar (2004).

[4] Which prohibits government borrowing from the Reserve Bank from 2006–7 except by way of ways and means advances (WMAs) or under exceptional circumstances. The RBI credit to SPVs under government guarantee can make the budget FRBMA compliant, but will go against its spirit.

years, there is still considerable excess capacity in the Indian economy. Hence, the third section is devoted to an examination of the impact of PCS when the economy operates with some slack. The fourth section extends the analysis of the previous two sections by considering alternative policy options and suggests how PCS requires modifications in some important respects for furthering the objective of growth with fiscal and balance-of-payments viability. The final section concludes.

Planning Commission Scheme (PCS) in a Full-employment Economy

In order to appreciate the motivation behind PCS, consider a neo-classical open economy with full employment of resources. Assume further that:

(a) in the initial situation accumulation of forex reserves exactly matches the net inflow of foreign capital, implying that the country's net exports of goods and services are zero;
(b) it is extremely difficult and costly to raise the tax–GDP ratio or public sector saving;
(c) paucity of infrastructural facilities poses a serious obstacle to private investment and has a dampening impact on productivity of labour and other types of capital; and
(d) the stock of foreign exchange reserves is far in excess of what is required for meeting external shocks.

Given these conditions and the fact that while investment in infrastructure is essential for stepping up growth and the private businessmen are chary of venturing into this area, the solution seems to lie in an increase in the government (or government-supported) investment for removing infrastructural bottlenecks. The problem, however, is that if such investment is financed through market borrowing, the resulting rise in interest rates crowds out private investment; leads to an increase in the general price level;[5] and adds to the burden of public debt. Again, in a full-employment situation monetized financing of the government expenditure does not constitute a policy option: an increase in the money supply causes an equi-proportionate rise in the general price level and leaves the government's command over real resources unaffected.[6]

The important point to note in this connection is that if the tax–GDP ratio cannot be raised and private saving is not very sensitive to changes in

[5] Since an increase in interest rate reduces the demand for money balances so that prices rise even without any increase in money supply.

[6] Government's command over real resources may rise (up to a point) through an increase in the growth rate of money supply, not its one-off increase (Rakshit, 2005).

interest rates, an increase in domestic investment requires recourse to foreign saving through an increase in current account deficit (or a fall in current account surplus). This can be brought about through sale of foreign currency by the central bank[7]: the resulting appreciation of the real exchange rate permits an increase in the domestic investment without a corresponding rise in the domestic saving. But, this on its own does not help extension of infrastructural facilities since the private sector does not find investment in this sector attractive.

The impact of policy instruments considered above indicates the economic rationale behind PCS. The primary objective of the scheme is to effect an increase in infrastructural investment without crowding-out private investment, creating inflationary pressure, or aggravating the fiscal imbalance. Recall that PCS involves an increase in the public (or government-supported) investment through monetized deficit. At the same time, there is an equivalent sale of foreign currency on the part of the Reserve Bank so that money supply remains unchanged. In the benchmark situation[8] (when reserves accretion equals foreign capital inflows to begin with) the impact of PCS will be only on public investment, the real exchange rate, and the current account balance; but prices, interest rates, and hence private investment, remain unaffected. Rigorous derivation of the results for the benchmark (as also for other) situations is given in Part A of the Appendix 8.1. However, since these results do not conform to the perceptions of many Indian analysts, some intuitive explanation may be in order. This we propose to do while examining the main concerns expressed regarding the scheme mooted by the Planning Commission.

Monetized Deficit, Prices and Inflation

Recall that under PCS, despite an increase in monetized deficit, the money supply does not change. Hence, there will be no tendency for prices to rise when the initial current account balance is close to zero. The reason is not far to seek. In the benchmark situation the exchange rate appreciation due to the RBI sale of foreign currency is such that the rise in current account deficit (or the import–export gap) equals the additional public investment and the interest rate remains unaffected. With both money supply and interest rates remaining unchanged, there will be no change in prices either. In fact, when there is a current account surplus to begin with, PCS will tend

[7] Note that the depletion of forex reserves implies a fall in the country's foreign assets and, hence, an increase in the country's net liability to the rest of the world.

[8] Impact of infrastructural investment on private investment demand is also ignored in the benchmark case.

to reduce prices as the exchange rate appreciation and the consequent fall in the current account balance are larger than in the benchmark case[9]: the increase in net imports is larger than the additional public investment so that the commodity market equilibrium requires a fall in interest rates. Similar logic suggests that prices tend to rise when the initial situation is characterized by a current account deficit.

However, it is important to distinguish between a rise in the general price level and inflation. The latter refers to a continuing rise in the price level, not to its one-shot increase in equilibrium following some shock or policy intervention. In the absence of persistent shocks, price increases over time depend primarily on growth rates of the GDP and the money supply. Thus so long as the Reserve Bank's targeted growth rate of money supply remains unchanged, PCS will have no inflationary impact. In fact, larger infrastructural investment (reinforced by crowding-in of private sector capital accumulation) makes the medium-run growth higher and hence the equilibrium inflation rate lower. This also suggests how misplaced is the critics' focus on inflation expectations: rational economic agents would, our analysis implies, expect the inflation rate to go down, not go up!

It is often argued that since many infrastructural projects are relatively labour- and non-tradables-intensive, PCS is likely to cause an increase in prices, especially during the adjustment process, even though prices of tradables fall. The first point to note in this connection is that the major part of additional demand generated through infrastructural projects will be for tradables such as basic consumer goods,[10] steel, cement, and machinery and equipments. An exchange rate appreciation under the PCS, will reduce prices of these goods along with an increase in their imports. Second, it is important to distinguish between a change in relative prices and that in the general price level. Under PCS prices (and production) of non-tradables may rise relatively to that of tradables,[11] but this does not imply an increase in the general price level: under the neo-classical system there is a dichotomy between the determination of relative and absolute prices, with the latter being governed primarily by money supply and 'aggregate output', not its

[9] The fall in current account balance measured in terms of domestic goods and services consists of two parts: (a) a fall in the value of reserves accretion over capital inflows due to an appreciation of the exchange rate; and (b) sale of foreign currency itself. In the benchmark case the first part is zero so that the fall in net exports equals only (b). It is also clear that if initially there is a current account deficit, the increase in the deficit due to PCS will be less than the rise in public investment.

[10] Road projects are no doubt labour-intensive, but additional employment requires an increase in the availability of food, clothing, and other consumption items.

[11] When the production possibility frontier is concave to the origin.

composition. Be that as it may, the result relating to changes in relative prices does not affect our conclusion that the impact of PCS is disinflationary in the medium run irrespective of whether the short-run equilibrium price level goes up or down.[12] The disinflationary effect is magnified or dampened to the extent there is crowding-in or crowding-out of private investment. What is no less important to recognize, prices of exportables will rise relatively to that of importables.

Crowding-in and Crowding-out

Since in the benchmark situation PCS leaves the real rate of interest unaffected, there is no crowding-out of private investment despite full employment and enlargement of fiscal deficit. The reason is that resources for additional public investment are secured directly or indirectly (see footnote 3) from the rest of the world, not the domestic economy: the increase in the country's net imports, as we have already noted, equals the additional investment undertaken by the government. It is also fairly clear that if accumulation of reserves is initially larger than capital inflow, the PCS will have a positive impact on private investment. In this situation, the increase in net imports is in equilibrium larger than that in public investment so that there is a fall in the interest rate and private investment goes up along with some decline in domestic saving.

It is only when capital inflows exceed reserves accretion that PCS can cause crowding-out. However, even in this case, not only is the quantitative significance of crowding-out likely to be small, but there is also a high probability of crowding-in. Low interest elasticity of investment demand prevents a significant fall in private investment when (with an initial current account deficit) the PCS leads to a hardening of interest rates. What is much more important to recognize, the fact that the government is implementing a programme for improvement of infrastructural facilities, should send a positive signal to the business community and tend to raise private investment demand.[13] Hence, the likelihood of short-term crowding-in, contrary to the conventional wisdom.[14]

The debate relating to crowding-in/crowding-out often ignores some fundamental issues. Suppose public infrastructural investment ends up

[12] As we have explained in the preceding sub-section, the price level goes up or down according as the initial current account balance is negative or positive.

[13] Especially for fixed capital, characterized by some gestation lag.

[14] In order not to clutter the algebra, in the formal models in Parts A and B of Appendix 8.1, we have left out the direct impact of infrastructural investment on private investment demand.

reducing private investment through an increase in interest rates. Does it mean that the government should not undertake the investment in such cases? In the context of acute shortage of road, railway network, irrigation, electricity, and other infrastructural facilities, the answer is a resounding 'no'. Note first that to the extent the net marginal productivity to the economy of private and public investment are roughly equal, there is an increase in the growth rate despite the crowding-out, remembering that it is partial. The impact on growth will be positive even in the (unlikely) case of one-for-one crowding-out since the marginal productivity of public investment is higher in view of severe infrastructural bottlenecks prevailing in the economy.

Second, the crowding-out, if any, is a short-run phenomenon; with the rise in the economy's (full employment) production and saving on the completion of infrastructural projects, there will be scope for raising both public and private investment in the medium and the long run. In other words, for judging the merit of a public investment programme, one should not take a myopic view of its impact on private or even aggregate capital accumulation.

Third and related to the second, it is hard to overemphasize the role of infrastructural investment in boosting aggregate supply through a variety of ways. Easy transport and communication, development of market centres, and extension of electricity and irrigation pave the way for productive employment of hitherto unemployed or underutilized resources in remoter parts of the country;[15] enable firms to reduce wastage by adopting just-in-time production process and cutting back on inventory holding;[16] and magnify the gains from international trade and commerce. The important point to note here is that in countries like India, the ratio of infrastructural to other types of capital stocks is significantly below its optimum. In such a situation, for any given level of investible resources, full-employment growth of the economy will be higher for a larger share of infrastructural investment in aggregate capital accumulation.

Public Debt and Fiscal Viability

Government investment under the PCS does involve an enlargement of fiscal deficit[17] and public debt; but contrary to the common belief, this will contribute towards, not erode, budgetary viability in the medium and the long run. In their discussion on fiscal sustainability, most Indian analysts

[15] We shall presently discuss the significance of such 'structural unemployment' in formulation and selection of public investment projects.

[16] This is closely linked with efficient transport, communication, and trading (Rakshit, 1993).

[17] Ignoring the window dressing under which the borrowing is through SPVs under government guarantee.

(following the official procedure) include RBI holding of government bonds in public debt and net RBI credit to the government in fiscal deficit—something which makes their analysis less than satisfactory, if not thoroughly misleading (see, for example, Rangarajan and Srivastava, 2003). As we have argued for umpteen times (Rakshit, 1994, 2000, 2001, 2004, 2005), since the government's interest liability to the RBI stands on a completely different footing from that to private lenders,[18] for analysing the longer term consequences of some budgetary stance it is important to distinguish between the government indebtedness to as well as borrowing from the public and the Reserve Bank.

Given the above perspective, PCS, it is important to note, does not involve any increase in the government debt or interest obligations to the public; the borrowing is entirely from the Reserve Bank so that additional interest payments should find their way back to government coffers by way of extra dividend from the central bank. There is, however, a reduction in RBI (and, hence, government) earnings from the US Treasury Bills and other foreign government securities. But since interest rates on such securities are fairly small in relation to returns on infrastructural investment to both the economy and the government, PCS should raise not only national income but also help in strengthening the government finances.

To see how, consider the benchmark situation where the increase in infrastructural investment equals the fall in forex reserves, that is, there is no crowding-in or crowding-out. Assume further that the marginal productivity of infrastructural investment to the economy is 16 per cent, the direct return to the government is 2 per cent, and the interest rate on foreign government securities 2.5 per cent. With a marginal tax–GDP ratio of 20 per cent, the direct-cum-indirect return to the government totals 5.2 per cent. Since the opportunity cost of infrastructural investment to both the economy and the government approximates the interest foregone on forex reserves,[19] the return to the economy (in terms of the net national product) would be (16.00-2.50) per cent or 13.5 per cent, and that to the government (by way of the incremental net revenue) amounts to (5.20-2.50) per cent or 2.7 per cent. It is also fairly simple to show that the return to the economy and to the government will be larger (smaller) than in the benchmark case when there is some crowding-in (crowding-out), especially through direct impact of public sector capital accumulation on private investment demand.

There are other and no less important routes through which PCS is likely to improve the financial position of the government. As of now, the net RBI

[18] The former constitutes a liability to one of the government's own organs.

[19] Taking the marginal cost of external sector risk (due to the cut-back in forex reserves) to be negligible. We shall turn to such costs if any in the next sub-section.

holding of government securities accounts for a negligible part of reserve money.[20] The sharp fall in its stock of government bonds has already forced the Reserve Bank to adopt, with the concurrence of the government, what is called the market stabilization scheme. Under this scheme the RBI issues on behalf of the government market stabilization bonds (MSBs), the proceeds of which are not available for government expenditure and, hence, constitute a fall in reserve money. Sale of MSBs is not included in the fiscal deficit but their implications for the burden of public debt and future interest payments are no different from that of other government borrowings from the public. Already more than Rs 51,000 crore worth of MSBs have been issued during the current financial year (2004–5), involving about Rs 2,200 crore net revenue loss per year[21] to the government. Under the PCS, RBI holding of government bonds will rise and, hence, enable RBI to discharge its liquidity adjustment function without large-scale issue of MSBs.

The most serious flaw in the arguments of fiscal fundamentalists lies in the neglect of the ways in which stepping up growth through public intervention widens the scope for fiscal correction and contributes towards sustainability of government finances. We have already emphasized how infrastructural investment helps improving the fiscal balance even when the major part of return on such investments does not directly accrue to the government. It is also important to recognize that the difficulties and costs of tax collections and imposing user charges tend to fall with a rise in the per capita income and increasing importance of the organized sector of the economy. Again, even when distortionary or other costs of taxation are slow to come down, an increase in the economy's productive capacity raises the real value of monetized deficit (seignorage) the government can incur (extract) without raising prices or pushing inflation beyond some 'acceptable' rate (Rakshit, 2000, 2001, 2005). Finally, the need for large scale public investment declines over time as government policy initiatives make the ratio of infrastructural to total capital stock approach its optimum level. Given the impact of infrastructural investment on the time profile of the government's revenue (including seignorage) receipts on the one hand and its expenditure requirement on the other, preoccupation with short-term fiscal deficit without any reference to the longer term implications of the underlying budgetary programme verges on 'fiscal fetishism' (Rakshit, 2004, 2005).

[20] Thus on January 28, 2005 the RBI holding of government securities amounted to only Rs 13,530 crore, but net foreign exchange reserves were a whopping Rs 5,61,595 crore.

[21] Taking the interest differential between GOI securities and the US Treasury Bills to be about 4.5 per cent.

Balance-of-payments

Critics have drawn attention to two main reasons why depletion of foreign exchange reserves under PCS is likely to have adverse balance-of-payments consequences and make the economy susceptible to an East Asia-type currency crisis. First, the counterpart of the country's external assets in the form of foreign currency reserves is said to be its short-term liabilities (or accumulated net capital inflows) to (from) the rest of the world. Hence, reduction of reserves along with an increase in infrastructural investment tends to produce a liquidity mismatch in the country's asset–liability structure: under PCS while the liability side remains unchanged, on the asset side there is a substitution of long-term, highly illiquid capital stocks for easily marketable foreign government bonds. Second, returns on infrastructural capital are in terms of domestic, not foreign currency, so that on this score also the country's balance-of-payments position becomes vulnerable to external shocks. Such apprehensions are sought to be supported by the fact that use of relatively short-term external loans for financing real estate investment in countries like Thailand played an important role in aggravating if not triggering off the 1997–8 Asian currency crisis.

Note, however, that India's external sector asset–liability position is radically different from that prevailing in the crisis countries in 1996–7. In mid-2004, the country's short-term external debt accounted for only 5.2 per cent of the total debt and was no more than 4.9 per cent of the forex reserves (Reserve Bank of India, 2004). In fact, forex reserves exceed the country's total debt by nearly 10 per cent. A substantial part of the country's external liability, it is true, consists of accumulated foreign institutional investments (FIIs). However, for such items the liability is in terms of rupee, not foreign currency so that the exchange rate risk is borne by foreign investors. Even so, since FIIs are liquid and easily reversible, they do constitute a source of balance-of-payments vulnerability (Rakshit, 2002, 2003). But even on this score India's position is quite comfortable: aggregate short-term debt and non-debt reversible liabilities are only about one-third of foreign exchange reserves. Remembering that the PCS involves a reduction of reserves of only USD 10 billion, there appears little reason for being worried on grounds of liquidity mismatch.

Again, the argument that infrastructural projects are not foreign exchange earners ignores some fundamental economic principles. First, what is relevant for balance-of-payments viability is the impact of the overall investment package on productivity of the tradable sector. The fact that foreign currency reserves are reduced in the process of raising infrastructural investment should be of no concern so long as public and private investments taken together sharpen the tradables' competitive edge in the international market.

In the context of the near universal perception among entrepreneurs that poor infrastructural facilities constitute the most serious impediment to raising the country's export, PCS cannot be faulted on the ground that infrastructural services (themselves) are not exported.

Second and more fundamental, the touchstone of any investment project is its net contribution to the country's consumables directly or through exports. The implication is that though there is no improvement in productivity of the country's tradable sector due to a project, its external financing may still be justified. Thus projects for extension of basic health services and provision of drinking water may raise productivity in the non-tradable relatively to that in the tradable sector. In such cases servicing of external debt requires a decline in the country's consumption of tradables for generation of an export surplus. Even so such projects are often worth undertaking because there is generally a net gain to the economy after allowing for the welfare loss on account of the cut-back in consumption of tradables.

Third, for the tradable sector, the role of infrastructural investment lies in raising the efficiency of resource use rather than providing special thrust to some specific exportables. Improvement in ports, transport, telecommunications, information network, and supply of electricity generally changes both the volume and pattern of exports and imports and enables a country to take fuller advantage of international trade and commerce. The part the State has to play in this regard consists in ensuring easy availability of infrastructural facilities and leaving it to entrepreneurs to decide whether or how much to invest in particular exportables or importables on the basis of their production costs and prospective prices in the international market.

Finally, enlargement of opportunities for profitable investment in the domestic economy constitutes the most effective bulwark against balance-of-payments shocks. The experience of China and other East Asian economies suggests how large-scale infrastructural investment (along with rapid human resource development) provides a boost to other types of capital formation, draws in a torrent of FDI, makes exports highly competitive in the world market and, what is crucial, enables producers to adjust quickly to changing demand and supply conditions in the international market.

PCS in a Demand-constrained Economy

There are two important reasons why it is necessary to consider the consequences of PCS when the economy is characterized by an output gap. First, though India's growth rate has picked up over the last two years, the slack still remaining in the economy is by no means insignificant. Second, even when the economy initially enjoys full employment of resources, some policy interventions, as we shall discuss in the next section, can cause a contractionary impact in the short and medium run—an impact which is similar to that in a demand-deficient economy.

Our analysis of the effects of PCS in the presence of an output gap is based on an open economy aggregate demand–aggregate supply (AD–AS) model. The formal model and its results are presented in Part B of Appendix 8.1. In the text we provide an intuitive explanation of the effects and suggest some extensions considered relevant for the Indian economy as of now.

Recall that PCS involves two policy instruments: (a) an increase in public investment financed through monetized deficit; and (b) an equivalent sale of foreign currency by the central bank (leaving the money supply unaffected). The first gives rise to an expansionary process, causing an increase in income and a depreciation of the exchange rate.[22] The equilibrium increase in income, as is to be expected in a demand-constrained situation, is a multiple of the incremental investment.[23] At the same time since an increase in income tends to push up interest rates (along with prices) and widen the import–export gap, private investment falls and the exchange rate depreciates. With an initial zero current account balance, there is, however, no change in net imports in equilibrium: depreciation of the exchange rate prevents the incipient fall in the trade balance.

Consider now the macroeconomic consequences of a sale of foreign currency by the central bank. The immediate impact of the sale is to cause an exchange rate appreciation and, hence, a fall in the country's net exports—something which sets in motion a negative multiplier process. As in the case of a change in public investment, in this case also the equilibrium change (fall) in income will equal the initial (or first round) reduction in net exports[24] times the multiplier. The fall in income, it is fairly easy to see, is

[22] Remembering that an increase in income raises imports and, hence, demand for foreign currency.

[23] The multiplier under the open-economy AD–AS system is, however, different from that in the simple model. The former tends to be smaller than the latter to the extent the rise in interest rates (due to an increase in income and prices) produces some crowding-out effect of private consumption and investment. But since the expansionary process also effects a depreciation of the exchange rate the fall in net exports tends to be smaller and the multiplier larger than in the textbook model. Recall that in the simple Keynesian model the exchange rate is taken to be fixed so that the leakage from the domestic income stream to the rest of the world (due to a unit increase in income) is nothing but the marginal propensity to import. Under a flexible exchange rate regime, the leakage is less since currency depreciation tends to raise net exports. In fact, as we shall presently see, the marginal leakage can even be negative, implying a higher multiplier in an open than in a closed economy!

[24] Due entirely to the exchange rate appreciation (at the initial income level) following the central bank sale of foreign currency. The adjective 'initial' or 'first round' is used only in this sense and does not have a temporal (or real time) connotation.

accompanied with an appreciation of the exchange rate, a decline in prices and interest rates, an increase in private investment,[25] and an improvement in the current account balance.

Given the fact that the macroeconomic effects of an increase in public investment and of a reduction in foreign exchange reserves are in the opposite direction, the consequences of PCS are not completely unambiguous. However, the results are straightforward and similar to those under the full-employment model when initially accretion of forex reserves exactly matches capital inflows: GDP remains unchanged and so do prices, interest rates, and private investment;[26] only the exchange rate appreciates and the consequent fall in net exports equals the increase in public investment.

As under the full-employment situation, the results tend to be different when initially accumulation of reserves exceeds or falls short of the capital account balance: the net effect of PCS will be contractionary in the former and expansionary in the latter situation.[27] The consequences for the interest rate, prices, and private investment are immediate once we know the impact of PCS on the gross domestic product. When the impact is expansionary, prices and interest rates rise, and private investment tends to fall. The effects are the opposite when PCS aggravates the problem of demand deficiency.

Before we examine more closely (in the fourth section) the suitability of PCS for the Indian economy as of now, it is important to indicate the implications of two factors, which though highly relevant in the Indian context do not figure in the orthodox AD–AS model. One is the direct, positive

[25] Note that the fall in income makes the equilibrium exchange rate appreciation less than the initial fall when production and income were yet to adjust. Under the conventional AD–AS model (where private investment depends only on the interest rate), the result relating to the rise in private investment is unambiguous.

[26] Abstracting from the direct impact of infrastructural investment on the private propensity to invest.

[27] The simplest way of appreciating the sources of these differences in outcome is to consider the first round impact on demand of an increase in public investment and of an equivalent reduction in forex reserves (measured in terms of domestic output). So far as public investment is concerned, the impact is direct and unambiguous: the rise in aggregate demand equals that in investment. The first round impact of the sale of foreign currency is indirect and operates through a fall in net exports due to exchange rate appreciation (with no change in adjustment in production and income as yet). Our earlier analysis of the effect on exchange rate under full-employment conditions suggests that the first round fall in net exports is greater than, equal to, or less that the sale of foreign currency according as reserves accumulation is larger than, equal to, or less than the quantum of foreign capital inflow. Thus the impact of PCS on income and employment will be neutral, expansionary, or contractionary according as the initial current account balance is zero, positive, or negative (remembering that the current account balance equals the difference between the reserves accretion and the capital account balance).

impact of infrastructural capital accumulation on private investment demand—something whose economic rationale we have already noted in the previous section. The other is the role of capacity utilization and profits in governing private investment. An increase in capacity utilization and in profits go hand-in-hand in a demand-constrained economy, and produce a positive impact on business expectations. No less important under highly imperfect capital market conditions is the fact that larger profits provide greater scope for self-financing of investment and make it easier for firms to raise funds by way of loan or equity capital.

The implication of the second factor is that (in the short run) private investment is positively related to the gross domestic product. Hence, the value of the multiplier in this case is larger than in the canonical AD–AS model. This, however, is a double-edged sword. When PCS is otherwise expansionary, not only is the effect magnified, but despite the increase in interest rates there may be crowding-in of private investment. However, when the economy has been running a current account deficit, the fall in GDP due to the PCS becomes larger and private investment may go down even though interest rates decline.

When private capital accumulation is positively related to the infrastructural investment, the multiplier remains the same, but there is an increase in the first-round aggregate demand due to public capital expenditure under PCS. Hence, not only does income rise when the current account balance is positive or zero to begin with, but even in the case of an initial current account deficit the result may be expansionary. Needless to say, in this situation PCS will tend to have a favourable effect on private investment.

An Alternative Policy Programme (APP)

Our analysis in the second and third sections suggests that there is little merit in the arguments relating to the adverse consequences of PCS by way of inflation, crowding-out, fiscal fragility, or balance-of-payments difficulties. But this does not mean that the scheme constitutes the best policy option as of now or that all its effects are salubrious for the economy. Indeed, not only is PCS inappropriate in the context of prevailing excess capacity, but for stepping up the country's medium- and long-term growth potential, the scheme requires drastic modification even after the output gap has been eliminated.

Policy Options in a Demand-deficient Economy

Recall that in the benchmark case PCS does not raise aggregate demand so that there is no increase in income and employment. There is, to be sure, an increase in investment, but its financing involves an avoidable cost to the economy. Since additional investment equals the rise in current account deficit, there is an increase in net external liability of the country (which is what the fall in forex reserves implies). However, in the presence of underutilized capacity it does not make sense from the viewpoint of the *economy as a whole* to rely on foreign resources for raising domestic investment: while the marginal opportunity costs of domestic resources are zero, an increase in net imports entails a diminution of the country's future national income[28] (Rakshit, 2003). The loss to the economy is larger when (with the country running a current account surplus) PCS (through a sharp exchange rate appreciation) aggravates the problem of demand deficiency and leads to a fall in output and employment. Even if the net effect of PCS is expansionary there is still an increase in the country's net external liability in bridging the investment–saving gap—something which does not constitute an optimum when there are unemployed or underemployed resources.

Given the huge infrastructural requirement for realizing the growth potential of the economy, presence of an output gap provides an opportunity for making up the shortfall without creating inflationary pressure, eroding fiscal viability, or storing up balance-of-payments problems for the future. As we have explained elsewhere (Rakshit, 2003), the basic policy package under this condition consists of an increase in infrastructural investment financed through net RBI credit to the government. The resulting increase in money supply prevents hardening of interest rates and helps crowding-in as private investment demand rises with an increase in capacity utilization and profits, and expectations of an early removal of infrastructural bottlenecks. Government finances are strengthened since (a) additional tax collections and PSU dividends cause a fall in short–run revenue deficit both in absolute terms and as a proportion of GDP; (b) borrowing from the Reserve Bank does not raise the government's debt or interest burden; and (c) a step-up in public and private investment boosts revenue receipts in the medium and the long run.

So far as the balance-of-payments position is concerned, net imports will tend to rise along with income; but if the rupee is allowed to depreciate, there is no need for an increase in current account deficit or a reduction in forex reserves: as we have argued earlier, a sale of foreign currency (or a rise in the country's net liability to the rest of the world) is not required in the presence of an output gap. The main problem with letting the exchange rate fall is that too sharp a depreciation may have a disruptive impact on trade and relative prices, and may affect resource allocation not in line with the country's

[28] Under PCS, the diminution consists in the foregone interest earnings on forex reserves.

longer-term comparative advantage. Hence, despite demand deficiency the Reserve Bank may have to sell foreign currency in order to moderate the fall in the exchange rate. However, even when the RBI intervention keeps the exchange rate unaffected, the reduction in forex reserves will be a fraction of the additional investment undertaken by the government.[29] The implication is that the net RBI credit to the government will be larger than the sale of foreign currency so that money supply goes up.

The important thing to note in the context of demand deficiency is that high power money, public investment, and the RBI sale of foreign currency are all independent policy instruments and can generally be manipulated to attain the three targets, viz., the output gap, the exchange rate, and the interest rate. Thus if the authorities want to close the output gap with no change in the exchange rate and the interest rate (to guard against crowding-out), the macroeconomic relations in the system give the required combination of the three instruments and their impact on government finances. To illustrate, take the multiplier to be 2.5 when through open-market operations along with an intervention in the foreign currency market, the Reserve Bank keeps the interest and exchange rates within narrow bands.[30] Let us take the marginal revenue collection,[31] the demand for reserve money and for import[32] with respect to an increase in the GDP to be roughly the same as their average values, viz., 0.2, 0.16, and 0.18, respectively. For a unit increase in the public investment (with no direct effect on private capital accumulation) there will then be an increase in the government revenue by 0.5; in the reserve money by 0.4; and in the net imports by 0.45 unit. The conventionally measured fiscal deficit[33] per unit increase in public investment is thus 1.0-0.5 unit or 0.5 unit. Since the RBI lending to the government can go up by 0.45 without any increase in the reserve money,[34] meeting the fiscal deficit through central bank finance involves an increase in the reserve money by 0.05 unit. However, the increase in reserve money required to meet its

[29] Remembering that the marginal propensity to import is a part (and a relatively small part in India) of the marginal leakage from the domestic income stream.

[30] For this purpose the Reserve Bank will have to raise the supply of reserve money and sell foreign exchange as demand and production go up in the process of working out of the multiplier. Note that keeping the interest rate unchanged prevents crowding-out and, hence, enlarges the expansionary effect; but the policy of not allowing the exchange rate to depreciate (as demand for imports goes up) has an opposite effect.

[31] Including both tax and non-tax revenue, the latter also being positively related to GDP.

[32] Of both goods and services.

[33] Defined as the difference between total government expenditure and non-debt creating receipts which in this case consist only of revenue receipts.

[34] The RBI sale of foreign currency being 0.45 for keeping the exchange rate unaffected.

additional demand (for price stability) being 0.4, the Reserve Bank also needs to buy 0.4-0.05 unit or 0.35 unit of government security (hitherto) held by the public.

In order to appreciate the fiscal implications of the scheme outlined above, note first that a fall in the outstanding government liability to the public[35] by 0.35 unit entails a reduction in the government's interest outgo by nearly 0.0228 unit, taking the interest rate on government securities to be 6.5 per cent. Again, with a 4 per cent interest differential between the GOI securities and foreign Treasury Bills, a sale of 0.45 unit of foreign currency raises the RBI's net earning and, hence, government revenue by 0.018 unit. Thus the yearly net revenue gain of the government, exclusive of the increase in the revenue arising from the supply-side impact of infrastructural capital accumulation, amounts to (0.00228+0.018) × 100 or 4.08 per cent of such investment. Assuming user charges cum incremental revenue from additional output (due to the increase in capital stock) to be a modest 5.5 per cent of infrastructural investment, the overall net return amounts to a substantial 9.58 per cent. Incurring fiscal deficit in funding infrastructural investment thus turns out to be not only growth promoting, but a most potent means of fiscal correction!

Let us indicate the absolute magnitudes of the additional public investment and other variables under the programme suggested above. With a 81.5 per cent capacity utilization in industries and none-too-insignificant slack in the services sector, a conservative estimate of the country's overall output gap would be 15 per cent.[36] From the advance estimate of GDP at market prices (at Rs 31,08,561 crore) for 2004–5, the output gap[37] may thus be put at nearly Rs 5,59,500 crore. For closing the gap infrastructural investment can be raised by (Rs 5,59,500 crore ÷ 2.5) or Rs 2,23,800 crore—a figure which is ten times the first year's investment (at USD 5 billion) under PCS. The RBI sale of foreign currency will also be larger[38] at USD 22.89 billion or Rs 1,00,710 crore. The magnitude of reduction in forex reserve should not, however, be a cause of concern since not only does the reserves depletion help in raising the gross national product[39] and reducing

[35] This equals the official measure of public debt less government securities held by the Reserve Bank.

[36] With an 80 per cent capacity utilization in industry and services taken together, and no short-term slack in agriculture, the output gap is 15.6 per cent when agriculture's share in GDP approximates 22 per cent.

[37] With an estimated output gap at 15 per cent of 'full employment' GDP, the gap amounts to 18 per cent of the actual or realized GDP.

[38] Taking the marginal propensity to import to be 18 per cent.

[39] Since the return on infrastructural investment is higher than that on foreign bonds held by the Reserve Bank (Rakshit, 2003).

quasi-fiscal costs,[40] but the current foreign exchange reserves (of around USD 142 billion) are substantially larger than the amount needed to guard against external shocks: given India's debt profile and the pattern of trade, the probability that the Reserve Bank will find it difficult to manage the country's balance-of-payments with a forex reserve of about USD 120 billion appears extremely low. Note also that for keeping the interest rate unaffected, it is necessary to raise the reserve money by (5,59,500 × 0.16) or Rs 89,520 crore so that the RBI holding of GOI securities goes up by (1,00,710 + 89,520) or Rs 1,90,230 crore. This has two important implications. First, the Reserve Bank's ability to conduct open-market operations and sterilize sudden surges of capital inflows without issuing MSBs will be greatly enhanced.

Second, with an increase in tax collections by (5,59,500 × 0.2) or Rs 1,11,900 crore, even after financing the entire increase in government investment the Reserve Bank will have to buy from the market GOI securities worth (1,90,230-1,11,900) or Rs 78,330 crore so that there is a considerable diminution of the government's liability and interest obligations to the public. The main significance of the scheme lies in effecting an enduring improvement in the investment climate and budgetary balance. The short-term impact of APP on the government budget consists in a substantial reduction of revenue deficit both in absolute terms and as a ratio of GDP: while additional revenue collections make the deficit lower by Rs 1,11,900 crore, as a ratio[41] of GDP it comes down to 0.7 per cent compared with 4.5 per cent in the financial year 2004–5. The impact may not appear salubrious so far as the fiscal deficit is concerned: the deficit increases[42] by Rs 1,11,900 to 11.6 per cent of GDP from 8.9 per cent in 2004–5. However, this sharp rise in fiscal deficit is in fact conducive to the viability of government finances in the medium run. Under the scheme, the government's net yearly revenue gain exclusive of direct and indirect returns from infrastructural projects will amount to (Rs 2,23,800 × 0.0408) or Rs 9,131 crore at 2004–5 prices. When these returns are taken into account, the figure jumps to (Rs 223,800 × 0.0958) or Rs 21,440 crore, that is, nearly 0.7 per cent of the 2004–5 GDP. The present value of this yearly net revenue gain, taking the interest rate (or rather the government's borrowing rate) to be 6.5 per cent, totals a whopping Rs 3,14,620 crore or more than 10 per cent of current

[40] The quasi-fiscal cost refers to the cost the government incurs on account of the RBI holding currency assets at the expense of GOI securities. See Rakshit (2003) for details relating to quasi-fiscal and other costs of holding large forex reserves.

[41] The ratio falls because of a rise in both revenue receipts and GDP.

[42] Because of the values of the multiplier (2.5) and the marginal revenue receipts (0.2), the increase in revenue and the rise in fiscal deficit happen to be the same.

GDP. To put the matter in a different manner, the scheme will reduce the ratio of the effective government liability to GDP by at least 10 percentage points. Add to that the effects on GDP and the fisc operating through (short- and long-term) crowding-in, increase in FDI, enlarged scope for (non-inflationary) seignorage,[43] and other supply-side forces set in motion by infrastructural investment, and the case for a policy package akin to APP cannot seriously be in doubt.

Before considering issues related to framing and implementation of APP let us note how some of its features (and outcomes) are markedly different from those of PCS. Under the former the magnitude of both public investment and reserves depletion are much larger and differ significantly from one another: compared with the PCS figure of USD 5 billion for infrastructural investment as well as for sale of forex reserves in the first year of the programme, the corresponding figures under APP are USD 51 billion and USD 23 billion, respectively. Second, APP (unlike PCS) does not involve any appreciation of the exchange rate even while the import–export gap widens by USD 23 billion. Third, money supply (and prices) remains unchanged under PCS; but with the net RBI credit to the government exceeding reduction in reserves by Rs 89,520 crore under APP, money supply goes up substantially (even though this does not cause any rise in prices). Fourth, while PCS is not designed to augment capacity utilization, the thrust of APP is on closing the output gap without creating a pressure on the price level or the exchange rate.

It is the last difference which, we emphasize, is central, and the others are closely related to it. It is not very difficult to see that the first three differences are due to a specific policy package which may not be necessarily optimum. Thus APP presumes that changes in interest rates and exchange rates (which affect private investment and current account deficit) from their current levels will be deleterious for the economy—a presumption which is by no means certain. More generally, since the policy instruments at the disposal of the authorities are public investment, the magnitude of sale of foreign currency, and the net RBI credit to the government,[44] while closing the output gap the government, *a la* the Tinbergen principle (Tinbergen, 1952), can still choose any two of the following targets: private investment, the current account deficit, and the price level.

[43] See Rakshit (2005).

[44] We have ignored taxes as a macro policy instrument not only since the government has repeatedly failed to attain the targeted tax–GDP ratio, but also because stability of tax rates is considered desirable. Note also that policies relating to sale of foreign exchange and net RBI credit to the government together give the change in reserve money so that it is not a separate policy instrument.

To illustrate, assume that the authorities are averse to depletion of forex reserves as well as to crowding-out of private investment. The implications of such preferences are fairly straightforward. In the absence of the RBI intervention in the foreign currency market, the exchange rate has to depreciate in response to an increase in income so that there is no change in the current account balance. Again, in order to keep private investment unaffected, interest rates have to be kept unchanged. Given the (estimated) values of the multiplier (with no crowding-out and no leakage from the domestic income stream by way an increase in net imports), the output gap, and incremental demand for reserve money with respect to an increase in income, the values of variables such as increases in public investment, budget deficit, and the net central bank credit to the government are then immediate. Thus let the multiplier[45] be 3, the incremental revenue–GDP ratio be 0.2, and the marginal demand for reserve money be 0.16. The additional infrastructural investment that eliminates the output gap is then (Rs 5,59,500 crore÷3) or Rs 1,86,500 crore. Since this raises government revenue by (Rs 5,59,500 crore × 0.2) or Rs 1,11,900 crore, the conventionally measured fiscal deficit goes up[46] by (Rs 1,86,500 crore-Rs 1,11,900 crore) or Rs 74,600 crore. Note, however, that since for avoiding crowding-out of private investment reserve money needs to go up by (Rs 5,59,500 crore × 0.16) or Rs 89,520 crore, not only is the entire fiscal deficit financed through borrowing from the central bank, but the RBI has to buy an additional Rs 14,920 crore worth of government securities. It is also not very difficult to see that if an increase in private investment is deemed desirable (without any depletion of forex reserves), the increase in reserve money has to be larger[47] and that in public investment smaller. Hence emerges the importance of evaluation of the relative returns on the two types of investment from the viewpoint of the economy as a whole. Our earlier illustration (under APP) also suggests that a reduction in forex reserves permits (through a widening of the import–export gap) an increase in aggregate investment, public or private. But such policy combinations are more appropriate when there is no longer any output gap.

Policy Options under Full Employment

As we have already noted, the PCS is framed under the presumption that the economy is supply, not demand, constrained. However, even under these

[45] Note that the multiplier is larger than in the previous exercise since the exchange rate depreciation eliminates the incipient current account deficit.

[46] Note, however, that the revenue deficit goes down by Rs 1,11,900 crore which is close to 3.5 per cent of gross domestic product.

[47] So as to bring down the interest rate for stimulating private investment.

conditions the size as well as the overall approach of the programme seems to require substantial revision. First, given the vast scope for productive investment in infrastructure, the figures suggested by the Planning Commission appear quite inadequate. The main problem in this respect seems to lie in framing and prioritizing investment projects—something which the Planning Commission should urgently undertake on a continuing basis.

Second, there is no reason why the step-up in infrastructural investment should be tied to the release of foreign exchange. Though the amount spent on new infrastructural projects may in equilibrium equal the RBI sale of forex reserves for additional imports,[48] imports of foreign goods and services are likely to constitute only a fraction of the total expenditure on the projects. Again, the main role of infrastructural investments, it is universally recognized, lies in facilitating private investment. Hence, for reaping the full benefit from the projects, release of foreign exchange should be related to their potential crowding-in effect; otherwise the effect will fail to materialize, with an increase in the interest rate choking off additional private investment demand[49] (see Part A of Appendix 8.1). Given the huge 'excess' reserves being held by the Reserve Bank, sale of foreign exchange for supporting both infrastructural projects and the additional investment demand resulting therefrom appears eminently sensible from the viewpoint of raising the gross national product and strengthening the government's budgetary balance. To illustrate, let the increase in (short-term) private investment demand due to infrastructural projects be 100 units; the RBI's (additional) sale of foreign currency balanced by purchase of government securities from the market of the same magnitude; and the marginal returns on private investment, foreign exchange reserves, and government securities be 15 per cent, 2.5 per cent, and 6.5 per cent, respectively. The resulting increase in gross national product (GNP) is then (15.0-2.5) or 12.5 units; and in net government revenue (6.5-2.5) or 4 units, exclusive of the tax revenue from additional GNP accruing to the private sector.[50]

Third, the above line of reasoning suggests a more fundamental flaw in schemes like PCS which do not form an integral part of an overall budgetary and planning programme. Such schemes are then likely to be sub-optimal and liable to be treated as appendages to the main policy package (as happened to PCS in the 2005–6 budget proposals). Given the close connection between the monetary, fiscal, and exchange rate policies, it is difficult to

[48] Or for bridging the (equilibrium) import–export gap, to be more accurate.

[49] Remembering that saving is not very sensitive to changes in interest rates.

[50] Note that the increase in GNP is estimated by taking the opportunity cost of sale of foreign exchange (which reflects the rise in the country's net liability to the rest of the world) to be 2.5 per cent.

overemphasize the need for eschewing piecemeal measures and ensuring that, under the constraints faced by the economy and given the nature of interdependence among its major sectors, the policy programme needs to be framed on the basis of the basic economic and social objectives it is expected to promote.

Finally, in view of the leads and lags or differences in rapidity of adjustment of production, prices, the exchange rate, and other variables in the system, sequencing or phasing of measures assumes enormous importance. To see why, let us grant that the economy is indeed supply constrained and that PCS is optimal. Consider now the following process of implementation of the scheme. The Reserve Bank sells USD 5 billion and extends an equivalent amount of (rupee) loan for infrastructural investment. Even if the investment projects are taken up immediately, the adjustment process (in its initial stages) is likely to be characterized by a fall in output and employment. The reason is that since the foreign currency market clears almost instantaneously, while the (Keynesian) multiplier takes time to work out, the contractionary effect of appreciation of the exchange rate will tend to dominate. Note also that the initial rate of appreciation (with practically no change in the country's demand for importables) will be higher than in the new equilibrium (when the demand generation impact of investment has spilled over to the external sector). Hence, the contractionary phase can last for quite some time and the adjustment process is likely to be cyclical. Thus while the authorities need to estimate the optimal levels of investment, reserves depletion, or net RBI credit to the government, no less important for smoothening the adjustment process are proper phasing of policy instruments and their adjustments over time to evolving conditions in the commodity, financial, and foreign currency markets.

Summary and Conclusion

(a) The Planning Commission Scheme (PCS) for using USD 10 billion worth of foreign exchange reserves for investment in infrastructure has met with strong opposition from an overwhelming majority of Indian economists. The main concern of the critics centres round (a) the inflationary potential of the scheme; (b) the enlargement of fiscal deficit causing crowding-out of private investment and an increase in the already onerous burden of public debt; and (c) the weakening of the balance-of-payments position or shock absorptive capacity of the country. A close scrutiny of the macro linkages of the Indian economy suggests, however, that contrary to the critics' concerns PCS is likely to raise private investment and rein in inflationary tendencies. Again, although the scheme involves an increase in the conventionally measured fiscal deficit and public debt, through a decline in the quasi-fiscal cost of forex holdings and an increase in the tax-cum-non-tax revenue generated directly and indirectly through infrastructural investment, PCS will in fact tend to reduce the burden of public debt and contribute toward fiscal viability. Finally, apart from the fact that the RBI holding of forex reserves is far in excess of what is required as a cushion against external shocks, removal of infrastructural bottlenecks, it cannot be sufficiently emphasized, constitutes a most potent means of raising export competitiveness and making the country an attractive destination of FDI.

(b) In the presence of a near 15 per cent output gap in the Indian economy as of now, PCS requires drastic modifications in more ways than one. First, the projected increase in infrastructural investment is paltry in relation to not only the scope for (or 'need' of) such investment, but also the amount required to close the output gap. Again, underutilization of capacity also implies that for stepping up infrastructural investment it is neither necessary to raise net imports (through depletion of forex reserves) nor does the government need to borrow from the public for financing new projects: extension of net Reserve Bank credit to the government in support of infrastructural investment will, apart from promoting growth and strengthening government finances, also help the central bank in managing capital flows.

(c) Only when there is no slack in the economy does reduction in reserves (or foreign borrowing) become necessary for stepping up domestic capital accumulation. However, even after the output gap has been eliminated, a much bolder investment programme than what has been mooted by the Planning Commission appears essential for bridging the infrastructural gap. Again, since removal of infrastructural bottlenecks tends to raise productivity of private investment, the optimal reduction in forex reserves will be more than the increase in public investment.

(d) While public infrastructural investment, net RBI credit to government, and depletion of forex reserves have to form integral parts of an overall policy package, from an operational viewpoint it is not generally desirable that they are strictly tied with one another and implemented at one go. The reason is that while adjustment in the forex market is near instantaneous, implementation of investment projects and adjustments in the commodity market involve some time lag. Hence arises the need for phasing of investment projects, sale of foreign currency, and changes in net RBI credit to the government such that transition to the new, high-investment–high-growth equilibrium is relatively smooth, not bedevilled by sharp fluctuations or large over/undershooting of major economic variables.

References

Chandrasekhar, C.P. (2004), 'Beyond the Forex Proposal', *Economic and Political Weekly*, 39(52), 5563–5, 25 December.

Lal, D., S. Bery, and D.K. Pant (2003), 'The Real Exchange Rate, Fiscal Deficits and Capital Flows: India 1981–2000', *Economic and Political Weekly*, 38(47), 4965–76, 22 November.

Patnaik, P. (2004), 'On Financing Infrastructure on the Strength of Reserves', *Economic and Political Weekly*, 39(52), 5565–7, 25 December.

Rakshit, M. (1993), *Trade, Mercantile Capital and Economic Development* (R.C. Dutt Lecture on Political Economy), Orient Longman, Hyderabad.

——— (1994), 'Issues in Structural Adjustment of the Indian Economy', in Edmar L. Bacha (ed.), *Economics in a Changing World: Development, Trade and Environment*, Macmillan, London.

——— (2000), 'On Correcting Fiscal Imbalances in the Indian Economy: Some Perspectives', *Money & Finance*, 2(2), 19–58, July–September.

——— (2001), 'Contentious Issues in Fiscal Policy: A Suggested Resolution', *Money and Finance*, 2(7), 23–60, October–December.

——— (2002), *The East Asian Currency Crisis,* Oxford University Press, New Delhi.

——— (2003), 'External Capital Flows and Foreign Exchange Reserves: Some Macroeconomic Implications and Policy Issues', *Money & Finance*, 2(13–14), 63–95, April–September.

——— (2004), 'Some Macroeconomics of India's Reform Experience', in K. Basu (ed.), *India's Emerging Economy: Performance and Prospects in the 1990s and Beyond*, MIT Press, Cambridge, Massachusetts.

——— (2005), 'Budget Deficit: Sustainability, Solvency and Optimality', in A. Bagchi (ed.), *Readings in Public Finance*, Oxford University Press, New Delhi.

——— (2005a), 'Budgetary Policy Making in India ', *Money & Finance*, 2(20–21), 45–64, January–June.

Rangarajan, C. and D.K. Srivastava (2003), 'Dynamics of Debt Accumulation in India: Impact of Primary Deficit, Growth and Interest Rate', *Economic and Political Weekly*, 38(46), 4851–8, 15 November.

Rao, M.G. (2004), 'Forex and Infrastructure', *Business Standard*, 16 November.

Reserve Bank of India (2004), *Annual Report 2003–04*, Mumbai.

Tinbergen, J. (1952), *On the Theory of Economic Policy*, North-Holland Publishing Co., Amsterdam.

Virmani, A. (2004), 'Need for a Hybrid Proposal', *Economic and Political Weekly*, 39(52), 5559–62, 25 December.

Appendix 8.1

The analysis and policy conclusions in the text are based primarily on two open-economy macro models, the first for a (neo-classical) full employment and the second for a demand-deficient economy. Both models are fairly standard, though the assumptions relating to the foreign exchange market are somewhat hybrid. In consonance with the prevailing exchange rate regime in India, it is assumed that the rupee is fully current account convertible and on a dirty float, but capital movements are not fully free. For simplicity of exposition without losing any essential element for the policy debate we assume that given the regulations in force, net capital inflow (or outflow) is exogenous or amenable to control by the authorities.[51]

Part A: An Open Economy Full-employment Model

Consider a neo-classical model characterized by the following equilibrium conditions:

$$S[r;\overline{Y},G,T]-[I^{v}(r)+I^{b}]=NX(e;\overline{Y},Y_{f}), \tag{A.1}$$

$$NX(e;\overline{Y},Y_{f})=e(X-F), \tag{A.2}$$

[51] Under the regulations currently in force, capital account transactions of residents are restricted and of a minor order, but changes in domestic and international economic environment affect foreign capital inflows and outflows. Out of the three principal components of foreign capital, non-resident Indian (NRI) deposits, foreign direct investment (FDI), and foreign institutional investment (FII), the interest differential seems to affect mostly the first; however, in their case the terms of and interest on the deposits are adjusted by the Reserve Bank with a view to keeping their magnitude at some 'desirable level'. FDI is determined primarily by the foreign investors' perception of long-term fundamentals rather than by short-term behaviour of the economy. FII constitutes the largest and most volatile component of foreign capital. Such inflows are mostly governed by (and in their turn affect) the short-term behaviour of the stock market rather than by the interest rate per se. This makes their modelling in a macroeconomic framework quite tricky. Hence, we take the simple way out and consider capital flows as exogenous or a target variable. In order not to distract attention from the main theme of the paper we do not go into the problem of what should be the target or how it is to be attained—something which involves issues relating to the of appropriate exchange rate regime. See, however, Rakshit (2002).

$$\frac{M}{P} = L(r + \Pi^e; \bar{Y}), \tag{A.3}$$

where S is the aggregate saving; $\bar{Y}$ the full-employment output; G the government consumption; T the taxes less transfers; I^v the private investment; r the real rate of interest; I^b the government investment; NX the net exports; e the real exchange rate;[52] Y_f the foreign income; X the accumulation of foreign exchange reserves; F the net inflow of foreign capital; M the money supply; P the general price level; L the demand for real balances; Π^e the expected rate of inflation; and $r+\Pi^e$ the nominal interest rate.

Equations (A.1), (A.2), and (A.3) represent, respectively, the commodity market, the foreign exchange market, and the money market equilibrium conditions. While the policy parameters[53] are G, T, I^b, M, and X, the endogenous variables in the system, determined through Eqs (A.1), (A.2), and (A.3), are e, r, and P, given $\bar{Y}$, Y_f, F, and Π^e. *FF*, *CC* and *PP* in Figure A8.1 provide diagrammatic representation of Eqs. (A.2), (A.1), and (A.3), respectively, with e_0, r_0 and P_0 showing the initial equilibrium values of the three variables for a given set of policy parameters and exogenous variables. Once the values of e and r are known, $S(.)$, $I^v(.)$, and $NX(.)$ yield, respectively, the equilibrium values of aggregate saving, private investment, and current account balance.

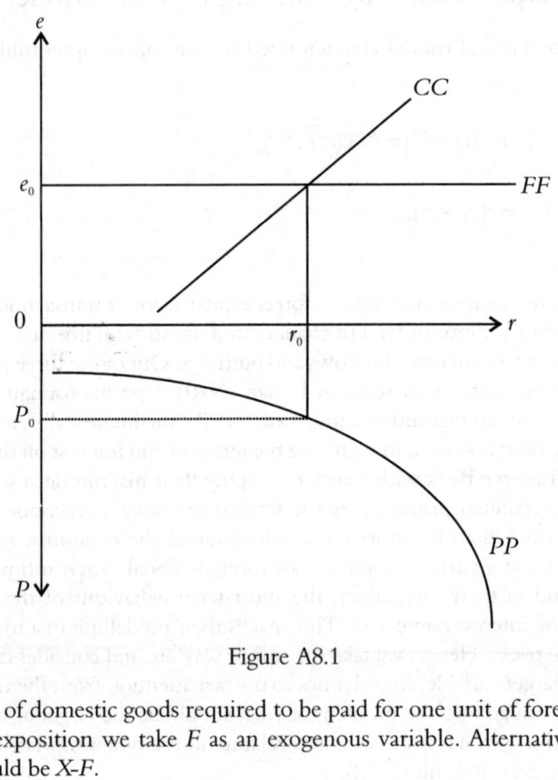

Figure A8.1

[52] Amount of domestic goods required to be paid for one unit of foreign goods.

[53] In our exposition we take F as an exogenous variable. Alternatively, the policy parameter could be X-F.

Before considering the PCS note that an increase in X through enhanced supply in the foreign currency market effects an appreciation of the real exchange rate, implying a downward shift of FF (Figure A8.1). Additional public investment tends to raise domestic demand and hence pushes CC to the right. From Eq. (A.3) it is also obvious that an increase in money supply at any given r causes an equiproportionate rise in the price level, that is, PP undergoes a downward displacement in Figure A8.1. As is to be expected in a neo-classical model, changes in M affect only P, but not r, e, or other real variables in the system. For subsequent discussion, it is useful to use some simple algebra for deriving the effects of changes in the three policy instruments, X, I^b, and M, on e, r, $NX(.)$, r, $I^v(.)$, and P:

$$de = \frac{edX}{NX_1 - X - F} > 0; \tag{A.4}$$

$$d(NX) = \frac{NX_1}{NX_1 - X - F} edX > 0; \tag{A.5}$$

$$dr = \frac{1}{(S_r - I^v_r)} \left[\frac{NX_1}{NX_1 - X - F} edX + dI^b \right] > 0; \tag{A.6}$$

$$dI^v = \frac{I^v_r}{(S_r - I^v_r)} \left[\frac{NX_1}{NX_1 - X - F} edX + dI^b \right] > 0; \tag{A.7}$$

$$dP = \frac{1}{M/P} \left[dM - \frac{PL_1}{(s_r - I^v_r)} \left(\frac{NX_1}{NX_1 - X - F} edX + dI^b \right) \right] > 0. \tag{A.8}$$

The economic interpretation of Eqs. (A.4) to (A.8) is straightforward, given the usual signs of the partial derivatives and the modified Marshall–Lerner condition for stability of equilibrium in the foreign exchange market[54]:

$$NX_1 - X - F > 0. \tag{A.9}$$

An increase in the central bank's purchase of foreign currency tends to cause depreciation and hence raise net exports. Since this implies an increase in the demand for domestically produced goods and services, the commodity market equilibrium

[54] Which, as may be seen from Eq. (A.9), implies that an increase in e (i.e., a depreciation) will tend to raise the net supply of foreign currency.

requires an increase in the interest rate so that private investment falls and the price level tends to go up.[55] It is in this context that neo-classical economists (e.g., Lal et al., 2003) would advocate the RBI sale of foreign currency[56] for raising domestic capital accumulation along with a fall in the general price level to boot.

However, even when production is supply constrained, the impact of a reduction in X on domestic investment will be small in a country like India. Such a policy leaves unaddressed the problem of infrastructural bottlenecks bedevilling the economy and acting as the most serious impediment to private investment. The implication is that given the paucity of infrastructural capital stock as of now, I^v_r is near zero so that the increase in investment following a cut-back in X will be negligible [vide (A.7)]. Hence arises the need for stepping up I^b. But as is evident from Eqs (A.6) and (A.7), this pushes up interest rates and tends to crowd-out private investment. Low-interest sensitivity of private investment makes crowding-out relatively small. But since (with an unchanged X), the increase in investment is entirely financed from additional domestic saving, the interest rate has to rise significantly in view of low interest sensitivity of saving. A fall-out of this is that even though money supply remains unchanged there is a rise in the general price level.[57]

PCS is designed to (a) raise government (or government supported) investment in infrastructure; (b) avoid crowding-out of private investment; and (c) keep the price level stable. Under the scheme the RBI sale of forex reserves is to equal the increase in public investment, that is,

$$dI^b = -edX. \tag{A.10}$$

Money supply is also slated to remain unchanged, with the increase in the net RBI credit to the government balancing the reduction in forex reserves in the portfolio of the central bank.[58]

Given Eq. (A.10) and $dM=0$, the effects of PCS on e, NX, r, I^v and P are immediate from Eq. (A.4) to (A.7). Changes in e and NX under PCS are the same as those indicated by Eq. (A.4) and (A.5), respectively;[59] but that in the other variables take the following form:

$$dr = \frac{1}{(S_r - I^v_r)} \left[\frac{X - F}{NX_1 - \overline{X - F}} \right] edX; \tag{A.6'}$$

[55] Remembering that a rise in r reduces the demand for money balances.

[56] Or rather, non-intervention in the foreign currency market when there is an inflow of foreign capital. It is easily verified that a fall in X and a rise in F have exactly the same effect on NX and other relevant variables.

[57] In order not to clutter the algebra we have refrained from specifying I^v as being positively related to I^b. In view of this relation the increase in the interest rate and the general price level would be larger than what is shown in Eqs (A.6) and (A.8).

[58] So that reserve money and, hence, M remain unaffected.

[59] The reason, as the perceptive reader must have realized, is that unlike in Mundell–Fleming-type models, here domestic interest rates do not (or are not allowed to) affect net capital inflow.

$$dI^v = \frac{I_r^v}{S_r - I_r^v}\left[\frac{X-F}{NX_1 - X - F}\right] edX; \tag{A.7'}$$

$$dP = \frac{1}{M/P}\,\frac{PL(.)}{s_r - I_r^v}\left[\frac{X-F}{NX_1 - X - F}\right] edX. \tag{A.8'}$$

Thus when the initial current account balance equals or is close to zero, the three objectives of PCS listed above are clearly fulfilled. The appreciation of the exchange rate is just enough to make the increase in the import–export gap equal the additional public investment. Interest rates remain unaffected, and so do private investment and the general price level. Remembering that with huge excess reserves at the disposal of the Reserve Bank, the opportunity cost of their depletion is only the interest rates on the US or EU Treasury Bills. The yearly increase in net *national* product and in net government revenue due to PCS will be $(r^s - r_f)dI^b$ and $(r^g - r_f)dI^b$, respectively, where r^s is the the social return[60] on infrastructural investment; r_f is the return on RBI holding of foreign assets; r^g is the government's marginal tax-cum-non-tax revenue from investment in infrastructure.

The results are somewhat modified when the initial situation is characterized by a current account surplus or deficit. From (A.5), (A.6'), (A.7') and (A.8') it is clear that when $dI^b = -edX$ and $dM = 0$,

$$\left.\begin{aligned} d(NX) &>,=,< edX \\ dr &>,=,< 0 \\ dI^v &>,=,< 0 \\ dP &>,=,< 0 \end{aligned}\right\} \text{according as } X >,=,< F. \tag{A.11}$$

The crucial result in Eq. (A.11) from which the others automatically follow is that relating to the change in NX. When $X > F$, the fall in the current account balance (or rise in the current account deficit) is larger than the depletion of reserves since the exchange rate appreciation itself lowers the value of the initial excess of X over F, measured in terms of domestic goods. With the increase in the current account deficit exceeding dI^b $(=-edX)$, there tends to be an excess supply in the commodity market which is eliminated through a fall in interest rates. Hence, there is crowding-in of private investment along with a fall in the general price level. Deviation of the results from the benchmark case, with $X = F$ or $NX = 0$, is not simply of academic interest: when, X differs from F, PCS can have a significantly

[60] Including positive externalities which can be quite important in the case of infrastructural investment.

positive or negative impact on private investment.[61] Hence while drawing up the policy programme it is necessary to consider the optimal changes in public and private investment as also the cost of depletion of forex reserves. Such considerations acquire special significance when infrastructural investment raises the productivity of private investment. In this case, the central bank's release of forex reserves needs to be more than what is suggested in PCS. The resulting larger net imports help realizing higher investment along with larger GOI securities at the expense of foreign assets in the RBI's portfolio and, hence, promote medium-term budgetary viability.

Price Level and Inflation in a Full-employment Economy

Though we have discussed how policy instruments affect the price level, under the neo-classical set-up this is of little consequence because changes in nominal prices do not affect any of the real variables. What about inflation expectations—the bug-bear of many a critic of PCS? Apart from the fact that prices remain unchanged in the benchmark case and falls when $X > F$, it is elementary but important to recognize that inflation implies a continuing rise in the price level, not its one-off increase in response to some temporary shock. The most important factors governing inflation, as may be seen from Eq. (A.3), are (a) the growth rate of full-employment output and (b) the growth rate of money supply.[62] Hence even if there is an increase in money supply and a rise in aggregate investment, so long as the growth rate of money supply is kept unchanged, the inflation rate will tend to come down on completion of new projects.

Part B: An Open-economy Aggregate Demand–Aggregate Supply (AD–AS) Model

In order to examine the consequences of PCS in an economy with an output gap it is useful to work with the standard open-economy AD–AS model with some modification (as in Part A) in the equilibrium condition for the foreign exchange market. In this model Y is an endogenous variable and so are[63] P, r, and e:

$$P = P(Y), \quad P' > 0; \tag{B.1}$$

$$S[Y, r; G, T] - [I^v(r) + I^b] = NX(e, Y; Y_f); \tag{B.2}$$

$$M = PL(Y, r); \tag{B.3}$$

[61] With some simple algebraic manipulation Eq. (A.5) can be written as $d(NX) = [\varepsilon/(\varepsilon-1)]edx$, where ε is elasticity of NX with respect to e. The implication is that if $\varepsilon = 2$, a USD 5 billion cut-back in X (along with an equivalent increase in I^b) raises private investment by about USD 5 billion when domestic saving is relatively interest-insensitive.

[62] Interest rate variations over time also affect the temporal behaviour of the price level. But unless the marginal productivity of capital undergoes a continuous increase despite capital accumulation, interest rate changes cannot be a source of inflation.

[63] Note that given the foreign price level, the nominal exchange rate is given by e and P.

$$NX(e,Y;Y_f) = e(X-F). \tag{B.4}$$

Unlike in the neo-classical full-employment model all the endogenous variables in the AD–AS model are jointly determined through interaction between aggregate supply [Eq. (B.1)], aggregate demand [Eq. (B.2)], the money market [Eq. (B.3)] and the foreign exchange market [Eq. (B.4)]. For a diagrammatic exposition it is useful to eliminate P and r. From Eqs. (B.1) and (B.3), r may be written as a function of Y and M:

$$r = r(Y;M), \quad r_1 > 0; r_2 < 0. \tag{B.5}$$

(Note that $r_1 > 0$ since both L_1 and P' are positive[64].)

Plugging Eq. (B.5) into Eq. (B.2) we get the commodity market equilibrium condition with Y and e as the only endogenous variables:

$$S[Y, r(Y;M); G,T]-[I^v(r(.))+I^b] = NX(e,Y;Y_f). \tag{B.2a}$$

Given the policy parameters and exogenous variables, the combinations of e and Y satisfying Eq. (B.2a) are shown by CC in Figure A8.2. The curve is positively sloped since an increase in e (i.e., a depreciation of the real exchange rate) tends to raise aggregate demand so that Y needs to go up for preserving equilibrium in the commodity market. The other blade of the pair of scissors, represented by FF, is obtained from Eq. (B.4). This is also positively sloped since while an increase in Y tends to reduce net exports, for a real exchange rate appreciation, the effect (on NX) is in the opposite direction. Fairly standard analysis suggests that for stability of equilibrium in the system at the intersection point of the two curves CC has to be steeper. The arrows in Figure A8.2 show the direction of adjustment in e and Y when the initial situation differs from the equilibrium one and indicates how the two variables move to their equilibrium position at E.

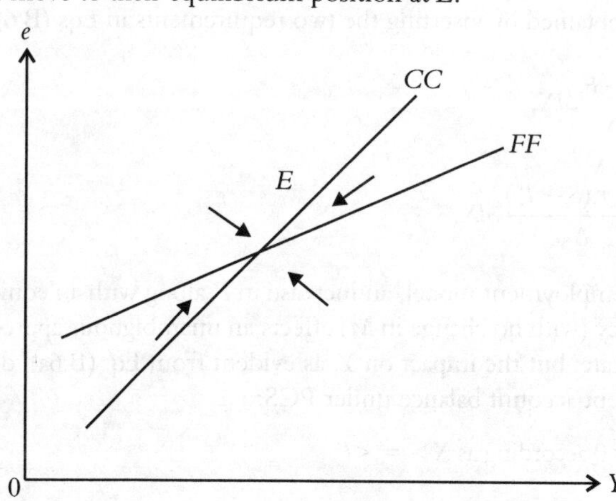

Figure A8.2

[64] Differentiation of Eqs (B.1) and (B.3) yields: $\delta r/\delta Y = -(LP'+PL_1)/(PL_2)>0$; $\delta r/\delta M = -(1/PL_2)<0$.

Consider now the effects of policy intervention. An increase in I^b shifts CC' to the right, but leaves FF unaffected. The result, as is to be expected, is an increase in income; a depreciation of the real exchange rate; a widening of the current account deficit;[65] and a fall in private investment.[66] On the other hand, sale of foreign currency by the central bank pushes FF downward and produces opposite effects: output falls, the exchange rate appreciates, the current account balance goes down;[67] and private investment goes up. It is also easy to see that an increase in the money supply shifts CC rightward so that the effects on Y and e are similar to that of a rise in I^b; but the two policies differ radically in respect of their effects on private investment and interest rates: an increase in the money supply reduces r and raises I^v.

For examining the economic consequences of PCS we need as before to use some algebra. Taking the differential of Eqs (B.2a) and (B.4), the effects of changes in I^b, X, and M on income and the exchange rate are as follows:

$$dY = \frac{1}{\Delta}\left[\left(NX_1 - \overline{X-F}\right)dI^b + NX_1 edX - \left(NX_1 - \overline{X-F}\right)\left(S_r - I_r^v\right)r_2 dM\right], \qquad \text{(B.6)}$$

$$de = \frac{1}{\Delta}\left[\left\{S_Y + r_Y\left(S_r - I_r^v\right) - NX_2\right\}edX - NX_2 dI^b - NX_2\left(S_r - I_r^v\right)r_2 dM\right], \qquad \text{(B.7)}$$

$$\text{where } \Delta\left\{S_Y + r_Y\left(S_r - I_r^v\right)\right\}\left(NX_1 - \overline{X-F}\right) - NX_2(F-X) > 0$$

(for stability of equilibrium).

Since under the Planning Commission programme $dI^b = -edX$ and $dM = 0$, changes in Y and e are obtained by inserting the two requirements in Eqs (B.6) and (B.7):

$$dY = \frac{X-F}{\Delta}edX, \qquad \text{(B.6a)}$$

$$de = \frac{S_Y + r_Y(S_r - I_r^v)}{\Delta}edX. \qquad \text{(B.7a)}$$

As in the full-employment model, an increase in I^b along with an equivalent sale of foreign currency (with no change in M) effects an unambiguous appreciation of the real exchange rate; but the impact on Y, as evident from Eq. (B.6a), depends upon the initial current account balance under PCS:

$$dY >,=,< 0 \text{ according as } X >,=,< F. \qquad \text{(B.8)}$$

[65] Though exchange rate depreciates, it cannot raise NX since depreciation itself is the result of an expansion in government investment expenditure.

[66] Since r rises along with an increase in Y.

[67] The reason is similar to that in fn. 65.

The effects of PCS under the three cases ($X = F, X < F$, and $X > F$) are shown in Figure A8.3. Thus in the benchmark case (with $X = F$), there is no change in Y, the interest rate[68] and, hence, private investment. The additional I^b is financed entirely through a widening of the current account deficit. However, when there is a current account deficit to begin with ($X < F$), income, interest rate and prices go up so that there is some crowding-out effect. The opposite will be the consequences for Y, r, P, and I^v when the initial situation is characterized by a positive current account balance. For an appreciation of the economic mechanism behind these effects, it is helpful to write Eq. (B.6a) in the following form [putting $dM = 0$ in Eq. (B.6) and rearranging the terms in Δ]:

$$dY = \frac{1}{\Delta_l}\left[dI^b + \frac{NX_1}{NX_1 - \overline{X - F}} edX \right], \qquad \text{(B.6b)}$$

where Δ_l (marginal leakage from the income stream)[69]

$$= \{S_y + r_y(S_r - I_r^v)\} + \frac{X - F}{NX_1 - \overline{X - F}} NX_2 > 0 \text{ for stability.}$$

Consider the two terms within the third brackets in Eq. (B.6b). The first indicates the first-round increase in domestic demand due to the increase in government investment. $NX_1/(NX_1 - \overline{X - F})$ is the increase in net exports due to a unit increase in *purchase* of foreign currency (effected through an exchange rate depreciation, given the level of domestic production). Hence, the second term gives the first-round

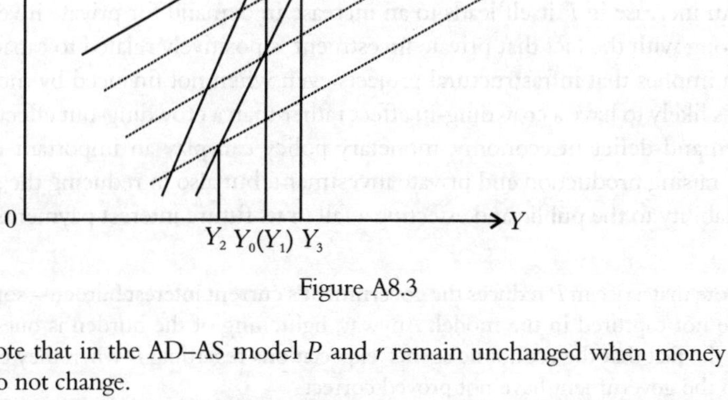

Figure A8.3

[68] Note that in the AD–AS model P and r remain unchanged when money supply and Y do not change.

[69] Which is the reciprocal of the (autonomous expenditure) multiplier in the AD–AS model.

increase in domestic demand due to edX. When $dI^b = -edX$ and $X=F$, the first-round demand-generating effects of the two policies cancel out so that Y remains unchanged in equilibrium. It is also clear that the positive impact of dI^b will outweigh (fall short of) the negative impact of ($-edX$) in the first round when $X<(>)F$ so that the change in Y will be a multiple of the net first-round effect (positive or negative). Given this perspective, it is easy to appreciate the consequences of PCS for the interest rate, prices, private investment, and the current account balance.

Objectives and Instruments

As we have already discussed in Part A, though most of the critics' misgivings relating to PCS are ill-founded, even in a full-employment situation the scheme requires some major modifications for promoting the basic objectives of economic policy. The need for reformulation is greater as of now, with the economy saddled with an output gap. Elementary economic principles suggest that when there is excess capacity, borrowing from abroad or reduction of forex reserves is not necessary for stepping up domestic investment: an increase in I^b (with no reduction in X) will, through a rise in Y, generate additional domestic saving that is enough to keep the initial investment–saving gap or the current account deficit unaffected (in the benchmark case). However, an increase in I^b, with no changes in X and M, will also cause some crowding-out, an exchange rate depreciation, and a rise in the general price level. There is also a fiscal fall-out which may weigh heavily with the authorities: the increase in government borrowing from the public at enhanced interest rates may tend to erode fiscal viability,[70] especially if the government is unable to capture the return on infrastructural investments through user charges or tax collections out of additional income.

The upshot of our argument is that, with three policy instruments at its disposal, I^b, X, and M, the government can generally attain three macroeconomic objectives. In case there is an output gap, the overriding objective should perhaps be to close the gap. The other objectives may be promotion of private investment, strengthening fiscal viability, and avoiding major variations in the exchange rate and the price level. An increase in I^b itself leads to an increase in demand for private investment. This along with the fact that private investment is positively related to capacity utilization implies that infrastructural projects even when not financed by monetized deficit is likely to have a crowding-in effect rather than a crowding-out effect. Again, in a demand-deficient economy, monetary policy can play an important role not only in raising production and private investment, but also in reducing the government liability to the public and effecting a fall in its future interest payments.[71] One

[70] Note that a rise in P reduces the government's current interest burden—something we have not captured in the model. Anyway, lightening of the burden is one-off and reflects the fact that the economic agents' expectations regarding P when they extended loans to the government have not proved correct.

[71] We have examined the issues relating to public debt and fiscal viability in some detail in Rakshit (2005).

need not worry about the rise in P, remembering that given the supply side impact of enlarged investment, inflation will in fact go down if the central bank keeps the growth rate of money supply unchanged over the medium run.

Thus, in the presence of excess capacity, through appropriate choice of dI^b, dX, and dM the government may raise output, promote private investment, and lighten the burden of public debt.[72] When there is no excess capacity, an increase in I^b requires a widening of the current account deficit. Since changes in M no longer affect the real interest rate, it cannot impact domestic saving either. Hence for any targeted increase in dI^b, it is necessary to have an appropriate cut-back in X in order to attain some prestipulated I^v. The main difficulty with PCS thus appears to be that the programme is ad hoc, not based on the nature of the constraints faced by the economy and the policies required for attaining the main objectives.

[72] Once the three instruments are fixed, changes in the net central bank credit to the government become an endogenous variable.

9

On Liberalizing Foreign Institutional Investments*

There is nothing people can't contrive to praise or condemn and find justification for doing it.

Moliere, *The Misanthrope*

Introduction

A major feature of economic reforms in India since 1991 has been a progressive liberalization of external capital flows, especially non-debt creating ones such as the FDI and FII. This has led to a surge of capital inflows and strengthened the country's balance-of-payments position. While except for a few strategic sectors (e.g., defence production and public sector banking) most entry barriers to FDI have been dismantled or lowered considerably, FIIs are still subject to a number of regulations and controls. The reason is that such flows can be volatile and make the financial system vulnerable. However, since FIIs, it is strongly believed in official circles, have a major role to play in providing a boost to the country's growth rate, the government appointed a Committee in 2002 and an Expert Group (EG) in 2004 in order to suggest measures for liberalizing FII without making the capital markets vulnerable. The terms of reference of the EG are wider in scope and its proposals include those already suggested by the Committee[1] (Government of India, 2004, 2005). Hence, our focus will be on the report of the EG (REG), its recommendations, and their economic rationale.

It is interesting to note that EG is called upon to suggest ways of 'encouraging FII flows' along with adequate safeguards against speculative investments engendering volatility in the capital market. Thus the Group is not

* Reprinted from *Economic and Political Weekly*, Vol. 41, No. 11, March 18–24, 2006.

[1] The chairman of the Committee also headed the Expert Group.

required to examine either the desirability or the optimum level of FIIs so long as their volatility (if any) can be contained. For its part, the EG regards the investment (and growth) -enhancing effect of FIIs as unquestionable, and is of the view that volatility of FII flows has not been of much significance for the Indian economy. No wonder, the EG does not pay sufficient attention to factors which govern the salubrious or deleterious impact of these flows on the health of the macroeconomy and the nature of monetary/fiscal policy problems they often create;[2] nor does REG contain well-thought-out suggestions for checking speculative capital flows. The main problem with FII, according to the EG, arises from the possible use of the route for money laundering or tainted transactions.

Given the above perception of the EG, its recommendations are intended primarily to (a) encourage FII and (b) preserve market integrity through prevention of contaminated flows, and only secondarily for (c) making FII relatively stable.[3] The recommended measures under (a) consist of the following:

(i) As in the original 1992 stipulation,[4] ceilings on FII if any are to be set over and above the prescribed sectoral caps for FDI.
(ii) Where there is a composite cap for both FDI and FII, the policy may continue as a purely transitional arrangement, but this composite cap should be set 'at a sufficiently high level'.
(iii) In order to augment the supply of good quality equities which FIIs will feel tempted to invest in, the EG suggests disinvestment in PSUs and encouraging companies executing large investment projects 'to access the domestic capital market'.

Capital Market Integrity and Stability

The EG is in agreement with a number of analysts who have identified FII inflows through participatory notes (PNs) and sub-accounts as major areas of concern since they can undermine market integrity and produce volatility in the system. Sub-accounts are underlying entities (e.g., private firms, public companies, pension funds, or individuals) on whose behalf an FII, registered

[2] RBI's Note of Dissent on recommendations of the Expert Group refers to the need for addressing 'the macroeconomic implications of volatility of capital flows' (Government of India, 2005). No less important, however, as we shall see, are the implications of the flows (even when not volatile) for counter-cyclical policies and optimal use of foreign resources for domestic investment from a long-term perspective.

[3] Though in line with its terms of reference the Group brackets measures under (b) and (c) as those intended to prevent vulnerability of the capital market to FII flows.

[4] Which allowed FIIs into the Indian capital market for the first time.

with the Securities and Exchange Board of India (SEBI), invests in the Indian capital market. PNs are derivative instruments issued (against some underlying Indian securities) by FIIs to their overseas clients.[5] Since sub-accounts and PNs may not be regulated anywhere, it is not very difficult to use these routes for shady transactions. This is especially so for PNs since the identity of their ultimate beneficiaries is not easily known or verified.

Large-scale use of PNs and sub-accounts is also liable to make the capital market unstable. Apart from the fact that derivative instruments like PNs when not properly regulated can engender volatility, hedge funds (outside the control of any supervisory authority) can use sub-accounts and PNs for playing in the Indian market. FIIs may also use the sub-account route to get round the ceiling (currently at 10 per cent) on holding in one firm by an FII: when an FII's own holding and holdings of its sub-accounts are treated as separate holdings, it is possible for an FII to corner through sub-accounts the entire amount of equities permitted under the sectoral cap. This defeats the objective of diversification of equity holding and makes capital markets, driven by operations of a smaller number of investors, more volatile.

In view of the above considerations the thrust of REG is on prevention of the FII route, through PNs, sub-accounts, or other devices, from being used for unsavoury and speculative inflows. The following constitutes the main recommendations of the Group intended to serve the objective:

(a) EG emphasizes the need for drawing up a list of tax havens and barring entities under their jurisdiction from being registered as FIIs.
(b) EG suggests continuance of the January 2004 SEBI stipulation regarding PNs. Under this stipulation (i) no further PNs are to be issued to an unregulated entity; (ii) FIIs are to follow strictly the 'know your clients' (KYCs) principle; and (iii) existing non-eligible PNs must expire or be wound down within a period of five years, whichever is earlier. FIIs should also be obliged to provide any information sought by SEBI concerning the final beneficiaries of the PNs.
(c) In order to address the problem of concentration of share holding through sub-accounts and the tendency for 'herding' arising therefrom,[6] EG suggests that the 10 per cent ceiling should be for the sum of holdings of an FII in a firm and all the sub-accounts having a common beneficial ownership as the FII (with the onus of establishing the absence of common beneficial interest of some sub-account lying entirely with the FII). For preventing unclean flows, it is also

[5] So that they enjoy income or capital gains from these securities.

[6] Herding refers to similarity of behaviour of a large group investors.

recommended that 'entities which do not have reputational risk or are unregulated', may be prohibited from registration as sub-accounts.[7]

The recommendations listed above are intended to serve the dual goal of market integrity and stability. There are two other proposals which are addressed solely for lending stability to the capital market. First, participation of domestic pension funds in the equity market, it is suggested, will augment diversity of view in the market and tend to make share prices less volatile. Second, the EG recommends that FIIs be permitted to switch between equity and debt instruments. Such operational flexibility, it is claimed, 'will induce more "balanced" strategies' on the part of FIIs and contribute toward stabilization of domestic capital markets. This along with the fact that FII investment in debt is denominated in domestic currency[8] warrants, according to EG, a progressive switch from the current ceiling on the aggregate stock of (FII held) debts to a cap on their annual flow.

The approach and recommendations of the EG raise several important analytical and policy issues. The most crucial of these relate to effects of FII flows on (a) aggregate and sectoral investment; (b) behaviour of financial including foreign currency markets with special reference to their volatility; and (c) efficacy of fiscal and monetary instruments in attaining the objectives of macrostabilization and growth. Our analysis of these issues and appraisal of REG are organized as follows. The second section abstracts from volatility of FII flows, examines their macroeconomic impact in light of the Indian experience, and draws some policy conclusions regarding the role of such flows. The third section addresses the issue of volatility in the Indian context. Drawing on the analysis in these two sections, a critique of the EG recommendations follows in the fourth section. The final section concludes.

FII Inflows, Investment, and Growth

Behind the terms of reference and the EG recommendations lies the presumption that (absent volatility) FII flows are always investment and growth promoting. The same can presumably be said of other forms of capital inflows, for example, FDI, NRI deposits, and commercial borrowing or funds raised through American Depositary Receipts (ADRs)/GDRs by domestic companies from the international market. The basic logic behind the presumption is as follows. To the extent a country can secure foreign capital, it can raise its investment rate above what would be permitted by

[7] Such entities will be given sufficient time to wind up their account.

[8] So that the potential balance-of-payments problem due to such debts is less than in the case of external borrowings denominated in foreign currency.

domestic saving: excess of domestic capital accumulation over saving, elementary economics tells us, exactly equals the net inflow of foreign capital. Before examining the relevance and implications of this line of reasoning for policies relating to external capital inflows in general and FII in particular, it is instructive to take a look at the temporal behaviour of investment, capital account transactions, and other related variables in the Indian economy over the period 1992–2005.[9]

Table 9.1 provides a profile of some macroeconomic and external sector indicators during the reference period. The trajectory of the indicators does not support the conventional wisdom regarding the role of foreign capital summarized above. There was little relationship during the period (especially over 1992–2002) between aggregate investment and the capital account balance, that reflects the net aggregate inflow of foreign capital other than the change in the RBI's external asset–liability position.

What is perhaps the most important for policy prescription, except for 1992–3 and 1995–6, during the entire thirteen-year period the capital account balance exceeded, often by a substantial margin, the country's current account deficit, with the three-year spell ranging 2001–4 being characterized by a surplus in both the current and the capital account. Since the EG makes no mention of this important macroeconomic phenomenon, a few words on its significance for policy purposes appear to be in order.

An excess of capital account balance over current account deficit implies that a part of foreign capital is being used for acquiring financial assets abroad, not for bridging the investment–saving (or the import–export) gap.[10] When capital inflows are positive despite the country running a current account surplus—as was the case in India during 2001–4—a part of the country's saving along with the entire amount of (net) capital inflow is lent or invested abroad. Under these conditions, the short- and long-run consequences of foreign capital for the macroeconomy as well as the government finances are far from salubrious. In order to appreciate why, it is useful to identify the routes through which capital inflows affect investment, income, and other macroeconomic variables.

Under the neo-classical economic analysis, inflow of foreign capital tends to cause an exchange rate appreciation and hence an increase in net imports of goods and services. The consequent fall in domestic demand lowers the interest rates which in its turn helps raising investment and reducing saving. Thus even in the orthodox model, foreign capital does not cause an

[9] Only from 1992 were FIIs permitted to invest in the Indian capital market.

[10] Ex-post investment–saving gap (as per national income accounting) is the mirror image of the export–import gap.

TABLE 9.1

Some Macroeconomic (including External Sector) Indicators

(Figures, unless specified otherwise, are as percentage of GDP)

	1992–3	1993–4	1994–5	1995–6	1996–7	1997–8	1998–9	1999–2000	2000–1	2001–2	2002–3	2003–4	2004–5
GDP growth	5.12	5.90	7.25	7.34	7.84	4.79	6.51	6.06	4.37	5.78	3.99	8.51	6.91
Total investment	23.61	23.09	26.00	26.90	24.48	24.60	22.57	26.29	24.36	22.95	25.19	27.25	30.10
Private corporate investment	6.46	5.61	6.91	9.58	8.05	7.97	6.39	7.23	5.74	5.59	5.75	6.84	8.25
Current account balance	–1.71	–0.42	–1.05	–1.65	–1.19	–1.37	–0.96	–1.05	–0.78	0.16	0.81	1.44	–0.95
Capital account balance	1.59	3.54	2.84	1.31	2.96	2.47	2.01	2.48	2.11	1.80	2.13	3.43	4.62
FDI & foreign portfolio investment (FPI)	0.23	1.52	1.59	1.38	1.59	1.31	0.58	1.16	1.48	1.70	1.18	2.67	2.09
of which													
FDI	0.13	0.21	0.41	0.60	0.73	0.87	0.59	0.48	0.88	1.28	0.99	0.78	0.80
FPI	0.10	1.30	1.19	0.77	0.86	0.44	–0.01	0.68	0.60	0.42	0.19	1.89	1.29
Reserve (increase +/decrease –)	0.33	3.18	1.44	–0.82	1.52	0.94	0.95	1.38	1.32	2.48	3.33	5.22	3.73
Net foreign exchange assets of RBI	3.03	5.98	7.38	6.24	6.93	7.61	7.92	8.56	9.44	11.57	14.54	17.55	19.73
Net RBI credit to the government	0.59	0.10	0.22	1.67	0.21	0.72	1.00	–0.22	0.27	–0.07	–1.28	–2.75	–2.32

Source: Reserve Bank of India (2005), Government of India (2006).

equivalent increase in investment: a part of the flow ends up in augmenting domestic consumption. The macroeconomic effects of capital inflows become radically different when the economy is bedevilled with demand deficiency or the price mechanism fails to ensure full employment in the short and medium run. The reason is that (in the absence of central bank intervention) the exchange rate adjusts immediately to capital inflows, but interest rates (especially the lending rates of financial institutions), wages, and product prices are slow to fall in response to a decline in the aggregate demand. Hence arises the danger of large-scale capital inflows causing a reduction in output and employment rather than fuelling an increase in domestic investment. In fact, the associated decline in capacity utilization and profit is likely to reduce investment and magnify the negative impact of foreign capital on the level of domestic economic activity.

In terms of the chain of causation operating under sluggish wage–price–interest adjustment, it is not very difficult to appreciate why surges in capital inflows into the Indian economy have been accompanied with a declining trend in GDP growth and domestic capital formation. Thanks to a fall in public especially infrastructural investment from 1995–6 onward and the monetary squeeze effected in that year, the period since the mid-1990s has been characterized by demand deficiency, fall in capacity utilization, and slowdown in private investment. Under these conditions external capital receipts may be expected to aggravate the problem of demand deficiency and make private producers still more chary of adding to their productive capacity (Rakshit, 2004). It is in this context that the Reserve Bank, faced with burgeoning capital inflows, undertook massive purchases of foreign currency, since otherwise there would have been a sharp rise in the value of the rupee and a further widening of the output gap. However, the resulting accumulation of reserves was not costless to the economy. Since these costs figure nowhere in the EG's discussion, it appears important to reiterate their nature and significance for the Indian economy.

Note first that the yield on the RBI's forex reserves, held in the form of short-term US or EU government securities, is significantly less than that on foreign capital invested in India. This implies a diminution of the country's GNP on account of holding forex reserves in excess of what is required for management of the external account. Taking the yield differential to be 6 per cent and the excess reserves to be USD 100 billion, the income loss on this account thus comes to USD 6 billion, or more than 1 per cent of the country's net national product.[11]

[11] Estimated at USD 579.5 billion for 2004–5. While estimating the cost of foreign exchange reserves held by developing countries, Rodrik (2006) uses the spread between

No less important are the fiscal (or quasi-fiscal) costs of accretion to forex reserves. In order to keep the money supply at the targeted level, the RBI had to undertake sterilization of reserves on a massive scale, balancing its purchase of foreign currency with the sale of government securities. Indeed, the cumulative sale of government securities had been so large that by 2003–4 the RBI holding of GOI securities became too small to conduct open-market operation on the required scale (Table 9.1). Hence a new financial instrument called market stabilization bond (MSB) had to be introduced for sterilization of accretions to reserves. Issue of MSBs (like that of ordinary government securities) adds to public debt, but their proceeds cannot be used by the government for financing its expenditure. These developments have produced three types of adverse effect on the budgetary balance.

The first has occurred through a sea change in the Reserve Bank's asset-liability position, with a massive switch to low yielding forex reserves from (relatively) high-interest GOI bonds. This causes a fall in RBI profits and hence in government revenue, remembering that the central bank profits accrue to the Treasury by way of dividends. Such a fall in government revenue is due to reserves accretions in the past, not to current capital inflows leading to a cut-back in the net (flow of) RBI credit to the government. The cut-back involves a loss of seignorage revenue for the government and constitutes the second source of quasi-fiscal cost. Since, while at a conservative estimate, the safe level of seignorage lies between 1.5 per cent and 2.0 per cent of GDP, with persistently negative net RBI credit to the government in recent years, the cost by way of loss of seignorage revenue has by no means been negligible (Table 9.1). The third type of cost arises from MSBs. The government expenditure financed through borrowing adds to public debt no doubt. But against that there is also benefit, present or future: while public consumption is welfare enhancing in the current period, government investment raises GDP and future revenue. For issuance of MSBs against the increase in public debt and the consequent (future) cost of debt servicing, there is no increase in current welfare or the

---

'the private sector's cost of short-term borrowing abroad and the yield that the Central Bank earns on its liquid foreign asset' as the measure of per unit cost of reserves holding. Our measure of the cost is based on the consideration that though the capital inflows augmenting the reserves have not contributed to domestic capital formation, foreign investors' return on them approximates the marginal productivity of investment (it can be more or less according as there are capital gains or losses in a given period). This consideration makes the spread between the return on capital in the domestic economy and the yield on the central bank's foreign assets the more appropriate measure of the net national product (NNP) loss.

government's revenue potential. There is thus little economic sense in encouraging capital inflows if instead of promoting investment they find their way into the RBI holding of forex reserves.

Finally, as we have argued elsewhere (Rakshit, 2003), in a demand-deficient economy the cost of foreign capital is significant even when it is used for financing domestic investment: from the viewpoint of the economy as a whole, the opportunity cost of domestic resources in such an economy is zero,[12] but the use of capital inflows involves the burden of meeting foreigners' claims on domestic income due to these flows. Hence, reliance on foreign capital may be justified when (a) the economy operates close to its full employment level and (b) the return on investment does not exceed at the margin the cost of a cut-back in private or public consumption.[13]

FII and Domestic Capital Formation

The foregoing analysis suggests some glaring deficiencies in the EG's views on the investment-enhancing role of the FII. These limitations arise primarily from a lack of macroeconomic perspective and an appreciation of linkages between capital inflows and the behaviour of the domestic economy. Particularly noteworthy in this regard is the absence of any mention of excess capacity, declining trend in investment, accumulation of forex reserves, sharp fall in the RBI holding of public debt, issue of MSBs, and the negative net RBI credit to the government—features of the Indian economy that are closely related to capital inflows and of immediate relevance for policies related to FII and other forms of external funds. No wonder, the main issues concerning the FII in India are hardly addressed in the report.

The EG does not seem to realize that measures for encouraging or controlling FIIs should form part of an integrated policy package for all major categories of capital receipts—FDI, FII, commercial borrowing, ADRs/GDRs, NRI deposits. The reason, our earlier analysis suggests, lies in the fact that macroeconomic consequences of FII depend (among other things) on the magnitude of total capital inflows. Encouraging FIIs without any reference to other types of capital receipts may well reduce domestic investment and/or saving and produce considerable fiscal stress. Again, as we shall presently discuss in the next section, since the 'country' risk perceived by international investors is positively related to the scale and composition of

[12] Since it is possible to raise both consumption and investment without any use of foreign resources.

[13] Otherwise, before accessing external funds, it would be better to raise domestic saving. Note that included in the cost of reducing domestic consumption are resources-cum-distortionary costs of government policies intended to promote saving.

external liabilities of the country, a partial approach to setting policies for different categories of capital flows is prone to end up making their costs larger than benefits.[14]

There is also little recognition in REG that for reaping the benefit of external capital, absence of output gap is not enough; it is necessary to ensure that the investment demand exceeds full-employment saving. We have discussed how in an economy with an output gap capital inflows have negative consequences for investment, growth, and fiscal viability. Now consider the case where with no demand deficiency to begin with, the country receives large foreign capital, but there is no change in the investment demand. Under instantaneous adjustment in the exchange rate but not in prices, wages, and interest rates, the result will be a fall in output, employment, fiscal balance, and investment—a process that may be fairly long drawn and generate its own momentum before being reversed. It is for this reason that foreign capital inflow is beneficial when it follows or accompanies a surge in domestic investment. This has some major policy implications which figure nowhere in the analysis or recommendations of the EG.

First, apart from macro policies for keeping the economy close to the full-employment level, rapid expansion of infrastructural facilities is essential before measures for encouraging external capital inflows are put in place. In fact, the (first) two policies constitute the most effective means of boosting private investment, domestic as well as foreign, and paving the way for productive use of external capital receipts.

Second, capital inflows which are directly linked to setting up or expansion of production facilities are much more investment and growth enhancing than those which are not so related: unlike the latter, the former effects an immediate enlargement of the gap between investment demand and (full employment) saving, apart from providing the wherewithal to finance the import–export gap. This consideration makes FII inferior to many categories of capital inflows. FDI used for setting up production units and domestic companies accessing international financial markets for executing investment plans push up domestic demand as well as the means of meeting the additional import bill arising therefrom. Hence, compared with FIIs and NRI deposits (which are not linked to an increase in investment

[14] The perceptive reader must have realized that the basic reason lies in negative externalities. There are two sources of such externalities. First, when capital inflows into a country are large in relation to aggregate global flow, the average cost schedule tends to be upward rising so that the marginal cost to the economy is larger than the cost to the domestic recipient of foreign funds. Second, though capital receipts in countries like India are relatively small, the country risk makes the average cost schedule positively sloped and the marginal cost exceed the average (Rakshit, 2001).

demand), these inflows tend to have a larger impact on domestic capital formation, effect a smaller fall in aggregate saving, and create less problems for monetary and fiscal authorities.[15]

Third and related to the second, encouraging FIIs (and NRI deposits) may be justified when there is a large demand for infrastructural and other productive investments in the economy over and above the demand coming from FDI and producers who can directly tap the international capital market. In other words, FIIs should follow an increase in investment demand rather than be augmented to kick-start domestic capital formation.[16] However, even when FII inflows supplement domestic saving in financing investment, they tend to make the economy vulnerable to both internal and external shocks—something relating to which the EG's analysis leaves much to be desired.

Vulnerability of Financial Market

There is a general agreement among economists that unlike FDI, which is governed by long-term fundamentals of the economy, FIIs are driven mostly by short-term expectations, characterized by 'herd' behaviour, and are prone to be volatile. Hence, these flows tend to make financial markets vulnerable and may end up landing the country in a currency/payments crisis. While considering the optimum scale and composition of capital inflows, policy-makers (apart from the factors noted earlier) have thus to take into account volatility of the flows and the costs associated therewith. As the exchange rates, interest rates, and share prices become volatile due to sudden surges in inflows and outflows of foreign funds, there is a rise in the

[15] To the extent FDI is for takeover of some existing firm, its impact is similar to that of FII or NRI deposits, except for the fact that there is often an improvement in productivity through induction of superior technical/organizational know-how and gradual diffusion of this know-how in the rest of the economy.

[16] The EG suggests that the rise in share prices due to FII inflows should have a favourable impact on investment. However, apart from the fact that the relation between prices of shares and (even) corporate investment is far from robust in the Indian economy, the EG, our earlier analysis implies, ignores some crucial macroeconomic linkages. In a neo-classical model (with two financial assets, money and bond) capital inflows raise investment (though by less than the amount of the flow) as the real interest rate falls in response to an exchange rate appreciation. Even with perfectly flexible wages, prices, and interest rates, the investment augmenting effect of the inflows will be less than what is suggested in the model since the heightened share market activity raises transactions demand for money balances and hence tends to harden interest rates. With sluggish adjustment of prices and interest rates, capital inflows, as we have explained in the text, can end up reducing investment. This is yet another example of the danger in macroeconomic analysis of relying on 'common sense' instead of a coherent model.

amplitude of fluctuations in output and employment; producers become wary of investing or entering into any long-term commitment; and economic activities get seriously distorted. It is for this reason that FIIs and other easily reversible capital flows pose serious hurdles to monetary and fiscal authorities in attaining the twin objectives of macrostabilization and growth.

A country may seek to resolve the aforementioned problems by (a) controlling capital flows, especially those which are volatile, or (b) building up adequate forex reserves, as many Asian nations (including India) have been doing since the East Asian currency crisis. However, accumulation of reserves as we have seen entails significant loss which may outweigh the benefit of foreign capital. This is especially true of FII. To see why, consider the case where not only is output gap zero, but there is a surge in investment demand—a most favourable scenario where FII can be expected to augment domestic capital accumulation. Even in this case, however, the net contribution of FII to aggregate investment may not amount to much since (a) for preventing balance-of-payment vulnerability the central bank has to add a significant part of such flows to its reserves (Rakshit, 2002); and (b) there is a fall in domestic saving. Add to that the additional income accruing to foreign investors and the GNP increase on account of FII may well turn out to be negative.

What is no less important to recognize, adequate foreign exchange reserves may enable the central bank in a country like India to maintain orderly movements in the exchange rate and counter speculative attacks on the country's currency, but not generally in preventing capital market volatility or formation of stock market bubbles. This is the trilemma policy-makers face in having a relatively stable exchange rate, effective control over money and capital markets, and unrestricted cross-border capital flows. The trilemma becomes particularly acute when the flows are volatile.

The EG does consider the problems of volatility of FIIs and vulnerability of capital markets arising therefrom. However, the problems are not considered very significant for the Indian economy. This judgement is based primarily on Gordon and Gupta's findings (Gordon and Gupta, 2003) that (a) FII investments are negatively related to stock market returns and (b) macroeconomic factors have a significant impact on these flows. The first implies negative rather than positive feedback trading, the second the relative insignificance of purely speculative behaviour on the part of FIIs. Under these conditions, one would not expect FII flows to be volatile. This is what Gordon and Gupta find in their empirical analysis. Since the Group's recommendations have been influenced so much by these findings, it is important to examine their robustness and relevance for framing policies relating to FII.

The Gordon and Gupta study is based on the monthly data of FII flows during the period 1993–2000. There are two major drawbacks which make the findings inappropriate for policy formulation. First, the Asian crisis marked a structural break in the nature and determination of FII (Chakrabarti, 2001)—something which the study misses altogether. Second, for examining the degree of volatility and drivers of FII flows, it is necessary to use daily, not monthly, data. In fact, taking cognizance of the regime change and use of daily data lead to results that are radically different from those of Gordon and Gupta.

Chakrabarti's empirical analysis for the period 1993–9 provides some support to the hypothesis that during the pre-Asian crisis period the causality ran from FII flows to Bombay Stock Exchange (BSE) returns; but after the crisis BSE returns became the sole driver of these flows (Chakrabarti, 2001). This return-chasing behaviour of FIIs and the relative insignificance of fundamentals of the domestic economy were confirmed in a later study based on daily data for the period 1999–2002 (Mukherjee et al., 2002). Other important findings of this study are (a) absence of diversification motive behind FII investments in India and (b) autocorrelation or inertia of capital flows. These findings suggest strong possibilities of volatility of FII flows and generation of stock market bubbles. In fact, using the same data set a further study reveals that (a) FII and stock market returns in India exhibit high volatility in terms of both extent and duration; and (b) volatility of the two is interrelated (Coondoo and Mukherjee, 2004). One cannot but wonder at the EG's making light of the danger of volatility of FII flows on the basis of an inadequate empirical exercise even though much more careful studies yield diametrically opposite results.[17]

There is a much more fundamental issue that seems to have escaped the attention of the EG. Suppose there is clear empirical evidence that FIIs in India have not been volatile. Does this support the case for encouraging FIIs? Clearly not. The reason is that results under a specific regulatory regime may not hold when there are major changes in rules under which economic entities operate. This consideration makes it difficult to assess how or whether relaxation or tightening of rules relating to FIIs will affect

[17] It is interesting to note that the EG does refer to Chakrabarti (2001) and Mukherjee et al. (2002) in Chapter 2 of the Report in a survey of the literature, but while considering policy options in Chapter 4, makes no mention of these studies and cites only Gordon and Gupta (2003) to buttress its position. One cannot help remembering in this connection one of the most important aspects of the theory of cognitive dissonance. According to this theory, when someone has already a predilection for some position, on hearing arguments for and against it, he remembers only the weakest arguments against and the most plausible arguments in support of the position.

volatility of FII investment or the underlying relation between it and other variables. A study by Bose and Coondoo (2004) is of some relevance in this connection. On the basis of a time-series intervention analysis of the impact of major policy initiatives relating to FIIs during the period January 1999 to January 2004 it is found that (a) liberalization policies produce not only an expansionary impact on FII inflows, but also raise their inertia and sensitivity to BSE returns; and (b) restrictive measures also raise the inertia of the flows and their sensitivity to domestic equity returns, but do not show any significantly negative effect on net inflows. While these results are by no means conclusive, they strongly indicate the possibility of heightened volatility of FII flows in the wake of major liberalizing measures.

Policy Recommendations of the Expert Group

In light of our analysis in the previous two sections, we examine how far recommendations of the EG, summarized in the first section, are likely to promote investment and growth, and contribute toward reduction of vulnerability of the financial market to external or internal shocks. Let us first consider the efficacy of the individual measures grouped under the two heads, encouraging FII flows and vulnerability to FII flows.

Encouraging FII Flows

A basic presumption of the EG seems to be that there is a direct if not a one-to-one effect of FII inflows on domestic capital accumulation—a notion we have tried to disabuse in some detail in the second section. In the absence of an output gap FIIs, as we have emphasized, can help raising investment when preceded by a step-up in domestic private or public investment demand not directly financed through other types of capital inflows; otherwise, the economy is likely to pay a heavy price in terms of a fall in investment, GNP, and government revenue including seignorage. Viewed in this context the Group's recommendations for reckoning FII ceilings over and above the prescribed FDI sectoral caps[18] and for raising (as an interim arrangement) the composite caps 'at a sufficiently high level' do not on their own appear justified from the viewpoint of promoting domestic capital formation. This is apart from the fact that a high composite cap widening the scope for large FII flows will tend to make the capital markets vulnerable and enhance volatility of share prices.

[18] The Group's citation in support of its recommendation of the original 1992 rule, under which the FII ceiling was exclusive of the FDI limit, is somewhat odd: unlike in a court of law, analysis and empirical evidence, not precedent, should be the touchstone of a policy conclusion.

The economic logic adduced by the Group for disinvestment of public sector undertakings (PSUs) also seems seriously flawed. There may be compelling reasons for disinvestment, but enlarging the supply of 'good quality equities in adequate volume' in order to draw FII flows is certainly not one of them. Disinvestment per se does not raise investment demand. The government may use the proceeds to retire some public debt or borrow less; nor need FII inflows be the best way of financing social sector or other investments when sale of PSU shares is tied (as it is under the National Common Minimum Programme) to an increase in such expenditure by the government.

The recommendation that companies executing large investment projects 'should be encouraged to access the domestic market' (so that there is a rise in supply of 'good quality equity') is also somewhat odd. It is possible that FII inflows being associated with a rise in these investments are justified. But the decision regarding whether the companies are to finance the projects through internal funds, term loans from Life Insurance Corporation (LIC) or other financial institutions, ADRs/GDRs, or issue of shares and debentures in the domestic capital market, should not be guided by the 'objective' of encouraging FII flows. In fact, as we have already noted, in view of their effect on volatility and country risk, the FII route is likely to be inferior to ADRs/GDRs or even long-term commercial borrowing from abroad.[19] It is also important to recognize that 'encouraging' companies to follow a particular mode of raising funds makes economic sense only if there is some positive externality associated with that mode; otherwise the encouragement violates the spirit of economic reforms!

Vulnerability to FII Flows

The EG's recommendations for preventing 'unclean' flows, for example, having a negative list of tax havens and prohibiting unregulated entities (including high net-worth individuals) from using the sub-account/PN route for purposes of investment, are unexceptionable. However, as the Reserve Bank's note of dissent records, since the beneficial ownership of PNs is extremely difficult to ascertain by the Indian regulatory authority and they can act as easy vehicles for illegal transactions, banning PNs altogether would address better the concern relating to market integrity.

So far as measures intended to curb volatility are concerned, the suggestion for operation of domestic pension funds in the equity market is well taken. The only rider is that individuals should be offered a menu of

[19] Provided there is no significant bunching of repayment (for the economy as a whole).

pension schemes under which the proportion of funds invested in equities may vary, but be subject to certain ceiling: this will allow less cautious individuals to try their luck in the share market, but restrain them from becoming too improvident.

There is also merit in the recommendation for including holdings of all sub-accounts as an FII's own holding while applying the limit on holding by the FII in any one company. However, this may not be enough in curbing volatility in share prices. If the Group's suggestion for raising the composite limit (for FII and FDI) sufficiently or reckoning the (overall) FII limit in a sector over and above the prescribed sectoral cap is implemented, the existing 10 per cent limit for an individual FII holding will in many cases be significant compared with the quantum of floating shares. This is apart from the fact that practically all FIIs, as empirical evidence suggests, are driven by the same factors so that for volatility what matters more is the total FII holding, not simply its degree of concentration.

Particularly inappropriate in the current context appears to be the recommendation to permit FIIs to switch between equity and debt instruments and to replace the current limit on aggregate debt holding of FIIs to a cap on annual debt flows. In view of a grossly under-developed private bond market, FII's dealings in the debt market trade are almost wholly in GOI securities. It is important to recognize that the extent of volatility in this market due to FII operations depends on the stock of government securities held by FIIs in relation to the volume of actively traded securities. So long as the FII holding is small, monetary authorities can exercise some control over interest rates without triggering off large capital inflows or outflows. As the RBI's note of dissent records, removal of the cap on aggregate debt holding of FIIs when there is a substantial interest differential between major world economies and India will make it extremely difficult to manage the exchange rate and the interest rate and preserve stability in the financial market.

Policy Package: Some Yawning Gaps

Whatever the merits of individual measures suggested by the EG, in the absence of a sound macroeconomic perspective they do not add up to a coherent package for tapping FII flows for promotion of basic economic objectives. Given the resource endowment and economic structure of the country, the optimum amount of FII inflows depends crucially on receipts of other types of foreign capital as well as on the aggregated demand for investment. Yet the Group's recommendations are made without any reference to these two factors. Closely related to this are two fundamental omissions which cast serious doubt on the worth of the whole exercise.

First, there is no proper analysis and estimate of the impact of FIIs on major macro variables such as investment, saving and GNP; nor does the Group go into the monetary/fiscal problems FII flows often create. Second, the Group makes no attempt at evaluating the relative merits of promoting/restricting alternative types of capital inflows under the current and expected configuration of the Indian macroeconomy—an evaluation which is essential for recommending policies for FIIs or any other major category of foreign capital.

Absence of an overall perspective and a somewhat cavalier approach to important issues also characterize the Group's stance on sectoral caps. Any economist approaching this issue would like to have answers to the following questions. What should be the criteria for fixing the cap in a particular sector? Why should or should not the FDI and FII caps be composite or separate? If the two caps are separate, how or whether the FII and the FDI caps should be related to one another? Why should the Board of Directors or the majority of shareholders of a joint stock company decide on the upper limit on FII or FDI shareholding, remembering that (a) there is no such provision for holding on the part of domestic institutional investors and (b) it is not for a company to decide whether there should be discrimination between foreign and domestic investors? Why should the caps be uniform or separate for different sectors? What are the implications for aggregate capital inflows and their composition for setting (or changing) sectoral caps or caps on an individual FII in a particular firm? Precise answers to such questions are no doubt difficult to provide. But posing the right questions is an essential step toward advancement of knowledge of what are the relevant considerations and important factors to take into account in addressing a particular issue. Otherwise, policy formulation ends up in ad hocism and churning out figures from thin air.

The EG's last recommendation is for initiating a research programme on 'Capital flows and India's Financial Sector: Learning from theory, international experience and Indian evidence'. This is certainly a major improvement on the terms of reference of the Group; but the ultimate focus of the research should be on capital flows and India's macroeconomy of which the financial sector constitutes *an* but not *the* most, important segment.

Summary and Conclusion

(a) There is something seriously amiss in setting up a committee to suggest measures for 'encouraging FII flows' on the presumption that when their volatility is contained such flows invariably boost domestic capital formation and growth. The presumption is supported by neither economic logic nor empirical evidence. When there is an output gap and investment demand is positively related to capacity utilization and profits, FII tends to have a negative impact on both output and investment. This is apart from the fact that in the presence of under-utilized capacity, investment through foreign capital does not make macroeconomic sense. It is only when domestic investment demand exceeds *full-employment* saving that tapping foreign capital may become a desirable course of action for raising domestic capital formation. No wonder, the surge in foreign capital inflow when the Indian economy was suffering from excess capacity went hand-in-hand with declining trends in investment and GDP growth.

(b) Even when there is enough demand for investment, reliance on other types of foreign capital, for example, FDI, ADRs/GDRs, or long-term borrowing, may be superior to FII for bridging the investment–saving gap. The reason is that when some capital inflow is linked directly to investment demand (which FII is not) a greater part of the capital inflow is translated into investment and chances of a fall in aggregate demand are less. FIIs can contribute toward capital formation and growth when direct foreign funding of some highly productive investment is difficult to secure. The implication is that policy formulation relating to FIIs requires (i) a macroeconomic perspective; (ii) a careful analysis of the current and prospective economic scenario; and (iii) an assessment of pros and cons of alternative types of foreign capital inflows. These considerations are totally missing in the terms of reference set for the EG.

(c) The EG for its part also seems to subscribe completely to the presumption(s) underlying its terms of reference. There is no coherent macroeconomic model behind its analysis and recommendations; no appraisal either of the optimal scale of capital inflows or the relative merit of FII vis-à-vis other categories of capital receipts at the current juncture of the economy; and no examination of monetary/fiscal problems associated with FII or of the quantitative impact of such flows on investment and other macro variables. Indeed, the Group seems to have been so swayed by its terms of reference that it advocates measures, such as, disinvestment of PSUs and encouraging companies implementing large investment projects to make capital issues in the domestic market, solely on grounds of attracting FIIs, without any reference to any other consideration.

(d) Recommendations of the Group for checking vulnerability of domestic capital market are sensible as far as they go; but the package as a whole appears inadequate to meet the objective. The problem in this case arises from three sources. First, there is little appreciation of the fact that vulnerability depends on the stock of the country's external liability, its composition, and flows of different types of foreign capital, not on FII flows alone. Second, the Group ignores the substantial empirical evidence on volatility of FII flows in India and shows little awareness of the fact that liberalization measures are generally followed by an increase in volatility of these flows. Third, despite the series of stock market scams and a large number of companies vanishing with impunity after raising funds, the EG reposes strong faith in the ability of the market watchdog to prevent unclean transactions through PNs or other devices in a liberalized FII regime.

(e) In the context of the recent surge in investment and GDP growth, a rise in capacity utilization and current account deficit, and the projected increase in infrastructural investment demand, issues relating to the use of different types of foreign capital for supporting domestic investment have assumed much greater importance now than in 1996–2003. It is also noteworthy that for the first time since 1995–6 capital inflows during the current year have been fully used for financing the investment–saving gap, not augmenting the RBI's holding of forex reserves. While these developments have raised the possibilities of productive use of foreign funds, for addressing issues arising in this context it is necessary (i) to go deeply into the interlinkages between capital inflows and domestic economic activity and (ii) consider measures relating to FII as an integral part of a policy package encompassing all types of external capital.

References

Bose, S. and D. Coondoo (2004), 'The Impact of FII Regulations in India: A Time Series Intervention Analysis of Equity Flows', *Money & Finance*, 2(18–19), 54–83, July–December.

Chakrabarti, R. (2001), 'FII Flows to India: Nature and Causes', *Money & Finance*, 2(7), 61–81, October–December.

Coondoo, D. and P. Mukherjee (2004), 'Volatility of FII in India', *Money & Finance*, 2(15–16), 85–102, October–March.

Gordon, J. and P. Gupta (2003), 'Portfolio Flows into India: Do Domestic Fundamentals Matter?', *IMF Working Paper* No. 03/20.

Government of India (2004), *Report of the Committee on Liberalisation of Foreign Institutional Investment*, Ministry of Finance, New Delhi, June.

——— (2005), *Report of the Expert Group on Encouraging FII Flows and Checking the Vulnerability of Capital Markets to Speculative Flows*, Ministry of Finance, New Delhi, November.

——— (2006), *Economic Survey 2005–6*, New Delhi.

Mukherjee, P., S. Bose, and D. Coondoo (2002), 'Foreign Institutional Investment in the Indian Equity Market: An Analysis of Daily Flows during January 1999–May 2002', *Money & Finance*, 2(9–10), 21–51, April–September.

Rakshit, M. (2001), 'Globalisation of Capital Market: Some Analytical and Policy Issues', in S. Storm and C.W.M. Naastepad (eds), *Globalisation and Economic Development*, Edward Elgar, Cheltenham.

——— (2002), *The East Asian Currency Crisis,* Oxford University Press, New Delhi.

——— (2003), 'External Capital Flows and Foreign Exchange Reserves: Some Macroeconomic Implications and Policy Issues', *Money & Finance*, 2(13–14), 63–95, April–September.

——— (2004), 'Some Macroeconomics of India's Reform Experience', in K. Basu (ed.), *India's Emerging Economy*, MIT Press, Cambridge, Massachusetts.

Reserve Bank of India (2005), *Handbook of Statistics on the Indian Economy*, Mumbai.

Rodrik, D. (2006), 'The Social Cost of Foreign Exchange Reserves', *NBER Working Paper* No. 11952, January.

10

Banking under the Emerging Economic Environment*

Golden rule for bankers: 'Don't lend to anyone who needs money'.

Introduction

With a rapidly changing domestic and global economic environment, the financial sector in India has undergone a sea change since the early 1990s. The purpose of the chapter is to focus on the developments that have immediate implications for banks; examine the opportunities and difficulties for banks under the new environment; and identify, from a broader, economy-wide perspective, some areas of concern which need to be addressed if the financial sector is to play an effective role in furthering economic and social objectives.

Changes in Economic Environment

For an appreciation of the challenges bankers have been facing under the evolving economic scenario, it is useful to distinguish among three types of developments over the last fifteen years: (a) changes in the regulatory environment under which financial entities operate; (b) developments in the non-financial sector of the domestic economy; and (c) increasing integration of domestic and international markets for goods and services as well as for financial products.

Banking Reforms

Financial sector reforms since 1991 have mostly been gradual or incremental; but their cumulative impact has been far from marginal. The thrust of

* Reprinted from *Money & Finance*, Vol. 2, Nos 22–3, July–December 2005.

the reforms programme was on (a) promotion of efficiency through competition and market orientation and (b) strengthening the shock absorptive capacity of the system through adoption of prudential norms and tightening of supervision. Entry of a number of private sector banks and foreign banks has added considerably to competitive pressure in the banking system. Though public sector banks (PSBs) still account for the lion's share of bank credit and deposits,[1] unlike in the olden days these banks (many of which have undergone partial privatization) are now guided almost wholly by commercial considerations and compete with one another as well as with private sector and foreign banks.

Market orientation of banks has been promoted through a number of policy initiatives. The most significant of these is the switchover from a fixed to a flexible interest regime: except for the interest rate on savings deposits,[2] banks are now free to fix their own rates for all categories of deposits and credit. At the same time, interest rates on GOI securities have also become aligned with the market rate so that the government can no longer borrow from banks (or other financial institutions) at rates significantly below the market rates of interest.

The flexible interest rate regime has been accompanied with much greater freedom for banks in respect of deployment of their assets. With a 38.5 per cent statutory liquidity ratio (SLR) and a 15.0 per cent cash reserve ratio (CRR) prior to liberalization, the major part of bank finance was pre-empted by the government. Remembering that the ratio of cash in hand to total deposits amounted to around 9.5 per cent[3] in those days, banks' freedom regarding use of funds extended to only 37.0 per cent of their deposits. The corresponding figure as of now stands at about 65 per cent as SLR and CRR have been reduced to 25.0 per cent and 5.0 per cent, respectively, and banks' cash in hand has fallen to 5.4 per cent of their deposits.[4] Even allowing for

[1] Between 1990–1 and 2003–4, the share of PSBs in aggregate commercial bank deposits and credit declined from 89.7 and 88.1 per cent to 77.9 and 75.5 per cent, respectively. During the same period, private banks' share in total deposits and credit went up from 4.5 and 4.1 per cent to 17.1 and 18.4 per cent, respectively. Foreign banks lost some ground, but not significantly.

[2] Which continues to be fixed by the Reserve Bank.

[3] Strictly speaking cash in hand constitutes a part of assets which banks are free to choose. However, since assets for meeting SLR and CRR requirement constituted 53.5 per cent of total deposits, banks had to carry relatively large cash for meeting their day-to-day transactions needs. The point to note here is that the greater the freedom of banks in holding their assets, the smaller tends to be the optimum cash in hand, the asset with zero return.

[4] See the previous footnote. Apart from the greater freedom of banks in deployment of their assets, adoption of commercial principles by PSBs has also contributed toward the decline in the ratio of cash in hand to total deposits.

the fact that the priority sector lending requirement is still in force, there is little doubt that a significantly higher share of bank assets is market driven now than in the pre-reforms era.

The enhanced market orientation and freedom of banks in respect of asset holding and setting of interest rates have been tempered with imposition of prudential norms and tightening of regulation and supervision. Of particular significance has been the adoption of CAMEL rating under which the Reserve Bank while assessing the financial viability and performance of a bank focuses not only on its capital adequacy (C) but also on asset quality (A), management (M), earning (E), and liquidity (L). Indeed, the regulatory norms set for banks in India are by and large international best practice and the country is also slated to be one of the first among emerging market economies (EMEs) to adopt Basel II (from March 31, 2007), the revised prudential and regulatory framework set forth by the Basel Committee on Banking Supervision (BCBS).

Domestic and International Economic Environment

Financial sector liberalization has been accompanied with wide ranging reforms in other areas—reforms which have radically altered the environment facing domestic entrepreneurs. With de-reservation of industries, discontinuance of the licensing system, and large-scale withdrawal of other restrictive rules on production activities, private entrepreneurs are now free to invest and operate in practically all lines of business. Entry of foreign firms in domestic industries and services is much easier now than in the early 1990s. Not only have a number of public sector enterprises (PSEs) undergone partial privatization, but PSEs have become subject to market discipline and been made to compete on an equal footing with private firms, including foreign enterprises.

No less important has been the increasing integration of domestic goods and financial markets with their international counterparts. Such integration is to be sure in tune with the globalizing trend of the world economy; but in the Indian instance the process has been triggered off through trade liberalization and significant lowering of barriers to cross-border capital movements. Quantitative restrictions on imports have been abolished; tariffs substantially reduced; exchange controls on current account transactions abandoned. So far as capital inflows and outflows are concerned, while there is no bar to outflow of foreign capital invested in the Indian market, there has also been considerable withdrawal of restrictions on inflow of foreign investment, both direct and portfolio. Rules limiting acquisition of foreign assets by domestic residents are still in force; however, select enterprises are permitted to invest abroad as also to access the international capital market.

Finally, liberalization of trade and capital movements has been accompanied with switchover to a market determined exchange rate regime, though the Reserve Bank often intervenes in the foreign currency market to avoid undue volatility of the rupee and keep its value vis-à-vis other currencies in tune with the country's economic fundamentals.

Opportunities and Challenges for Banks

With financial sector liberalization banks, as we have noted, now enjoy much greater freedom relating to choice of assets and setting of interest rates on deposits and advances; but at the same time they are subject to stricter regulatory and supervisory norms. In order to appreciate the scope for exercising this freedom and significance of the regulatory rules, it is useful to consider how changes in the economic environment noted above have created opportunities as well as difficulties for bankers.

Business Opportunities

De-reservation of industries and discontinuance of licensing along with sharp reduction in duties on imports of capital goods, raw materials, and components have opened up considerable investment opportunities for private producers—something which is reflected in an increase in private investment as a ratio of both GDP and aggregate capital formation,[5] the former by more than 3.2 percentage point and the latter by 11 percentage points.

Perhaps the most noteworthy development in the Indian economy since the early 1990s has been in the sphere of international trade and finance as well as the domestic capital market. Over the period 1980–90 trade in goods and services as a ratio of GDP increased only marginally, from 16.0 per cent to 16.8 per cent. In sharp contrast, between 1989–90 and 2004–5 the ratio rose from 16.8 per cent to 41.6 per cent, reflecting increasing openness and allocative efficiency of the Indian economy. Again, thanks to the large number of Indians working abroad and the demise of the black market in foreign currency with the switchover to the new exchange rate regime, India has become the largest recipient of remittances[6] which during 2002–5 averaged more than 3.3 per cent of GDP compared with 0.87 per cent in the period 1987–90. Relaxation of controls on capital movements has over time triggered off a flood of foreign investment, especially foreign portfolio

[5] Between the two five-year periods, 1986–91 and 1999–2004, the average ratio of private investment to GDP went up from 13.5 per cent to 16.7 per cent and the share of the private sector in aggregate capital formation from 57.3 per cent to 68.3 per cent.

[6] In absolute terms.

investment[7] (FPI). The quantum jump in FII, entry of large private mutual funds, de-materialization of stocks, electronic trading system, all these have had a mutually reinforcing effect in boosting turnover in the foreign exchange,[8] money and capital (including the government bond) markets.

The developments summarized above have opened up a wide range of business opportunities for banks. Greater market orientation resulting in larger investment and production in relatively high yielding lines of economic activities widened the scope for bank loans to more creditworthy ventures. Remembering that inter-country trade has traditionally been dependent on bank advances, the significance of the rapid rise in the trade–GDP ratio for banks can hardly be overemphasized. No less important are non-interest revenues through provision of a variety of services that banks provide—services that have gained prominence in the context of ever widening financial transactions and growing demand for instruments facilitating their easy settlement. Among others the services include automated teller machine (ATM) and credit card facilities, transfer of funds, currency transactions, holding accounts of de-materialized stocks, and investment advice. Apart from such fee incomes, investments in financial instruments along with operations in the government securities market[9] have become important sources of bank revenue in recent years.

Challenges

The new environment has also posed serious challenges to bankers and requires them to develop expertize in some crucial areas. The most important of these challenges relates to evaluation of borrowers' creditworthiness in the context of mounting competitive pressure and increasing integration of domestic and international markets. In the pre-reforms period licensing, protection from foreign competition, export subsidy, and cheap, directed credit made life relatively easy for domestic producers. Importance of public investment, licensing of industrial capacity, relatively low trade–GDP

[7] In the pre-liberalization era FII was barred and foreign direct investment (FDI) was about 0.1 per cent of GDP. In recent years net foreign capital inflow, of which FII constituted the major part, averaged around 2.0 per cent of GDP. Since the daily two-way movement of FII is substantial even when the net amount may not be large, foreign currency transactions due to capital movements are many times the official figure for net foreign investment.

[8] Transactions in the foreign exchange market as a ratio of GDP amounted to 418.6 per cent of GDP in 2004–5 compared with 168.8 per cent during 1996–7. Comparable data for earlier years are not available; however, figures for trade and capital account balances and absence of FII suggest that the ratio was significantly less in the early 1990s.

[9] Banks' exposure to the share market is strictly controlled by the Reserve Bank.

ratio, and severe restrictions on cross-border capital movements implied that the main imponderable in the Indian macroeconomy consisted in vagaries of the monsoon. However, the impact of even a monsoon failure on the non-agricultural output and GDP came down significantly by the 1980s as the weight of the primary sector in the country's output had declined and the overall increase in agricultural productivity enabled the authorities to undertake fairly effective buffer stock measures.[10]

Since 1991 the importance of agriculture in the Indian economy has fallen further. But possibilities of business plans of entrepreneurs going awry are much higher now as the frequency as well as intensity of shocks of various categories—firm- or industry-specific, economy-wide, or global—has increased manyfold. Thanks to a sharply declining trend in the cost of transport, communication, and accessing information, competitive pressure on the producer's profit margin has led to a significant step-up in technological, organizational, and financial innovations; however, since many of these innovations are quite disruptive, under the new environment industries are often characterized by high rates of what Schumpeter called 'creative destruction'.

Easy transport and communication, facilitating increasing globalization, have also proved disruptive for a firm, an industry, and the national economy. A typical producer now secures various kinds of raw materials, components, and services from suppliers located all over the world. This has promoted efficiency, but raised substantially the chances of the production process getting clogged due to unforeseen shocks somewhere in the widely dispersed supply chain. As the fortunes of semiconductors, automobiles, airlines, and iron and steel suggest, competition for exploiting scale economies and capturing larger market shares in a profitable line of business often cause serious coordination failure, reflected in creation of excess capacity at the global level. Such industry-specific difficulties can produce an economy-wide impact since the tendency for particular economic activities to be concentrated in regions where they enjoy a cost advantage is much stronger in modern days. This is apart from the fact that increasing trade–GDP ratio everywhere has made international transmission of business cycles faster and more pronounced.

The greatest source of volatility may, however, be traced to the integration of global financial markets. Not only are exchange rates, interest rates,

[10] In 1986–8 below-normal monsoon reduced the growth of primary sector GDP to 0.2 and -1.0 per cent, respectively, in the two years. Even so, industries posted higher growth (at 6.2 per cent and 7.2 per cent respectively) compared with their growth (at 4.7 per cent) in 1985–6, and the average GDP growth of 4.1 per cent during the two years was not significantly lower than the 4.4 per cent growth in 1984–6.

and share prices in a country now dependent on developments in both the domestic and the international economy, but thanks to the dominance of non-FDI capital flows, self-fulfilling expectations[11] have made an EME prone to currency/financial turmoil and to contagion from a crisis raging elsewhere. At the same time it is now extremely difficult for authorities of an individual EME to curb volatility in the financial market and ensure macroeconomic stability.[12]

Risk and Return

Given the heightened competitive pressure in the financial market and the large imponderables affecting the fortunes of business ventures, managing risk and ensuring adequate return on assets now call for considerable expertise on the part of banks. Under the new environment, an evaluation of the expected return and the risk of a loan[13] involves assessment of the borrower's ability-cum-integrity as also of his vulnerability to various types of shocks noted above. Banks' problem becomes relatively tractable when firms seeking loans have been graded by credit-rating agencies. Such information (which is in the public domain) when supplemented with in-house knowledge of the borrower's financial health can considerably ease a bank's risk management.[14] However, not only are the vast majority of enterprises not credit rated, but competition among lenders tends to turn banks' margin on advances to relatively highly rated enterprises paper thin. The implication is that banks now have to put in place a fairly sophisticated system of (a) assessing the prospective yield and risk of alternative ways of deployment/raising of

[11] Thus if currency traders believe that a country's exchange rate is going to depreciate soon, there will be rush for exiting from the currency and the expectation becomes self-fulfilling.

[12] Consider the dilemma facing a modern-day policymaker. With a higher trade–GDP ratio imported inflation acquires greater significance so that exchange rate volatility translates into sharper variations in inflation rate. If on the other hand, the central bank adjusts interest rates to keep the exchange rate stable, cyclicity of output and employment gets more pronounced.

[13] Roughly speaking, the expected return on a loan means the average return a bank can expect on a sufficiently large number of similar loans. Riskiness is indicated by some measure of volatility (e.g., the coefficient of variation—the ratio of standard deviation to mean).

[14] Since it is the borrowing companies, not lenders, who pay the rating agencies, use of publicly available information relating to rating by banks (and other lenders) implies that credit rating generates positive externalities, making its social benefit exceed the cost at the margin! Lest the argument, appearing as it does in the ICRA Bulletin, may seem biased if not self-serving, we hasten to add that in view of the oligopolistic nature of the rating market, subsidization is unlikely to be the most effective means of removing the inefficiency.

funds; and (b) choosing optimally the combination of assets and liabilities keeping in view the requirement of liquidity and return on the one hand and moderation of overall risk on the other. The need for such a system arises not only for advances but for investments in financial instruments as well. Credit risk of government securities (or bonds of highly rated corporates) may be negligible and their liquidity quite high; but the increase in interest rate volatility requires banks to carefully scrutinize the risk-return profile of these investments before deciding on their optimum holding.

Small is not Beautiful

A moment's reflection on the problem of risk management or striking the right balance between return and risk suggests how heavily the stakes are now loaded against small or medium banks. There was a time when banks could survive or even thrive by catering to a small group of clients in some locality or some particular line of business. That is now history. The reasons are aplenty. Perhaps the most important is the enormous increase in fixed costs in evaluation of credit worthiness and management of risk. Keeping track of developments and trends in specific sectors as well as in the domestic and international economy, installation of computers and softwares for storing/sifting/analysing the enormous amount of relevant data, employment of highly skilled personnel, all these involve huge expenses that are basically overhead. Even processing of individual loan accounts becomes less time consuming and costly once these facilities are in place. And so is provision of various banking services, for example, ATM, credit card, transfer of funds, currency transactions, investment advice. The bigger banks thus enjoy a major cost advantage over their smaller rivals in undertaking both traditional and newer functions.

Second and no less important is the advantage of size in risk management. Globalization and the associated volatility have tended to make smaller banks non-viable since concentration of loans to a limited number of firms and business activities goes against the cardinal principle of risk management, viz., diversification or not putting all eggs in the same basket. For reducing risk it is necessary to distribute the loan portfolio among a large number of borrowers whose earnings are not highly and positively correlated, that is, do not generally move in a similar manner. However, diversification entails considerable cost (for any given amount of total loan). The major part of the cost of giving loan to a borrower, let us remember, is on account of assessment, monitoring, etc. and, hence, fixed.[15] This makes the average cost decline sharply with an increase in the amount of an advance. At the same

[15] i.e., the extra cost of giving loan to a borrower is marginal.

time, given the amount of fund earmarked for lending, its allocation among a smaller number of borrowers raises the overall risk of the loan portfolio. Hence the importance of scale economy in modern day banking.

Finally for the cost of raising funds. Wider range and better quality of services provided by a bank enables it to mobilize larger deposits at lower interest rates (even when fees are charged for the services). With lower operating cost and better risk management, a bigger bank has also greater access to cheaper loan and equity capital in both domestic and international markets. This is apart from the fact that the 'too big to fail' rule followed by many a government[16] provides almost sovereign guarantee to debts of large enough banks.

The above does not mean that the size alone ensures good financial performance or viability of banks. But even when they are relatively efficient it is necessary for small banks to have a medium-term plan for rapid growth either organically or through merger and acquisition.

Regulatory Compliance

In view of the importance of sound banking as a bulwork against financial/currency crisis,[17] central banks in all EMEs have enforced prudential norms for banks in line with recommendations of the BCBS. As of now the norms laid down for banks in India (and most other countries) are those suggested in the 1988 BCBS proposal, known as Basel I. The proposals are intended to raise the shock absorptive capacity of banks by requiring them to follow prescribed rules relating to assets classification, provisioning for non-performing assets (NPAs) and the minimum ratio of capital to risk-adjusted assets ratio (CRAR or capital adequacy ratio). The Reserve Bank conducts regular supervision not only to ensure that the prudential norms are being strictly adhered to, but also to assess the quality of management and financial viability of banks, recommend corrective measures for weak banks, and take steps like restraining a bank from accepting fresh deposits or cancellation of its license if deemed necessary.

From March 31, 2007, the banks in India are scheduled to operate under Basel II, the revised BCBS proposal suggested in 1998. Of the three pillars of Basel II, the first relates to capital adequacy. This allows banks to choose from a menu of approaches [including the internal rating based (IRB) approach] for computing their minimum capital requirement in the

[16] Most governments are extremely reluctant to let a big bank go bankrupt in view of the large negative consequences for the economy, including systemic troubles such bankruptcies tend to produce.

[17] Weak banking, as the Latin American and the East Asian experience suggest, tends to aggravate if not trigger off a currency crisis.

context of credit risk, market risk, and operational risk their asset portfolio is subject to. Initially banks in India will follow the standardized approach and only when some bank develops adequate risk management capability will the RBI permit it to adopt the IRB approach. Pillar 2 covers the supervisory review process. While ensuring that banks maintain adequate capital, the central bank under Pillar 2 is to evaluate the implications of risks not covered in Pillar 1 (e.g., liquidity risk and domestic or international shocks that are external to the bank) and if necessary mandate a higher minimum capital than is required under Pillar 1. The objective of Pillar 3 is to enhance the efficacy of market discipline by requiring banks to follow a formal disclosure policy so that market participants are kept abreast of the true state of banks' financial health.

Both Basel I and Basel II are designed to promote viability of banks and avoid systematic crisis in the financial sector. However, costs of regulatory compliance are not insignificant for banks. There are two types of costs banks have to bear in this regard. The first is the administrative and other expenses in connection with regular compilation and provision of the requisite information. The second and more important arises from the fact that the central bank mandated prudential norms limit banks' freedom relating to choice of assets and sources of funds. This means that financial performance of banks, even when they are fully alive to various kinds of risk and capable of taking effective steps for their management, tends to suffer under a rigid regulatory regime, as Basel I is. What is more damaging, under such constraints banks may not find it worthwhile to invest in developing risk management capability. The disincentive will be significantly less under Basel II when banks with adequate skill are allowed to adopt internal rating based approach to risk management.

However, compliance with Basel II is on the whole going to be more demanding for banks. Compared with the regulatory stance as of now under Pillar 2 and Pillar 3, the norms and rules will be more wide-ranging and supervision much stricter. Thus challenges to banks are likely to be greater and it is the larger ones which in general will be better able to meet the challenge. Again, since the minimum capital requirement is slated to be less and freedom relating to composition of the balance sheet more for banks with superior risk management skill, they will enjoy a competitive edge over their rivals. The life of laggards is going to be much more difficult under the proposed regulatory environment.

Post-reforms Banking in India: Strengths and Weaknesses

The performance of commercial banks in India since the initiation of financial reforms and adoption of the international best-practice regulatory framework has been most impressive. As Table 10.1 attests, both PSBs and the other category of banks have successfully overcome the hurdles posed by the new environment. Between 1996–7 and 2004–5, the gross NPAs of scheduled commercial banks as a ratio of total assets and total advances were brought down from 7.0 and 15.7 per cent to 2.5 and 5.2 per cent, respectively. Banks also undertook a massive cleaning up of their balance sheet through loan-loss provisioning so that at end-March 2005 net NPAs as a proportion of total assets and advances were no more than 0.9 per cent and 2.0 per cent, respectively. More noteworthy in this regard was the performance of PSBs: though they were initially saddled with much larger NPAs, by 2005 their ratios to assets and advances were not significantly different from those of private and foreign banks.

Progress in respect of other indicators of banks' financial health, viz., CRAR and profitability, has been equally impressive. The overall capital adequacy of banks, which had already risen to 8.9 per cent in 1995–6, reached 12.9 per cent in March 2005, nearly 4 percentage point larger than the stipulated minimum.[18] Despite the rise in CRAR and stringent norms relating to asset classification and provisioning under the new regime, bank profits, especially of PSBs, have shown a healthy trend since the mid-1990s. Indeed, India stands second (to Hong Kong) among the Asian nations in terms of return on bank assets and is now widely regarded to have one of the strongest financial systems among EMEs.

Areas of Concern

While there can be little doubt regarding the significantly improved performance of the financial sector in the post-reforms period, there are also areas of major failure, especially from the viewpoint of the economy as a whole. These failures are often structural or systemic; but in some instances the responsibility lies with the banks themselves. For purposes of policy prescription it is important both to identify the deficiencies and locate their sources.

Long-term Lending

Among the negative developments perhaps the most important has been the demise of development financial institutions (DFIs) and their reincarnation as commercial banks. This in a way is a fall-out of both the overall and financial sector reforms programme. DFIs (like commercial banks) became subject to market discipline so that they could no longer rely on

[18] The minimum of 9.0 per cent is for each bank individually.

TABLE 10.1

Financial Profile of Banks in India

(Per cent)

	1994–5	1995–6	1996–7	1997–8	1998–9	1999–2000	2000–1	2001–2	2002–3	2003–4	2004–5
Public sector banks											
Gross NPA/total assets			7.80	7.00	6.70	6.00	5.31	4.89	4.21	3.50	2.74
Net NPA/total assets			3.60	3.30	3.10	2.90	2.72	2.42	1.93	1.28	0.99
Gross NPA/gross advances			17.80	16.00	15.90	14.00	12.37	11.09	9.36	7.79	5.53
Net NPA/net advances			9.20	8.20	8.10	7.40	6.74	5.82	4.53	2.98	2.06
Scheduled commercial banks											
Gross NPA/total assets			7.00	6.40	6.20	5.50	4.90	4.60	4.00	3.30	2.50
Net NPA/total assets			3.30	3.00	2.90	2.70	2.50	2.30	1.90	1.20	0.90
Gross NPA/gross advances			15.70	14.40	14.70	12.70	11.40	10.40	8.80	7.20	5.20
Net NPA/net advances			8.10	7.30	7.60	6.80	6.20	5.50	4.40	2.90	2.00
Capital adequacy ratio											
Public sector banks		9.0	9.80	11.53	11.23	10.91	11.20	11.80	12.60	13.20	12.90
Scheduled commercial banks		8.9	10.05	11.59	11.44	11.29	11.40	12.00	12.70	12.90	12.80
Profitability (% of owned capital)											
Public sector banks	4.28	–1.30	9.31	12.34	7.78	11.11	8.65	14.45	18.75	20.89	15.50
Scheduled commercial banks	6.91	2.53	10.36	11.79	8.17	11.14	9.13	12.88	15.64	18.94	14.09

(Table 10.1 contd.)

(Table 10.1 contd.)

	1994–5	1995–6	1996–7	1997–8	1998–9	1999–2000	2000–1	2001–2	2002–3	2003–4	2004–5
Spread											
Public sector banks			3.16	2.91	2.81	2.70	2.86	2.73	2.91	2.98	2.92
Scheduled commercial banks			3.22	2.95	2.78	2.73	2.85	2.57	2.80	2.88	2.84
Operating profit (% of total assets)											
Public sector banks			1.6	1.58	1.37	1.46	1.34	1.88	2.31	2.68	2.22
Scheduled commercial banks			1.82	1.84	1.47	1.66	1.53	1.94	2.4	2.7	2.2
Operating profit (% of banks' own capital)											
Public sector banks			26.72	25.20	25.27	28.32	27.66	37.72	45.31	49.59	39.46
Scheduled commercial banks			27.68	26.55	24.52	28.06	27.76	33.81	39.95	45.12	34.60
Operating profit and interest expended (% of total assets)											
Public sector banks			8.13	7.77	7.58	7.68	7.33	7.86	7.75	7.14	6.24
Scheduled commercial banks			8.48	8.16	7.88	7.90	7.56	7.64	7.90	7.10	6.08
Provisioning and contingencies (% of total assets)											
Public sector banks			1.03	0.81	0.95	0.89	0.92	1.16	1.36	1.55	1.33
Scheduled commercial banks			1.15	1.02	0.98	1.00	1.03	1.19	1.39	1.54	1.29
Provisioning and contingencies (% of banks' own capital)											
Public sector banks			17.24	12.86	17.49	17.21	19.01	23.27	26.56	28.71	23.66
Scheduled commercial banks			17.50	14.76	16.36	16.96	18.76	20.69	31.68	30.66	23.54

Source: Reserve Bank of India (2005, 2005a, 2005b).

heavily subsidized funds and extend long-term loans to enterprises that were insulated from domestic and foreign competition. Dismantling of the licensing system and opening up of the economy seriously eroded profits of erstwhile borrowers of DFIs and made many of their loans non-performing. Also, the institutions did not possess or acquire adequate expertise to manage risk related to long-term borrowing and lending. No wonder, DFIs tried to find salvation is venturing into commercial banking, starting from a clean slate and investing heavily in new technology and human resources.

The strategy has helped the institutions survive (or even thrive) under the new environment; but this has created a yawning gap in supply of finance for long-term capital accumulation. The problem is compounded by the fact the market for private debt instruments is extremely thin; given the nature of their obligations and risk management skill, insurance companies are wary of long-term lending (without adequate collateral); and commercial banks, commanding the overwhelming part of funds mobilized through the financial sector, cannot extend long-term loans on a significant scale without creating problems of inadequate liquidity and maturity mismatch in their asset–liability position. The problem is not that difficult for large, reputed corporates: apart from issue of shares, they can rely on undistributed profits, term-loans from commercial banks, private placement of debentures, or even international financial markets for borrowing or issuing ADR/GDRs. It is the small and medium enterprises (SMEs) or farmers trying to raise their productive capacity, and new entrepreneurs seeking to enter a market that face stiff obstacles in executing their plans. The problem is no less serious in the case of infrastructural investments, characterized as they are by substantial gestation lag and yields stretching over a long time horizon. Given the lumpiness and magnitude of funds required for an infrastructural project, and the highly uncertain nature of returns, it is not difficult to appreciate why not only commercial banks, but other financial institutions also are extremely wary of financing such investments. However, whatever the reason the fund constraint inhibiting fixed capital accumulation by SMEs and in infrastructure, everybody recognizes, poses a serious hurdle in realizing the country's growth potential.

A fuller discussion of issues related to long-term finance is beyond the scope of the present chapter. Here we remain content with examining if commercial banks, with their overwhelming presence in the financial market, can help in promoting investment in fixed capital without compromising on sound norms relating to yield, liquidity, and risk. Remembering that deposits are mostly short-term, extension of long-term loans on a large scale makes bank assets relatively illiquid and their riskiness unacceptably high. This should not, however, preclude medium-term loans to SMEs.

The reason is two-fold. First, when a bank has already found an enterprise creditworthy (for short-term advances), the evaluation and administrative cost of providing a term-loan is marginal. Second, when the amount lent to a borrower is relatively modest, distribution of term loans among a large number of enterprises engaged in different types of activities tends to make the risk manageable, especially when the aggregate amount of such loans forms a relatively small part of total assets. The implication is that an increase in the average size of commercial banks should have a favourable impact on medium-term lending to SMEs.

Financing large infrastructural or other fixed investments by commercial banks requires structural changes or financial innovation. Ideally, funds for such projects should be raised through equity and debt instruments. When these instruments are easily marketable, they can become part of a commercial bank's optimum asset portfolio: up to a point substitution of these instruments for advances and other assets raises liquidity and reduces risk, remembering that portfolio investments are divisible and can be distributed widely among a number of debt instruments. There is scope for a substantial increase in bank funding of long-term including infrastructural investment provided an adequate system of credit rating of borrowers is in force and there is an active secondary market for (non-government) debts. With the implementation of the proposal for shifting from rating of individual issues to issuers, it should be easier for efficient enterprises to finance economically viable projects. But for this to happen large banks, insurance companies and pension funds need to be innovative and seek to exploit opportunities of being market makers in the initial stage of development of the bond market. Meanwhile consortium lending by a group of banks will remain the major means of financing large projects though this is unlikely to bridge significantly the gap created by the disappearance of DFIs.

Loans and Investments

Perhaps the most unforeseen development during the post-reforms period was the significant switch in bank assets from loans to investments and from commercial sector credit to government securities. Between 1990–1 and 2003–4 banks' investments as a ratio of loans rose sharply, from 64.5 per cent to 80.5 per cent. At the same time, there was large-scale substitution of GOI bonds for 'other' approved securities: the ratio of investments in 'other' approved securities to bank advances fell from 21.6 per cent to 2.7 per cent along with a commensurate rise in the ratio of government securities to bank credit, from 42.9 per cent to 77.9 per cent. The implication is that the share of bank credit going to the government registered a quantum jump at the expense of credit to the commercial sector. While banks' investments in government securities as a ratio of credit to commercial sector was 31.0 per cent in 1990–1, by 2003–4 the ratio rose to a whopping 69.0 per cent.[19]

The irony of the situation is that one of the major objectives of financial sector reforms was to augment the flow of credit to the commercial sector, away from government securities. With this end in view, SLR was progressively reduced from 38.5 per cent to 25.0 per cent and restrictions on interest rates on bank advances were abolished. With the benefit of hindsight it is not very difficult to see what went wrong, and why banks despite their holding of government securities far in excess of the SLR requirement went on accumulating these assets rather than extending loans to the commercial sector or investing in non-government bonds. First, with the unfreezing of interest rates there was a jump in the yield on government securities. Second and no less significant, the large and growing size of government bonds, interest rate flexibility, entry of private mutual funds and other entities actively taking positions in the GOI securities market, electronic trading facilities, all these factors helped in developing a fairly deep market for government securities and added greatly to their liquidity.

Third, regulations relating to prudential norms tilted the balance heavily in favour of government securities. Given the significantly lower risk weight of these securities compared with those of other assets, an increase in the share of government debts in a bank's total asset raises its CRAR. The mark-to-market rule for corporate debentures but not for government bonds makes investments in the latter more attractive.[20] Regulations relating to asset classification and provisioning imply that an increase in advances at the expense of GOI securities raises the probability of deterioration in asset quality and, hence, of an increase in provisioning requirement. Continuance of the rule that banks have to set aside 40 per cent of their total loan for the priority sector has also reduced the relative attractiveness of advances: given the high administration cost and riskiness of priority sector credit, a switch from loans to investments, enabling a reduction in advances required to be made to the priority sector (by 40 per cent of the amount switched), may appear a paying proposition to many a banker.

Finally, the industrial slowdown from the mid-1990s produced an adverse demand as well as a supply side impact on bank credit to the commercial sector. Demand deficiency induces a decline in firms' planned borrowing for working capital and long-term investment. At the same time,

[19] There has been some reversal of the trend since then, but the ratio is still far in excess of their pre-reforms magnitude.

[20] This is apart from the larger risk weight and lesser liquidity of corporate debt instruments. This differential has among other things made development of an active government securities market easier.

banks become reluctant to extend loans to borrowers whose bottomline has been hard hit by the demand slowdown. Since in such situations non-performing loans tend to rise, there is a decline in the banks' capital adequacy ratio and, hence, their ability to meet demand for advances. While the tendency for bank credit to the commercial sector to fall and for banks' holding of government bonds to rise during the downward phase of the trade cycle was also present earlier, such pro-cyclicity has been greatly accentuated with the adoption of Basel I. All economies face this problem, but it is much more serious for countries like India where the overwhelming part of transfer of funds from savers to investors is routed through banks. Hence arises the need for moving toward a system that contributes toward sound risk management, but does not make bank credit a major source of volatility or inefficiency of the macroeconomy.

Credit and Risk Management

Decline in bank lending to the commercial sector has been accompanied with a much steeper fall in credit to agriculture and SMEs, something which not only has grave social implications but is also sub-optimal from a broader economic perspective. For suggesting remedial measures it is useful to examine the main deficiencies of the current regulatory system and banks' management of risk and return under the system.

Consider first the way in which some of the prudential norms in force stand in the way of appropriate risk management and flow of bank funds to most productive lines of business. Neither the risk weights for bank advances nor rules concerning asset classification and provisioning are related to the nature of economic activities the borrowers are engaged in or their efficiency and track record. Thus the nature of risk faced by some farmer is quite different from that of a producer of gems and jewellery: the farmer is subject to vagaries of the monsoon; for gems and jewellery manufacturers fortunes of the global economy and exchange rate movements are crucial. The appropriate risk weights for banks' exposure to the two businesses are thus likely to be quite different. Note also that given the nature of the monsoon cycle, the fact that a farmer has defaulted for two to three consecutive quarters in a draught year need not be a serious concern for a banker provided he has distributed his advances over a large number of borrowers engaged in activities that are subject to quite different types of risk. This implies that (a) risk weights for different industries should not be the same; (b) rules concerning asset classification and provisioning must be related to the nature of the cycle affecting the fortunes of an industry; and (c) the required capital adequacy ratio should be related to the overall risk arising from concentration of loans not only to a small number of borrowers, but also to activities returns on which are highly correlated. Under Basel II banks with adequate risk management capability will be free to choose their minimum capital. Hopefully, these issues will then be properly resolved and a much larger share of bank funds flow to the commercial sector, including small borrowers in both agricultural and non-agricultural sectors. However, banks' track record relating to the disbursal of credit and risk management suggests the need for significant overhaul in their mode of operation if they are to deliver results under the new rules and environment.

It appears that the procedure of assessing creditworthiness and granting/renewing loans of many a bank is still archaic or mechanical. Rules of thumb rather than analysis of industry-cum-firm-specific factors often remain dominant in evaluation of credit risk. For borrowers deemed creditworthy, the amount of loan sanctioned or renewed is generally a pre-stipulated fraction of the past value of output with little reference to the prospective inflation[21] or the borrower's ability for profitable deployment of larger funds.[22] To be sure, banks have also been hiring skilled personnel and using sophisticated technology for judging creditworthiness or managing risk. This no doubt is a move in the right direction, but not free of problems. In most instances an evaluation or assessment is little more than feeding data into the computer and the software does the rest. The nature of the data required is also specified in the software package. The result is that not only is it akin to a black box to top managers of a bank, but even the persons running the programmes cease to apply their mind or fathom the rationale of the programmes.

Bank management in India seems by and large to underestimate the value of in-house expertise not only in use of software packages supplied by some specialized agency, but also in modifying them (or even developing new ones) to suit specific instances under a rapidly changing economic scenario. It is important to recognize that (a) a bank's decisions need necessarily to be forward-looking; and (b) past regularities or volatilities (on the basis of which software programmes are formulated) are crucially governed by the economic structure of a country, the policies that were being pursued, and the international trade and financial system that was in force. Thus, major changes in any of these factors require drastic modification in the method of assessment and risk management—something which bank management will fail to carry through unless they are thoroughly conversant with the basic factors affecting risk and returns, the specific methodology behind the programmes and conditions under which they will or will not yield the

[21] Which erodes the real value of loans (fixed in nominal terms).

[22] Banerjee et al. (2003).

right answer.[23] Such expertise will go a long way in helping development of innovative financial products and modus operandi for exploiting hitherto neglected opportunities, remembering that financial innovations are a rare phenomenon in Indian banking and this constitutes a major reason behind the grossly inadequate coverage of banking facilities and existence of large credit gaps in major sectors of the economy.

How not to Serve Small Borrowers

That there is something seriously wrong with operations of banks in India is illustrated by some recent developments. The post-reforms period was, as we have discussed, marked by a steep fall in the share of bank funds going to farmers and other small borrowers. This was in spite of continuance of the priority sector lending requirement and the fact that a special agricultural credit plan (SACP) had been in force since 1994–5. However, banks, thanks to the government pressure and initiatives taken from the mid-2004, have significantly stepped up the flow of credit to agriculture and small enterprises. For agriculture the initiatives include a 30 per cent increase in credit in 2004–5 and a 20 per cent to 25 per cent rise in subsequent years; extension of loans during a year to at least 100 new farmers by each rural and semi-urban branch of banks; restructuring/rescheduling of debts of farmers in arrears and making them eligible for fresh loans; provision of credit to tenant farmers and oral lessees; and financing capital-intensive farming and technological upgradation, etc. In order to augment the supply of credit to the 'tiny' sector banks have been 'advised' to dispense with collateral requirements for loans upto Rs 5 lakh and raise the limit to Rs 25 lakh for 'deserving' borrowers.

In the context of the huge shortfall of credit in the informal sector, there is undoubtedly an immense scope for productive deployment of bank funds by small farmers and enterprises. A recent World Bank–National Council for Applied Economic Research (NCAER) survey reports that only 24 per cent of farmers in Andhra Pradesh and 19 per cent in UP have access to formal credit; the corresponding figures for households having formal credit facilities are 56 per cent and 51 per cent, respectively. Despite the increase in loans extended through self-help groups (SHGs) in recent years, the credit gap in the unorganized sector remains yawning. According to some analysts, the estimated demand for loan by poor but creditworthy borrowers is

[23] One is reminded in this connection of Robertson's cautionary note in his *Lectures*. After setting forth Hick's forbidding expression summarizing the laws of derived demand (for inputs), Robertson in his inimitable way advises the reader not to commit the formula to memory unless he is a trained mathematician.

of the order of USD 40 billion, forty times the current supply (*The Economist*, November 5, 2005).

Notwithstanding the enormous potential for expansion of credit to the tiny sector, the recent spurt in bank advances to this sector appears unhealthy and reflects poorly on bank management. The reason is that the increase is driven by government 'advice', not banks' own reassessment of the risk-return profiles of such loans. It is highly unlikely that before giving loans to 50 lakh new farmers during 2004–5 under the June 2004 government initiative, banks could properly evaluate their creditworthiness. As the experience of directed (and subsidized) credit, especially of loan *melas*, suggests, expansion of credit through government initiative can not only be a direct source of misallocation of bank funds and piling up of NPAs, but it tends to undermine banks' initiative in developing their ability to manage risk and exploit opportunities under a changing economic scenario. The most worrisome aspect of the development is that banks in general and public sector banks in particular do not seem to have acquired enough freedom to follow sound banking practices.

The government as well as bank management is responsible for the deficiency in supply of credit to small borrowers. That a top-down policy of fixing yearly targets for additional credit or the number of new loans in some sectors/locations is seriously flawed is not very difficult to appreciate. The government does not have the necessary expertise to fix either quantitative targets for loans to a sector (not to speak of individual branches of banks), or special prudential norms[24] for particular categories of borrowers. Such targets and norms create moral hazard problems and do not often meet the needs of small enterprises having high-return investment plans.

The important point to note in this connection is that violation of commercial principles in disbursement of credit is not generally an effective means of promoting social objectives or reducing poverty, let alone allocative efficiency of resource use. What small or poor borrowers need is timely and adequate not cheap credit, remembering that they pay astronomical interest rates in the informal market. Indeed, with proper alignment of lending rates to both riskiness and operational costs of banks, flow of credit to the tiny sector can rise manyfold. In the process, the bottomline of enterprising banks would improve substantially, and so would both incomes of the poorer sections of the community and the overall productivity of the economy.

So far as banks are concerned, their failings lie in not developing during all these years of liberalisation, an efficient system of evaluation of

[24] Over and above those in force for all loans.

creditworthiness of small borrowers, an economical way of loan disbursal and recovery, and optimum pricing rules for different category of borrowers in the unorganised sector. The failure is particularly glaring for large banks which, as we have seen, have an inherent advantage in terms of economizing cost, reduction of risk, and raising (risk-adjusted) return. One reason for this failure was the reluctance to charge small borrowers interest rates higher than those for other loans. However, such reluctance, while understandable in the context of both official and social attitude, is not of much help to the vast majority of poor but creditworthy borrowers: not only does it sharply reduce the amount of loan that can be profitably extended to these borrowers, but the excess demand associated with cheap credit almost inevitably breeds corruption and bad debt as high-yielding projects are often deprived of funds and middlemen (in collusion with the bank personnel) appropriate the difference between the demand and actual price of loans making borrowers feel morally justified in defaulting on their debt.

This does not mean that the government has no role to play in raising the flow of credit to the unorganized sector. Provision of transport and communication facilities, easy access to information concerning prices of inputs and outputs vital to small producers, development of marketing centres, and crop and health insurance, all these generate positive externalities and require active support by the government. These facilities not only raise productivity of small enterprises, but what is relevant for our theme, reduce considerably banks' risk and cost of assessing viability of loans given to borrowers in this sector.

In order to exploit the huge market opportunities in the unorganized sector, banks for their part need to focus on proper evaluation of risk and return of prospective borrowers. Remembering that a major part of such cost is one-off and high marginal productivity of borrowers enables banks to charge a commensurate rate of interest, from a medium to long-term perspective lending to the tiny sector should be highly lucrative. At the same time it is imperative for banks to be always on the look-out for the best strategy in the context of specific markets and economic conditions they operate in. To illustrate, banks serving in rural areas and having a thorough knowledge of their customers can act as agents of insurance companies and provide term loans for investment in cold storage, warehouses, or mobile telephone centres (or cyber cafes). These operations can not only be profitable on their own, but are also likely to make bank financing of working capital of farmers and small entrepreneurs much more viable than it otherwise would be. Indeed, in banking as in other commercial activities excellence depends ultimately on attention to details as well as on innovation and ability to adjust promptly to the emerging environment.

Conclusion

(a) Going by the conventional yardstick, financial performance of banks under the post-reforms economic environment has been quite impressive. NPAs have come down significantly; the capital adequacy ratio has risen by 4 percentage points above the stipulated minimum; profits have shown a healthy trend.

(b) However, there have also been major shortcomings, especially from the viewpoint of the economy as a whole. The most important of these relate to drying up of funds for long-term including infrastructural capital accumulation; sharp rise in investments in government securities at the expense of credit to the commercial sector; and grossly inadequate supply of loan to farmers, SMEs, and other borrowers in the unorganized sector. Part of the reason for this is structural or policy related, not due to inefficiency of individual banks. The demise of DFIs has not been compensated through development of an active market for non-government debts. Rules relating to the priority sector lending militate against bank advances relatively to investments. The prudential norms in force tilt the balance heavily in favour of government securities. What is more damaging, not only do the norms raise pro-cyclicity of bank loans, but they are not related to the nature of risk of different types of economic activities or to the *overall* risk arising from banks' portfolio of assets and structure of liabilities.

(c) Deficiency in operation of banks themselves is by no means venial. They have yet to put in place an adequate system for assessing creditworthiness and risk-return trade-off. Decisions relating to granting/renewal of loans appear to be based more on rules of thumb than careful evaluation of borrowers' prospective profits. Even when sophisticated technologies are used, banks, lacking sufficient in-house expertise, have failed to modify them to suit specific conditions or to develop innovative financial instruments for exploiting the vast, untapped market potential, especially in the unorganized sector. The most glaring instances of banks' failings are absence of initiatives for becoming market makers in private debt instruments; sub-optimal pricing and supply of loans to small borrowers; and grossly under-utilized benefits from synergy of combining advances for working capital with term loans and other services in carefully chosen areas or regions.

(d) Our analysis highlights the need for changes in both regulatory norms and banks' own operation and management in some crucial areas.

At the same time it is important to recognize that banks in India are not large enough to function efficiently under the emerging environment, to undertake sufficient investment in skill formation, and to come up and experiment with innovative ways of exploiting the opportunities and meeting the challenges thrown up under a rapidly changing economic scenario.

References

Banerjee, A.V., S. Cole, and E. Duflo (2003), 'Bank Financing in India', MIT Website.

Reserve Bank of India (2005), *Handbook of Statistics on the Indian Economy 2004–5*, Mumbai.

——— (2005a), *Report on Trend and Progress of Banking in India 2004–5*, Mumbai.

——— (2005b), *Statistical Tables Relating to Banks in India 2004–5*, Mumbai.

Author Index

Banerjee, Abhijit V. 279, 284
Barro, Robert J. 43, 59, 100, 137
Bernanke, Ben S. 14, 33
Bery, Suman 196, 205, 234
Blinder, Alan S. 16, 22, 33
Bose, Amitava 150, 166
Bose, Suchismita 254, 255, 260, 261
Bruno, Michael 180, 205

Chakrabarti, Rajesh 254, 260
Chandrasekhar, C.P. 208, 230
Chenery, Hollis B. 180, 205
Cole, Shawn 279, 284
Coondoo, Dipankor 254, 255, 260, 261

Domar, Evsey D. 101, 136, 137, 139, 155, 166
Duflo, Esther 279, 284
Dutt, Amitava K. 54, 59

Flood, Robert P. 185, 205

Gordon, James 253, 254, 260
Gupta, Poonam 253, 254, 260

Lal, Deepak 196, 205, 234

Marion, Nancy P. 185, 205
Mukherjee, Paramita 254, 260, 261

Obstfeld, Maurice 180, 185, 205

Pant, Devendra K. 196, 205, 234
Patnaik, Prabhat 208, 230

Rangarajan, Chakravarthi 214, 230
Rao, M. Govinda 208, 230
Rodrik, Dani 248, 261
Rogoff, Kenneth 180, 205

Samuelson, Paul 40, 60, 109, 138
Srivastava, D.K. 214, 230
Stiglitz, Joseph E. 15, 34
Strout, Alan M. 180, 205

Taylor, Lance 54, 60, 76, 86, 90, 150, 151, 166
Tinbergen, Jan 225, 230

Virmani, Arvind 208, 230

Weiss, Andrew 15, 34

Subject Index

above poverty line (APL) families 62–3, 66n, 87n
administered interest rates 13, 15, 21, 21n
advances/credit, priority sector 264, 277, 280, 283
adverse selection 15n
aggregate demand–aggregate supply (AD–AS) framework/model, 218–20, 218n, 219n, 236–40
  an open economy, multiplier in 218n, 218–20
agriculture–industry interaction/imbalance 53–4, 66n
allocative efficiency 30, 30n, 42, 126, 131n, 149, 152, 265
  and income distribution 115n
anti-cyclical policies 50, 126, 128, 148
Antyodaya (Anna) Yojana 64, 67, 68n
asymmetric information 15n

balance of payments (BoP), crisis/vulnerability/viability 20, 31, 167, 169, 174, 187, 197, 203, 203n, 208, 216–17, 221, 242, 245n
  and capital account convertibility 186, 197–8, 201
  and holding of foreign currency reserves 167, 187, 189–92, 224
Balance of Payment, High-level Committee on 169
balance-sheet effect 76n, 174
  and bankruptcy 52
bank, 'too big to fail' rule 270, 270n
  credit to small and medium enterprises (SMEs) 280–2
  regulation 264, 270–1, 277
  performance, post-reforms 271–2, 275–8
banking (financial) reforms 262–4
banks' cash in hand 263, 263n
Basel Committee on Banking Supervision 264
Basel I (see also prudential norms) 270–1
  and cyclicity of bank credit 278
Basel II (see also prudential norms) 264, 270–1
  and bank credit 279
below poverty line (BPL), families 62, 64, 67–8, 76, 77, 88
  quotas 67–8, 69n, 70–1, 72n, 77–8, 84, 87–9
British Code of Fiscal Stability 50n
budgetary programmes, second best 108, 111–16, 133, 137
budgetary viability 36, 85, 99, 103, 107–8, 107n, 112, 120, 144, 199, 213, 236
buffer stocks 54, 62, 63n, 64
burden of taxes 40n, 41n
  inter- and intra-generational 39–42

call money rate 13
CAMEL 264
capacity, excess 22, 41, 73, 79, 80, 82n, 90, 101n, 104, 148, 151, 176, 182, 187, 198–9, 204, 240–1, 259, 267
utilization 26–7, 32, 41, 54, 75, 79, 83, 92, 104, 150n, 157, 182n, 190, 204, 220, 221, 240, 248, 259–60
capital, adequacy 264, 270, 272–3, 278
control 173, 186n, 187, 197–8, 201, 253, 265
to risk adjusted asset ratio (CRAR) 270, 272, 277
capital account, convertibility 186, 197–8, 201–2
liberalization 197–8
capital flows, two-way 203, 266n
capital inflows (see also foreign capital) 5--7, 173, 174, 191, 193, 201, 204, 231n, 251–2, 258–9, 264
and investment 86, 180, 181–4, 192, 202, 212, 219, 245–52, 252n, 255, 260
and reserves accretion 176, 181–4, 191–3, 210, 211n, 212
control on (see also capital control) 197–8, 201
Capital Issues (Control) Act, 1947 18
capital market volatility 242, 243n, 244, 253, 255
cash drain 12, 16, 18
cash reserve ratio (CRR) 12, 13, 15, 17, 75n, 263, 263n
commercial bank credit to the government 9–10, 276
commercial papers (CPs) 13, 14, 19, 20
Committee on Fiscal Responsibility Legislation 35
Report of the 3n, 47
compensation criterion 150n
Comptroller and Auditor General of India (CAG) 57n, 63n
contingent liability 38
convertible debentures 18
coordination failure 27, 126, 267
core reform scenario 160–1
countervailing duties 24, 30, 30n, 31–2
country risk 201, 250, 251n, 256
credit, bank 13, 15–17, 263, 263n, 176–8
non-bank 15–18, 21n
credit, delivery system 54, 199, 204
credit constraint/rationing, 2, 9, 14–16, 18, 22
sectoral 22
credit rating, India's 11, 27
crowding-in and crowding-out, financial 16, 82n, 105–6, 105n, 212–13
effects of government borrowing 18, 103–5
effects of public investment 81, 153, 208, 212–13, 218n, 220, 221, 234–5, 240
current account deficit, optimal level of 145, 200
currency crisis (see also BoP crisis) 174, 174n, 186, 201, 208, 216, 270

debt dynamics 144, 154–6, 158
debt trap, internal 121, 137
debt–GDP ratio 37, 98, 99, 101, 103, 118, 120, 145, 154–6, 158–9, 162, 203
and primary deficit 154–5
debt-service ratio 174, 175, 187, 190, 203
deficit, revenue and fiscal (see also fiscal deficit) 10, 37, 57–8, 81–2, 99, 103n, 117, 134, 135, 152, 152n
anti-cyclical variations in 58
demand and supply constraints, coexistence/simultaneous operations of, 15–17, 121n, 150–2, 198
policy implications of 151–2
demand and time liabilities (DTLs) 12

depreciation 52, 76n, 77, 83, 183, 185, 200, 201, 218, 218n, 221–2, 226n, 233, 233n, 237, 238n, 239, 240
its effect on domestic market 83, 83n, 183–4
balance-sheet impact of 76n
de-reservation 264, 265
development financial institutions (DFIs) 272, 283
disembodied technical progress 44–5
disintermediation 16
disinvestment 56n, 74n, 108n, 156, 243, 256, 259
Domar condition/results 136, 139, 155n
duality of individual preference 44
dualism, financial 53

easily reversible external liability (EREL) 216, 253
East Asian currency crisis 52, 186n, 191, 270
easy money policy 53, 187
failure of 53
economic cost, FCI's 62–3, 66n, 68n, 69
efficient policy combination 72, 72n
Eleventh Finance Commission 96, 98, 126, 134–5
employment schemes 114n
equity, inter-generational 35–6, 39–40, 42–3, 45, 45n, 46–9, 58
euro-convertibles 21
euro-issues 11, 19, 25
exchange control (see also capital control) 169, 264
exchange rate, expectation 52, 185, 268n
dirty float 190, 190n
pure float 52
volatility 52, 245, 265, 267–8, 268n
Exim policy 24n
Expert Group (EG) 242–60
export of foodgrains 3, 69–70, 74
external, balance/imbalance (see also BoP) 83, 84, 86, 94, 190
balance-sheet 174
debt 25, 97, 169, 174, 192n, 197, 203, 217
external sector asset-liability, India's 216

feed-back effect 66n, 72, 72n
financial sector, liberalization 7, 11, 20, 264–5
vulnerability 266–8
fiscal and monetary policy, separation of the roles of 51–2
fiscal deficit, and disinvestment 106–8, 136n
concept of 106–8
cyclical 143, 147–8
structural 143, 147–8
fiscal, correction targets 163–5
fetishism 152n, 215
gap 117, 118, 135, 136
imbalance 143, 148, 210
restructuring schemes 134–6, 144–6, 151–2, 154–6, 160–3, 164–5
fiscal policy, anti-cyclical 50, 58, 126, 128, 148
expansionary 49, 53, 79, 79n, 81–2, 104, 128, 148n, 196–7
Fiscal Policy Strategy Statement 36, 38
fiscal programme, second-best 49n
Fiscal Responsibility and Budget Management Act (FRBMA) 144, 145, 208
Fiscal Responsibility and Budget Management Bill (FRBMB) 35–7
and cyclical fluctuation 50, 58
food constraint and capacity utilization 53–4
Food Corporation of India's (FCI's) excess stocks, macrotheoretic approach 78–83
FCI losses, underestimation of 71

food-for-work programme/scheme (FFP) 54, 83–4, 90–5
and public investment 91–3
food policy 62–72
general equilibrium approach/ framework 78
partial equilibrium approach/ framework 65–66, 65n, 66n, 70–2, 73n, 77, 87
food security 62
food stock, excess/surplus 64–71, 78–81, 83, 84–5, 87–94
foodgrains prices, seasonality of 62
two-tier system of 62–3
foreign capital (see also capital inflows) 5, 24, 177–81, 200–1, 201n, 231n, 245–6, 248, 250, 253, 257–8, 259–60
foreign direct investment (FDI) 27, 83, 171, 182, 187n, 202, 204–5, 217, 225, 231n, 242–3, 247, 255, 258
foreign exchange reserves (see BoP and holding of foreign currency reserves)
adequacy of 184–7, 202, 205
and net RBI credit to government 193, 229
and output gap 187, 192n, 202, 221, 229
cost of holding 187–90, 229, 248–50, 248–9n
for pre-payment of external debt 197, 203
for infrastructural investment (see Planning Commission Scheme)
sterilization of 249
foreign institutional investment (FII), and BoP vulnerability 259–60
and financial volatility/vulnerability 243, 252–5
and stock market return 253–4
and tainted transaction 243
inflows, investment, and growth 245–8, 250–2, 252n
in debt and equity 257
optimal inflows of 257–8
sectoral cap on 255, 257–8
foreign institutional investors 18, 216
foreign portfolio investment (FPI) 171, 182, 186, 202, 205, 247
foreign trade multiplier 73, 181–2, 196n, 218
and currency appreciation 181–2, 181n, 182n
of foodgrains export 73–5
Friedman on lags in monetary policy 51–2n
full-employment output 142, 146–50
and debt-financed government expenditure 105

general equilibrium analysis/ framework 66n, 72, 72n, 73n, 75–6, 78
global depositary receipt (GDR) 182, 256, 259
globalization, of trade 264
of financial markets 251, 264, 267
golden rule 42, 43n, 47–8, 161
and public investment 48n
goods and financial markets, integration with the global market 264
government borrowing, net interest cost of 117, 119, 119n, 120n
government expenditure, composition of 41–2, 105, 108, 142
government guarantee (see also contingent liability) 38, 207n, 208n, 270
growth, full employment (NAIRU) (see also NAIRU) 50, 51, 126, 148, 161, 164, 213
-interest differential 117, 120, 120n, 144–5, 155–6, 157

hedge funds 244
Hegel-type approach 46
herd behaviour 26, 52, 252

herding 244, 244n
heterodox policies 152
high-cost borrowing instruments
133–4, 133n
household, disposable income of 40, 41n, 100, 101, 124
household saving, 124–5, 132, 153, 156
paradox in India 132

immunity schemes 168, 168n
incremental capital-output ratio (ICOR) 161n, 179
industrial growth, deceleration of 80, 121, 128, 137, 204
inflation expectations 211, 236
infrastructural, bottlenecks/ constraint 27, 73, 126, 127, 148, 151, 163, 209, 213, 229, 234
finance 156, 221
investment/capital accumulation (see investment in infrastructure)
internal rating based (IRB) approach 270–1
International Monetary Fund (IMF) 98, 168, 168n
international trade and finance, post-reforms 265–6, 266n
inter-temporal budget constraint, of government 43n, 111–13, 115, 132–3
intra-generational inequality 79n
investment in agriculture, public and private 27
investment multiplier 16
investment–saving gap 182, 188–9, 196n, 205, 240, 246n, 260
investment and capital flows 182
investment in infrastructure 6, 80–1, 126, 153, 182, 210–14, 216, 217, 221, 223n, 227, 248, 275
economic and budgetary consequences of 80, 215, 223, 226
and net RBI credit 221, 229
investment programme, optimal 163
isolation paradox 46

Japan 51, 147, 153

Keynes (Treatise)-Kaldor-Kalecki results 153
know your clients (KYCs) principle 244

Latin American currency crisis/ turmoil 169, 201, 270
lender of last resort 185
Life Insurance Corporation of India (LIC) 18, 256
liquidity, excess 9, 11–13, 19–21
mismatch 216
Lucas principle 27
longer term debt scenario 156

macroeconomic stabilization 28, 50, 51, 54
marginal cost, of borrowing 180, 201
of external finance 201, 203, 251n
of taxation 158
market stabilization, bonds (MSBs) 159, 215, 249, 250
scheme (MSS) 159, 215
mark-up/cost-plus pricing 78n, 80, 90
maturity mismatch 275
Medium-Term Fiscal Policy Statement 36, 38
merit goods 146
microcredit agencies 114
minimum support price (MSP) 61–3, 67, 68n, 73n
modified value-added tax (MODVAT) 30
monetary authority/Reserve Bank, role of 51
accommodating monetary policy of 76n, 82n
anti-cyclical monetary policy of 128

monetized deficit/seignorage 16, 19, 37, 49, 59, 96, 105, 110, 112, 124, 133, 135, 136–7, 208, 210, 218, 240
prices and inflation under 106, 106n, 162n, 112, 112n, 210–12, 215
with no tax constraint 110
with tax constraint 112, 158
money multiplier 12, 15, 17, 19, 173n
monsoon failure 150–1, 267
moral hazard 15n
multiplier, credit 16–20
foreign trade (see foreign trade multiplier)
money (see money multiplier)
sectoral 75n, 76, 81, 151n
Mundell–Fleming results 51, 234n

National Council of Applied Economic Research (NCAER) 280
National Savings Certificates (NSCs) 16, 133
new growth theories 101n, 154
non-accelerating inflation rate of unemployment (NAIRU) 147n
non-bank financial institutions 15–16, 20–1, 30, 53, 256
non-food advances/credit 12, 13–14, 74
NRI (non-resident Indian), deposits 250–2
remittances 197–8, 265

oil price shock 152
open economy AD–AS model 218–20, 218n, 219n, 236–40
open economy full-employment model 209, 231–6
open market sales of foodgrains 62, 66, 78, 84–5
(general) equilibrium impact of 76, 78
multiplier effect of 75
optimal saving ratio 43–7, 161
output, potential/trend levels of 41, 86, 142, 147
output gap 128n, 142, 149, 164, 181, 182, 187, 202, 204, 222–3, 225, 229, 258–9
and reserves depletion 192n, 223, 225

partial equilibrium approach/framework (see food policy, partial equilibrium approach/framework)
participatory notes (PNs) 243
payments crisis, 1991 168, 186n, 193n
Pigou effect 24n
Plan and non-Plan expenditure 146, 146n
Planning Commission Scheme (PCS) 207–8, 216–17, 221n, 228, 238–9
economic rationale behind 185, 210
implications for public debt and fiscal viability 213–14
policy, sequencing of 228
targets, intermediate and final/ultimate 109n, 200–3
political economy of fiscal management 57
primary deficit 145, 154n, 155–6
and debt–GDP ratio 154–5
primary issues 37
prioritization of targets 163
private investment 27, 36, 56, 74, 79, 92, 103n, 104–5, 109–10, 130, 148, 151, 157–8, 199–200, 204, 209, 216, 218–20, 225–6, 228–9, 251
production loan 16, 20, 22
project imports 24, 30
prudential norms (see also Basel I and Basel II) 264, 270–1, 277, 278, 283
and bank credit 22
and demand for government securities 283

and monetary policy 13–14, 22, 53, 283
public distribution system (PDS) 61–3, 85, 114n
Targeted Public Distribution System (TPDS) 62
public consumption 40, 100n, 124, 141, 249
public investment 27, 42, 48n, 55–6, 79, 91–4, 103n, 109–10, 126, 131n, 137, 157, 190, 199, 204, 210–11, 216, 219, 222, 229
demand and supply side effect of 157
public liability 117, 118
public sector saving 48, 48n, 49, 143
public debt, burden of 40n, 79n, 99–100, 209, 228, 229, 241
and government securities 102, 209, 241
canonical views on sustainability of 100–1
composition of 209, 241
held by the Reserve Bank 97, 102, 118
TFC concept of (see TFC, concept of public debt)
public goods 40, 42n, 100, 100n, 109, 113n, 114, 146, 154
optimum amount of 40n, 51, 109n, 141
Public Provident Fund (PPF) 133
public saving and inter-generational equity 58
public sector undertakings (PSUs), disinvestment in 106–8, 156, 243, 256, 259
savings of 48n, 125

quasi-fiscal costs 159–60, 224n, 229, 249

rating agencies 268n
real effective exchange rate (REER) 170, 203
revenue balances 47, 57, 76, 81, 92, 162n
Reserve Bank of India (RBI), autonomy of 37,
credit to the government 6, 29, 156, 158, 159, 193, 207, 221, 229, 247, 249
responsibilities of 51
reserves, excess 14, 19, 199, 203, 227, 235, 248
their opportunity cost 193, 235
reserves adequacy/requirement (see foreign exchange reserves, adequacy of)
restructuring programme, optimal (see TFC/fiscal restructuring programme)
reversible capital flows (see easily reversible external liability) 216, 253
Ricardian equivalence 43n, 100n
risk management 203, 268–71, 278–80
Robertson's cautionary note 280n

safety net for workers 150n
saving–investment relation, under full-employment 153–4, 154n
under output gap 153
saving, optimum (see optimal saving ratio)
Securities and Exchange Board of India (SEBI) 18, 244
self-fulfilling expectations 185, 187, 268n
self-help groups (SHGs) 280
seignorage (see also monetized deficit) 112, 156, 156n, 157, 158, 162, 193, 249, 255
and inflation 106, 106n, 112, 112n, 162n, 210–2, 215
impact on debt–GDP ratio 162
safe level of 249
services growth 121, 121n
small saving 97

social cost of taxation 161
Solow residual 154
speculative attack 83, 174, 185, 253
State Trading Corporation (STC) 64
statutory liquidity ratio (SLR) 10, 13, 16, 53n, 105, 112–3, 133–4, 137, 263, 277
  securities 133n
sterilization, of capital inflows/reserves 159, 173, 183–4, 249
Structural Adjustment Programme (SAP) 9, 13, 19, 20, 31, 33
sub-accounts 243–5, 257
subsidies, and poverty 62, 65, 67, 70, 77, 80, 89
  fertilizer 114, 131n, 152
  food 23n, 62, 63, 66–7, 63n, 68n, 81, 89, 91, 93, 114, 131n
suppliers' credit 19, 24
supply of food, excess 85

tax constraint 109, 112, 113, 137
Tinbergen principle 225
time preference 43, 109, 161
trilemma of policy makers under capital mobility 253
Twelfth Finance Commission (TFC)/ fiscal restructuring programme 4, 142–65
  concept of public debt 158–9
  definition of full-employment and potential output 146–8

Unit Trust of India (UTI) 13, 18, 29
United States 14, 151, 153, 168 180, 199
unsterilized intervention 183, 184
user charges 56, 130, 132, 145, 152, 215, 240

wealth effect 100, 101, 162n
wheat export at below cost 64, 64n, 65, 69, 69n, 71n
World Bank 98, 168n, 181, 182, 204, 280
working capital 19, 282, 283